Edward Blackmore

The British Mercantile Marine

Edward Blackmore

The British Mercantile Marine

ISBN/EAN: 9783337415907

Printed in Europe, USA, Canada, Australia, Japan

Cover: Foto ©ninafisch / pixelio.de

More available books at **www.hansebooks.com**

THE
BRITISH MERCANTILE MARINE

A SHORT HISTORICAL REVIEW,

INCLUDING

THE RISE AND PROGRESS OF BRITISH SHIPPING AND COMMERCE
THE EDUCATION OF THE MERCHANT OFFICER; AND
DUTY AND DISCIPLINE IN THE MERCHANT SERVICE.

BY

EDWARD BLACKMORE,

MASTER MARINER; ASSOCIATE OF THE INSTITUTION OF NAVAL ARCHITECTS;
FORMERLY A RESIDENT JUSTICE OF THE PEACE FOR THE COUNTY
OF RENFREW, N.B.; AND A MEMBER OF THE INSTITUTION
OF ENGINEERS AND SHIPBUILDERS IN SCOTLAND.

LONDON:
CHARLES GRIFFIN AND COMPANY, LIMITED,
EXETER STREET, STRAND.
1897.

[*All rights reserved.*]

THIS LITTLE VOLUME IS

Dedicated

TO THE MEMORY OF

PETER DENNY, LL.D.,

A DEPUTY-LIEUTENANT AND JUSTICE OF THE PEACE FOR THE COUNTY
OF DUMBARTON, SHIPBUILDER AND SHIPOWNER, WHO, EMINENT
IN HIS PROFESSION AND MAGNANIMOUS AS AN EMPLOYER,
WAS DISTINGUISHED BY A CAREFUL SOLICITUDE FOR THE

EDUCATION

OF THE YOUTH OF HIS NATIVE TOWN, AS WELL AS OF THOSE IN HIS
EMPLOY; WHOM HE, MOREOVER, AIDED BY GENEROUS ASSISTANCE.
AS A SINCERE FRIEND AND A SAGACIOUS ADVISER HIS LOSS
WILL EVER BE REGRETTED BY ALL WHO, WITH THE
AUTHOR, ENJOYED HIS LIFE-LONG FRIENDSHIP
AND BENEFITED BY THE WISDOM OF
HIS COUNSEL.

PREFACE.

The following pages are founded upon a Series of Papers written for, and read before, the Shipmasters' Society of London. As these papers were well received by the Members of that Society, it was more than once suggested to me that they should be collected and published as a volume. Being diffident of their possessing sufficient value for wider dissemination, however, I from time to time waived the idea until the present "Nautical Series" of works, intended by the Publishers as an Educational Series for young sailors, opportunely presented itself.

This little book does not, of course, pretend to be in any way exhaustive of the history of the British Mercantile Marine; nevertheless, it is hoped that it will afford a sufficient outline of its Past and Present to be both interesting and instructive to those who care to know anything of the rise and progress of our Merchant Navy. In full detail this is not to be found in any less important work than Mr. W. S. Lindsay's "History of Shipping," a book which is both too expensive for the general reader, and, moreover, was written fully twenty years ago.

The principal works referred to in the following pages, in addition to Mr. Lindsay's, are: Anderson's and Macpherson's "Histories of Commerce"; Prof. Thorold Rogers' "Industrial and Commercial History of England"; Tooke's "History of Prices"; H. Zimmern's "Hansa Towns" (*Story of the Nations* Series); various articles in the *Encyclopædia Britannica, Encyclopædia Americana,* and the *Nautical Magazine;* together with the Blue-books and Departmental Papers of the Board of Trade; to all of which, as well as to many other sources of information, the author acknowledges his indebtedness.

The love of the sea which fascinated our ancestors, and enabled them to surmount obstacles with which, in these days, we are totally unacquainted, still holds its own among the British race. The difficulties which our sailors now have to encounter are not those which met their ancestors, who battled with the elements in small shallops no bigger than a modern fishing-smack, amid the dangers of unknown and unsounded seas. Rather is the modern difficulty that of dealing with the splendid instruments of commerce now in vogue, and the immense increase in traffic, especially in the narrower seas—conditions which require in those who have the responsibility a higher scientific training and a greater alertness in the avoidance of accidents than was needed at any previous period of our history. Rush! is the order of the day; and there seems to be no time for the ordinary old-fashioned precautions which used to be taken in order to keep ships clear of the rocks or of each other. To meet such a state of matters, the officers of the Mercantile Marine require a higher education to quicken their mental capacity, and a higher sense of responsibility to endow them with greater readiness and wariness of action, than was perhaps needed in the "good old seaman" of former days.

If, in dealing with the subject of Education, the author may seem to have taken a somewhat pessimistic view of its past, or even its present state, let the reader be assured that his desire is to improve, not to detract from the position of the Mercantile Marine. Among its members we already number men of high scientific training. Let us not rest satisfied till all attain the same standard!

With a view to affording the Merchant Officer an opportunity for self-training and cultivation, the Publishers have promoted their "Nautical Series" of works treating of the various sciences with which it is absolutely necessary that the modern Merchant Officer should be acquainted. These works will speak for themselves. Should the present volume be in any way conducive to the stimulation of further inquiry into the History of our Merchant Navy, or to the progress of education, it will be a great and sufficient reward for any trouble or pains taken in its compilation.

EDWARD BLACKMORE.

CONTENTS.

PART I.
HISTORICAL.

CHAPTER I.
FROM EARLY TIMES TO 1486.

Early Population of England—Ancient Britons' knowledge of Shipbuilding—Alfred the Great—Athelstan rewards Foreign Adventurers—Edward the Confessor creates the Cinque Ports—Richard the First's Fleet—Les Roles d'Oleron—Hanseatic Laws—Trade in the reign of Edward the First—Rivalry between the Cinque Ports and the French—Letters of Marque—King Edward the Third's Fleet—Sea Fight off Sluys—Increase of English Exports—The Hanse Towns—The Flemings in London—Wat Tyler's Rebellion—Richard the Second's Act of Protection for English Shipping—State of England—The Kings of England and the Hanseatic League—Henry the Fifth—Improvement in Shipbuilding—The King of Sweden's large Ship—Enterprise awakening in European Countries—The Road to India—The Portuguese double the Cape . . . . pp. 1–9

CHAPTER II.
PROGRESS UNDER HENRY THE EIGHTH.

State of Arts and Commerce—Christopher Columbus and Henry the Seventh—Sebastian Cabot discovers Labrador and Newfoundland—Henry the Eighth builds a Royal Navy and founds Dockyards—Sir Edward Howard and the King's Fleet—English Commerce hampered by the Hanse Towns—London Merchant Adventurers—Froude's picture of the English People . . . . pp. 10–14

CHAPTER III.

FROM HENRY THE EIGHTH TO THE DEATH OF MARY.

New Activity and Intelligence—Henry the Eighth sends Cabot and Sir T. Port on a new Voyage of Discovery—Their return—Cabot retires to Spain—The Reformation—Henry prepares for Defence by Sea—English Mariners—Trade with Newfoundland—West of England Fishermen—Will Hawkins—Edward the Sixth and the Russian Ambassador—Oppressive Measures of the Hanseatic League—Sir Richard Chancellor discovers Archangel—The London and Muscovite Company—Queen Mary succeeds and marries Philip of Spain—Mary's attempts to restore the Roman Catholic Supremacy disturb the Country—Philip's influence—English rovers—Mary's death . . pp. 15-20

CHAPTER IV.

THE MERCANTILE MARINE DURING ELIZABETH'S REIGN.

Effect of British Protection—Elizabeth repeals Navigation Laws—Her general Policy—She curtails Hanseatic Privileges—Treaty of Commerce with Hamburg—The Hansa Power broken—Seymour and his Allies—Quarrel between Elizabeth and Philip—The Inquisition—The Queen supports Holland—John Hawkins sails to the Gold Coast—Drake's Surveys of the West Indies—The Queen commissions Drake—He sails round the World—Portugal friendly to England—Philip determines to crush England—Elizabeth's Self-confidence—Her Fleet—The Spanish Armada—Drake and his Privateers—The Armada reaches the English Channel—Off Plymouth meets the Fleet and Drake's Ships—The Duke de Medina tries to separate them—The superior sailing qualities of the English Ships now seen—A worrying Fight up Channel—The Spaniards chased into Calais Roads and the North Sea—A remnant of the Armada returns to Spain . pp. 21-28

CHAPTER V.

MERCANTILE PROGRESS UP TO THE REIGN OF WILLIAM THE THIRD.

Chaucer's Seaman—The English People—West of England Mariners—Judge Prowse's History of Newfoundland and Trade—Art School of Shipbuilding—Tobias' Letter to the Queen—Fishing industry, a school for Sailors—Trade with Portugal—The Russian and Levant Companies—The East India Company, its first Fleet—James the First forbids Piracy—Encroachments of the Dutch—Van Tromp and Blake—

Cromwell's Act—Dutch Trade in the English Colonies—Charles the Second's Navigation Laws—Sir Joshua Child's opinion—Other Navigation Laws—Bounty for building large Ships—Progress of Trade—William the Third encourages the Marine—Success of the East India Company—Tonnage at the commencement of the Eighteenth Century

pp. 29-38

CHAPTER VI.

PROGRESS TO END OF THE EIGHTEENTH CENTURY.

Queen Anne—South Sea Company—Bubble Companies—State of Shipping—Trade of American Colonies—Newfoundland—Supply of Seamen—American Smuggling in the West Indies—Naval Operations there—Survey of the St. Lawrence by James Cook—Revolt of the States—Their Independence achieved—Effect of the War on British Shipping—French King's proposals for reciprocal Trade—Convict Colony in New South Wales—Trade of Liverpool—Renewal of E. I. Charter—State of Navigation—Reward offered by British Government for the best method of determining Longitude at Sea—John Harrison's Timekeepers—Government grants for Lunar Tables—Nautical Almanac

pp. 39-49

CHAPTER VII.

PROGRESS DURING EARLY PART OF THE NINETEENTH CENTURY.

Nineteenth Century—The Slave Trade—Hampering effect of Legislation—Scarcity of Seamen—Advantage of Americans as Neutrals—The right of search a cause of another American War—*Shannon* and the *Chesapeake*—East India Trade thrown open—Depression in Shipping—The Reciprocity Acts—Laws regulating Emigration—General revision of Marine Acts in 1825—Low state of Tonnage—China Trade thrown open in 1833—Reform Bill and its effects—Shipping Acts, 1834 and 1835—Compulsory Apprenticeship—Increase of American Ships—Conduct of British Shipmasters—Public meetings on Shipwrecks, &c.—Royal Commission of 1836—Report of Commissioners—W. S. Lindsay's opinion of British Officers—Past training of Seamen and its effects upon Character—Proposed remedies—Mr. Silk Buckingham's Bill—Opposition of the Shipowners—The defeat of the Bill—Further Commissions of Inquiry—Mr. Murray's Letter to Consuls abroad as to the conduct of British Shipmasters—Act of 1844—Mr. Poulett Thompson's idea of Voluntary Examinations—State of Marine Officers compared—East India Company's Officers—Ordinary Shipmasters and Officers—London Passenger Ships and their discipline—Education of British and Foreign Seamen compared . pp. 50-67

CHAPTER VIII.
INSTITUTION OF VOLUNTARY AND COMPULSORY EXAMINATIONS.

Unsatisfactory condition of the British Marine—Voluntary Examinations for Masters and Mates instituted by Order in Council, 1845—Boards of Examiners—American competition and its effects—Repeal of the Corn Laws—Shipowners fight for Protection—Decline in English Shipbuilding—Navigation Laws repealed, 1849—Effect of the Voluntary Examinations—Compulsory Examinations instituted, 1851

pp. 68–79

CHAPTER IX.
THE RISE AND PROGRESS OF STEAM PROPULSION.

Rise and Progress of Ship Propulsion—Blasco Garay—James Watt—Newcomen's Engine—Henry Bell—The *Comet*—The *Rob Roy*—The *Enterprise* reaches Calcutta—Iron as a material for Shipbuilding—The Leviathan class of Steamers—Dr. Lardner and Steam across the Atlantic—The *Sirius* and the *Great Western* cross successfully—Francis P. Smith's Screw Propeller—New Steamship Companies—The Cunard and other Lines—The *Great Britain*—The Screw Propeller superior to the Paddle—Collins Line—The advance of Steam steadily progressive . . . . pp. 80–92

CHAPTER X.
DEVELOPMENT OF FREE TRADE.

New Departure under Free Trade—Mr. Richard Green and the Americans—Iron and Steam—Goldfields of California and Australia—Increase of Shipping—Speed of American Ships—China Trade—British Tonnage Laws—Mr. Moorsom's Plan of Measurement becomes the basis of Legislation in 1854—Improvement in Ships—Parliament relieves burdens upon Shipping—Effect on British Seamen—Coasting Trade thrown open, 1854—American Coasting Trade—Shipping Laws consolidated, 1854—Apprentices—Russian War—High Freights—Indian Mutiny—Glut of Shipping in Eastern Seas—Increase of Foreign Shipping in British Ports—Competition in the China Trade—*Thermopylæ* and *Sir Lancelot*—French Bounties—Conclusions . . pp. 93–100

CHAPTER XI.

SHIPPING LEGISLATION, 1862-1875.

Shipping Legislation, 1862—Engineers' Examinations—American Blockade—Origin of the Suez Canal—Canal condemned by the English—Increase of Steam Trade to India through the Canal—Mr. Plimsoll and Loss of Life at Sea—Mr. Fortescue's Act, 1871—Marine Department of Board of Trade invested with full control of British Shipping—Mr. Plimsoll's Book—Lord Carlingford's Bill—Ships sold to Foreigners—Royal Commission, 1873—Mr. Plimsoll's Bill, 1874—Report of the Commissioners—Sir Charles Adderley's Bill, 1875—Mr. Plimsoll's conduct—Painful incident in the House—"Stopgap" Act, 1875—Excitement amongst Shipowners . . . . . pp. 101-111

CHAPTER XII.

"LOCKSLEY HALL" CASE—SHIPMASTERS' SOCIETIES—LOADING OF SHIPS.

Further Legislation, 1876—Wreck Commissioner—*Locksley Hall* case—Unjust Sentence on Captain Barnes—Shipmasters and the Prime Minister—Formation of Shipmasters' Society of London—Court of Appeal for Inquiry into Shipping Casualties—Serious Losses at Sea—Stowage of Grain Cargoes—Mr. Martell's paper on Losses at Sea—Port of Montreal—Capsizing of the *Daphne*—Inquiry by Sir Edward Reed and his Report—Detention of Overladen Ships—Loadline Committee—Royal Commission of 1884 " On Loss of Life at Sea "—Wreck Reports . . . . pp. 112-119

CHAPTER XIII.

SHIPPING LEGISLATION, 1884-1894.

Mr. Chamberlain's Bill—Opposition of the Shipowners—Depression in Shipping, 1885—Full Report of the Commission in 1887—The effects of late Legislation described—Its apparent inability in preventing Loss of Life—Papers by Professors Elgar and Jenkins—False Competition and careless Stowage—Amount of Shipping Legislation
pp. 120-127

CHAPTER XIV.

STATISTICS OF SHIPPING.

Board of Trade Returns—British Tonnage—Its increase compared with Foreign—Steam Tonnage—Fluctuations in Shipbuilding—Gradual decrease in number of Ships since 1865—Increase in size of Ships and decrease in Crews—Large Vessels in 1850—And 1884—Shipbuilding in 1895—Comparison of the largest Steamers in existence—North German Lloyd's new Steamer—Increased competition in building in Foreign Countries—Causes of British success—Speculation—Improvement in economy of Engines—Principal sources of foreign opposition in Shipping . . . . pp. 128–140

PART II.
PERSONNEL OF THE MERCANTILE MARINE.

CHAPTER I.
SHIPOWNERS.

Shipowners—Tenure of Shipping Property—Sixty-fourths—Different kinds of Companies—Limited Liability Acts—Mr. Thomas Gray's opinion of them in connection with Ships—Reasons for adoption by Ship Managers . . . . pp. 141–145

CHAPTER II.
THE MARINERS, OR THE EMPLOYED.

The Mariners—Master Mariner—The Mates—Their qualifications—Petty Officers, &c.—Able Seamen—Apprentices—Engineers and Firemen—Cooks, Stewards, &c. . . . . . . pp. 146–149

CHAPTER III.
THE DUTIES OF THE PERSONNEL.

Early years of Commerce—Duty of the Shipowner—Master and Owner—Effect of rapid communication on Master's position—Master's Duties—Limitations—Duties of the Mates—Relation between Masters and Officers—Owners and Seamen—Result of the abandonment of compulsory Apprenticeships—Engineers and Engine-room Crews—Necessity of true Discipline . . . . . . pp. 150–161

CHAPTER IV.

THE PRESENT POSITION OF THE PERSONNEL.

The Mercantile Marine Service not a homogeneous one—Its division into Classes—The Shipowner—Company Directors—Private Ship Managers—Effect of high competition in Shipbuilding and Owning—Merchants and Shippers—Home Trade—Shipmasters—Their responsibility—Position decaying—Number of Certificated Masters unknown—Annual Passes in the various Grades—Competition of Aliens—Reasons for employing Foreigners—First Mate, his Duties and Position—Junior Officers—Ocean Tramps—Want of consideration in Masters—Seamanship less required than formerly—Engineers, their improved Position and Education—Remuneration—Experience valuable both at Sea and on Shore—Advantages of Engineers greater than those of Sailors . . . . pp. 162–173

PART III.

EDUCATION OF THE MERCANTILE MARINE.

CHAPTER I.

BACKWARD STATE OF EDUCATION.

Deficiency of Education in the early part of the Century—Recommendation of the Royal Commission *re* Nautical Schools—Apprentice System as a means of Education—Its failure—What has the Board of Trade done to promote Education?—Action through Board of Education's Science and Art Department—Grants to Nautical Schools—Alteration in 1862 fatal to Nautical Education—Schools in connection with South Kensington—Results of their Teaching—Honours Examinations—Another change in 1892—Falling off of Scholars in consequence—Divergence of Board of Trade and South Kensington Examinations—Why has the Government not done more for Nautical Education?—Mr. Bolam's Evidence . . . . . pp. 174–181

CHAPTER II.

GENERAL RESULTS OF THE SYSTEM OF EXAMINATIONS.

Results of the Voluntary Examinations—Lowering of the Standard for Compulsory Examinations—Its effect—Promise of the Board to raise the Standard—System of Examination productive of Cramming—

Evil results adverted to in 1870 by a Writer to Lloyds—Board of Trade's recommendation to Officers to Educate themselves never acted upon—Neglect of the Primary Sciences in Board of Trade Examinations—Comparison with Foreign Nations—Men of fifty years ago—System rendered Shipowners and Masters careless of the Education of Young Sailors—Passports to Service, their intention—Promotion, an Owner's question . . . . . pp. 182-187

CHAPTER III.
OUR YOUNG SAILORS.

Attractions to a Sea Life—The different classes of Lads who go to Sea—Changes in Life at Sea—Age of going to Sea—Advice to Parents—A special Education the first necessity for any Profession
pp. 188-191

CHAPTER IV.
A SEAMAN'S EDUCATION: WHAT IS EMBRACED IN IT.

What a Seaman's Education should be—Changes from Sail to Steam—Qualifications of a Seaman—The Science of Navigation—What it requires—How to acquire the necessary Knowledge—The Law silent on this point—Difficulty attending Education—Various types of Officers . . . . pp. 192-195

CHAPTER V.
THE PRESENT MEANS OF EDUCATION.

Education as a Seaman—Training Ships—Education as Navigators—Where to be found—Christ's Hospital—Endowed Nautical Schools—Liverpool Nautical College—College of Navigation at Liverpool—School Ships *Conway* and *Worcester*—Deficiency of Schools in London—The Drapers' Company—Evils of the present System . pp. 196-201

CHAPTER VI.
HINTS ON EDUCATION.

Elements to be acquired—The first five Rules—Course recommended—To be tested by Preliminary Examinations—*Worcester* Examinations—The Nautical Colleges *Conway* and *Worcester*—Little assistance given by Government, &c., to Young Sailors—New Regulations for

Examinations—New element in Extra Master's Examination—What will be its effect?—It will be a *dilettante* exercise—The true meaning of the Fifth Rule of Arithmetic—The two methods of Education—Shipmasters' and Officers' Memorial for Honours Examinations—Opinions of Shipowners—Adverse to theoretical Education—Officers' Duty as to Education—"Survival of the Fittest" . . pp. 202–210

PART IV.

DISCIPLINE AND DUTY IN THE BRITISH MERCANTILE MARINE.

(*A Paper on "Duty and Discipline" as read to the Shipmasters' Society.*)

Discipline and Duty—Relation between the Shipowner and the Crew—Between the Master and Crew—Duties of Mates, Petty Officers, and Seamen, Engineers and Engine-room Crew—Mutual respect enjoined
pp. 211–231

POSTSCRIPT.—The Serious Decrease in the Number of British Seamen, a matter demanding the Attention of the Nation . . pp. 232–236

APPENDIX: (A) A List of the Ships forming the Fleet of King Edward the Third—(B) Description of the Shipman from Chaucer's Prologue—(C) An Abstract of the Passes and Classes of Masters and Mates under an Order in Council, 19th August, 1845, prior to December, 1849—(D) Apprentices in the Mercantile Marine—(E) List of Navigation Classes in British Isles—(F) Passes in connection with South Kensington Classes—(G) Educational Standard required by various Maritime Powers for Masters and Mates . . . . pp. 237–243

INDEX . . . . . pp. 245–248

THE BRITISH MERCANTILE MARINE

PART I.

HISTORICAL.

CHAPTER I.

FROM EARLY TIMES TO 1486.

CONTENTS.—Early population of England—Ancient Britons' knowledge of shipbuilding—Alfred the Great—Athelstan rewards foreign adventurers—Edward the Confessor creates the Cinque Ports—Richard the First's fleet—Les Roles d'Oleron—Hanseatic laws—Trade in the reign of Edward the First—Rivalry between the Cinque Ports and the French—Letters of Marque—King Edward the Third's fleet—Sea-fight off Sluys—Increase of English exports—The Hanse Towns—The Flemings in London—Wat Tyler's rebellion—Richard the Second's Act of Protection for English shipping—State of England—The Kings of England and the Hanseatic League—Henry the Fifth—Improvement in Shipbuilding—The King of Sweden's large ship—Enterprise awakening in European countries—The Road to India—The Portuguese double the Cape.

Early Population of England.—The bulk of the population of the sea coasts of Great Britain, especially on the eastern side of the Island, is for the most part of Saxon origin, with a considerable mixture of the Danish or hardy Norseman blood; on the western parts it is more purely British with a strong intermixture of the Saxon. The Danes never penetrated into Cornwall, Devon, or Wales, so as to settle there and largely affect the population, as on the East. After the Norman conquest the followers of William the Conqueror became the great landowners of England, but the Saxons, &c., remained the trading and farming bulk of the population, and retained their peculiar characteristics.

Ancient Britons' Knowledge of Shipbuilding.—The knowledge of maritime affairs possessed by the ancient Britons must have been very slight, and their coasting voyages in "coracles" could not have afforded much room for seamanship. Whatever knowledge of actual shipbuilding—*i.e.*, of planked and framed vessels—they had must have been derived from the Romans during their occupancy of the Island. In after years they were no match for the Saxons, who easily possessed themselves of the coast lines, and with them the command of the sea. The Saxon Angles in their turn fell a prey to the superiority of the hardy Norsemen, sea dogs from their cradles. It was to these mingled races, with their sea-roving instincts, that the Englishmen of succeeding ages owed that confidence on the rocking element, and delight in the amphibious life of a seaman, which has made him the "natural master of the vessel and the wave."

Alfred the Great.—During the Saxon period many attempts were made to encourage a race of mariners. Notably, Alfred the Great, after he had conquered the Danish invaders and restored peace to his kingdom, fostered foreign adventure and trade, even as far as the Mediterranean and the Levant, then the furthest limits of the European world, by building and hiring vessels to merchant adventurers, and even supplying them with means for the purpose of trading.

Athelstan.—Thirty years after his death his successor Athelstan urged his subjects to foreign voyages, by ordaining "that every merchant who made three voyages to the Mediterranean on his own account should be raised to honour, and enjoy the privileges of a gentleman."

Edward the Confessor creates the Cinque Ports.—A hundred years later Edward the Confessor gave protection to the mariners of Kent and Sussex, by enfranchising the Cinque Ports—Sandwich, Hythe, Dover, Romney and Hastings—and conferring privileges upon their seamen. After the Norman conquest by William the Conqueror, in 1066, that monarch confirmed these privileges and extended them, by granting these ports a kind of Palatine jurisdiction under "gardiens," or wardens, in each port, the whole being supervised by a superior named the Lord Warden, and thereby freeing them from the civil and military administrations of the counties of Kent and Sussex. This was for the purpose of creating and fostering ship-building and -owning, as well as a race of mariners for the protection of the shores of these counties, which were the key of the kingdom, against foreign invasion.

After the Norman conquest a gradual fusion of the various races, Norman, Saxon, and Danish, took place, and they became in time one people, speaking the same language and governed by the same laws; and we then begin to find further traces of foreign adventure.

Richard the First's Fleet.—Richard the First, an illustrious warrior and traveller, did much to encourage seamen. In 1197, when he raised a great fleet to take part in the third Crusade, English shipbuilding must have reached some perfection, for Geffre de Vinisauf, who was with the expedition, says, that "the people of Messina in Sicily where the English and French Fleets rendevouzed, *never saw, or ever will see*, on their coasts so great and so fine a fleet as that of England." Each vessel was manned by 15 sailors, 14 rowers, and 40 soldiers with their horses. The entry of this fleet into Messina, with colours flying and trumpets blowing, is painted in vivid colours by the old chroniclers. It is to be feared that none of all that fleet ever reached home again, for Richard returned a wanderer, and alone, after enduring many hardships and long imprisonment.

Les Roles d'Oleron and Hanseatic Laws.—He is said to have been the author of the celebrated laws, for the guidance of shipping affairs, entitled "Les Roles d'Oleron," but his claim is doubtful.

The people of Rhodes, who are mentioned by Homer in the "Iliad" as a powerful maritime race, flourished exceedingly 200-300 B.C., and excelled all other nations as jurists. Their excellent laws relating to navigation were introduced into the Roman Code, and, without doubt, formed the foundation of the "Roles d'Oleron" attributed to Richard, as well as of our system of maritime law, which was brought to such perfection by Lord Mansfield in the middle of the last century.

As some of the provisions of the "Roles" throw considerable light upon maritime manners and customs of that day, one or two, relating to Masters and Mariners, are quoted.

The 12th Article enacts: "That the master, having hired his crew, was to be invested, in the first place, with the duty of keeping the peace," that is, the law gave him magisterial authority. "If any man gave the lie to another at table, where there was bread and wine, he was fined four deniers; but if the master himself offended in that way, he had to pay a double fine.

"If any sailor impudently contradicted the master, he was fined eight deniers, and if the master struck him he was required to bear that blow; but if the master struck more than one blow, the sailor might defend himself; whereas, if the sailor committed the first assault, he was fined 100 sous, or condemned to lose his hand."

It would appear that "the master might call the sailor opprobrious names," and in such case the sailor was advised "to submit, or to hide himself in the forecastle out of sight;" but if the master "followed the sailor, he might stand upon his own defence—for the master ought not to pass into the forecastle."

Article 13 enacted: "That if a difference arose between the master and the seaman, the former ought to deny the seaman his mess thrice before he turned him out of the ship; if the latter offered satisfaction, and was refused, and then turned out of the ship, he could follow the ship to her port of discharge and claim full wages;" and

"The master not taking any seaman in his stead, in such case rendered himself liable for any damage occurring."

The Hanseatic laws required the master "not to give the seaman any cause to mutiny;" nor "to provoke him by calling him names," "nor wrong him, nor keep from him that which was his; but to use him well, and pay him honestly that which was his due."

There were also some curious laws as to meals. The custom of serving out a specified allowance seems very ancient.

The "Roles" enacted: "That the seamen were to have one meal a day, and wine allowed them; but if there were no wine, then two meals were to be served."

"Pilots causing loss of life, or ship, from ignorance or otherwise, with no power to make it good, were to lose their heads, and the masters had power to inflict the penalty!"

The laws against piracy were very severe, and "pirates caught red-handed might be hanged upon the spot."

These laws breathed a spirit of simple, if rough, justice to all alike.

The laws of ownership and the regulation of freight, wages, &c., were complete prototypes of those which have been in force down to this century—details have been multiplied, particulars have been added from time to time—but the general principles remain the same, forming the nucleus of the existing laws of nations regarding shipping.

The officers of the vessels referred to in the "Roles" are the Master or Pilot, the Mate, another officer who gave the word to the rowers and served out the provisions, and a fourth whose especial duty it was to look for shoals and rocks, and to direct the ship with long poles. The usual course of the voyage was by creeping along the land in daylight, and anchoring at night; hence the duties of the above-named officers are easily understood. Without compass, or chart, navigation was a matter of experience or experiment, and, as the sounding was performed by a pole, the vessels could have had no great draft of water.

Rigid discipline was maintained, and those who failed in their duty were often punished with great severity. The punishment of keelhauling, not unknown in the English service, dates back to this period, and perhaps earlier. The crews, as detailed in Richard's fleet, were divided into sailors and rowers, whose duties were quite distinct; the sailors never being compelled to labour at the oars except in cases of emergency.

Trade in the Reign of Edward the First, 1294.—In King Edward the First's reign commerce seems to have gained ground, notwithstanding his numerous wars. In addition to the trade with the Hanse towns * and Norway, there was a large trade in wool, which was exported to Flanders, and large quantities of wine and other produce were imported from Gascony and Guienne, the principal port of which was Bordeaux. A fast increasing commerce was maintained with Italy and Spain. Ships were now being gradually transformed from galleys impelled by oars, and the occasional use of sails, into decked vessels fitted with suitable masts and sails.

Rivalry between Cinque Ports and French.—An intense rivalry existed between the Cinque Ports seamen and the French of the opposite shores. This in Edward the First's reign culminated in open warfare, and a sea fight took place between them, in which it is said 8000 Frenchmen were slain. This being the case, the Cinque Ports must have been very powerful, and the seaman population very considerable. The king desiring to avert an open war with the French, threatened the men of the Cinque Ports with pains and penalties, and a withdrawal of their privileges. This they resented, and, with much independence, said, "Be the King's Majesty and council well advised, that if any wrong or grievance be done them in any fashion against right, they will sooner forsake wives, children, and all that they have, and go seek through the seas where they shall think to make their own profit." An unveiled threat of open piracy! Notwithstanding all the king's efforts, the dispute with the French continued, and was one of the causes of the celebrated hundred years' war between the two countries.

Letters of Marque.—Letters of marque are said to have been first issued by Edward, who, finding his efforts at peace unavailing, made use of the valiant Cinque Ports seamen, and gave them licence to prey upon the French.

Edward the Third's Fleet. Battle off Sluys.—In the reign of Edward the Third the war still continued, and he, assembling a great fleet from all parts of the kingdom, proved the British naval superiority in an engagement off Sluys, on the 22nd of June, 1340, by completely routing the French fleet. It must be remembered

* A combination of towns in the north of Europe for purposes of trade and self-protection.

that the ships employed were ordinary merchants' vessels,* there being no Royal navy in existence. In addition to the crews of the vessels, soldiers were put on board to do the fighting. It will be observed from the list of Edward's fleet that London, although undoubtedly the largest emporium of British trade, sent fewer ships than many of the out-ports to join him.

Increase of English Exports; Hanse Towns; Flemings in London; Wat Tyler's Rebellion.—Although English commerce had increased, and Edward obtained a revenue of £80,000 a year from the export duty on wool, it did not bring a corresponding benefit to the London shipowners. The reason of this was, that the trade in wool and other exports was in the hands of the Germans of the Hanse towns. These towns were scattered all over the North of Europe, and had banded themselves into a league, and, from the twelfth century to the reign of Queen Elizabeth, monopolised and controlled the trade of Europe. Soon after the Norman conquest the Flemings had settled in London in considerable numbers. They had warehouses on the north side of the Thames, on a spot now covered by the Cannon Street Railway Station, around which grew up a German colony, which controlled the exports and imports of London to the detriment of the native merchants; and as they employed the ships of the Hansa instead of those of the English, it was to the detriment also of the native shipowner and mariner. Of this competition the London citizens complained bitterly, and it was one of the leading causes of Wat Tyler's Rebellion, in which the foreigners were attacked by the mob, and many of the houses of the German quarter, known as the Steel Yard, were burnt.

Richard the Second's Act of Protection.—To allay the anger of the citizens the first step was made towards the protection of British shipping, for by the Act 5 Richard the Second, c. iii., it was enacted: "That for increasing the shipping of England, of late much diminished, none of the king's subjects shall hereafter ship any kind of merchandise, either outward or homeward, but only of the ships of the king's subjects, on forfeiture of ships and merchandise; in which ships also the *greater part of the crews* shall be the king's subjects."

Such an enactment as this, a sufficiently provident one, in a state commercially weak but politically strong, was hardly suitable to the Germans of the Steel Yard, or the Frenchmen of the Vintry, in whose hands were largely both the export and import trades of the country, and who, of course, preferred to use ships of their own. To carry out such a measure was necessarily difficult, as English ships were scarce, and trade was consequently

* See *Appendix* **A.**

hampered, to say nothing of the opposition of these foreign merchants, who were disgusted at seeing the trade, of which they had reaped most of the profits, taken out of their hands.

It would appear that Parliament itself felt the difficulty, for in the very next year we find an enactment (6 Richard the Second, c. viii.) which re-opened to them the door, and which " permitted the merchants, *where no English ships were to be had*, to export or import in foreign ships."

Nine years subsequently we find what must be called a New Act of Navigation. "All English Merchants were bound to freight only in English ships" always provided "that the freight was *reasonable* and *moderate*"; a very just precaution, but one very difficult to work.

State of England.—When we reflect upon what has occurred in our own day, it is curious to note the efforts of a small and growing people to attract and keep trade within its own grasp. England up to this time had been a fertile country, with a sparse population, producing food and cattle more than sufficient for its own wants. Its flocks of sheep were large, and its wool famous and plentiful. Such a country does not fly readily to manufactures for a living. The wool was exported into Flanders and came back woven into cloth. Naturally the Flemings, as manufacturers, would send their merchants here to buy their wool in the cheapest possible market, and, having woven it, send it back for sale in the dearest. To do this, it was necessary to keep the traffic in their own hands, and in their own ships. The English rulers, constantly engaged in Continental wars, felt the want of a navy, both for fighting and transport, for which they were wholly dependent upon the Mercantile fleet; and the English merchants grudged the foreigners their immense profits! How, then, could they help themselves but by some sort of protective legislation? And in time it bore fruit, but slowly.

For a time this effort at protection had little success. The resources of the English were not sufficiently advanced to maintain the traffic; trade suffered and with it the King's revenues, and this close protection had to be relaxed.

Hanseatic League.—During the succeeding reigns of the house of Lancaster, the country, disturbed and harassed by the Wars of the Roses, had little opportunity of fostering commerce. The Hanseatic League, favoured by the Kings, who found in the Germans a ready means of providing funds for carrying on their wars and lenient bankers who did not press for repayment, as long as their privileges remained intact, grew in power and importance. Notwithstanding many efforts to repress this power it continued to prevail until the Elizabethan period.

Henry the Fifth's Navy.—In the year 1417 Henry the Fifth seems to have made a serious attempt at the creation of a Royal Navy. Three large vessels, the *Trinity*, the *Grace de Dieu*, and the *Holy Ghost*, were built at Southampton to enable Henry to compete with the large vessels hired by the French from the Genoese and the Spaniards. He also built two Royal Yachts, the *King's Chamber* and the *King's Hall*, which were sumptuously fitted internally, and had sails of purple silk, whereon were emblazoned the Arms of England and France. This was evidently a great advance in naval architecture, and these vessels were no doubt looked upon with wonder and astonishment by the good people of Southampton.

Improvements in Shipbuilding. The King of Sweden's Large Ship.—The art of shipbuilding was making great strides in the northern countries of Europe as well as in England. In 1455 the Swedish King sent a large ship of 1000 tons to England, with a request that she might be permitted to trade and reload with lawful merchandise. This is supposed to be the largest ship ever seen in England at that time. Henry the Sixth did much to encourage shipbuilding, and rewarded the patriotism of John Taverner of Hull in building a vessel "as large as a carrack;" and, for Taverner's encouragement, he was permitted to load her free of dues. Wm. Comyngs of Bristol possessed ships of 400 and 500 tons burthen and one of even 900 tons. These vessels he probably purchased from the Baltic men, as, if they had been built in England, such notice would hardly have been taken of Taverner's ship.

Enterprise awakening in European Countries.—The spirit of enterprise and discovery was now rife in all the maritime states of Europe, especially in Portugal. The loss of trade with India *viâ* Egypt, which had been closed to the Christian States by the Saracens, vexed them sorely; and the great question of how to reach India by sea was filling the minds of the Portuguese navigators.

The Road to India. The Portuguese double the Cape.—Whilst England was absorbed in domestic strife, the Portuguese, under the patronage of their enlightened Prince Henry the Navigator, were struggling down the coast of Africa to find, around it, a way to the East. After many rebuffs from bad weather and sickness, in 1486 A.D. Bartholomew Diaz rounded its southern point, and saw the land trending to the N.E. That point, from the difficulty he had had in reaching it, he named the Cape of Storms; but on his return the King of Portugal named it "El Cabo d'Esperanza" (The Cape of Good Hope). Eleven years after, another expedition, under Vasco di Gama, doubled the Cape and reached India.

In the meantime Columbus had discovered, not a road to India across the Atlantic, but a new world. These two events had an unprecedented effect upon the trade of the world, and opened up to its mariners a field of adventure and discovery before unknown, in which those of England were destined in the future to take their full share.

The defeat of Richard the Third, of the House of York, by Henry, Duke of Richmond, of the House of Lancaster, on the field of Bosworth, in 1485, put an end to the Wars of the Roses, which had deluged the country with blood, injured its trade and resources, and the nation had peace to pursue its commercial avocations.

CHAPTER II.

PROGRESS UNDER HENRY THE EIGHTH.

CONTENTS.—State of Arts and Commerce—Christopher Columbus and Henry the Seventh—Sebastian Cabot discovers Labrador and Newfoundland—Henry the Eighth builds a Royal Navy, and founds dockyards—Sir Edward Howard and the King's fleet—English commerce hampered by the Hanse Towns—London merchant adventurers—Froude's picture of the English people.

State of Arts and Commerce.—Leaving behind us a period of internecine struggle for victory, whether in conquest or commerce, we now arrive at one of great change and progress in the world's affairs. The invention of the art of printing had revolutionised learning, and rendered the communication of ideas easy; and the invention of gunpowder had completely changed the art of warfare, making it no longer a struggle of hand to hand combat. The progress of these arts was slow but sure. The former had been brought to England by Caxton in the reign of Edward the Fourth, and one of its first patrons was Richard, Duke of Gloucester, the king's brother, who, whatever his faults, was an enlightened prince, and during his short reign fostered English commerce by several enactments. The art of shipbuilding had grown by slow degrees, and ships had passed from the stage of mere galleys, partly propelled by oars, into stately vessels fully rigged and dependent upon sail power for their navigation. The perfection of the mariner's compass enabled the navigator to find his way from point to point without closely hugging the intermediate shores; and improvement in the sciences of astronomy and geodesy afforded a lantern to his path. The north star and the rising and setting sun were no longer the only beacons by which he might direct his course.

The settlement of the true form of the earth as a sphere, and the invention of the astrolabe, a graduated circular rim with sights attached for taking altitudes of the heavenly bodies, paved the way for reliable astronomical observations. The latitude of many places had been fairly settled, but the relation of various parts of the world in distance east and west was still vague, as position by longitude was in a very incomplete condition.

Hitherto charts had been only roughly conceived, and grotesque maps of land and sea, sketched by the imagination rather than by science, were useless for purposes of navigation as understood in more modern times. Timekeepers or watches were still unknown. The world was, however, waking to new ideas in both science and practice, and their fruits were soon to be seen in new discoveries.

Christopher Columbus.—Whilst the Portuguese had been struggling to get round Africa on the road to India, Christopher Colon, or Columbus, was endeavouring to obtain assistance to carry out his great project of trying to proceed to the Indies and Cathay by a westerly route across the Atlantic. Foiled in Portugal and Italy, he sent his brother to England to try and secure the good offices of Henry the Seventh. That monarch listened to his story, and although not wanting in intelligence enough to make him see the advantage of success in such an undertaking, dallied with it until too late.

Columbus finding aid in Spain, before Bartolomeo's return, had discovered the New World, and all the benefits derived from it fell into the lap of the Spanish monarch instead of that of the English king.

Sebastian Cabot discovers Labrador and Newfoundland. —Henry, finding too late what he had lost, and willing to aid his subjects in the discovery of unknown lands, gave to John Cabot, of Bristol, and his sons, Sebastian and another, a patent of discovery and conquest. In the beginning of 1497 Sebastian sailed from Bristol in a ship named the *Matthew*, and on the 24th of June sighted the coast of North America, supposed to have been the coast of Labrador, in about 56° of north latitude; he is said to have explored the coast southward as far as Florida. He also discovered Newfoundland. These discoveries were long thought to have had little effect upon British trade and commerce, but the researches of Judge Prowse, of Newfoundland, of which the results are to be found in his lately published history of that island, have thrown an entirely new light upon them. The failure of one or two attempts to colonise the island in the sixteenth century may have given rise to the idea that it was of little value to us; but Judge Prowse has fully proved that this was quite beside the truth.

John Cabot was a native of Venice, and may therefore well be supposed to have had an acquaintance with Italian literature, and speculations as to a western passage to India. He knew of the Spanish discoveries, and the latitude in which Columbus had struck land, and the idea occurred to him that he might get round that land to the north; but finding himself blocked there, he steered south, hoping to find a passage through until he reached Florida, and found it impossible. That this idea was in his mind we shall see hereafter.

Henry the Eighth builds a Royal Navy and founds Dockyards.—The idea of a royal navy, adapted for fighting purposes, was further promoted by Henry the Seventh, who built the *Great Harry*, a three-masted vessel, and the earliest war vessel of any size. His successor, Henry the Eighth, a monarch zealously devoted to the aggrandisement of England, following his example, built several large vessels, notably the *Harry Grace à Dieu*, of 1000 tons burthen, and 80 guns, in 1515. This ship was fitted with port-holes, which were invented by a native of Brest named Deschayes. The dockyards of Portsmouth, Deptford, and Woolwich were created by Henry. He was himself fond of shipbuilding and made quite a study of the art. At his decease he left a fleet of fifty ships manned by 8000 seamen. He also settled the ranks of the officers of the navy, dividing them into admirals, vice-admirals, and captains, &c., and it was in his reign that ships began to be reckoned by tons burthen and the number of their guns.

Sir Edward Howard and the King's Fleet.—As a curiosity of history, and to show the manner in which fleets were managed in that day, it may be related that in 1512 Henry the Eighth fitted out a fleet of about thirty ships and 3000 men, the former being from 100 to 1000 tons burthen, to join the King of Spain in guarding the seas against the French. The command of this fleet he gave to Sir Edward Howard, who contracted with the King to manage and provide for it on the following terms, viz., A salary of ten shillings *per diem* for himself, and one shilling and sixpence *per diem* for the captains; the sailors, soldiers, and gunners were to receive five shillings per month as pay, and the same for victuals. The King was to have half of all the prize-money, and the other half, in due proportion according to rank, was to be distributed amongst the officers and men of the fleet. Taking the value of money as being from four to five times what it is now, this pay appears small, and therefore prize-money must have formed a considerable part of the remuneration for service in the King's ships.

English Commerce hampered by the Hanse Towns.—As to trade and commerce, the English were making slow progress, the principal part of it being still in the hands of the Hanseatic League. During the reign of Henry the Seventh their privileges had been well maintained, and Henry the Eighth confirmed and even extended them for political reasons.

London Merchant Adventurers.—The citizens of London were now bestirring themselves in earnest, and a number of merchants formed themselves into a company somewhat upon the principles of the Hansa, which was named "The Merchant Adventurers"; and on their part carried on their business with almost as much arrogance as the "Hansa" itself, which begot them the name of the "New Hansa."

The Hanseatic League was still strong, and the Germans of the Steel Yard having most of the London trade, the company of "The London Merchant Adventurers" had a hard struggle to make way against them. Wheeler, writing in defence of that company in 1601, drew a very poor picture of London shipping. He says: "That about sixty years before he wrote there were not above four ships (beside those of the Royal Navy) that were above 120 tons each within the River Thames." Whatever progress British shipping had made was in the out-ports rather than in London.

Froude's Picture of the English People.—The spirit of foreign adventure had not yet filled the English with any very serious aspirations. Mr. Froude, writing of the English people in 1530, gives a vivid picture of them as traders of that period.

He says: "Until the fall of Wolsey, the sea-going population of England, with but few exceptions, moved in a groove, in which they lived from day to day with unerring uniformity. The wine brigs made their annual voyages to Bordeaux and Cadiz; the hoys plied with such regularity as the winds allowed them between the Thames and the Scheldt. Summer after summer the 'Iceland Fleet' went north for cod and ling, which were the food of the winter fasting days; the boats of Yarmouth, Rye, Southampton, Poole, Brixham, Dartmouth, Plymouth, and Fowie fished the Channel. The people themselves, though hardy and industrious, and though as much at home upon the ocean as their Scandinavian forefathers, or their descendants in modern England, were yet contented to live in an unchanging round, from which they neither attempted, or desired, to extricate themselves."

"The officials of the London companies ruled despotically in every English harbour; not a vessel cleared for a foreign port, not a smack went out for the herring season, without the official licence; and the sale of every bale of goods, or hundredweight of fish, was carried on under the eyes of the authorities, and at prices fixed by Act of Parliament."

To such a people, careful of protecting home industries, and happy in doing as their forefathers had done, there was little room for expansion and less desire for it. To them the rich trade of the East or the El Dorados of the West were a vain temptation. But the succeeding age will unfold a different picture.

In the earlier days of English commerce and shipping the people had been confined in leading-strings which largely affected freedom of action; they were dependent upon the will of the Sovereigns, who regulated affairs for their own ends, and granted monopolies to such people as suited themselves—not considering the general welfare of the nation, but their own revenues. No monopoly was granted that did not procure them a large revenue, or give them ample return in services compulsorily rendered in case of the King's need. In this manner succeeding monarchs gave monopolies to foreigners, such as the Hansa, who retained their privileges by means of large bribes, to the great disadvantage of the nation's own merchant adventurers; and this continued more or less until the time of Elizabeth.

CHAPTER III.

FROM HENRY THE EIGHTH TO THE DEATH OF MARY.

CONTENTS.—New activity and intelligence—Henry the Eighth sends Cabot and Sir T. Port on a new voyage of discovery—Their return—Cabot retires to Spain—The Reformation—Henry prepares for defence by sea—English mariners—Trade with Newfoundland—West of England fishermen—Will Hawkins—Edward the Sixth and the Russian Ambassador—Oppressive measures of the Hanseatic League—Sir Richard Chancellor discovers Archangel—The London and Muscovite Company—Queen Mary succeeds and marries Philip of Spain—Mary's attempts to restore the Roman Catholic supremacy disturbs the country—Philip's influence—English rovers—Mary's death.

New Activity and Intelligence.—The reign of Henry the Eighth was a period of transition from old ideas and customs to a new activity and intelligence. The new learning, aided by the printing press, was having an influence on the minds of men to whom learning had before been a sealed book. In connection with navigation and discovery, the travels of Amerigo Vespucci, a competitor with Columbus for the discovery of America, were widely read. Cabot had written an account of his voyage; Sir Thomas More his *Utopia*, or ideal commonwealth, which he tells us was suggested by a conversation with a sunburnt sailor, whom he accidentally met in Antwerp, and who proved to have been a companion of Amerigo Vespucci in those voyages to the New World, "that now be in print, and abroad in every man's hand."

Voyage of Cabot and Port.—In the early days of Henry's reign the trade of India and America was in the hands of Spain and Portugal, protected by the Pope's bulls; therefore open commerce by the English with these countries was forbidden. The king, desirous of fostering the merchants of England, in the year 1517 employed Sebastian Cabot to proceed on another voyage of discovery to find a north-west passage to India, in company with Sir Thomas Port (or Perte). During this voyage Cabot seems to have again visited Newfoundland, and penetrated Hudson's Bay to the latitude of $67\frac{1}{2}°$ N.; but of this voyage, as of many others, no details have been preserved. It is known, however, that he·

was compelled to return through the ill-will of Sir Thomas Port, who behaved very spitefully towards him, and the mutinous conduct of his crew. On his return Cabot, in disgust, gave up the English service and entered that of Spain.

The Reformation. Henry prepares for Defence by Sea.—Henry the Eighth's quarrel with the Pope and the Roman Catholic monarchs of Europe, caused by his adoption of the Reformation, opened up a new vista for thought and action in the minds of English mariners. Henry, himself threatened with the vengeance of these formidable foes, had to look to his defences; and naturally thinking that with command of the sea he could keep them at bay, turned his mind to the creation of a fleet of ships more fitted for war than those in existence. The art of shipbuilding had been a favourite study of Henry's, and the dockyards of Woolwich and Deptford, in which the best foreign naval architects were employed as teachers, became great schools of the art, producing such ships as had never before been seen in England.

English Mariners and the Cod Fishery.—The English mariners caught the spirit of the times, and new expeditions were set on foot. Withheld from trespassing on the shores of Africa and America by the fear of offending the monarchs of Spain and Portugal, backed as they were by the power of Saint Peter's successors at Rome, the English had sought for adventure in other directions. The enormous quantity of fish to be found on the shores and banks of Newfoundland had been reported by Cabot, and of this immediate advantage was taken by the fishermen of the West of England, who had been in the habit of yearly visiting Iceland for the cod fishing to be found there. The shipbuilders of the west found the vessels for this trade, and the ships of Bridport, Bideford, Dartmouth, and many other western ports became famous. The cod fishery, pursued by the men of Devon and Cornwall, first in Iceland, and then to a much greater extent at Newfoundland, made them hardy sailors. No wonder, then, that we find them the first to stretch further south when the way seemed opened.

Will Hawkins.—Will Hawkins, of Plymouth, "armed out," says the quaint language of the times, "a tall and goodly ship," and sailed for the Gold Coast in 1530. Thence he crossed to the Brazils and opened a trade, which was continued principally by the merchants of Southampton with much success until 1580, when Portugal fell under the Spanish crown. Hakluyt remarks "that Hawkins' ship, being of 250 tons, was thought exceedingly large."

A large trade was also kept up by the shipowners of the West of

England with the wine ports of Spain, Portugal and the Canaries. In this occupation Hawkins had been brought up, and therefore had an opportunity of knowing the kind of trade they were doing in Africa and America. Another voyage was made by him in 1532 with great success. At this time also the London merchants sent ships (one, it is said, of 300 tons, carrying one hundred persons) to Sicily, Candia and Chio, and sometimes to Cyprus, Tripoli and Barrutti (Beyrouth in Syria). The voyage usually occupied a year, and the journals of those old voyages show that they were considered "exceedingly difficult and dangerous," no doubt from the depredations of the Barbary corsairs, as well as the dangers arising from the poor vessels and the meagre instruments of navigation then in use.

Edward the Sixth and the Russian Ambassador. Hanseatic League. Sir R. Chancellor.—In 1547 Henry the Eighth died, leaving his throne to his young son, Edward the Sixth. In the first year of his reign there came a Russian ambassador to the English Court bearing kindly messages from the Tzar Ivan, with whom Edward concluded a treaty of peace and amity between the two nations. This was one of the first blows to the trade of the Lubeckers and the Hansa, who had converted the Baltic Sea into a secluded inland lake, carefully excluding the English as well as all other foreigners from entering its portals, or having any communication with either their own ports or those of any other nation on its shores; but the days of the League were numbered. After severe fighting the Scandinavian nations had freed themselves from its grip, and their vessels traversed the Sound without let or hindrance. The League had governed the whole of Russian trade, forcing themselves as far as Novogorod. They bound it down by severe and offensive laws; a German creditor was to be paid before a Russian; they kept a close watch that no non-Hanseatic should learn Russian, and they permitted no Russian to live in their provinces. The English treaty, and the subsequent discovery of a passage into Russia by way of Archangel, was such a check as they never before received. The discoverer of this new ocean route was Sir Richard Chancellor, who, with Sir Hugh Willoughby, had been sent by the London merchant adventurers to discover a way to China by the northern icy sea, in three ships, named the *Bona Esperanza*, the *Bona Confidentia*, and the *Edward Bonaventura*. At the North Cape, the last, which was commanded by Chancellor, got separated from the others and never saw them again. Sir Hugh, with his crew, penetrated to a harbour in Lapland, where they all perished from cold and starvation. More fortunate, Sir Richard Chancellor reached

B

Archangel, whence he travelled to Moscow, and was well received by the Tzar Ivan. He then returned to England with a letter from that monarch to King Edward, desiring more intimate relations between the two countries.

The London and Muscovite Company.—The English, taking advantage of the terms of trade offered, formed a commercial company to trade with Russia, which was entitled "The London and Muscovite Company." Sebastian Cabot, who had returned to England, and had been named "Grand Pilot" by Edward, was made the first governor of this company. He was a shrewd far-seeing man, and sought to make England a grand *entrepôt* for all kinds of foreign produce.

Commerce under Queen Mary.—Before the arrangements were complete the young king died, and his sister Mary had come to the throne. Edward the Sixth had strongly supported the London merchants, and curtailed the privileges of the League in England, which Mary at first restored, Philip of Spain (whom Mary had married) being at that time at amity with the League. Not a long time, however, was taken to prove the oppressive nature of these privileges upon the citizens of London. A return at the time showed that the League exported from England 36,000 pieces of cloth as against 1100 by the English. The League's representatives were summoned before the queen in Council and a long list of grievances put before them, one of which was that their action was prejudicial to the English navy, because they refused to employ any vessels but their own. The council decided that the Hansa should abstain from importing English cloth into the Netherlands, with many further restrictions; and it was further informed that any infraction would result in loss of all their privileges. Even the influence of Philip, who did everything to stifle British trade in favour of Spain and the Netherlands, was insufficient to make the Queen of England and her council cut the throat of her commerce by maintaining such outrageous privileges to foreigners. The Hansa retaliated by threatening to withdraw from all intercourse with England, but quickly discovered that that would have ended their days there, and that even their power over their own towns was not what it had been.

Such, then, was the state of English commerce at the end of Mary's reign. External influences had tended to keep native shipping, except in fishing and coasting craft, at a very low ebb indeed. Manufacturers had increased, especially in those branches which found their supply on the native soil—viz., those of woollen and linen cloth. Tin and lead, sheep and rabbit skins, were, in addition to wool, still the chief exports. The chief imports were iron and horses from Spain and Portugal; and from France came wines, in which English shipping participated; velvets, linen, and fine cloths from the Flemish manufacturing towns; herrings, pitch, furs, and timber from the Baltic; the silks, velvets, and glass from Italy were imported by foreigners. Throughout the Middle Ages a Venetian fleet annually visited our shores, bringing silks, satins, fine damasks, and cottons; also the rare Eastern spices, camphor and precious stones. English vessels did not penetrate the Mediterranean until the sixteenth century, and it is a sign that our commerce had increased when we find that the last visit of the Venetians occurred in 1532, such visits being no longer profitable. From some cause our trade with the Levant was suspended from 1553 for about twenty-five years, and was not resumed until the middle of Elizabeth's reign. The fact that most of our ships of burden were bought from the east countrymen on the shores of the Baltic proves that the building of such ships had not taken place in England, except for war or under special circumstances, such as have been mentioned.

Attempt to restore the Roman Catholic Supremacy.—As external influences were not favourable to the progress of British commerce, so the internal affairs of the kingdom during Mary's reign were little conducive to it. The queen, always sincerely Catholic, had never approved of her father's or brother's support of the Reformation, and on her accession immediately proceeded to restore the Roman supremacy. In the foregoing years great numbers of the English people had, however, become as sincerely Protestant, and looked upon a return to the Roman communion with aversion. The marriage of Mary, early in the second year of her reign, to Philip of Spain, a bigoted Catholic, accentuated her own religious feelings, as well as her power; and induced her to determine upon wiping out the Protestant faith and restoring that of the Church of Rome in its integrity. This threw the country into the convulsion of a religious civil war, and many of the Protestants, refusing to change their religion, chose rather to suffer persecution, which Mary was not slow to use. Amongst these were some of the best families in the kingdom, especially in the south and west of England.

English Rovers.—Flying from the Marian persecutions and irritated by the cruelties practised by the Inquisition upon the crews of English ships in the ports of Portugal and Spain, whither they resorted for the purpose of peaceful trade, numbers of young Englishmen became roving chiefs. With small handy vessels built in the western ports, they roamed the channels, and preyed upon the ships of Spain and the Netherlands as their natural enemies. In this they were joined by Huguenot Frenchmen, who suffered a like persecution at the hands of the Duke of Guise, an ardent Catholic, who was now all-powerful in France, and so they jointly revenged themselves upon their persecutors.

So far indeed did these lawless rovers carry their schemes, that at one time Sir Thomas Seymour, one of their principal leaders, formed an intention of seizing the Scilly Islands, there to form an independent State and secure a place of safety for their vessels and their prizes. Failing this, and not being able to bring their prizes into English ports, they either took them to Ireland or, what was worse, having plundered the vessels of all their valuables, both ships and crews were destroyed! A striking picture of the lawlessness of the times!

Mary's Death.—Under such conditions of life commerce was stifled—trading became difficult and dangerous; and as long as Mary lived, Philip, whose influence was predominant, did all he could to destroy it in favour of that of Spain and the Netherlands, his own dominions. Fortunately Mary's reign was short, or England might have sunk into such a state of appanage to Spain as Philip intended, and wished it to be. At her death in November 1558, her sister Elizabeth, as staunch a Protestant as Mary had been a Catholic, succeeded to the throne. Seizing the reins of government with a firm hand, she restored the Protestant faith, and the nation awoke to new life and enterprise.

CHAPTER IV.

THE MERCANTILE MARINE DURING ELIZABETH'S REIGN.

CONTENTS.—Effect of British protection—Elizabeth repeals Navigation Laws—Her general policy—She curtails Hanseatic privileges—Treaty of commerce with Hamburg—The Hansa power broken—Seymour and his allies—Quarrel between Elizabeth and Philip—The Inquisition—The Queen supports Holland—John Hawkins sails to the Gold Coast—Drake's surveys of the West Indies—The Queen commissions Drake—He sails round the World—Portugal friendly to England—Philip determines to crush England—Elizabeth's self-confidence—Her fleet—The Spanish Armada—Drake and his privateers—The Armada reaches the English Channel—Off Plymouth meet the fleet and Drake's ships—The Duke de Medina tries to separate them—The superior sailing qualities of the English ships now seen—A worrying fight up Channel—The Spaniards chased into Calais Roads and the North Sea—A remnant of the Armada returns to Spain.

Effect of British Protection.—A system of protection for British ships and merchants having been inaugurated by Richard the Second, this policy was pursued by succeeding monarchs down to the period at which we have now arrived, with very varying and doubtful success. Jealous of the action of the British rulers, those of foreign States retaliated by shutting their ports against British vessels and traders.

Navigation Laws repealed. Elizabeth's Policy.—This had made unpleasant changes in the old system of navigation and commerce, and when Elizabeth came to the throne, she, with unusual sagacity, saw the effect it had upon British commerce. With the consent of her Parliament she, by the Act 1 Eliz. c. 13, repealed all the restrictions of her predecessors, and allowed all merchants to use whatever ships they pleased, subject only to the necessity of their paying aliens' duty if they used the ships of an alien. In this she was not neglectful of British interests, but sought, by such a measure of liberality, to disarm foreign opposition; at the same time she reserved the coasting trade to British ships. Always averse to war, it was her policy to gain her ends by diplomatic cunning rather than by attempted force. Indeed, she was at times induced to carry this policy too far almost for safety, as will presently be seen.

Hanseatic Privileges curtailed ; Treaty made with Hamburg and Hansa Power broken.—Almost immediately on her accession the Hansa approached her, demanding a renewal of their ancient privileges. She received them graciously, but soon let them see that the interests of her own subjects and realm were with her paramount. The merchant adventurers in their turn made their claim, which was the destruction of the Hanseatic privileges and freedom of trade for themselves with Europe. By this time the cohesive force of the League was much weakened; many of the towns, grown rich, were becoming independent of such a " mutual protection " society, and ambitious of their own especial welfare. The Queen, backed by her trusty minister, William Cecil, Lord Burleigh, insisted upon her subjects being put upon an equal footing with those of the Hansa. She restored all Edward the Sixth's tariffs, and claimed free admission for her ships into their ports, and, when they refused, curtailed their export to 5000 pieces of cloth in the year. When the Hanseatic towns found her obdurate, they attempted retaliation, which had no effect. Quarrelling with each other for a share of the London trade, the astute Queen and her Minister played with them in turn, and it ended by Hamburg making a treaty with the London merchant adventurers for ten years. The Hansa League bitterly opposed this, but their power was broken. As their power waned, so did the influence of England increase, until in 1598 they were expelled from London. After some years the Steel Yard was restored to them, but they were traders only on sufferance— their privileges were gone for ever. And so we may bid them adieu.

Seymour and his Allies. Quarrel between Elizabeth and Philip.—On Elizabeth's accession Seymour and his semi-piratical allies returned to their allegiance, and by her were taken into favour. The country being at peace with both France and Spain, their semi-warlike depredations were for a while stayed, but this did not last long. Philip, regretting the death of Mary, and still more his hold upon England, offered marriage to Elizabeth; but this honour the Queen declined. Her mind was bent upon reestablishing the Reformation, and Philip, who was at this time endeavouring to bring back the Netherlands under the power of the Inquisition, would have been an unsuitable husband; their quarrels were thenceforth incessant, although war was not actually declared. For years a sort of unacknowledged warfare was carried on between the two kingdoms. British mariners, notwithstanding, undauntedly maintained their trade with Spain and Portugal, fearless of the terrors of the Inquisition, which lost no chance of imprisoning the *heretics* upon the slightest pretence. The presence of a Bible in a ship was a sufficient conviction of heresy. The West of England men revenged themselves for such cruelties by pouncing upon every stray Spaniard they could lay their hands on, and confiscating his property as a lawful prize. The Queen, supporting the Reformers of Holland by every means in her power but open warfare, quietly shut her eyes to the proceedings of her subjects. She encouraged trade with the rebellious Lowlanders, supplying them with means to carry on the war, and even went so far as to impound some Spanish vessels carrying money and stores to the Duke of Alva, Philip's general in the Netherlands. Philip stormed and raved; and his ambassadors prayed and besought the obdurate Queen to alter her policy; but she, fully aware of Philip's pretence to the throne of England, and knowing full well that the defence of Holland was the defence of England and her own throne, pursued the even tenour of her way—flattering and cajoling the Spanish ambassador at one moment, placing him at open defiance the next; and so the struggle went on for years.

Up to the middle of the fifteenth century Bruges had been the great *entrepôt* in the Lowlands for British trade, but, on its fall in 1482, caused by the cutting of the canal which connected it with Sluys, by the Emperor Maximilian, in revenge for a rebellion in which the Liegois took part with Ghent and other towns, Antwerp had risen into importance and remained without a rival as the medium of European trade, until the period at which we have now arrived in our history. In the war raging between Philip and the Lowlanders, Antwerp was taken, and sacked, by Alva, and the best of the trade was transferred to London; numbers of the persecuted Flemings, flying thither to find a home, received encouragement from Elizabeth, and her sagacious Minister, Cecil. Besides aiding our manufacturers they materially aided our commerce, and London became the general mart of Europe.

John Hawkins sails to the Gold Coast.—In 1562 the West of England men entered with zest upon foreign trade. John Hawkins set on foot another expedition to the Gold Coast. Assisted by the subscriptions of sundry gentlemen, he fitted out three ships (the largest being 120 tons and the smallest 40), and having learned that negroes were a very good commodity in Hispaniola, he sailed to the Guinea Coast and took in a cargo of them; proceeding to Hispaniola he sold his negroes and English commodities, then loaded his vessels with hides, sugar, ginger, and precious stones, and, returning home in 1563, finished a profitable voyage. This seems to have been the first slaving voyage performed by Englishmen!

Hawkins made another voyage in 1564 successfully, but during the next, in 1567, he got into collision with the authorities in the

Spanish main, and losing many of his ships returned to England with two only, after suffering great hardships. In this voyage Hawkins had been joined by Francis Drake; but Drake had no love for the "blackbird" trade and never entered upon it again. This was Hawkins' last voyage in that trade, but by no means his last act of service to his country. The Queen conferred upon him the post of Superintendent of H.M. Dockyards, in which it will hereafter be seen he did good work.

Drake's Surveys of the West Indies.—Francis Drake, descended from a good Devonshire family, was a seaman from his boyhood, and had taken part in many of the frays in the English Channel with the ships of Alva and Spain. Twenty-five years of age when he joined Hawkins in that last unfortunate voyage, he lost all his property. Bringing the vessel he commanded safely back to Plymouth, he had gained a character for courage and ability. Filled with desire of revenge upon the Spaniards, he gathered about him a company of sea adventurers, who found sufficient money to fit out another vessel, and with them made several voyages to the Spanish West Indies, intent upon learning the navigation of those parts and gaining useful intelligence, combined with picking up such riches as fell in his way, of which, we read, he obtained "much store," by "playing," says Camden, "the seaman and the pirate."

Elizabeth commissions Drake. Drake's Voyage round the World.—The Queen, meeting the plots carried on by Philip and the Catholics against her crown and life, by counter-plots and undeclared warfare, granted a commission to Drake to "sail the seas," and he started in 1577 upon what proved to be his famous voyage round the world, the first ever performed. His fleet consisted of five ships, the largest of which was 100 tons, and the smallest only 15. Making his way down the east coast of South America and passing through the Straits of Magellan, he proceeded up the west coast to Chili, Peru, and Panama. On the way many a rich galleon, ignorant of the presence of an enemy, fell into his clutches; amongst them the immense carrack, the *Cacafuego*, filled with gold, silver plate, and "great store of diamonds, emeralds, and pearls." With full ships he attempted to sail northwards and find a passage that way into the Atlantic, not daring to return as he came by the Straits of Magellan, as the Spaniards were now on the alert and he feared capture. At last he sailed west from California, and feeling his way through the Moluccas and by the north coast of Java, passed through the Straits of Sunda, and round the Cape of Good Hope, reaching home on the 26th September 1579. He was graciously received by the Queen, who created him a Knight upon the deck of his own ship. For years afterwards he was employed upon expeditions against the Spaniards all over the world.

These buccaneering expeditions did not commend themselves to Cecil, Elizabeth's cautious Minister, who could not persuade himself that any good would come of these "water thieves" as he called them, and "believing that piracy was detestable and could not last, he tried hard to persuade Elizabeth to withdraw her covert support;" but she was poor, and her cupidity (for she was a partner in almost every adventure) and the very times were too strong for him; yet buccaneering, combined in an irregular manner with trade and religion, became the very source of England's power at sea. However unwise and indefensible were the deeds of Drake and his companions, we cannot but be conscious that it was their hardy prowess and daring valour which fostered in the nation that obstinate disdain of external control which was so soon to be needed and sorely tried!

Portugal friendly to England.—Although such was the state of matters between Spain and England, the Portuguese had on the whole been more friendly towards us. In 1572 a treaty of peace had been concluded with Portugal; freedom of trade to the Gold Coast and the Brazils had been secured, and all former disputes adjusted. This was taken advantage of by our Southern ports, especially Southampton, whose merchants carried on a flourishing trade with the Brazils, until 1580, when Portugal became joined to the Spanish crown.

Philip determines to Crush England.—Philip, now all-powerful in Europe, the whole of the Spanish peninsula, Austria, the Netherlands, and a great part of Germany being under his sway, with the whole power of the Papal Court at his back, determined to make an effort to maintain his claim upon the English crown, and put Elizabeth and her truculent subjects under his feet. The attacks of Drake upon the West Indies, the looting of so many valuable carracks, and the burning of the ships in Cadiz Harbour, stung the Spanish nation to the quick. Philip and Elizabeth were both averse to open warfare, but the Pope, filled with rage at the loss of England, urged Philip on by every possible means to attack her, and at last the slowly moving Emperor prepared a fleet of overwhelming force to make the attack.

Elizabeth's Self-confidence.—Elizabeth, confident in her own power of cajoling both monarch and ambassadors, would scarcely believe Philip, after the failure of oft-repeated threats of vengeance, to be in earnest; amused by diplomatic efforts for a treaty of peace between herself, Philip and the Netherlands, she would not accept the possibility of war, and even went so far as to restrain Drake from any further acts of piracy, and apologise for the attack upon Cadiz; absolutely without fear and swayed by her penurious disposition, she dismantled her own fleet and ordered it to be laid up at Chatham; she even went so far as to enter into a treaty of amity with Philip. Burleigh, in despair and knowing well the preparations Philip was making, advised her to send out Drake to the Azores and put him in fear for his gold ships, but she would not listen. "She was," says Mr. Froude, "in one of her ungovernable moods." "Never," said Lord Howard, the English High Admiral, "since England was England, was such a stratagem made to deceive as this treaty. We have not hands left to carry the ships back to Chatham."

The Spanish Armada.—At last, in the spring of 1588, news came that the Armada was about to sail—a mighty force of 130 ships, from 700 to 1300 tons each, with 30,000 fighting men, which seemed irresistible. Alva had also prepared a fleet to land an army from the Netherlands. All this time Elizabeth was obdurate; she refused to supply money, men or victuals. To her advisers she seemed bent upon destruction. In the end she was forced to yield. Her fleet, of which she possessed only 38 ships, she reluctantly ordered to be prepared. Fortunately some of these had been built by Hawkins, an able shipbuilder, pirate and slave hunter though he had been, who, using his experience, built them upon new principles; the usual high sterns and forecastles were made lower, and the vessels themselves longer on the keel and of fine lines. The older seamen shook their heads, and foretold disaster; but the wisdom of Hawkins was seen when the fight came.

To meet the immense Armada, which was now undoubtedly coming, Lord Henry Seymour was left with five ships to watch the Dover Straits and the Netherlands contingent, and Howard joined Drake at Plymouth with eighteen sail. The western privateers headed by Drake, their chosen chief, lay in Plymouth Sound, making about forty sail of light craft, but well armed and manned. On July 23, after many false starts and misadventures, the Armada sailed from Corunna with undiminished numbers. After a somewhat stormy passage they were off the Lizard, sailing up the Channel in fighting order. Off Plymouth Howard was discovered with eleven ships, and Drake inside with about 40 sail, which seemed the whole British force. The Spanish Admiral, the Duke di Medina Sidonia, despising this apparently small force, offered battle, and endeavoured to divide the two fleets of Howard and Drake. The effect of the new style of ship was now seen. Howard's ships, close-hauled, passed easily to windward of the Spanish ships, out of range of their guns, and joining Drake, the whole English fleet passed close-hauled in line behind the Spaniards, raking them with their guns of longer range at a safe distance with deadly effect. The great ships of the Armada and their crews were thrown into disorder and completely demoralised. The Duke, seeing he could do nothing with the wasps of ships, which both out-sailed and out-cannoned him, bore away and sailed up the English Channel, the English fleet following. Two of the largest ships, the *Santa Catalina* and the *Capitana*, getting into difficulty fell a prey to Drake and his privateers, proving a rich booty, and, what was of more importance to Drake, well supplied with gunpowder. The Spanish officers, furious at this loss, besought Medina to attempt a rescue; but it was growing dark, the heavy lumbering Spaniards could not get near the English ships, and he sailed away leaving them to their fate. Off Portland on the Monday the fight was continued with the same result, the Spaniards being out-sailed and badly manœuvred. At the end of this day the English powder was exhausted, but the authorities on shore were now aroused from their slumber, and fresh privateers poured out from the Dorsetshire ports bringing supplies of every kind.

A Worrying Fight up Channel.—The Duke di Medina observing that his enemies were growing numerous, had made up his mind to run for the Solent, land his 10,000 troops, take the Isle of Wight, and then wait for news from the Prince of Parma in the Netherlands. Now he must fight another battle. On the Wednesday the two fleets lay becalmed, the English taking in their supplies. The next day the Duke hoped by the help of his galliasses to bring the English to close quarters; but this hope failed him. The wind rising brought up Drake again, and again the terrible cannonade ensued. The Spanish shot flew high over the low English privateers, whose every shot told upon the Spanish hulls; the very guns seemed to the helpless Spaniards heavier than before. The Duke's ammunition began to fail; he had counted upon one fight, he had now fought three. Losing heart, he gave up the attempt to make for the Solent, and sailed away to Calais roads, where at least he might find safety. During the Friday he sailed on without interruption from the English, and on Saturday at dusk dropped anchor in Calais roads. The English fleet, from which he hoped now to be clear, to his intense disgust he saw also anchor within half a league astern of him. And so passed from the shores of England that fine fleet which Philip had provided to carry out the decrees of Providence. But Providence takes no account of, nor aids, weak and ignorant commanders, and the Duke, although a Spanish grandee of the finest water, was ill fitted for the command of so well provided and powerful a fleet; and well for England that it was so.

Dispersal of the Armada.—We have not space to linger upon the after events—of how Howard and Drake drove the Spaniards from Calais roads into the North Sea—of how Providence, in the shape of severe storms, completed the work so well begun and so valiantly carried out—of how in a few weeks that formidable Armada was scattered to the winds, and only 54 ships with about 9000 to 10,000 men returned to the ports of Spain, to relate such disasters as had overtaken them at the hand of God as well as man. So ended the vainglorious dream of Philip—so ended the last real attempt of a foreign enemy to plant a foot upon the English land!

Had it not been for Drake and his merchant fleet what would have happened? England might have become an appanage of Spain; America, a Spanish province; the United States never have existed, and the Inquisition have been triumphant over the world! Most happily for England it was otherwise. The failure of that last great attempt upon our land and liberty left her free to pursue that course of Mercantile and Maritime adventure which has proved to her such a source of wealth and power, and given her that sovereignty of the seas which has never since been taken from her by force, though frequently challenged by the Spaniard, Dutch and French in turn.

CHAPTER V.

MERCANTILE PROGRESS UP TO THE REIGN OF WILLIAM THE THIRD.

CONTENTS.—Chaucer's seaman—The English people—West of England mariners—Judge Prowse's History of Newfoundland and Trade—Art school of ship building—Tobias' letter to the Queen—Fishing industries, a school for sailors—Trade with Portugal—The Russian and Levant Companies—The East India Company, its first fleet—James the First forbids piracy—Encroachments of the Dutch—Van Tromp and Blake—Cromwell's Act—Dutch trade in the English colonies—Charles the Second's Navigation Laws—Sir Joshua Child's opinion—Other Navigation Laws—Bounty for building large ships—Progress of Trade—William the Third encourages the Marine—Success of the East India Company—Tonnage at the commencement of the eighteenth century.

Chaucer's Seaman.—In describing the course of English commerce and shipping in the foregoing pages, we have been able to say little of the actual people engaged in it, for little is left to tell us of the mariners of those early days, but a characteristic glimpse may be got from the description of a seaman in Chaucer's prologue, written in the latter half of the fourteenth century, and in the reign of King Edward.

The character, drawn so quaintly, roughly resembles his descendants; he is ready to join any expedition, a good seaman and pilot, and yet not over nice or scrupulous about the manner of obtaining his desires.*

Character of the English People.—Speaking of the English people in the early part of Elizabeth's reign, Mr. Froude says: "In the English nature there were and are two antagonistic tendencies; on the one hand, a disposition to live by rule and precedent, and to maintain with loving reverence the customs, convictions, and traditions which have come down from other generations; and, on the other hand, a restless, impetuous energy, pressing forward into the future, regarding what has been done as only a step, or landing place, leading upwards and onwards to higher conquests."

West of England Mariners.—This description was clearly illustrated by the men of Elizabeth's day. Hawkins, Raleigh,

* See *Appendix* B.

Drake, Seymour, and their followers, were men filled with the love of their country as well as of adventure—tinged, possibly, with the superstition of the times—and, however unwise and indefensible appear to us, in these days of more freedom and enlightenment, to have been many of their deeds, they were fully determined to act upon their own responsibility; it was their hardy prowess and daring valour which stretched forth the arms of English commerce and paved the way for England's subsequent greatness. Had it not been for the assistance of these west of England mariners, where would Elizabeth have been in her extremity? How—the question arises—how was it the west of England could, in the emergency, have produced such mariners? In what school had they been taught, and where had they gained their experience? This is a question that seems to have been passed over by historians in a marvellous manner. Even Mr. Froude says little on the subject. The solution must be sought for in the fisher folk, who, from the discovery of Newfoundland, and its valuable fisheries, went forth year after year in increasing numbers to fish for cod upon its shores and banks. It had been the custom of the fishermen of the West from Bristol, Bideford, Dartmouth, &c., to join the fishermen of the East coast in the cod-fisheries of Iceland; but henceforth the Iceland fishery, although not all at once abandoned, was forsaken for those of Newfoundland, in which they were joined by fishermen from the ports of Northern Spain, France and Portugal in great numbers.

Judge Prowse's History of Newfoundland and Trade.— "These traders," says Judge Prowse, "escaped the notice of kings and chroniclers; their humble calling insured their safety for the first half-century. In Newfoundland they carried on, besides the fisheries, a great free trade: oils, wines, and fruits of France, Spain and Portugal, were exchanged for English cutlery and West of England cordage, cloth, hats, caps and hosiery. The business was most profitable all round; it built up the west of England. . . . It appears quite clear that taking one year with another, twenty years before Gilbert's time, at least fifty English vessels engaged in the transatlantic fishery, and from 2500 to 3000 men were employed in this business."

St. John's was the great rendezvous long before there was any settled Government, and there the various commodities were exchanged. Besides the fishing vessels there were larger vessels, built with a view to speed, to enable them to escape "the sea rovers," and to carry the salt, fish, and wines, with other articles of trade, between Devonshire, Newfoundland and Spain, &c. These vessels were built at Bideford, Bridport, Dartmouth, and Plymouth, and it was for that class of vessel these ports remained celebrated until the middle of this century. In the fishing season the fishermen chose an admiral from amongst their number, and as the English vessels were the largest, and the Englishmen the strongest, he was usually selected from them. Once invested with power, he administered justice with a rough and ready hand.

The idea entertained by historians, that, after its discovery by Cabot, Newfoundland was lost sight of and deserted for nearly a century, has been ably disposed of by Judge Prowse, who laughs at the idea "that the most pugnacious and pertinacious race in all the three kingdoms would enter upon a profitable business and then give it up."

Art School of Shipbuilding.—Here then was the school in which for a century before the day of the Armada, the West of England seamen were toughened and gained their experience, and were ready at the call of Hawkins, Drake and Gilbert in the day of need. Here was the art school in which were perfected the building and the lines of naval architecture found in the ships, which with ease walked like greyhounds round the lumbering galleons of Spain in the famous year of 1588, and sent them to their doom. In no other way can it be accounted for, that there were such ships and such men.*

Tobias' Letter to the Queen.—Providentially escaped from such an attempted blow at its liberty, the nation became, henceforth, convinced that its only safety lay in its ships and its sailors. The necessary duty, then, of all succeeding Governments was to foster and sustain the commercial marine, as the only source whence her defenders could be drawn.

To press this home upon the Queen and the nation, among many others, one Tobias, gentleman, fisherman, and mariner (as he styles himself), published a pamphlet, entitled "The Best Way to make England the Richest and Wealthiest Kingdom in Europe," in which he recommends the encouragement of the fishing trade by the construction of a "thousand busses upon a national design, in order to compete with the Dutch."

A "Busse" was a fishing or coasting vessel of about sixty to eighty tons burthen, and cost about £500.

Fishing Industry. A School for Sailors.—He appeals to the patriotism of the large city companies and other wealthy bodies to do this, and asks them to consider "the advantage it would be in the hour of need to have ready for service lusty fed younkers, bred in the busses, who could furl a topsail or a spritsail,

* De Witt, the great Pensionary of Holland, says, "The navy of England became formidable by the discovery of the inexpressible rich fishing bank of Newfoundland."

and shake out a bonnet in a dark and stormy night, and not shrink from their duties like the surfeited or hunger-pinched sailors, who made the southern voyages."

Even then, as now, our best sailors were bred in our fishing-boats, and our coasting-smacks and brigs.

Trade with Portugal.—It must not be forgotten, however, that there was another trade in which the southern and western ports had always been well engaged, and that was with the Portuguese. During the thirteenth, fourteenth, and fifteenth centuries a great friendship existed between the two nations. Numerous fleets bound for the Holy Land had rendezvoused at Lisbon filled with the flower of English chivalry. These, on passing, had greatly assisted the young kingdom of Portugal in its wars for independence against both Moors and Castilians; and a friendship was cemented which was not disturbed until, in the early part of the sixteenth century, the Inquisition which had been established in Portugal, waged a holy war against all heretics, amongst whom the English Reformers were included. The disruption was complete when Portugal fell under the Spanish crown in 1580. English ships could not visit the ports of the Peninsula without peril, and then it was that the traffic between the two countries was maintained by the peaceable fishing fleets meeting on the shores of Newfoundland.

"The years which followed the defeat of the Armada," says Mr. Froude in his History, "were rich in events of profound national importance. They were years of splendour and triumph. The flag of England became supreme upon the seas; English commerce penetrated to the furthest corners of the Old World, and English Colonies rooted themselves on the shores of the New."

Russian and Levant Companies.—In addition to the Russian Company, which now possessed a valuable trade, the Levant Company had been formed for trading with the East through the ports of the Levant, and it was securing an important share of the lucrative business which had in former ages been in the hands of the Italian merchants. Elizabeth had made a commercial treaty with Turkey, which placed her subjects on as favourable a footing as those of any other nation. A charter was granted to this company in 1581.

Tooke, in his "History of Prices," tells us that it was computed that in 1582 the Mercantile Marine of England comprised 135 ships, many of which were over 500 tons, but that twenty years later it had increased to 400 ships.

East India Company.—By far the most important event after the defeat of the Armada, was the formation of an association of merchant adventurers for the purpose of trading to the

East Indies. After much debating and squeamish reluctance on account of the jealousy shown by Philip of Spain, the Queen granted the company its charter upon the last day of the year 1600. The company was formed by a number of noblemen, aldermen, and councillors of the City, and other gentlemen, headed by the Earl of Cumberland, who is said to have been the first British subject who built in England a ship of 800 tons burthen.

Under Elizabeth's sanction two expeditions had been sent to India; one in 1582, commanded by Edward Fenton, and the second in 1589, under George Raymond. Both were failures. The first came back without doubling the Cape, and the second lost all its three vessels, as well as its commander, and most of the crews. Captain Lancaster, the second in command, found his way home overland, and arrived in a miserable plight, after many sad adventures.

The Company's First Fleet.—The first fleet belonging to the Company consisted of the *Red Dragon*, 600 tons, and 200 men; the *Hector*, 300 tons, and 100 men; the *Ascension*, 200 tons, and 80 men; the *Susan*, 240 tons, and 80 men; and a pinnace of 100 tons and 40 men—in all 1500 tons and 500 men. With a selected cargo for trading, and twenty months' provisions, this fleet sailed from Woolwich on February 13, 1601, under the command of Captain Lancaster. It returned in 1603, but Elizabeth did not survive to see it. The profit was large, but as usual in those days, a very considerable part was derived from the capture of a Portuguese ship fully laden. Fleets followed each other in rapid succession, and the first seven or eight voyages were full of encouragement, returning as much as 150 to 200 per cent.

James the First forbids Piracy, 1603.—James the First succeeded, and declaring himself at peace with all the world, put a stop to privateering, and called in all the privateers. To please the Spanish monarch, he stained his fame by beheading Sir Walter Raleigh, on his return from a voyage on which he had permitted him to go.

From this time forward there was no more open buccaneering. Piracy existed, it is true, but no longer received the sanction of crowned heads. From the days of the Norsemen downwards, the race was to the swift and the battle to the strong. A foreign vessel weak enough to be captured seemed to be fair game, but it was a strange morality which allowed Elizabeth to sanction such a course of action as she did. With regard to her acts towards Spain, doubtless there was cause given.

When we consider the imprisonment of English crews, and the

torture practised upon them in the ports of Spain, on account of their religion, we can hardly be surprised at the fearful reprisals made by Drake and his followers upon Spanish crews when occasion offered. Under James, who concluded a treaty of peace with Spain soon after he came to the throne, these religious asperities were somewhat abated, and an improved condition of trade existed between the two countries.

Encroachments of the Dutch.—In 1642 (Charles the First now being king), the East India Company employed about 15,000 tons of shipping. Its great rival, the Dutch East India Company, had grown immensely in power, and added largely to the riches of the Republic. With its riches had grown its insolence, and it had assumed a "Sovereignty of the Seas."

Van Tromp and Blake.—The Dutch had seized upon all the fishing grounds adjacent to our coasts, and in 1618 were said to have 3000 fishing-vessels and 50,000 men in this business, from which they attempted to drive our fishing vessels by force. Their audacity at last became unbearable, and the minds of the English people were filled with alarm and disgust. The unfortunate Charles was unable to protect his people, but Cromwell, when in full power, in 1651, carried through the Rump Parliament another Act of Navigation which stopped their trade with England, and declared their presence on the fishing-grounds illegal.* This was so serious a blow to the Dutch that war ensued, and the Dutch Admiral, Van Tromp, paraded the English Channel with a broom at his masthead swearing he would sweep the English from the seas. At first he seemed to be succeeding, as our fleet was completely beaten, but Admiral Blake, recruited with more and better ships, in a few years gained a succession of brilliant victories, which crushed the naval power of Holland, and it never again rose to its former height.

In 1606, the first colony had been founded in North America by Captain Smith. He was followed in 1620 by the Pilgrim Fathers in the *Mayflower*, and our colonial trade soon became an important business. Religious difficulties at home drove many

---

* Act passed by the Rump Parliament:—"That no merchandise either of Asia, Africa or America, including also our own plantations, should be imported into Britain in any but English-built ships and belonging to English or English plantation subjects, navigated also by an English Commander, and three-fourths of the sailors to be Englishmen; excepting, however, such merchandise as should be imported directly from the original place of their growth or manufacture, in Europe solely. Moreover, no fish should thenceforward be imported into England or Ireland, nor exported from thence to foreign parts, nor even from one of our own home ports to another, but what shall be caught by our own fishers only." This is commonly called Scobele's Act.

out of the country, and these were followed by a large number of Dutch and Swedes.

Cromwell's Act.—Cromwell in 1655 threw open the trade to India, hoping thereby to damage the Dutch East India Company, but, finding this did not answer, he re-established the monopoly again in 1657, and restored the English Company.

Prior to Elizabeth's reign many ineffectual attempts at establishing secure navigation laws had been made, but Elizabeth, as we have seen, repealed them all, and threw the trade of the country open to aliens under certain restrictions. The laws from her time until the Commonwealth very much resembled what is to be seen in many foreign countries at the present time, in carrying out ideas of reciprocity.

Dutch Trade in the English Colonies.—In the meantime Dutch commerce had largely increased. Antwerp was once more the emporium of Europe, and the Dutch were the carriers of the world. They had established a large trade with the English Colonies, in the ports of which were to be seen forty Dutch ships for one English. Cromwell never rested until he had driven the Dutch from the English fishing-grounds, and then out of the Colonies. As the Colonies had sided with Charles against the Parliament, this legislation was intended to punish both. It was, indeed, rigorous, perhaps injurious, but effectual, for it gave to Dutch commerce a blow, which, followed by the success of Blake, destroyed it, and from which it never recovered.

Charles the Second's Navigation Laws.—Henceforth the navigation laws took a new direction—viz., the preservation of the trade between the colonies and the mother country, for the benefit of British shipping.

In 1660, an Act, 12 Charles the Second, c. 18, was passed, adding still further to the protection of British and Colonial shipping; this has since been called "The Maritime Charter of England."

1662.—Another Act, 14 Charles the Second, c. 11, enacted "that no foreign built ship should have British privileges, although owned by Englishmen," and further privileges and exemptions from duties were added to encourage the building of ships of large tonnage.

These Acts were so effective, that at the peace of 1667 the Dutch struggled hard to get them rescinded, as they had destroyed their commerce, but without avail. The war which this peace concluded had principally been brought on by the quarrel between the English and Dutch merchants on the coast of Guinea, but this was really only one feature of the contest waged between the two nations for mercantile supremacy.

Sir Joshua Child's Opinion.—The Acts were not passed without great diversity of opinion—the mere merchant buyers and sellers would naturally be opposed to them, and there were not wanting many who affirmed that they would be destructive of commerce. Sir Joshua Child, who wrote "Discourses on Trade" in 1666 to 1668, writes: "Without these Acts we had not now been owners of one half of the shipping, or the trade, nor should have employed one half of our seamen." Anderson, in his "History of Commerce," supplements this in 1776, by saying: "So vast an alteration had these Acts brought about, that in a few years we were at length become in a great measure what the Dutch once were, that is, the great carriers of Europe, especially within the Mediterranean Sea."

Other Navigation Laws. 1664.—Another Act, 16 Charles the Second, c.6, compelled "British seamen to fight the Barbary pirates and defend their ships." The cause of this Act was the cowardice of many shipmasters and crews in giving up their vessels on condition of their lives being saved by the pirates. It is not pleasant to think that British seamen could have behaved so, but when we think of the crowds these pirates carried in their Xebecques, there may have been some excuse for poorly-manned and ill-armed vessels.

1685.—1 James the Second, c. 18, imposed a duty of five shillings per ton upon foreign vessels in our coasting trade.

The statistics of shipping in the seventeenth century are meagre enough, but it is stated * that at the Restoration in 1660 the tonnage cleared outwards amounted to 95,266 tons, and at the accession of William and Mary, twenty-nine years after, it was 190,533, or exactly double; and, from other sources, that the tonnage of merchant ships in 1688 was exactly double what it was in 1666, but no figures are given. These statements, at all events, prove substantial progress.

Bounty for building large Ships.—In 1694, a bounty of one-tenth of the tonnage and poundage duty was granted to builders of vessels having at least three decks, and of 450 tons burthen, and armed with 32 guns, and built within the next ten years. This to be allowed upon the first three voyages only.

Progress of Trade.—The population of England, which after the Conquest, as shown in the Domesday Book, only amounted to about 2,000,000, had risen in Elizabeth's time to 5,000,000, and the junction of Scotland with England by the accession of the King of Scotland to the English throne, brought peace and security hitherto unknown. The colonisation of Virginia by Sir Walter Raleigh, and the opening of trade to India by the East India Company, gave employment to an increased number of British ships

* Colliber's "History of English Naval Affairs."

and seamen, and the greatest industrial progress in England was in the direction of foreign trade. James suppressed piratical adventure, but was too timid to declare war against Spain, which throughout his reign, as well as that of Charles the First, maintained their monopoly of trade with their West Indian and American possessions. Cromwell, however, was no sooner safely in possession of the government than he at once demanded free trade with the Spanish colonies, and religious freedom for English settlers in them. When this was refused he immediately declared war, and his fleets seized Jamaica, which gave the English a secure footing in the West Indies. The Dutch had arrogantly attacked our fishing-grounds, and almost destroyed our east coast fisheries and fishermen. Cromwell, with a zealous care for his people, drove the Dutch from our coasts, and then protected our fishermen and our seamen by stringent laws.

William the Third encourages the Marine.—The accession of William and Mary secured peace between the two countries, and to a certain extent consolidated their aims and interests. This did not, however, make William neglect English interests; on the contrary, he evinced a fostering care for them, and, following the traditions of the nation and former rulers, he encouraged the marine by establishing a registry office for 30,000 seamen as a force to be relied upon for the defence of the country. As one of the inducements to the mercantile mariners to register, he granted them all the privileges of Greenwich Hospital and its pensions, in common with the seamen of the Royal Navy. "This Act," says Anderson, in his "History of Commerce," "was unfortunately repealed by an Act of Queen Anne a few years after."

Success of the East India Company.—During the seventeenth century the operation of the East India Company was one of the chief factors in the progress of shipping and commerce. In 1676 so flourishing we learn was its trade that its dividends amounted to 300 per cent. This success raised the cupidity of others who were not included in the monopoly, and various attempts were made to raise up opposition companies, and consequently the original company was not permitted to enjoy its charter in peace. Company after company was formed, the rivals only helping to kill each other, and it was not until 1708, when the two companies then existing (the original London company, and the new English company which had been empowered by the 9th William the Third, c. 44) were united into one grand Company, that henceforth the trade was carried on under propitious circumstances, with the three settlements of Bombay, Madras, and Fort William (now Calcutta) under one rule. Trade with America prospered, especially after the taking of New Amsterdam, now New York, in 1664, during Charles the Second's short war, which added to the consolidation of the New England colonies. The Hudson's Bay Company had received their charter in 1670, and very soon developed a profitable trade in furs, &c., with the Indians of that cold and inhospitable region.

Tonnage at the Commencement of the Eighteenth Century.—In 1701-2 we have the first authentic account of the tonnage registered in British ports, which was obtained in reply to questions addressed to the Commissioners of Customs throughout the kingdom. The total is returned as 3281 ships, estimated to measure 261,222 tons, and manned by 27,196 officers and men. Of these London possessed 559 ships, 84,882 tons, 10,065 men; Bristol, 165 ships, 17,338 tons, 2359 men, followed by Yarmouth, Exeter, Hull, Whitby, Liverpool, and Scarborough, in order averaging from 9000 to 7000 tons, and the remainder scattered over the minor ports of the kingdom; the crews of these averaging one man to every eight tons, and the ships averaging 80 tons burthen.

From this we see that London possessed rather more than a sixth of the ships, and a fifth of the tonnage of the whole.

And yet how slow the growth of commerce up to this date has been after all the fostering care bestowed upon it! Does it not strike us with surprise when we see what rapid strides it made later on?

CHAPTER VI.

PROGRESS TO END OF THE EIGHTEENTH CENTURY.

CONTENTS.—Queen Anne—South Sea Company—Bubble Companies—State of Shipping—Trade of American Colonies—Newfoundland—Supply of seamen—American smuggling in the West Indies—Naval operations there—Survey of the St. Lawrence by James Cook—Revolt of the States—Their independence achieved—Effect of the War on British shipping—French King's proposals for reciprocal trade—Convict colony in New South Wales—Trade of Liverpool—Renewal of East India Charter—State of Navigation—Reward offered for the best method of determining longitude at sea—Harrison's timekeepers—Government grants for lunar tables—Nautical Almanac.

Queen Anne.—In the beginning of 1702 A.D., William the Third lost his life by an accident—a fall from his horse—and was succeeded by Anne, youngest daughter of James the Second, who, like her sister Mary, had been brought up in the Protestant faith. Just before William's death the country had become once more embroiled in a war waged between England, Holland, and the German Emperor, on the one side, and France and Spain on the other. This has been commonly called the "War of Succession," and lasted through nearly the whole of Anne's reign. It was in this war that John Churchill, Duke of Marlborough, won his laurels, and gave such a deadly check to the power of France.

South Sea Company.—The commerce of England pursued its accustomed tracks. The two East India Companies, the English and the Dutch, now allies instead of enemies, carried on an increasing and valuable trade, and the trade between England and the American plantations grew year by year. Several Acts of Parliament were passed in aid of the latter and for the encouragement of the colonists. Regarded from a commercial point of view, the principal Act of Anne's life was the union between England and Scotland, which brought solidity to the trade of the two countries, and was the cause of future wealth and prosperity. Well would it have been for the country if all the Acts of her reign had been equally successful. The continued wars had accumulated an enormous amount of floating debt, bearing high interest, which the Government were anxious to provide for by creating a funded debt for its relief. To do this, and give a greater seeming security to subscribers, the Earl of Orford, then Prime Minister—in A.D. 1711—created the famous "South Sea Company," which was to take over the outstanding debt of nearly £10,000,000 sterling, to which Parliament guaranteed interest at the rate of 6 per cent. per annum, upon the credit of certain duties on spirits, tea, and other commodities. As an allurement to the subscribers a monopoly was granted to the Company of all the British trade with the coast of America, from the Orinoco southwards, round Tierra del Fuego, and up the west coast to the extreme north; but, as the monopoly of all the coasts of Asia was in the hands of the East India Company, the South Sea Company was forbidden to send its ships further into the Pacific Ocean than 300 leagues from the American coasts. Besides this monopoly the Company's charter provided for its entering upon whale and other fisheries, and their improvement; and indeed provided an open door for speculation of any kind, which in later years was carried on with such disastrous results.

For the South Sea trade several large ships were built, and also a fleet of twenty-four or twenty-five whaling ships. As a security for the trade on the south and west coasts, an "assiento," or contract for the supply of slaves to the Spanish West Indies, was entered into with the Spanish monarch, who in return granted the Company protection. This proved of little service, as the people of the Spanish colonies hindered the Company's trade in every possible way, and at last went so far as to seize the great ship *Prince Frederick* with a valuable cargo, and confiscate all the Company's property at Vera Cruz. When peace was made with Spain in 1728 the *Prince Frederick* was restored and returned to England with a valuable cargo, but it was insufficient to pay for the losses incurred. Of all the voyages made by the four great ships, of which we have record, only one is said to have returned a profit.

The whaling ships went out year after year for about eight years without success. This was hardly to be wondered at, seeing that all the officers, harpooners, boat-steerers, &c., had to be obtained from Holstein at a very heavy expense, the English seamen not knowing, or, from neglect, having lost the art of whale-fishing. This art was deemed so valuable to the nation, that, notwithstanding the failure of the South Sea Company to make it a successful business, a bounty of from £1 to £2 per ton burthen was offered by Parliament to those who built and sent out ships for the purpose, under certain conditions that insured its proper application and use. As the century progressed it became an established and valuable trade.

Bubble Companies.—As a trading company the South Sea Company was a failure; in fact, it never properly recovered from the discredit brought upon it by the crazy speculation of 1720, when fraudulent directors, by inflated promises of abnormal profits, caused such a run upon the shares as in a very few weeks sent them up to £1000 per share, by which the directors and their friends realised enormous fortunes. This sent the whole nation frantic, and bubble companies of all kinds and descriptions were set afloat. This did not suit the directors of the South Sea Company, and they prosecuted some of these speculators for infringing their rights. Once in the law courts their own proceedings were thrown open to public gaze, and alarm became general. It did not take long for this to have an effect upon the Company. A scrutiny being made, its affairs were found to be in an absolute state of rottenness. The shares immediately fell from 1000 to 300, and thousands of persons were reduced to ruin. On an inquiry by a committee of both Houses of Parliament, the corrupt practices of the directors were brought to light, involving some of the highest personages in the land, and it was found that £1,000,000 of fictitious stock had been created for the purpose of bribery. The estates of the directors were confiscated, and every means taken for recovery; but, on winding up, it was found that there was only about 33 per cent. of the subscribed capital to divide between the legitimate shareholders. Parliament came to their aid, and by sundry schemes of adjustment the pressure of loss was distributed over as large an area as possible. For many consecutive years the Parliament Roll was filled with South Sea statutes. Such was the end of an unfortunate system of financing then new to the world, which has had many successors, down even to the present day.

State of Shipping.—In spite of these untoward circumstances the general shipping trade increased. It is reported that, in the six years preceding A.D. 1729, English tonnage had increased by 238,000 tons. It is difficult to reconcile such a statement with another, of about the same time, which tells us that London possessed only 1417 ships of from 15 to 750 tons burthen, amounting altogether to 178,557 tons and 21,797 men of which there were only 213 above 200 tons. At Liverpool, on an Act being sought in 1739 to give powers to build docks and levy dues, it was stated there were 211 ships above 30 tons—from 200 to 400, seven ships—from 100 to 200, 78; and the remainder 90 tons and downward.

Trade of American Colonies.—Again in 1731 the trade with Virginia and Maryland seems considerable, for it is said to have employed 24,000 tons that year in bringing home 60,000 hhds. of tobacco, lumber, furs, walnut wood, boards, &c. Pennsylvania was building 2000 tons of ships yearly and employed about 6000 tons. New York sent fewer ships home than the other colonies, but their cargoes were richer in furs and skins. The freight on tobacco was £10 per ton.

Newfoundland.—Newfoundland, although but sparsely inhabited, was of great use as a "breeding ground" of able seamen in its fisheries. The trade of the colonies in the aggregate was said to be worth at least £1,000,000 per annum to Great Britain.

Supply of Seamen.—In 1740 it is computed that there were at least 200 British ships in the trade to Maryland and Virginia. In consequence of the war which had broken out with France, mainly in consequence of trade jealousies, seamen became scarce and the protective Acts were relaxed by the Act 13 George the Second, c. 3, in favour of the employment by our merchant men of foreign sailors, who were now admitted to the extent of three-fourths, instead of one-fourth, of the crews of British ships. An inducement also was offered to the foreigners, whereby, after two years' service in the Royal Navy, they became naturalised Englishmen. By the same Act British seamen over fifty-five years of age or under eighteen were free from impressment, and any persons following the sea were free for the first two years at any age.

Notwithstanding all inducements, legislative or otherwise, the demand for seamen was always outrunning the supply. The extension of the colonies and the constant wars created a drain which could not well be met.

The King's service was not popular with seamen of the Merchant service. The length of time men had to serve without relaxation, and the rough discipline, did not suit those who were accustomed to the easy habits of the coasting-schooner, or the fishing-smack, and, whatever their hardships otherwise, to a frequent return to the village and the fireside.

The difficulty of finding men for the navy caused the impressment of merchant sailors by King's officers. This often led to acts of violence and oppression, but its worst consequence—however legal it was, and that has never been doubted—was, that the best of our sailors fled the country to escape from it, and even the Merchant service became denuded of its sufficient number of seamen.

The American colonies formed an asylum into which it was difficult for men of war to follow them, although the right of impressment was as freely used there, when occasion served, as at home.

In 1742 an Act, 15 George the Second, c. 31, was passed which required all Colonial as well as British ships to be registered as British, and yet more strictly provided against the intrusion of any foreign ships in the trade between Britain and America or on their coasts.

A very strong attempt was at this time made to upset the East India Company's Charter and throw open the trade; but the Government thinking it would be unsafe to do this, as, in face of constant war, private traders would not be able to maintain themselves like the powerful ships of the Company in the face of the enemy, it was in 1744 A.D. renewed for another fourteen years.

American Smuggling in the West Indies.—During the war between England and France and Spain, the Colonies of America, thinking more of their own gain than loyalty to the mother country, carried on a strong illicit trade with the French West Indies and the Spaniards on the Mississippi, and the Mobile, under flags of truce, in contravention of the British Acts of Parliament; and all the endeavours of the Home Government, and any attempt the Colonial governors made to put a stop to it, failed to have any effect. The expanse of coast was too extensive to watch closely, so the smugglers slipped in and out without let or hindrance. This was the beginning of a contention between the parent country and its offspring which was doomed to beat hereafter with a stronger pulse.

Naval Operations there.—A considerable portion of the naval warlike operations were carried on in the West Indies, where, before the end of the war, the Havannah had been stormed by Admiral Pococke, and the *Hermione*, a Spanish ship from Cuba with bullion and rich merchandise, which fetched half a million of money, had been taken by two sloops of war. In the East, Manilla was taken by General Draper and Admiral Cornish, with a force despatched from India, when a galleon worth another half-million fell a prize to the captors. Canada had fallen before the sword of General Wolff.

Survey of the St. Lawrence by James Cook.—In 1763 the combatants, fully worn out, were glad to make peace; and a treaty was concluded at Paris. France ceded Canada, Cape Breton, Nova Scotia, and all the islands at the mouth of the St. Lawrence, and Spain ceded Florida to Great Britain. Shortly afterwards James Cook, R.N., made a survey of the coasts of Newfoundland, Labrador and the Saint Lawrence. Cook was born in 1727 at Whitby in Yorkshire, where he was apprenticed to a linen-draper, but disliking that business he engaged himself for nine years to the master of a collier. In 1755 he joined the navy, where by his personal merit he soon found his way to the quarter deck. Here, in the midst of warlike operations, he found time to study Euclid, and otherwise make up for a deficient education. There is reason to believe that he never attempted to draw a chart before he began the survey in 1759, which he completed to the entire satisfaction of the Admiralty. This was the Captain James Cook who afterwards became famous for his circumnavigation of the world and his many discoveries.

Revolt of the States. Their Independence Achieved.— After the close of the war the British Government attempted to carry out the Navigation Laws, by trying to put down the contraband trade with the Spanish colonies with a strong hand. This was borne with a bad grace by the colonists, but might not have gone further had not an attempt been made to lay direct taxes upon them for the benefit of the mother country, who naturally thought that her offspring ought to help her out with the debts which she had contracted partially, at least, in their defence. The unfortunate Stamp Act of A.D. 1765, and the taxes on tea, glass, paper, colours, &c., of A.D. 1767, set fire to the match of popular indignation which lit a blaze never to be quenched. A sullen endeavour to control, by a Ministry unaccustomed to rebellion and a monarch who thought himself absolute, was met by energetic defiance on the other side. The Ministry so far gave way as to repeal all the duties except that on tea, but that was not sufficient; any tax at all was deemed by the excited colonists a badge of slavery, and to be resented as such. In a riot, blood was drawn in the streets of Boston; overt acts of rebellion took place in quick succession, and in less than two short years the Twelve States proclaimed their independence on the 4th of July, 1776. For nearly eight years a desultory war was carried on, in which the colonists were aided by France, Spain, and Holland, each and all with a grievance against Great Britain, and only too glad to assist at what they believed would be the dismemberment of its empire.

Fleets of American privateers covered the ocean and even ventured into the narrow seas, to the great detriment of English and Irish trade. As the war progressed the commerce of England was almost destroyed; every ship was employed by Government either as a transport or a privateer, and it became almost impossible to find means for the export of the English corn, which was very plentiful. It was therefore provided that neutral ships should receive half the bounty paid to the nation's own vessels for its export.

The struggle was protracted until 1783, when the British nation, tired of its losses, and fearing the entire destruction of its commerce, almost forced the Government to give up the contest. Peace was proclaimed in September, and the States gained their freedom.

Our country, although depressed to a remarkable degree, came out of the war in better plight than the other nations. During the war the French merchant shipping was destroyed and the merchants thrown into bankruptcy. Communication with the French West Indies was kept up by neutral ships, and the Spaniards were in the same plight. The French navy, dependent upon the West India trade for its supply of seamen, must have been laid up if the war had lasted another year.

Effect of the War on British Shipping.—The loss of the American colonies to the mother country has been variously estimated, but perhaps on the whole it was a gain. It relieved the British Government of many costly charges and bounties granted in aid of the colonies; and perhaps one of the most important benefits was the restoration of shipbuilding in the British shipyards, which had in a measure been sacrificed to the zeal for colonial prosperity. During the war the British yards had been well employed, and yards had been opened in Wales and other parts, which utilised the fine timber grown on the spot, and, as they could produce ships cheaper than on the Thames by from 10s. to 30s. per ton, they found plenty of customers, especially those who had been accustomed to use the cheap ships of the colonies. In addition to the utilisation of the excellent timber of these parts of the kingdom, it gave employment to numbers of young men, who were encouraged to apply themselves to a trade upon which the prosperity of the country so much depended.

To show how this had operated during the eight years of the war, Mr. Anderson gives a table showing that, at the commencement, the proportions of British and American-built ships on the British Registry was 2 to 1, whilst at the end of the war it was 7 to 2; with a total loss of about 45,000 tons on the whole; but apparently this loss was more than compensated for by the large number of ships still in Government employ which were not included in the above figures; the average total tonnage being about 950,000 tons. It is, however, difficult to reconcile these figures with another statement at the end of the year in which it is said that the total number of ships belonging to the ports of Great Britain was 8342 of only 669,802 tons, and that the total entries of the year A.D. 1783 were 1,135,674 inwards and 1,039,045 outwards. No doubt a great many ships would have been taken off the register and transferred to the United States, but these could hardly have accounted for so much as 300,000 tons. It is very evident that all the statistics of those times were only approximations, and liable to considerable error. That the peace brought increased vitality to British trade is very evident, for the returns, commenced in 1783 and continued every year, in 1790 show the number of British ships to be 15,015 of 1,460,823 tons, having 112,556 seamen, or more than doubled in the seven years.

French King's proposals for Reciprocal Trade.—At this period a curious incident occurred, foreshadowing principles which have since found a home in Britain, if no where else as yet. Louis XVI. of France began his reign in 1774 with enlightened ideas as to necessary reforms, both constitutional and commercial, which, had he been able to put them into execution, might have saved the revolution of 15 years later that cost him his crown and life; but the *cliques* of aristocrats who had enjoyed power so long were too strong for him.

After the peace of 1783 he made a proposal to the British Government and others, to abolish exclusive trade, which meant not quite Free Trade as we now understand it, but a measure of reciprocity, which would admit of free intercourse between the nations. The English Ministry declined an answer to this until an answer was received from the Empress of Russia. This appears to have had no result, for two years after, when British manufacturers had made such way in France that the merchants wrote over their doors "Warehouse for English Goods," the French manufacturers and traders craved protection. The French monarch, in replying to his people's wishes, said in a most liberal spirit, that nothing could be more agreeable to his own wishes than a general liberty of trade which should permit the free circulation of the produce and manufactures of all nations, making them, as it were, but one nation in point of trade. "But," he continued, "until such a liberal system could become universally and reciprocally established, he must consult the interests of his kingdom by prohibiting the importation of white calicoes, stuffs of cotton and woollen mixed, handkerchiefs, dimities and nankeens, except those imported by the (French) East India Company's vessels licensed by a late decree." Bitterly must the English Ministry have felt their indecison in not complying with the King's desire for free trade, for this decree half ruined the English manufacturers and caused great distress to their workpeople. A better feeling was allowed to prevail in a year or two, and a most liberal treaty of commerce was entered into on the 26th September 1786 at Versailles, between Mr. Eden (Lord Auckland) on behalf of England and M. de Reyneval on the part of France. This did not last long enough to prove its value to both nations, for the French Revolution, ensuing almost immediately, upset the whole business, and such complete amity between the two nations has never been since regained.

Convict Settlement in New South Wales.—The year 1787 was signalised by the settlement of a Convict Station at Port Jackson (Sydney) in New South Wales, of which Capt. Arthur Phillips was appointed the first Governor. Botany Bay had been the chosen spot, but when Phillips arrived there it was found so unsuitable for the purpose that he determined to explore the coast further to the North, and discovered the lovely harbour of Port Jackson, in which all the fleets of the world might ride in safety. This was the commencement of a colony, which has proved and will still prove invaluable to Great Britain as long as the parent and child walk together in harmony, which we may hope will be for a long period yet.

Trade of Liverpool.—The trade of Liverpool had grown so great during the century, that whereas at its beginning the place was not much more than a village, it had now become the second port in the kingdom, taking the place so long held by Bristol. Between them these two towns had absorbed most of the trade with Africa, and with it the slave trade to the West Indies, upon which their merchants and shipowners had grown wealthy. Liverpool also had a large share of the American trade, and, backed by the manufacturing interest of Manchester and Lancashire generally, had no difficulty in outstripping her rival.

Renewal of E. I. Charter.—About this period (1792) Liverpool merchants were anxious about the slave trade, which had already aroused the sympathies of Clarkson and Wilberforce, who, with their friends, were agitating for its abolition. Fearing the loss of business, and looking round for means of employing capital which had been invested in the slave trade, the merchants of Liverpool turned their attention to the East, and thought themselves entitled to an East India Company of their own; but these wishes were not realised. The declaration of war by the French Republic against both England and Holland engrossed the attention of the nation; the slave trade had a respite for another ten years, and the East India Company enjoyed its privileges for another twenty. For the rest of the century the war found plenty of employment for British sailors in the Royal navy, as well as in hosts of privateers. The navigation laws were once more relaxed, and foreign seamen employed in great numbers.

State of Navigation.—In 1799 the number of ships returned by Anderson as belonging to the United Kingdom and its Colonies was 17,879 of 1,752,815 tons, manned by 135,237 seamen; and the ships built in that year, 858 of 98,044 tons.

Before leaving this period, it will be as well to show the progress made in the art of navigation as well as of its shipping. At the commencement of the century, the Cross staff, or its improved model the Back staff, were still the only instruments in use for the determination of altitudes at sea. Position in latitude had been fairly ascertained for the most prominent parts of the known world, but position in longitude was still in its infancy, consequently the art of cartography was in a hazy condition, although improvements had been slowly made. Indeed, until the middle of the eighteenth century, charts built upon the Ptolemaic principle were still in existence. The consequence of all this was that ships in finding their way about the world were dependent upon dead reckoning for their presumed differences of longitude, and it was not at all uncommon on a passage across the Atlantic for a man-of-war even to find herself five or six degrees out in longitude. The difficulty, therefore, of making the land or preserving security was precarious to the last degree, and required extreme carefulness. It was this which rendered our seamen observant of wind and weather, the signs of approach to land by discolouration of water, the presence of land birds, &c., whereas in the present state of the art of navigation, with perfect instruments and charts, little or no notice is taken of such incidents as indicators of position.

Reward offered for the best Method of Determining Longitude at Sea.—In 1687 Sir Isaac Newton published his "Principia," in which he developed the law of gravitation, and laid the foundation of modern astronomy; at the same time the study of the art of navigation attracted considerable attention. The Government, acting upon the advice of Sir Isaac Newton (then President of the Royal Society) and others, passed the Act, 12 Anne, c. 15, which offered a large reward for the discovery of a correct mode of ascertaining the longitude at sea. Several schemes had been proposed—it had been attempted, *e.g.*, to solve the problem by means of a watch or astronomical observations—but the difficulties attending these projects rendered them useless for sea purposes. As Sir Isaac Newton explained in the House of Commons " it was necessary that a watch should keep strict time, but that by reason of the motion of the ship, the variations of heat and cold, of moisture and dryness, and the difference of gravity, such a watch had never been found." He also explained "the difficulties of observing the occultation of Jupiter's Satellites, and the moon, &c.," but concluded that the offer of such a reward would be a proper thing to pass. The offer of so high a reward as £20,000 for the discovery was distinct testimony of the value placed by the Government and the nation upon any means of meeting the much-felt want of security in navigation.

Harrison's Timekeepers.—At the time when this reward was offered there lived in Yorkshire a man named John Harrison, who was, as an old writer terms him, "a heaven-born clock-maker," then just twenty-one years of age. Stimulated by the reward, Harrison worked on laboriously for twenty years, when in 1735 he took his first machine to London and laid claim to the reward. This was sent on board a ship of the navy to Lisbon, and was found accurate enough on the return voyage to correct a degree and a half error in longitude by D.R. After making further improvements and several trials to the West Indies and back, under rigid surveillance, Harrison produced a timepiece which was accounted sufficient to meet the demands of the Act of Queen Anne, and in 1767, when over seventy years of age, he received the full reward of £20,000.

Government Grants for Lunar Tables. Nautical Almanac.—It may be mentioned that the Commissioners had been empowered to expend £2000 in experiments and that power was continued for various sums up to £5000 until 1818 when the last Act was passed, which continued in force until 1828, when it was repealed as no longer required.

Under these Acts several sums were granted for experiments and several rewards, notably £3000 to the widow of Professor Mayer, of Gottingen, for his improvements in Lunar Tables, and £500 to Professor Euler of Berlin, for his assistance in the construction of Mayer's Tables. A Mr. Witchell also received £1000 to enable him to prosecute his work in the construction of a set of marine tables for the calculation of the longitude by the lunar method. That gentleman was also appointed with four others to compute an ephemeris to be published for promoting the sciences of Astronomy and Navigation. This was the foundation of the Nautical Almanac which was first published by Dr. Maskelyne, the Astronomer Royal, in 1767, and it remained under his editorship for forty years. Since that it has been published under sanction of an Act of Parliament by the Lords of the Admiralty.

CHAPTER VII.

PROGRESS DURING EARLY PART OF THE NINETEENTH CENTURY.

CONTENTS.—Nineteenth century—The Slave trade—Hampering effect of legislation—Scarcity of seamen—Advantage of Americans as neutrals—The right of search, a cause of another American war—The *Shannon* and the *Chesapeake*—East India trade thrown open—Depression in shipping—The Reciprocity Acts—Laws regulating emigration—General revision of Marine Acts in 1825—Low state of tonnage—China trade thrown open in 1833—Reform Bill and its effects—Shipping Acts, 1834 and 1835—Compulsory apprenticeship—Increase of American ships—Conduct of British shipmasters—Public meetings on shipwrecks, &c.—Royal Commission of 1836—Report of Commissioners—W. S. Lindsay's opinion of British officers—Past training of seamen and its effects upon character—Proposed remedies—Mr. Silk Buckingham's Bill—Opposition of the shipowners—The Defeat of the Bill—Further Commissions of Inquiry—Mr. Murray's letter to Consuls abroad as to the conduct of British shipmasters—Act of 1844—Mr. Poulett Thompson's idea of voluntary examinations—State of Marine officers compared—East India Company's officers—Ordinary shipmasters and officers—London passenger ships and their discipline—Education of British and foreign seamen compared.

Nineteenth Century.—We now enter upon the nineteenth century, during which the progress of shipping and commerce has been phenomenal. It would take volumes to write its history, which is impossible in the space of a work like this; therefore only the salient features which have led up to the present condition of prosperity can be given.

For the first fifteen years the country was engaged in a war fought to sustain the liberties of Europe against the ambition of one of the greatest military tyrants the world had ever seen, in which our commerce was tried to its utmost limits.

The Slave Trade.—One of the first important events was the suppression of the African slave trade in English ships, and by English crews. In 1807 it was abolished by 47 Geo. III. c. 36, but as by this Act only a money penalty was exacted from offenders, it had little effect. The trade was too profitable to be stopped by a mere money penalty, so in 1811 an Act was passed declaring its pursuit by British subjects "a felony," punishable by fourteen years transportation or imprisonment with hard labour. In course of time even this was not sufficiently deterrent, and in 1824 the act of trading in slaves was pronounced a "piracy" and punishable capitally if committed within the Admiralty jurisdiction. The British conscience was not yet (except in the breasts of the few philanthropists, who, by their earnest pleadings at last convinced the nation of its utter wrongfulness) taught to look upon it with abhorrence. Many of those who had been engaged in the trade gave it up with reluctance, especially when they saw other nations continuing the lucrative, though detestable, traffic.

Hampering Effect of Legislation.—As an instance of the manner in which trade was hampered by legislation and monopolies, when our shipowners who engaged in the whale fishery found it profitable to proceed into the Pacific Ocean in search of fish, it was found necessary in 1802 to pass an Act of Parliament to free them from the objections made by the East India Company and the South Sea Company. During the war merchantmen were strictly forbidden, even although they were willing to run the risk, to sail without convoy. To avoid this many vessels which were good sailors and were well-manned, in the West India trade especially, took letters of marque, which enabled them to sail how and when they pleased. Large fortunes, from the high rate of freight, were made in this way, from £20 to £30 per ton being no uncommon rate, and at times even higher. At the same time there was a large amount of unproductive voyaging in consequence of the Navigation Laws, which was brought about by what has been called the "sole market" theory; this was a doctrine which taught the nations to make the attempt of keeping all their own trade in their own hands, and to confine all foreign imports to their own ships, by refusing to receive the products of other countries in the ships of those countries.

As long as the American colonies were a portion of the British empire, English and American vessels sailed freely between English and American ports; but after the separation of the States their ships were treated as foreign vessels and fell under the same restrictions. As a set off against this the young republic in 1790-2 framed their own navigation laws upon the same basis, and English ships were prevented from importing British goods into the United States. Matters continued thus until after the American War of 1812-15.

Scarcity of Seamen.—The necessities of the English Naval Service during the French war created a demand for seamen which was supplied with difficulty, and impressment was enforced without stint. Every measure was taken to encourage the increase of persons following the sea as a profession. The rule as to three-fourths of the crew of an English ship being Englishmen was once more relaxed, and masters and apprentices of fishing smacks were freed from impressment, as long as the number of apprentices fixed by law was maintained in each vessel; the master was also to carry one seaman for every ten tons in his vessel free from seizure by the press gangs; and any landsman, above 18 and under 30, who might be actually employed in fishing, was also free for two years. But legislation had little effect. The revolt of the American colonies had raised up an independent maritime nation, speaking the same language, ruled by the same laws and governed by the same restless energy as ourselves. What wonder then that numbers of our best seamen sought shelter, from what they deemed oppression, in the country of their cousins across the water, who, having plenty of employment for them, received them with open arms?

Advantage of Americans as Neutrals.—Moreover as both English and French ships during these years were subject to capture, it gave an immense advantage to vessels sailing under the American flag, which was largely taken advantage of in England, and much English money was invested in American ships. At home shipbuilding timber was getting scarce, and consequently ships were dear to build. Notwithstanding these difficulties, our own shipping had never been employed better or at higher freights, but its increase during the war was less than it had been during the immediately preceding years. This may be accounted for by extra war risks, yet, although the price of ships was very high in England, the demand was constant. In 1809 freights were as much as £30 per ton for hemp, and other articles in proportion. Insurances amounted to 40 or even 50 per cent.

The Right of Search, a Cause of another American War.—The English Government, annoyed by the wholesale desertion to the American ships, insisted upon their right of search for British subjects. English men-of-war overhauled them wherever met, and took out those sailors who could not make good their claim to American citizenship; this became a prominent cause of the war declared in 1812. This war was indeed largely fought between Englishmen in the naval engagements; in some cases brother against brother, and father against son.

The "Shannon" and the "Chesapeake."—It was a calamitous war on both sides. American commerce was temporarily destroyed, and its effect was so severely felt that the New England States, which had never favoured the war, threatened to secede if peace was not made. In the course of the war several English men-of-war were taken, but in every case by vessels of much greater weight, both in men and guns. The English Government evidently undervalued the strength of their opponents, and met them with light undersized vessels, which stood little chance against the modern American ships, which outsailed and outweighted the English on every point; but when better ships were sent into American waters, the honour of the old flag was more than maintained. The ever memorable fight between the English frigate *Shannon*, and the American *Chesapeake*, in sight of Boston Harbour, when the latter was taken after one of the severest hand to hand fights ever known, turned the tables. In December 1814, both sides being sick of what had been a naval duel rather than a war, peace was signed.* The battle of Waterloo settled the French war six months after, and the nations laid down their arms to recruit their exhausted strength in a lengthened peace of forty years.

The result of the peace with America was that the navigation laws of both countries were, as far as concerned the trade between them, mutually rescinded; the ships of both countries were placed upon the same footing, and all discriminating duties abandoned. This was the first approach to reciprocity of trade granted by the English Government for centuries.

East India Trade thrown Open.—About this time also one of the great shipping monopolies was abandoned. When the East India Company's charter was renewed in 1793, the large commercial towns, especially Liverpool, already referred to, strenuously opposed the continuance of the monopoly, and insisted upon the trade being thrown open, but the Government, with the commencement of a war upon its hands, of which nobody foresaw the end, carried its point, and the Company's charter was renewed for another twenty years. A sop was indeed thrown to the complainants by compelling the Company to reserve a certain amount of tonnage in their ships for private enterprise, but the limited quantity so allotted, and the high freights charged, caused such dissatisfaction that it was foreseen that in any new charter much greater concessions would have to be made. Accordingly, when the charter was renewed in 1813, by the Act 53 Geo. III. c. 155, the trade to India, under certain restrictions, was thrown open to all parts of the East except the trade with China, which, with the tea trade, was still strictly reserved to the Company. Private ships trading to the East Indies were confined to the three

---

* This war proved ruinous to American trade, its foreign commerce being reduced from fifty to four millions in the three years.

ports of Calcutta, Madras and Bombay, of all those parts subject to the government of the East India Company. Trade to the coasts and minor ports of India required a special licence from the directors, and no ships under 350 tons were to be thus employed. This referred to British ships trading between the home ports and India; but in the next year trade was opened between the East India Company's settlements and ports in North and South America (not being British plantations), Madeira, the Canaries, Cape de Verde Islands, St. Helena, and the Cape of Good Hope, but this was strictly confined to British bottoms.

In 1815 Indian country built ships were admitted to the British register. At the same time Lascars were permitted to be carried in Indian ships as long as the European part of a crew amounted to seven men for every hundred tons burthen. In 1816, when the convention of reciprocity was carried out between England and the United States, ships of the latter were permitted to clear out of English ports for places in the East Indies, which permission was to last as long as the convention.

In the next few years the restrictions upon trade between the English possessions were gradually relaxed, and their ships permitted to pass freely between them. Thus the barriers created by the "sole market" theory were being broken down, and a door opened for freer trade everywhere.

The East India Company continued to run trading ships to India for a few years longer, but at length the trade proved unprofitable, and it was abandoned to the Free Traders, as the private ships were termed. The Company maintained their own ships for military and store purposes to India and in the trade to China.

Residence in India had been strictly reserved to the Company's own officers and servants, but now private traders were permitted to reside in the presidencies under licence from the Company, and the great London and Liverpool merchants soon established branch firms there.

Depression in Shipping.—The effect of peace and of the American convention was to depress British shipping, so that tonnage was absolutely at a standstill for many years. There were several reasons for this; in the first place, the accession of peace threw upon the market a large amount of tonnage which had been employed by the Government; and, in the next place, both British and American ships, which had been travelling the Atlantic in ballast, were now getting cargoes both ways, and not nearly so much tonnage was required; and the curious fact is seen that American tonnage was for years in the same position. On the other hand, the shipping of the British colonies, principally in Canada, doubled itself in twenty years.

The Reciprocity Acts.—Another circumstance now occurred which no doubt had some effect upon shipping. In 1823 Prussia, seeing the effect of the American protest against the doctrine of exclusiveness, also retaliated and shut up her ports to British ships. This led to the passing of the Reciprocity Acts (4 Geo. IV. c. 77, and 5 Geo. IV. c. 1), which empowered the King in Council to grant reciprocity to such nations as would place us on the same footing. Thus the back of our navigation law was broken, although it survived for some years longer.

Laws regulating Emigration.—After the peace the rage for emigration once more set in, and hundreds of poor people sailed for America and Canada. It is related that their sufferings were very great, not only from ignorance of the country they were going to, but also from the brutality with which they were treated by those who undertook to take them across the ocean to their destination. Stories are told of the unfortunate passengers being cheated in every possible way, and of their being landed at places far from their desired haven. Anderson, in his history of commerce, relates how one hundred such emigrants were taken on board a sailing ship on the Clyde, landed on the Island of Rathlin in Ireland, and robbed of the five guineas paid for their passage, their clothes, and their provisions. This was quite worthy of a slave-trading age. No government supervision was extended to passengers until 1817, when an Act—57 Geo. III. c. 20—was passed, forbidding ships to take more persons on board than one for every one and half tons of the registered tonnage, including the crew; it also provided that passengers should be landed at the place contracted for (evident proof of the foregoing tales), and that proper provisions and water should be supplied. In 1825 and 1826 that Act was extended, and a certain space allotted to each passenger. These Acts also provided that in vessels of only one deck, if cargo was carried in the hold, it should be platformed over, and a height of not less than $5\frac{1}{2}$ feet under the main-deck left for the accommodation of passengers. Such a provision is itself a proof of what had been going on—viz., that the unfortunates had been tumbled down below, treated as so much more cargo, and left to shift for themselves as they best could. Can one now imagine the scene? What an idea it leaves on the mind of the character of certain classes of shipowners and seamen in those days! No doubt such men thought themselves unjustly treated, and *their legitimate business* interfered with by Government care and supervision.

General Revision of Marine Acts in 1825.—A general revision of all the Navigation Acts took place in 1825, when all former Acts were repealed and summed up in a new Act—6 Geo. IV. c. 109. In this Act the restriction as to British crews was maintained—viz., three-fourths of the crew to be British seamen; but if one British seaman for every 20 tons was carried the rest of the crew might be foreigners.

Low State of Tonnage.—This year the tonnage was at a very low ebb, much less than in 1815, but this seems to have been the turning point. In the Atlantic trade the American ships were fast gaining the pre-eminence. Built for sailing as well as carrying, they ran off with the bulk of the passenger trades, making their passages in a much shorter time than the British built ships.

With the peace the British shipowner hoped his troubles were at an end, but it was a delusive hope. He soon began to find that the dear ships built at home contrasted badly from an economical point of view with the cheaper ships of America, or the colonies; the former he was forbidden to purchase, and the timber of Canada was very inferior to that of the States. The profits of the Indian trade enabled him to purchase and employ the first-class "river-built" ship, as those constructed on the Thames were termed, which still held their own in the eyes of Indian shippers, but in the American trade they could not compete.

China Trade thrown open in 1833.—In 1833, the East India Company lost their China Trading Charter, and henceforth the China trade was thrown open to all British subjects for ever.

Their ships were all sold in the following year, and the fine old fleet of double-banked ships soon disappeared.

The passenger trade from London to India was carried on by several fleets of fine passenger ships, owned by such well-known and honoured names as the Wigrams, Greens, Dunbar, Tindall, and many others; and a few single ships which maintained their standing for some years. We now pass on to a period of growing energy and vitality.

Reform Bill and its Effects.—Hitherto the landed interest of the country had been the ruling one in Imperial politics, but the growth of manufactures and of the manufacturing populations, in towns and districts, was enabling traders, day by day, to compete more unmistakably with the landed proprietors and agriculturists for power. In 1832, after a long struggle, the famous Reform Bill was passed, which threw more of that power into the hands of manufacturers and traders, and renovated the country.

Intellectual activity kept pace with the political, and movements were begun which have not seen any termination, but are going on with ever widening circles on the ocean of life in our own day.

In this enlargement of activity the Mercantile Marine participated, and in the next twenty years nearly doubled itself, while the ships grew rapidly in size and number.

Shipping Acts, 1834 and 1835.—In 1834, an Act, 3 & 4 Will. IV. c. 54, was passed, re-asserting and restricting the qualification for a British shipmaster to the natural born subjects of the Empire, or to persons naturalised by process according to law.

Compulsory Apprenticeship.—Another Act, 5 & 6 Will. IV. c. 19 (1835), consolidated the law relating to merchant seamen, the main features of which were a declaration that a British ship should be considered duly navigated if she had one seaman for every twenty tons of her registered tonnage, the regulation and binding of apprentices, and the manner of binding them to the sea service, and making it compulsory for every vessel to carry a certain number according to tonnage, that is to say:—

 Vessels of 80 tons and under 200 tons, one.
 Vessels of 200 tons and under 400 tons, two.
 Vessels of 400 tons and under 500 tons, three.
 Vessels of 500 tons and under 700 tons, four.
 Vessels of 700 tons and upwards, five.

And for every apprentice deficient a fine of £10 was to be inflicted.

It also provided that Justices of the Peace should adjudicate upon complaints as to ill-usage, or charges of assault, &c., committed on board ship by any member of a crew.

This is the first Act which made the carriage of apprentices as part of a crew *compulsory*. By this Act also a registry of seamen was established, which is still in existence. It has fallen into disuse, but has never been repealed, although it has been somewhat modified.

Increase of American Ships.—The distressed and low condition of our shipping continued, and nothing seemed to avail for its restoration. The American "marine," aided by every natural advantage, except a sufficiency of native-born seamen, increased by leaps and bounds, and it appeared as if we were to be beaten upon what we proudly conceived was our own ground.

Conduct of British Shipmasters. Public Meetings on Shipwrecks, &c.—Our shipowners complained of loss of trade from the undue and increasing competition of foreign ships. Our sailors complained of ill-usage, bad food, and miserable quarters; underwriters, of the increasing and abnormal losses, which they attributed to the incompetency and reckless carelessness of those in charge. Philanthropists complained of undue loss of life by shipwreck, and of brutality exercised by masters and officers upon their crews; indeed, the whole of the British maritime world was in a state of complete unrest, and the minds of shipowners, mariners, and the benevolent public were alike exercised to find a remedy. Public meetings were held throughout the country, notably in Edinburgh, and Parliament was inundated with petitions to inquire into the causes of such increased loss of life. The seamen and public of Sunderland did the same, specially referring to badly constructed and worn-out ships; marine insurance and its abuse; and *the incompetency of masters* as the prevailing causes —and *inter alia* prayed the House of Commons to "appoint an experienced nautical committee to examine vessels, their stores, the number of their crews and their berths, and into *the ability of commanders and officers.*"

The humanitarian feelings, which had up to 1834 been fully expended upon negro slavery, were now directed with full force upon the state and condition of our fellow countrymen who " go down to the sea in ships." In that same year, at the Annual Dinner of the Royal Humane Society, Captain Hyland, after saying that "prevention of loss of life" was the text upon which their society was founded, referred " to the great loss of life at sea caused by the *ignorance of shipmasters*, who were entirely *ignorant of the use of the sextant or chronometer;* and also by the difficulty of getting soundings from *neglect of using the best instruments* invented for the purpose." Such an expression of opinion in the City of London by one who spoke with some authority created an animated controversy. Letters were written *pro* and *con*, in attack or defence, and articles appeared in the "Edinburgh Review" and other journals of the day. Public opinion was much divided. The general public blamed the shipowner "for buying and owning imperfectly built ships and carelessness of loss being protected by over insurance"; the underwriter for "slackness of survey and gambling insurance, the greater the risk the greater the premium"; and the masters for "ignorance, carelessness, and insobriety." The shipowners, on the other hand, denied with vigour the allegations brought against them, and declared that the statistics upon which they were founded were erroneous; laid all their own difficulties which prevented profitable trade at the door of foreign competition and unrestricted reciprocity (which latter had been forced upon them by the peculiarities of American trade, and in which Prussia and other European nations followed suit), and deprecated any Governmental interference with themselves in the general management of their business, or with their sole control over their masters or crews.

The passing of the Act 5 and 6 Will. IV. cap. 19 (1835), rather added to than allayed the acrimony of the dispute. The shipowners, who had begun to look upon the system of apprenticeship as an unnecessary burden, resented the compulsory system, and their advocates wrote very bitterly against it—a system which appeared to the Government the only mode of keeping up the supply of seamen for H.M. service.

Royal Commission of 1836.—The consequence of this state of matters was the appointment of a Royal Commission in 1836 to consider the whole subject, and to inquire into and answer such statements and complaints as were now made respecting our Mercantile Marine, viz.,

"That the wreckage of British ships was largely on the increase and, consequently, loss of life.

"That foreign ships were being preferred in foreign ports to British ships, and were commanding better freights.

"That the reason for this was:

"That foreign ships were better built.

"That foreign shipmasters were better educated and more careful; and, that the ships were better manned than our own."

A *terrible indictment* for the ships and the men of the first maritime nation in the world—if true!

Report of Commissioners.— After hearing voluminous evidence on the subject the Commissioners state:

"That the abnormal amount of loss of life and British ships was due:—

"1st. To a bad system of classification, which depended upon the age of the ship and not her inherent worth.

"2nd. To competition with foreign shipowners, who were able to build and sail their vessels much more cheaply than we could.

"3rd. To the bad form of ships in consequence of the bad system of measurement.

"4th. To incompetency of masters and officers.

"5th. Drunkenness of officers and crews.

"6th. The system of marine insurance.

"7th. Want of harbours of refuge.

"8th. Imperfection in charts."

The replies of the Commissioners referred chiefly to the question of wreckage; but the charges against the *personnel* of the British marine are brought in incidentally, yet in no measured tone.

Shall we say that, in regard to the charges against the British sailor, the verdict was—guilty? One is reluctant to admit it. And yet such a Committee could hardly have come to such a conclusion, at least with regard to a large section of British shipmasters and officers, without just cause shown.

W. S. Lindsay's Opinion of British Officers.—Even Mr. W. S. Lindsay, in discussing this subject in his *History of Shipping*, cautiously says: "Although it can scarcely be said that the character of British seamen *degenerated* from the time of the Declaration of Independence by the American colonies till towards the close of the first half of the present century, there is no doubt that those of other nations were making rapid strides in advance of them;" and then, with his well-known "free trade" proclivities, he adds, "Indeed, many causes had combined to raise alike the position of the shipowners and seamen of foreign nations, not the least of these being the protection afforded to our shipowners by the Navigation Laws; as under that protective system, they felt it less necessary to exert themselves to contend with the foreigner as keenly as, under other circumstances, they would surely have done."

Past Training of Seamen and its Effects upon Character.—Protection had little or nothing whatever to do with the moral degradation of either shipowner or mariner, but, if a cause must be sought, it will be found in the low state of education then existing throughout England, and the fact that too many took to a sea life to escape from books and tutors, imposed upon by the idea that, for a sailor, book learning was unnecessary.

Throughout the preceding ages the life of the sailor was quite as much that of a fighter as of a trader. Harassed by an almost continual state of war, ships of every sort were more or less armed and crews kept upon the alert for defence against not only ships of the enemies' navies, but also a swarm of privateers and semi-piratical vessels. Armed merchantmen in their turn made use of the licence of the times and preyed upon the traders of other countries which were weak enough to be attacked.

The slave trade, in which numbers of our merchantmen engaged from the days of Hawkins onward, was not calculated to improve the habits or the morals of the men engaged in it. During the long wars a very large number of our traders carried letters of marque to enable them to prey upon the stray vessels of the enemy. The life of the sailor was one of continued excitement, ill calculated to tend to the intellectual or moral advancement of those who followed the profession. The shipmaster and his officers under such circumstances were petty tyrants whose word was the law of the moment, and he who hesitated or disobeyed was at once triced up to the triangle and received his punishment, or was cut down as a mutineer whose fate no one cared for or inquired into. In such a life the steady eye and the strong arm were of more value than a cultivated intellect, and the latter, when found in an uncultivated state, only gave the possessor the greater power of command or even tyranny. Recovery from such a state of life could by no possibility be sudden. Those to whom it did not commend itself, turned, like John Newton, from it in horror and disgust When wars ceased and privateering come to an end, it was difficult for the men brought up in such a school to weigh the moral effect of conduct upon themselves or their crews, and therefore an overbearing and licentious habit, incompatible with peaceful trading, for a long period after all necessity, if such there had been, for such conduct had ceased, was not only permitted, but continued to be practised until the light of reason dawned upon it, and efforts were put forth for its correction.

Another and more prevailing cause for the want of moral tone and intellectual cultivation in our seamen, was doubtless the fact that lads went to sea at a very early age with little or no education or moral training, and but few found opportunity of acquiring them in after life. There were good seamen in plenty, as seamanship—that is, the handicraft of a sailor's work, and coasting pilotage—can be acquired without much book knowledge. But the deeper parts of a navigator's art, and a thorough knowledge of the sciences upon which it is founded, as also general courtesy of behaviour and sobriety of conduct, are seldom attained without polite education and literary ability, the want of which had stamped the British sailor in the eyes of foreign nations with contempt and gave rise to the terrible revelations of his conduct as displayed in the reports of consular agents in foreign ports. The consequence of this was said to be shown in the fact that the good name of the British ship was lost; hence foreigners everywhere got the preference for security in the handling and transmission of cargoes, and the British shipowner was fast losing his trade. The position and character of the British sailor was the result of training rather than deliberate choice, and the immediate question which the Commissioners answered was, how were these to be improved.

Proposed Remedies.—The evils being admitted, what were the remedies proposed by the Commission? *Inter alia*, these, as affecting the mariner, viz.:

(1) The formation of a Mercantile Board to regulate the affairs of the Mercantile Marine.

(2) The formation of a standard of acquirement for officers by the establishment of examinations.

(3) Savings Banks for seamen.

(4) Asylum for worn-out seamen.

(5) Registry Offices, at which seamen's characters shall be recorded and kept.

(6) Nautical Schools.

(7) Courts of inquiry into shipwrecks, with power to *censure* and power to *reward* by money, medals, or otherwise.

(8) Tribunals for speedy settlement of disputes.

(9) Discouragement of drinking on board ship.

And, lastly, attention was called to the *vast superiority* in officers, crews, and equipment, and consequent superior success and growth of American shipping.

Mr. Silk Buckingham's Bill: Opposition of Shipowners.—With the view of carrying out the proposed remedies, Mr. Buckingham, Chairman of the Committee, in 1837, brought in a Bill embracing in detail all the proposals of the Committee, which, although it received the strongest support from Mr. Joseph Hume (himself the son of a shipmaster); who at that time was posing as a "financial reformer" and the "people's friend," Admiral Sir Edward Codrington, and many others, offered a policy which was not only revolutionary in character, but too cumbersome and expensive in its working clauses. Its advocates strongly urged that it could, if read a second time, be altered in Committee; but the Government looking askance at it, its success, as a private Bill, could hardly be hoped for. It received the uncompromising opposition of all the shipping members of the House, especially of the member for Sunderland, notwithstanding the petition of the mariners of that port, and their friends in favour of its principle.

Defeat of the Bill.—Mr. Poulett Thompson, the President of the Board of Trade, in moving the rejection of the Bill, expressed the Government's sympathy with much of its intention, but could not support its details, "which," he said, "were so hopelessly bad that, in his opinion, not a clause of it would survive its committal," and therefore it would be useless to take up the time of the House. In the course of his speech he threw out a hint, which, as we shall see, was not altogether lost sight of; it was to this effect, that "he thought that it might serve a good purpose if the authorities of the Trinity House of Deptford Strond *would institute voluntary examinations* for shipmasters and officers." The Bill, being pressed to a division, was lost by 176 votes to 28.

The debate had displayed some curious feelings. One maritime gentleman opposed the Bill because *nothing was said in it* as to the *cause* of shipwrecks. A second would not permit any examination because *a great many masters would be found un-*

trustworthy !—and the third declared the Bill *a legislative monstrosity !*

Further Commissions : Mr. Murray's Letters.—Mr. Buckingham and his friends were defeated, but neither did their opponents conquer, for between them they raised a " Frankenstein " which has outlived all its creators. The controversy continued, and inquiries by the Commissioners were furthered in 1839 and again in 1843 with varied success; but the general result was to emphasise the recommendations of 1836, especially as to the education and examination of officers in the Marine. It was in 1843 that Mr. Murray, of the Foreign Office, issued his now famous letter of inquiry to the British Consuls in Foreign ports, as to the qualities and conduct of British shipmasters when within their jurisdiction, and especially in regard to their comparison with foreign shipmasters.

Act of 1844.—After the reports of 1836, 1839, and 1843 ignorance of the facts could no longer be pleaded, and it was plainly the duty of the Government to try and set matters right, if possible, and so alleviate the evils complained of; yet the only answer at that time vouchsafed was the Act 7 & 8 Vict. c. 112 (1844), which further enforced the carrying of apprentices in proportion to tonnage; required every seaman to have a register ticket ; and gave power to punish crime on board ship.

In this Act the Government did not see their way to legislate decidedly upon education and examination. The thought of it was still apparently working in their minds, but the difficulty was how to do it. To make it the duty of a Governmental Department seemed too autocratic a proceeding towards persons not in Government employ, and to leave it in the hands of the local shipowners seemed fruitless.

After the loss of the Bill of 1837, the Sunderland shipowners and masters took the law into their own hands, instituted examinations for themselves, and enforced regulations which had been utterly opposed by their own member in Parliament. It was also proved on evidence that private firms had instituted examination of masters and officers for themselves. One firm, Messrs. Daniel & Co., of Mincing Lane, whose ships had been remarkably free from casualties (they having lost only one ship in twenty years), attributed their success to such a plan. The Sunderland Board does not appear to have been so successful as might have been hoped, for they were accused of being " a mere pilot board for Yarmouth Roads, Hasborough Gat, and up Swin," rather than paying attention to the higher arts of navigation and nautical astronomy; and also of favouritism towards those who presented themselves for certificates.

Mr. Poulett Thompson's Idea of Voluntary Examinations.—The idea thrown out by Mr. Poulett Thompson in 1837 was now, however, about to bear fruit, as in August 1845, the Lords of the Privy Council for Trade issued their order establishing the voluntary examination of masters and mates in the Mercantile Marine.

State of Marine Officers Compared.—Before proceeding further, and to gain a right understanding of its position, it will be necessary to take a slight survey of our mercantile marine as it had come down to us at this date. From the Elizabethan age there was a very evident difference between two sections of the mercantile marine—viz., those engaged in the service of the East India Company, and some few of the other great chartered companies on the one hand, and those employed in the ordinary trading vessels of the country generally, on the other.

East India Company's Officers.—The officers of the East India Company held a unique position, second only to that of the Royal navy in importance. They were governed by special regulations, and almost from the commencement were entrusted by Parliament with the power of exercising military discipline; they were also enabled to hold their own courts for the punishment of offences against discipline or crime. During the whole of the Company's trading wars were continued, and the ships were fully armed—equal in some respects to men-of-war—for even trading was only maintained by the strong hand. The officers were usually men of birth and standing, and fully as well educated as king's officers. The service was popular, and often preferred to the king's service by the sons of merchants and the gentry. They usually commenced their career as cadets or midshipmen.

A fourth mate had to be twenty years of age, and must have performed one round voyage of, usually, three years as a midshipman. A third mate, must have sailed two round voyages and be not under twenty-one years of age. A second mate must have sailed a voyage as third or fourth mate and be not less than twenty-two years of age. Chief mates must have served one voyage as second or third mate, and be not less than twenty-three years of age.

Every Commander was required to be twenty-five years of age, and must have performed one round voyage in the regular service of the Company, as chief or second mate, or have commanded a ship in the extra service. Every officer was put through a strict examination before taking each step in promotion.

The nominal pay was small, even of the commanders, but it was enhanced by so many privileges that their position was a very lucrative one. A certain amount of space in each ship was reserved for the commander, officers and petty officers upon a recognized scale, the commander getting the lion's share of something more than one-half of that space; and so on in proportion to rank down to the very lowest.

Ordinary Shipmasters and Officers.—In the ordinary merchant vessels, very few of which exceeded 500 tons, the simple rôle was that of master, mate and second mate or boatswain (carpenters were frequently second mates also), seamen and apprentices. All commenced life before the mast and served an apprenticeship of five to seven years. It was not uncommon then for lads to go to sea at twelve years of age. There were no statutory regulations for the maintenance of duty or discipline, but the common law recognized an unbounded authority in the master over his crew. The discipline was paternal rather than military, and the rope's end was as freely used on refractory sailors as the father's rod or the schoolmaster's birch. No doubt such power was sometimes abused when out of the reach of the secular arm of the law, but on the whole it bred a race of noble and brave seamen, who, if somewhat coarse in language and manner, were always ready at duty's call, and who learnt to command through learning to obey. As a race they were not the best educated of men, although many by sheer force of character and self-education raised themselves above the crowd. It was the ignorant and careless amongst them who, by their vicious life and conduct, brought such shame upon the whole race of sailors as was displayed in consuls' letters from abroad and in evidence before the House of Commons' Committees.

London Passenger Ships and their Discipline.—Such was the position of matters in regard to the *personnel* in the various branches of the Merchant Service up to the termination of the Company's Charter and exclusive trade to India. This had been the one principal passenger trade from London to the east, and the discipline maintained was semi-military under the sanction of Acts of Parliament. The other considerable passenger trades were those to the American continent, in which London divided the trade with Liverpool, Bristol, &c. In these the discipline was that of the ordinary merchant vessel. When the London passenger trade to the East fell into the hands of private owners whose ships were termed "Free Traders" in contradistinction to those of the East India Company, many of which were commanded and officered by men who had previously served in the chartered ships of the Company and also by naval officers, thrown adrift at the end of the war in 1815, the traditional discipline of the Company was maintained. The ships were well officered and manned, and care was taken to educate young officers as midshipmen. Of course the discipline was no longer maintained by Acts of Parliament as in the Company's ships, but *esprit de corps* remained, and was successful in preserving it intact; and although the officers were no longer invested with the powers of punishment accorded to the Company's officers, the moral force of character remained and had its due effect upon the crews; for the observance of due respect and modes of discipline in the officers, as between themselves, had the effect of impressing the same upon the men, and a better state of discipline was maintained than in the ordinary merchantman. By this it is not intended to convey the idea that there was no discipline on board the ordinary merchant ships, but it was not of so punctilious a character as in the better class of passenger ships. It was a rougher style of discipline and more readily enforced by brute strength, when supposed to be necessary, than by moral power. This difference is still to be traced in the different classes of British ships.

Education of British and of Foreign Seamen.—As a comparison had been drawn between the British sailor and his foreign competitor, which appeared so much to our discredit, let us now take a glance at foreign countries, and see how matters stood with regard to their merchant officers—premising that nothing had ever been done in this country by the Government to educate our merchant sailors, or to improve their general intelligence in any way whatever; to bind him to serve an apprenticeship was the utmost stretch of our national wisdom.

Long before we thought it necessary to institute any test of the capability of our officers, a most perfect system, not only of examination but of education, had been in use in nearly all, if not all, the countries of Europe.

In Denmark no seaman could undertake the command of a Danish vessel until he had made two foreign voyages as mate, or before he had passed an examination of the severest order. He had to prove himself an intelligent navigator by dead reckoning; by a knowledge of astronomy, and the motions of the sun, moon, and stars, and how to find their positions; by a knowledge of tides and currents, and a perfect knowledge of general seamanship.

In Norway and Sweden, they had to undergo a similar examination, and were required to have a general knowledge of ship's business, some knowledge of shipbuilding and the various parts of her construction, and an ability to measure a ship's capacity.

In Russia and Prussia an equally severe examination was made; and in addition to a competent knowledge of their own language, and the ability to write it with accuracy, there was required some knowledge of English and French.

In the Dutch ships the qualification for both masters and mates was considerable. Gentlemen of good families and superior education entered the Merchant Service of that country, and masters and mates of long-voyage ships were subjected to a severe examination.

But France had gone beyond all other countries in this respect. The combination of her naval and mercantile services is very complete, as the officers and masters of her foreign-going ships not only pass similar examinations as the lieutenants and sub-lieutenants of the Government service, but also thereby acquire substantially the same rank.

In all these countries schools had been set up in all the larger seaports, where not merely the rudiments of navigation were taught, but considerable attention was also paid to moral and intellectual improvement. In France, before one could obtain a certificate entitling the holder to command a foreign-going vessel, he had to attend a full course of study for at least six months at a Naval College, and not until then might he become a "Capitaine de long cours."

"In America," says Mr. Consul Peter, in a report made by him upon the American Marine, "a lad intended for the higher grades of the Merchant Service, after having acquired (in addition to the ordinary branches of school learning) a competent knowledge of mathematics, navigation, ship's husbandry, and generally French, is commonly apprenticed to some respectable merchant, in whose counting-house he remains a couple of years, or at least long enough to make him familiar with exchanges, and other commercial matters. He is then sent to sea as a junior mate, and gradually rises to the position of captain." He also adds: "An ignorant American native seaman was scarcely to be found"; and further ..... "Cases of disputes between native born Americans and their captains have ever been less frequent, both in this country and abroad, than between British masters and seamen, owing in great measure to the superior education, and the more vigorous discipline, on board American ships."

In the face of such educational advantages, was it any wonder that the foreign merchant sailor was a better educated man than the British, who was dependent entirely upon his own resources, and left to pick up his knowledge as best he could, unless indeed he, as sometimes happened, was a fairly well educated young man before he ever thought of going to sea?

CHAPTER VIII.

INSTITUTION OF VOLUNTARY AND COMPULSORY EXAMINATIONS.

CONTENTS.—Unsatisfactory condition of the British Marine—Voluntary examinations for Masters and Mates instituted by Order in Council, 1845—Boards of Examiners—American competition and its effects—Repeal of the Corn Laws—Shipowners fight for protection—Decline in English Shipbuilding—Navigation Laws repealed, 1849—Effect of the voluntary examinations—Compulsory examinations instituted, 1837.

Unsatisfactory Condition of the British Marine.—From the preceding chapters it will be seen that the Mercantile Marine, in part at least, was evidently not in a satisfactory condition, either in respect to its ships, shipowners, or mariners. The heart of the nation had been stirred to the very bottom by the terrible cost of life incurred; commission after commission had inquired without satisfactory results, and the Government seemed paralysed in its actions, finding the questions involved difficult to approach, and the remedy for acknowledged evils still undiscovered.

The Bill which Mr. Silk Buckingham had introduced in 1837 might have formed a good ground for legislation, although some of its details were hypercritical and unsuitable—perhaps unworkable—but the Government of the day, backed up by the shipowners, who, disliking any interference in the management of their property, and stating that any Government interference could only be partial and therefore unjust, opposed the second reading of the Bill and it was consigned to oblivion. The question was not, however, settled in this cavalier-like manner, and the agitation still went on. Even in 1844 the Government had not the courage to face the position, and left all reference to the education and examination of masters and officers out of the Bill of that year, which eventually passed as the Act, 7 and 8 Vict. c. 112.

This Act repealed the former Act of 1835, but re-enacted most of its provisions with additions. Agreements with the crews, payment of wages, the supply of medicines, punishment of desertion, were strictly enforced ; it maintained the registry of all seamen, and the compulsory apprenticeship according to tonnage, regulated the punishment of assaults committed on board ship, and provided for a survey of provisions upon the complaint of three or more of the crew.

The debates upon this Act had aroused in the minds of the Government a sense of the propriety, as well as the necessity, for taking some action in the question of the education and supervision of officers in the merchant service, but instead of immediate legislation they fell back upon Mr. Poulett Thompson's idea of the institution of voluntary examinations, and determined to set on foot a scheme for carrying that idea into effect.

Voluntary Examination for Masters and Mates Instituted.—In 1845 the first step was taken in connection with the officers.

Under an Order in Council, dated August 19, 1845, the Board of Trade made arrangements and regulations for examining masters and mates in the Merchant Service who should voluntarily offer themselves for examination.

These regulations acknowledged only the two classes, masters and mates, and to each was allotted three divisions or classes, evidently intended to apply to the class of vessel in which the recipients of the certificates were supposed to serve. To masters who showed higher attainments than those demanded to satisfy the first class, a certificate marked "Class I.—Extra," was to be supplied.

The examination for mates was to be based upon items required for masters of the same class, permitting them, under certain contingencies, to become substitutes for the masters.

Board of Examiners.—The Boards appointed to conduct the examinations (which service was performed voluntarily) were the Corporation of Trinity House of Deptford Stroud, for London; the Branch Boards, consisting of the Sub-Commissioners of Pilotage, at Beaumaris, Gloucester, Milford, Plymouth, Portsmouth, and Great Yarmouth; the Corporation of the Trinity House at Hull, Newcastle, and at Leith; the Board for licensing pilots at Glasgow and Liverpool; and the Ballast Board of Dublin.

At Dundee and Shields (North and South), committees of competent persons were appointed.

The actual examiners were to be members of the Boards, or proper persons appointed or employed by them respectively.

A curriculum of the conditions and subjects of examination was laid down by the Order in Council, and it was then left to the Boards to conduct their examinations in their own manner.

In London the Elder Brethren of the Trinity House appointed four of their number examiners, who were assisted by a very able mathematician, Boulter J. Bell, as scientific examiner. This example was followed by most of the other Boards; but some appointed nautical, as well as scientific, examiners—some none at all.

Under the regulations addressed by the Board of Trade to the Boards of Examiners, we find that the examinations were divided into three classes for both masters and mates, and were evidently intended to apply to the officers of three distinct classes of vessels, although not expressly so.

First class.—To ships engaged in the Indian and other over-sea voyages south of the Equator.

Second class.—To ships engaged in over-sea voyages north of the Equator, the Mediterranean, &c.

Third class.—Coasting voyages, the north of Europe, and the Baltic.

In this, to a certain extent, the same course was pursued as was found in practice in other European maritime countries, and it was undoubtedly relevant to the then existing state of the Marine, which was still comprised principally of sailing ships, and certainly to the general state of education found in the officers of these separate classes.

It must be remembered that at this time there was no single department with control over mercantile naval affairs, so the carrying out of the order was entrusted in the principal ports to such bodies, or marine corporations, as were in existence.

Of those who presented themselves for examination, masters were "to be 21 years of age, and must have served at sea not less than six years," and mates were "to be 19 years of age, and to have served four years." In the first order nothing was said as to the capacity in which the candidates had served for the stipulated periods; but on the 1st of May, 1849, it was ordered that the candidates for mastership must have served at least one year as first mate or two years as second mate; satisfactory certificates of service had to be produced for these periods, and particular stress was laid upon evidence of *habitual sobriety*.

On proceeding to examination the first requirement for every candidate was "that he must be able to write a *legible hand* and *understand* the *first five* rules of arithmetic."

All were to be examined as to their knowledge of seamanship, the rigging of vessels, the stowing of holds, &c. &c., and in navigation and nautical astronomy; those who were to be admitted to the lowest class of masters, viz., *the third class*, were "to be able to correct the courses steered by compass for variation, leeway, &c.; to work what is termed a *day's work;* to prick off the vessel's place on the chart, either by the calculated latitude or longitude, or by the bearings of the land by compass; to understand the use of the quadrant or sextant; to observe the sun's meridian altitude, and therefrom determine the latitude; to work the tides by the age of the moon from the known time of high water at full and change;" or, so much of the art of navigation, &c., as would be required in practice on the voyages which took the navigator off the coasts for very short periods or distances.

The *second class* examination was about on a par with those of the present ordinary master, as far as related to seamanship, navigation, and nautical astronomy, but was not so complete in magnetism, compass deviation, &c., as at present known.

The *first class* was equal to that of the present master extra, and the candidates were required " to show proficiency in *all* the practical branches of nautical astronomy, and also in seamanship in such cases as called for a higher order of resources;" but *further*, they were also to have " a competent acquaintance with geometry and plane trigonometry; they were to understand the construction of Mercator's charts so as to be able to correct any errors they may detect in those they possess; and also to have a knowledge of mercantile *book-keeping* at least by *single entry*."

In the event of a candidate for a first class master's certificate "proving himself to have still higher attainments, such as being well versed in great circle sailing (then being used more extensively, especially in southern voyages), spherical trigonometry, marine surveying, and a more extensive knowledge of astronomy, it was to be noted on the certificate, and entitled the bearer to *first class extra*."

The examination of mates in each class was to be on the same lines as those for masters, but extreme proficiency was not so rigorously exacted.

Although not specified in the Board of Trade regulations, the Trinity House authorities exacted an examination in the pilotage, lights, and soundings of the English and the mouth of the St. George's channels, as had been customary in the examination of officers in the Honourable East India Company's service.

Beyond issuing the order, the Lords of the Committee for Trade made no further attempt to interfere, but left each Board of Examiners to carry out the order in the manner they deemed most suitable; each scientific examiner formulating his own scheme of examination to suit the order in each case.

On the promulgation of the order of 1845, many of the various bodies addressed appointed examiners and set earnestly to work to carry it out. The van was led by the London Trinity House, with Dundee close upon its heels; followed early in 1846 by Plymouth, South Shields, and Newcastle; with Portsmouth, Glasgow, Leith, and Liverpool later on in the year.

"These regulations," says the Registrar-General of Seamen in the introduction to *The Mercantile Navy List* (then an official publication) " are called for, not only by the very general expression of opinion that *those in charge of life and property* should possess the qualification necessary for so important a trust, but in order the better to enable masters of British vessels *to compete with foreigners for freight in the markets of the world*, by the production of satisfactory credentials as to their competency."

Notwithstanding the value of such intentions the order was not so warmly received or acknowledged by the shipping community as it might have been. As for the shipowners, any interference with their power of appointing whom they pleased as their servants was the last thing they desired; and for the masters and officers themselves, they, with few exceptions, contemned the whole business—" as if *seamen could be proved* by examination!"

The candidates for examination did not come forward quite so freely as the promoters had hoped, and the Government soon felt that external pressure was needed. By the end of 1846 not quite 200, in the various ranks and classes, had passed—about one half of that number in London, and the remainder in the out-ports—so at last the whip was applied. The Admiralty issued an order "that on and after the 23rd of March, 1847, no vessel shall be taken up as a transport, convict ship, or freight ship unless the master and mates have obtained the required certificates;" and this regulation was soon extended to vessels carrying H.M. mails, transports and others over which the Government exercised control. This had a visible effect upon the number of candidates, as in 1847 nearly 400 presented themselves and passed, and there is no doubt that all who felt themselves capable were doing so in London and some of the ports at least. The numbers increased as the years passed on, and at the end of 1850 more than 3000 had passed, including almost all of the officers holding the higher positions in the mail and other contract Government services. There were several of these who had passed two examinations, but according to Mr. Murton there were in existence at the end of that year 2610 who exchanged their old certificates for new ones granted by the Board of Trade, in which were retained the classes under which the holders had passed the voluntary examination. Out of that number there were just 500 who held 1st class and 1st class extra, and 1530 second class (of whom several took the master extra subsequently under the new regulations) and the rest were 3rd class masters and officers.

The standard of examination at the Trinity House was of a very high order, whatever it might have been at the out-ports, requiring a very considerable mathematical training and knowledge. The examinations were conducted in such a manner as not only to test the accuracy of the candidates, but also their experience; and it need hardly be said that scarcely a man went up to pass these examinations who had not been *putting into practice* all the subjects, more or less, upon which he was to be examined, and needed little or no special training.

Before passing from this subject it may be useful to review the work done by the Voluntary Boards, as a "Mercantile Navy List" for June 1850, affords the required information. As already stated, the matter and manner of the examinations were left to the discretion of the various local boards so long as the general curriculum was fulfilled. A table, showing all the passes at the various ports in each year down to the end of the year 1849, will be found in the Appendix.* The result is very curious, and would seem to show that the London men were far behind those of many of the out-ports. But this was really not the case. The explanation is that men were passed as extra masters at the out-ports upon a much lower standard of examination. An example of this may be given. A master of a first class mail-line (no board of examination at the port from which he hailed having been established, when the Admiralty promulgated the order that all masters of mail and contract ships must pass and receive certificates of competency), was sent to London to pass. He did so, but could only get a first class certificate, not being able to pass the Trinity House extra first examination. Upon this coming to the knowledge of the owners of the line immediate steps were taken to set up a Board of Examiners at that port, and every other master in the service was passed as a first class extra master right away. This had the effect of attracting the attention of the Board of Trade authorities, who soon put their own value upon it, and when the examinations became compulsory they took care that they should be as nearly as possible upon the same lines in all the ports, although from what came to light in later years it was not easily attained.

American Competition and its Effects.—At this period the reciprocity laws were in full swing with most European countries as well as America, and the effect is visible in the growing proportion of foreign clearances—29 per cent. in 1845.

* *Appendix C.*

The Americans, with unlimited supplies of timber at hand, built finer and cheaper vessels than were produced in England, and soon after the opening of the trade between the two countries placed upon the Atlantic a splendid line of packets, which performed the passage in several days less than ours, and carried off a very large share of the trade.

Our shipowners felt the pinch of the foreign shoe more than ever, and unrest prevailed; complaints were made that the English ships were not what they ought to be. Foreigners were everywhere being preferred to British vessels, as being better handled and delivering their cargoes in better condition.

Dissatisfaction reigned supreme at the thought that we were being beaten out of the field we fondly hoped was our own. Royal commissions enquired into wrecks, the management and manning of ships, and everything connected with the Mercantile Marine. Seamen were said to be scarce, and certainly large numbers were joining American ships (who were the pick of our men), in which, although the work was hard, the pay, food, and treatment on the whole were superior to our own. To provide for this and to increase the number of sailors an Act was passed (7 & 8 Vict. c. 112)—compelling ships to carry apprentices in proportion to their tonnage, and authorising parish authorities to bind as apprentices to the sea such pauper boys as they wished to get rid of. Besides this, all sorts of nostrums were prescribed, without much effect, and were soon followed by the most drastic measures.

Repeal of the Corn Laws.—The manufacturing interests now became exceedingly powerful, and the manufacturers, led by Cobden and Bright, clamouring for cheap bread to enable them to keep down wages, succeeded in having all restriction upon corn withdrawn, and in 1846 the Corn Laws were repealed. Having got in the thin edge of the wedge, and setting their faces against all protection, they set on foot an agitation for the repeal of the Navigation Acts, to get cheap carriage for their wares, and cheap cotton for their mills.

Shipowners Fight for Protection.—The shipowners fought hard for protection, conscientiously believing that their very existence depended upon it.

Their great objection was that ships could be built much cheaper in many foreign parts than was possible in Britain, viz., in Dantzig for £10 per ton, in the States for £12, and in Canada for less; whereas a British ship could not be built for less than £15.

Decline in English Shipbuilding.—In fact the returns show that there were fewer vessels built in England in 1845 than in 1835 by thousands of tons. No less than forty shipbuilders had failed in Sunderland between 1841 and 1847. English wooden shipbuilding was killed by the cheap foreign and colonial timber, and it was not until the sound of the adze was replaced by the sound of the hammer that Sunderland recovered her trade.

Navigation Laws Repealed.—Despite all the opposition and outcry of the shipbuilders and shipowners, the Free Traders bore all before them, proclaiming loudly that when foreign nations discovered beyond all doubt that England was advancing on the path of Free Trade they would gladly follow the example, and commerce would reign throughout the world free and unshackled! The spirit of the times was in their favour, and in 1849 the navigation laws were repealed, and our foreign trade thrown open to the world.

Effect of the Voluntary Examinations.—Reference has already been made to a letter written by Mr. Murray, of the Foreign Office, to consuls abroad relative to British shipmasters. The answers to it revealed a state of matters not at all pleasant to contemplate. To cite them here would involve too lengthened a space, but it will suffice to say that they were laid before Parliament in 1848, together with Mr. Murray's report which states his conclusions, as follows:

" 1. That the character of British shipping has declined, and that of foreign shipping had improved.

" 2. That there was not sufficient control over British shipmasters either at home or abroad, while foreign vessels were subject to considerable control.

" 3. That there was no system of regular education for the merchant service of Great Britain, but that in foreign countries this matter was much attended to.

" 4. That the sort of education which a British subject receives when training for the higher grades of the merchant service, does not suffice to qualify him to represent with advantage the merchant by whom he may be employed in that merchant's interest, and that he may often neglect those interests, and the merchant not be aware of the fact.

" What was wanted," he continues, " was not merely a study of navigation and seamanship, but a *thorough knowledge of ship's husbandry*, and of the *stowage of cargoes*, of *exchanges*, and other *commercial information* which would qualify the master to act if necessary as the representative of his employer in the character of merchant; the commander of a ship being, in law, considered the representative of the owners of the property on board."

When the report was published, the shipowners strongly objected to it, and alleged that Mr. Murray's letter was couched in unfair language, as it seemed to put words into the mouths of the Consuls, which would naturally direct their answers partially and unfairly—that it had the effect of drawing attention to the bad features in the character of British mariners to the neglect of the good. We cannot sum up that matter better, perhaps, than in the words of Mr. Lindsay, who may be looked upon as an impartial authority, especially from the shipowners' point of view. "Strong objections," he says, "were, however, raised by the shipowners against *any* Government interference, on the ground that it would be partial, and, consequently so far, unjust; these objections being naturally strengthened by the manner in which Mr. Murray had set about the inquiry of 1843.

"It was, nevertheless, but too evident that, however much British shipowners might deprecate the assistance or interference of Government, a large proportion of their ships were commanded and navigated in a manner reflecting discredit on our national intelligence, and injurious to the interests of Great Britain; that the persons placed in command of them were too frequently unfit for their duties, and that while many of them were so habitually addicted to drunkenness as to be altogether incompetent for their position, not a few of them were almost without education."

Mr. Lindsay's summing-up of the evidence is most valuable, for not only were his sympathies largely on the side of the shipowner, as evidenced through his whole life work, but, as he had raised and educated himself from being a poor cabin-boy up to the proud position he afterwards attained, literally by his own exertions, he could also witness to the trials and difficulties inherent to the position of the British mariner, officer, and master, and sympathise with them. There was humour in him, too, for he says in a note: "In my own time I remember a shipowner saying to me that he never would have a 'scholar' in command of any of his vessels, *because* education taught him how to make up false accounts and the art of cheating; while another whom I knew only retained one 'educated' master in his service, because he was flattered by being invariably addressed as Mr. Joseph Perkins, Esquire!"

Compulsory Examinations Instituted, 1851.—Judged of at this distance of time, there can be no doubt that these consular reports must have applied to a portion only of British shipmasters, at the same time they left no doubt in the public mind as to the necessity for regulating the education and qualification of shipmasters and officers in a manner that had not been hitherto attempted. Consequently, the Government, encouraged by the success of the voluntary examinations so far as they had gone, and with the opposition of the shipowners disarmed by Mr. Murray's report, had no difficulty in passing the Act 13 & 14 Vict. c. 93, during the session of 1850, which made the examination of mercantile marine officers, who sought appointments higher than those they had previously held, obligatory after the 1st of January, 1851.

This Act formulated the system of examinations and accepted the certificates that had already been granted by the voluntary boards as valid, but recalled them, and new certificates were issued by the Board of Trade, which stated the class for which they were exchanged.

Finding from the experience of the attempt to make many of the older shipmasters pass an examination, in response to the Admiralty orders in regard to Government contract vessels, their inability or unwillingness to do so, the larger number of those already serving were granted certificates of service.

All idea of the classification of ships and officers was abandoned, and it was settled that all the future officers of foreign-going ships, irrespective of voyage or service, should be examined as for "second mates," "first mates," or "masters," to whom the appellation of "ordinary" was applied in contradistinction to the "master extra," to which step any master might *voluntarily* proceed. The requirements for any "ordinary master's" certificate were placed on about a par with those for a master of the second class in the voluntary scheme of examination; and that for the "master extra" with what had been required for the "first class master," with this exception—that no reference was made to geometry or trigonometry, plane or spherical—that is to say, all reference to the sciences upon which the art of navigation is founded were dropped out of sight, and have never since been revived. There was no regulation making the "extra" in any sense compulsory, although a faint attempt at classification seemed to be foreshadowed in the regulations as to extra masters, which said "it was intended for such persons as are desirous of obtaining command of ships and steamers of the first class." This kind of hinting regulation became a dead letter, as an ordinary master's certificate carried him all over the world, in all classes of foreign-going ships; and to navigate the Baltic (which is little better than a coasting voyage) required, and still requires, as stiff an examination as for long over-sea voyages to India, China, or the Pacific seas and coasts.

The effect of this change was not to bring up the education of the former, but to degrade the standard of the latter. The owners of first-class vessels may demand the extra or not, as they please, the Government does not interfere.

Let us now, for a moment, consider the necessary qualifications of age and service which entitles the candidate to apply for examination. From the printed regulations of the Marine Department of the Board of Trade, we find that a second mate must have served four years actually at sea (the breaks between the voyages not counting), and such service must be proved from his record in the office of the Registrar-General of Seamen and Shipping. He must also have certificates of ability and good conduct, and particularly of *habitual sobriety* from his former masters or employers.

In respect to the foregoing rule regarding actual sea service, there are two exceptions to be noted—the first is in regard to indentured apprentices for the term of four years or more in one employ, when four-fifths of that time is actually served at sea; and the second is applicable to time served on board training ships, part of which is to count as sea service not exceeding one year.

It is not, however, compulsory that the four years be served as a seaman, or seaman apprentice, for by Rule 24* the time may have been spent as a cook, steward, or carpenter, &c., as long as the Board of Trade or a Local Marine Board is satisfied that the party applying has a good knowledge of seamanship. This (the regulation says) "may *possibly* be proved by the production of satisfactory certificates from masters whom the applicants have served." Failing that, the applicant may be called upon to perform additional service in the capacity of "able or ordinary seaman." Now, when we consider that no man is entitled to the rating of A.B. unless he has served "four years before the mast" (see 43 & 44 Victoria, cap. 16, sec. 7), we are landed in the intricacies of a considerable puzzle; and the qualification for second mate, may, from a seaman's point of view, be something less than that for an A.B. Service in an engine-room excludes from the rank of deck officer (see Regulation 27).

In addition to the limitations of service, there is also one of age. No person can apply for a second mate's certificate until he is seventeen years old. To make this of any value to the applicant he must have gone to sea before he was thirteen.

A first or only mate must be nineteen years of age and have served five years at sea, one of which must have been as second mate, or as third or fourth mate, if he has had charge of a watch

---

* Of the regulations of 1888. Since this was written, by the newer code of 1894, time as a steward is not allowed to count, and for the cook, carpenter, or sailmaker, six years' service is required instead of four. Cooks not serving as seamen are precluded.

during the required period, and been in possession of a second mate's certificate the whole time.

A master must be twenty-one years of age, and have served six years; one as first mate, and one as second; or six years and a half at sea, two and a half of which must have been as second mate, during the last twelve months of which he must have been in possession of a first mate's certificate, &c.

By the same Act the Marine Department of the Board of Trade was created, and to it was entrusted the power of carrying its provisions into force. Local Marine Boards were appointed at all the prominent ports, the members of which were partly appointed by the Crown, and partly chosen by the registered shipowners. The municipal authorities were also acknowledged by making their mayors or provosts *ex officio* members, and the judicial courts by the appointment of the stipendiary magistrates or sheriffs in the same manner.

The public bodies, Trinity Houses, Ballast and Pilot Boards, &c., by whom the examiners under the Order in Council had been appointed, were set aside, and these duties were hereafter, with many others now for the first time created, entrusted to the semi-representative local marine boards, acting, however, under the central control of the Board of Trade, who issued regulations for general guidance. In doing this it became a serious consideration as to the standard which could possibly be maintained. Guided by the light of the past five years' experience, it was very evident that such examinations as had been enforced at the Trinity House, and elsewhere, could not be maintained with immediate success; so the new regulations for the guidance of the local marine boards and their examiners were a decided step down from those which were issued under the Order in Council of 1845. The officials of the Marine Department seemed to deplore the necessity for this, for the warning was issued at the same time that " it is the intention of the Board of Trade to raise the standard from time to time, whenever, as *will no doubt be the case*, the general attainments of the officers of the merchant service shall render it possible to do so *without inconvenience;*" and these gentlemen evidently thought that an educational renaissance would be begun, and bear fruit, to enable them to do so by the mere warning. We shall see, by-and-by, how far their sanguine hopes have been justified.

CHAPTER IX.

THE RISE AND PROGRESS OF STEAM PROPULSION.

CONTENTS.—Rise and progress of ship propulsion—Blasco Garay—James Watt—Newcomen's engine—Henry Bell—the *Comet*—The *Rob Roy*—The *Enterprise* reaches Calcutta—Iron as a material for Shipbuilding—The Leviathan class of steamers—Dr. Lardner and steam across the Atlantic—The *Sirius* and *Great Western* cross successfully—Francis P. Smith's screw propeller—New Steamship Companies—The Cunard and other lines—The *Great Britain*—The screw propeller superior to the paddle—The Collins line—The advance of steam steadily progressive.

Rise and Progress of Ship Propulsion.—In the early ages the chief mode of propelling vessels was, undoubtedly, the oar, or paddle, and we may suppose that the inception of the use of sail-power would arise from some tired rowers sticking up an oar, or paddle, and spreading upon it a handy garment. to help them along over some lazily-flowing stream. From this, man would, step by step, be encouraged to make further use of the winds of heaven as a means of propulsion, and sail-power grew in general perfection and adaptability from the one mast with its almost square-headed sail, fitted only for taking advantage of a wind which was fair, up to the magnificent rig of the modern ship, with its three or four masts, numberless yards, and wonderful cloud of canvas, capable of doing almost anything but proceed in the eye of the wind.

For long ages men's brains were puzzled in attempting to overcome this difficulty, and attempts were evidently made, very early in the Christian era, to accomplish ship propulsion by means of wheels hung over the ship's side, and attached to hand-gear within the vessel. This is proved by several drawings handed down to us from the Middle Ages.

Blasco Garay.—The first really important attempt, of which we have any account, was made by a Spaniard, one Blasco Garay, who made some experiments on a vessel with paddle wheels, in the harbour of Barcelona, in the middle of the sixteenth century.

The vessel he employed was one of about 200 tons, named the

Trinity, and the trial was made on June 17, 1543. It has been asserted that the power he used was *steam*, and that he had a boiling cauldron on board, but he would not permit any one to see his machinery. On the face of it, it could hardly have been steam power that was used, as a boiler, or cauldron, large enough to generate steam sufficient to move a vessel of 200 tons, could hardly have been put on board without being seen, although some writers have confidently stated that it was so. The archives of Spain have been well ransacked for proof of the assertion, but none is forthcoming. There is abundant evidence that Garay made some experiments with paddle-wheels, and whatever the power employed, the attempt was deemed worthy of reward by the Spanish Government, although nothing more came of it at the time. The idea of paddle-wheel propulsion slept for more than two centuries, waiting for the evolution of that present handmaid of the world—the power of steam.

James Watt.—The very mention of this power raises before our eyes visions of that wonderful man, James Watt, mathematical instrument maker to Glasgow College, working in his little room within the college precincts—boiling his kettle, and studying the properties of latent steam—manufacturing model engine after model engine—until he, as it were by an inspiration, lit upon the *condensation* of steam in a vessel separate from the cylinder.

Newcomen's Engine.—This had been done in Newcomen's engine by injecting water into the cylinder itself at each stroke, but the alternate heating and cooling of the cylinder, and all its parts, created such wastefulness of fuel that the cost was almost prohibitory of its useful application. It was said to have required 12 to 14 lbs. of coal to produce an effective horsepower.

In 1763, Watt was supplied with a model of Newcomen's engine, the defects in which soon became apparent to him, and he brooded over his experiments with it for many a day. Walking one Sunday afternoon upon Glasgow Green, in the spring of 1765, his thoughts were running on his experiments, when like a ray from heaven the idea of the separate condenser flashed upon him and the difficulty was solved. At last the world had presented to it a workable steam engine, and its practical application to ship propulsion was brought to a successful issue by Fulton in America, and Henry Bell in Scotland. Many attempts were made by others, but without any very practical results.

Henry Bell. The "Comet."—Some time in 1811 Henry Bell, who, although not a mechanic himself, had pursued the

F

idea of steam propulsion for ships for some years, entered into negotiation with Messrs. John and Charles Wood, of Port Glasgow, to build for him a vessel to be propelled by steam-power, and the *Comet* was built and launched in 1812. Her dimensions were 40 ft. keel, 10 ft. 6 in. beam, and 25 tons burthen. The engine was made by John Robertson, of Glasgow, and the boiler at the works of Messrs. Anderson, Campbell and Co., of Greenock, of which firm Messrs. Caird & Co. are the legitimate successors.*

Many difficulties had to be overcome, principally from mechanical and practical inexperience, before the *Comet* was finally ready "to ply, by the combined powers of air, wind and steam," as Henry Bell's advertisement quaintly puts it. These were, however, at last subdued, and the *Comet* began her voyages between Glasgow and Greenock. The venture was successful, and, as steamers are now fast superseding sailing-ships all the world over, so, from the moment she started, the days of the old-fashioned "fly-boats" of the Clyde were numbered.

She was the forerunner of a new era, and the commencement of a silent revolution destined to have more effect upon the wealth and comfort of mankind, and the civilization of the world, than all the efforts of the greatest conquerors from Alexander the Great downwards—more than all the discoveries of Galileo or Newton—or the physical researches of Bacon, or Des Cartes, and a host of followers;—a revolution which has brought man into touch with his brother man all the world over, and helped on that grand ideal which, although to our eyes yet far distant, shall teach men "to beat their spears into pruning-hooks and their swords into ploughshares."

The *Comet* began to ply in 1812, and several steamers were built in 1813-14.

The oldest steamer in existence, the *Industry*, was built in 1814—it is said at Fairlie on the Clyde—and her engine was made by Thompson of Glasgow. She continued to ply as a luggage-boat, between Glasgow and Greenock, down to the year 1862. The original spur-wheel gearing, coupling the main-shaft to the paddle-shafts, was in use to the last. Her hull is still lying at Bowling, on the Clyde.

Another boat built in this year was the *Marjory*, by William

---

* The *Comet's* engine is supposed to be the one shown as hers in the South Kensington Museum. There is also another at the Stobcross Engine Works, Glasgow, which claims the honour. As to which it is really due, we must leave the respective owners to decide, but it is hardly worth much controversy, as, in the main, they are counterparts of each other.

Denny, of Dumbarton. Her dimensions were 63 ft. long by 12 ft. breadth of beam, and her engine was a single side lever of 10 H.P., by Cook, of Glasgow. She is principally to be noted as the first steamer put upon the Thames, where she encountered a very violent opposition from the "watermen," always a notoriously conservative body. She plied successfully with passengers between London and Margate for a number of years.

The "Rob Roy."—The next most interesting vessel was the *Rob Roy*, built at Dumbarton in 1818, by William Denny, and was the first steamer built for over-sea trade. She was 90 tons burthen, and had an engine of 30 H.P., constructed by the afterwards celebrated engineer, Mr. David Napier, of Glasgow and London.

The *Rob Roy* was the first steamer that plied between Glasgow and Belfast. After remaining in this trade for some time, she was transferred to Dover, and, renamed the *Henri Quatre*, was the first mail steamer which plied between that port and Calais.

It is said that Mr. David Napier, before deciding upon building this steamer, crossed in a sailing-ship to Belfast in a heavy breeze, with the intention of watching the effect of the waves upon a vessel at sea, and became convinced that steam-power could be employed to overcome them.

He then made several experiments upon model boats, and as a result, determined to give his proposed steamer a sharper entrance than had been usual in the river steamers.

In 1819, Mr. Napier had built, by Messrs. Wood, of Port Glasgow, the *Talbot*, of 150 tons, which was fitted with a pair of his side lever engines, of 30 H.P. each. She was the first vessel placed upon the station between Holyhead and Dublin, and appears to have been an efficient vessel.

In the same year Mr. Napier established the first steam traffic between Glasgow and Liverpool, with the *Robert Bruce*, a similar vessel to the *Talbot*.

The first steamer entered in Lloyd's Book was the *James Watt*, 146 ft. long, and 25 ft. beam, built by the Messrs. Wood, in 1822. She was entered there as of 294 tons, but another authority describes her as of 448 tons. Her engines were by Messrs. Boulton and Watt, of Soho Foundry, Birmingham, and of 50 H.P. each. Her speed was said to be 10 miles per hour. Lloyd's officials, apparently, did not take upon themselves any interference with, or supervision of, the building of the early steamships; but the extension of the coasting lines, and the necessity for insurance brought them under their surveillance, and it soon extended. In 1830, we find no less than 81 steamers in Lloyd's book, and in 1832, 100.

The "Enterprise" reaches Calcutta.—In 1825 there was built upon the Thames a steamship named the *Enterprise*. She was built for the purpose of attempting the voyage to India, and sailed from Falmouth in the month of August, in that year, under the command of a Captain Johnson. Her tonnage is stated to have been 500, and she was propelled by engines of 120 H.P. Captain Johnson navigated her successfully to Calcutta, and received a gratuity of £10,000 from the Government for doing so.

Iron as a Material for Shipbuilding.—Another change of great importance took place about this time—viz., the use of iron as a material for shipbuilding instead of wood.

So far back as 1809, Richard Trevithick and Robert Dickenson had proposed a scheme for building large ships "with decks, beams, and sides of plate iron;" and in 1815 Dickenson patented an invention for "boats to be built of iron, with a hollow water-tight gunwale."

The first iron steamer, the *Aaron Manby*, was built in parts at Horsley in 1821, then taken to London, rebuilt and launched there. She was owned by Mr. Manby and Captain (afterwards Admiral Sir) Charles Napier, R.N., and by the latter was taken to France, and sold to the French. The Shannon Steam Packet Company were the first to employ iron steamers in river navigation in 1824. In 1832 Laird built the *Elburkah* for the Niger.

The use of iron did not find favour at the outset, and progress in iron shipbuilding was slow, for it was not until the year 1837 that a vessel built of iron is noted in Lloyd's book. This was the steamer *Sirius*, of 180 tons, which was built in London for French owners at Marseilles. In the same year, Messrs. Laird & Co., of Liverpool, constructed the first iron steamer owned by the General Steam Navigation Company—the *Rainbow*, 185 ft. in length, and 25 ft. beam; of 600 tons and 180 H.P.

These examples were not very rapidly followed. The late Mr. Scott Russell has left it on record that, talking once to an eminent naval architect, the head of one of her Majesty's royal dockyards, about the prospects of ships being built of iron for war purposes, he replied, with some indignation, "Don't talk to me of iron ships; it's contrary to nature!"

The danger of explosion in steamships seems from a very early stage to have caused alarm; so much so, that the House of Commons in 1817 appointed a Committee of the House to inquire into it. Upon their report legislative action ensued. It required all steamers to be registered and provided for the inspection of their boilers, which were to be constructed of copper, or wrought iron, and fitted with two safety valves. All boilers were to be tested to three times their working pressure, which was on no account to be more than one-sixth of the ultimate strength of the boiler. This regulation with some modification still exists.

The Leviathan class of Steamers.—In 1826 the first of the so-called "Leviathan class of steamers," *The United Kingdom*, was built by Messrs. Robert Steele & Co., of Greenock, for the trade between London and Edinburgh. She was 160 ft. by 26½ ft. and had engines of 200 H.P., by David Napier, of Glasgow. The value of steam-power had now been fully proved, and, early in the fourth decade of this century, all the principal coast routes of the United Kingdom were supplied with steamship lines, a great impulse being given thereby to communication between all parts of the Kingdom. But matters were not long to rest there, as attention was very soon paid to the possibility of extending the use of steam-power to over-sea voyages. The communication between America and Britain, which was most important to both countries, had hitherto been chiefly in the hands of American sailing-packets, but the desirability of shortening the passage was felt by all concerned in this trade, and it was much discussed.

Dr. Lardner and Steam across the Atlantic. — Dr. Lardner, then one of our most learned scientists, delivered a lecture on the subject in Liverpool in December 1835. After speaking of the great projects in hand in connection with rail and steamship, and advocating the approach to America by certain stages which he pointed out, taking the shortest distances between land and land, Dr. Lardner said: "As to the project, however, which was announced in the newspapers lately," *i.e.*, of making the voyage directly between New York and Liverpool, "it was, he had no hesitation in saying, perfectly chimerical, and they might as well talk about making a voyage from New York or Liverpool to the moon!" Dr. Lardner then went on to contend that it must be a commercial failure, as no steamers could carry sufficient cargo, and at the same time sufficient fuel, for the voyage to make it profitable. He had apparently fixed upon 800 tons and 9 knots, as the ultimatum of size and speed; but how he should have been led to that conclusion, in face of the great relative increase which had already taken place in the size of steamers, it is now impossible to imagine. He little dreamed how soon he would be shown to be a false prophet—and when afterwards he was rather scorned for having uttered such a dictum, he declared "that he never stated that it was a *physical impossibility*," seeing that steamships have already proved it feasible.

The first which had made the attempt was the *Savannah*, of 300 tons, in the year 1819, sailing from New York to Liverpool. She made the voyage in 31 days, partly sailing and partly steaming.

In 1829 a steamer named the *Curaçoa* of 350 tons and 100 N.H.P., was built in London for Dutch owners, and made many successful voyages between Holland and the Dutch West Indies.

And a third, the *Royal William*, of between 400 and 500 tons, was built at Three Rivers, in Canada, and was fitted with engines which had been constructed in England, and sent out to Saint Mary's foundry, at Montreal, where they were put on board. She sailed from Quebec on the 18th of August, 1833, and arrived at Gravesend on the 11th of September, following. It was not, however, attempted to send her back. She was sold to the Portuguese, and plied from Lisbon for some years.

The "Sirius" and "Great Western" cross successfully. —It did not take long to test Dr. Lardner's opinion, for in 1837 the *Great Western* was built by Patterson, at Bristol, for an English company, under the superintendence of Mr. (afterwards Sir) I. K. Brunel, and of course of wood. Great pains were taken to make her strong enough to brave the storms of the Atlantic; her frame timbers were as heavy as those of a first-class line of battle ship, and placed so close that they were caulked outside and in before the planks were put on. Her dimensions were 212 ft. keel, by 35 ft. 4 in. beam, and 23 ft. 2 in. depth of hold, and she was fitted with a pair of side lever engines by Maudsley and Field, having two cylinders each, 74 in. diameter by 84 ins. stroke of piston. Paddle wheels of radial type, 28 ft. diameter, and having each twenty-eight floats. Four boilers with return flues carrying a working pressure of 5 lbs. to the square inch. Her wheels made ten to eighteen revolutions according to their immersion, and her average passage between Bristol and New York was fifteen days. Her consumption of Welsh coal was about 8 lbs. per I.H.P. per hour.

Although the first vessel built in England for the Atlantic, she was not permitted to have the honour of being the first vessel to cross it, for a rival company chartered the *Sirius* of 450 tons -register, 700 tons burthen, and of 320 H.P., which had just been built for the London and Irish trade of the Saint George Steam Navigation Company, by Menzies, of Leith, and engined by Thomas Wingate, of Glasgow. She started from London a few days before the *Great Western* from Bristol, and arrived in New York a couple of days before her. The safe arrival of these two steamers in New York was hailed with immense acclamation. The *Great Western* continued for some time on this route, but was afterwards employed for some years by the Royal Mail Company in their West Indian Service. The *Sirius* being found too small for the

Atlantic, returned to the home coasting trade, and was wrecked in 1847.

Smith's Screw Propeller.—The year 1837 saw the dawn of another change—the introduction of the screw-propeller. In this year Francis P. Smith built the *Archimedes*, and fitted her with his patent screw propeller. She was so far successful that others followed, and in the fifth decade of this century several small screw-steamers were built, but it took many years for the screw-propeller to gain such a victory over the paddle-wheel as it eventually did, and which we shall have to refer to again in due course.

New Steamship Companies.—This year also saw the origin of a Steamship Company, which commenced its operations by trading first to the ports of the Spanish Peninsula, and has since extended its operations to the furthest confines of our Eastern Empire and China. This will be recognised as the now familiar and well appreciated Peninsular and Oriental Company. The Peninsular Company commenced with a couple of small paddle-steamers, and was the first steam company which entered into a contract with the Government for the carriage of foreign mails, viz., to Oporto and Lisbon.

The foreign postal service had for long years been carried on from Falmouth by a number of Government ten-gun brigs, which sailed regularly to Halifax, the West Indies, Lisbon, Gibraltar, and Malta. This was a fine service in its day as regards its *personnel*, and was the breeding-place for seamen for H.M. Service. The vessels were miserable craft, which received the apt cognomen of "ten-gun coffins," and tried the resources of their officers and crews to the utmost. Few men would have been found to go on year after year risking their lives as these men did but the true British sailor.

Falmouth in those days was a famous and flourishing port, which, as these postal packets were displaced, one after the other, by the various steam lines, fell into decay, from which it has but scarcely recovered.

The Cunard Line.—The success of the *Sirius* and *Great Western* in their trips across the Atlantic opened the road for further adventure in that direction. Shortly after Mr. (afterwards Sir) Samuel Cunard, convinced of the advantage which would accrue to both countries from the adoption of a regular communication by steam, came over from America, and was introduced to Messrs. Burns, of Glasgow, and Messrs. McIver, of Liverpool, who had been engaged for years in the Liverpool and Glasgow, and Glasgow and Belfast steam trades. He made such arrangements with them as enabled him to compete for and obtain a contract for the conveyance of the mails between Liverpool and New York. For this service they built first three steamers, to which almost immediately a fourth was added, viz., *Britannia, Acadia, Caledonia,* and *Columbia*—each about 207 ft. long, of 1156 tons B.M. and 425 H.P., and having a speed of $8\frac{1}{2}$ knots—a very modest attempt we should now say—and the working pressure of steam was advanced upon that of the *Great Western* by 2 lbs., making it 7 lbs. pressure. These vessels made an average passage of 12 to 13 days each way, and established the fame of a company which has never since wavered, for, spite all opposition, it still continues the favourite line with passengers on both sides of the Atlantic; and can make the proud boast of never having lost a life or a letter through default of either ship or officers.

In 1844 they built the *Cambria* and *Hibernia*, of 1422 tons, 500 H.P. Speed $9\frac{1}{4}$ knots. In 1848, the *America* and *Niagara*, *Europa* and *Canada*, of 1820 tons and 680 H.P., $10\frac{1}{4}$ knots, and pressure on the boilers now advanced to 13 lbs. In 1850 the *Asia* and *Africa*, of 267 feet by 40 feet 6 inches, by 27 feet 6 inches and $2128\frac{78}{94}$ builder's measurement; 265 feet by 37 feet 2 inches by 27 feet 2 inches and $2226\frac{24}{100}$ new measurement: N.H.P. 814, cylinders 96 inches by 9 feet, wheels 37 feet 7 inches diameter, 30 feet 10 inches effective. Four flue boilers, 20 furnaces, W.P. about 15 lbs. They had an average speed of 303 miles a day, or $12\frac{3}{4}$ knots. These are given somewhat in detail, as they were about the best type of ocean steamer built up to the latter date, and show the rate of progress that had been made in the decade."

Royal Mail Company.—In 1841 the Royal Mail Company, having contracted for the carriage of the West Indian mails, commenced its business with greater pretensions than any other Company had previously done. By this time the Government, having begun to build small war steamers for themselves (in 1838), saw the advantage of being able to command the services of as many steamers fit for war as possible, and laid this Company under heavy restrictions as regards the construction of their vessels. They were compelled to build them of a sufficient scantling to carry the ordinary guns then used in naval warfare, and also with their paddle-box tops fitted to be removable, and used as boats for conveyance of troops, &c. There were fourteen steamers built, and put upon the line from Southampton to Saint Thomas as the central point, and thence supplementary branches were carried to the principal West India Islands, and afterwards as far as Chagres. Thence the mails were carried overland to Panama, and so down the West Coast of South America, to Peru and Chili.

Peninsular and Oriental Company.—In 1842 the Peninsular and Oriental Company sent the *Hindostan, Bentinck* and *Precursor* to India, and their overland service was commenced by the arrival of the *Hindostan* at Suez with the Calcutta mails in February, 1843, the homeward half of the service to and from Alexandria being served by the *Oriental* and the *Great Liverpool*.

The " Great Britain."—In 1843 the first large iron steamer, the *Great Britain*, was built at Bristol by Patterson, for the Great Western Company. Her dimensions were 289 feet length of keel, 51 feet beam, and 32 feet 6 inches depth of hold, tonnage 2984 N.M. She was fitted with a pair of screw-propeller engines of 1000 H.P., and fully established that mode of propulsion for large sea-going steamers. She sailed from the Mersey on July 26, 1845, for New York, arriving there on August 10. Unfortunately, on her second voyage from Liverpool, she was run ashore in Dundrum Bay, Ireland, and lay there stranded for nearly two years. By the strenuous efforts of Messrs. I. K. Brunel, and Bremner, she was eventually floated off on August 27, 1847, taken to Liverpool, and repaired. This gave a convincing proof of the strength of iron ships, which soon led to the building of large fleets of iron screw steamers. When the demand for large passenger vessels to the Australian colonies took place, her six masts were removed, and she was fitted as an ordinary three-masted auxiliary steamship. In that trade she ran for some years with great success, and was broken up only a few years ago at Barrow.

Screw-Steamers.—In 1845, Messrs. Robert Napier & Sons built the first screw-steamer constructed on the Clyde—the *Fire Queen*, of 135 tons and 80 H.P. One of the first screw-steamers for foreign trade was the *Dumbarton Youth*, of 238 tons and 34 H.P. nominal. She was built at Dumbarton by William Denny & Brothers, and her engines were by Caird & Co., of Greenock. She made many successful voyages to the Mediterranean.

In 1850, the first iron screw-steamer for the Liverpool and Glasgow trade was the *Princess Royal*, built by Messrs. Tod & Macgregor. In the same year they also built the *City of Glasgow*, screw-steamer of 1609 tons for the trade between Glasgow and New York, but she was soon transferred to Liverpool, and became the pioneer of the now famous Inman Line of steamers.

The Screw Propeller superior to the Paddle.—The establishment of this line of screw-steamers may be said to have sealed the doom of paddle-steamers for over-sea purposes. The power of the screw propeller proved itself superior to the paddle for many reasons. The great difficulty of the paddle-steamer was the varying immersion of the paddle-wheels with the varying draft of water. When the vessel was deep laden they were so much immersed that the wheels were choked, and the engines could not get away at a proper rate of speed, which, consequently, was slow at the beginning of a voyage and gradually improved, as the fuel became exhausted and the draft of water thereby lessened, allowing the wheels fairer play. The screw-propeller overcame this difficulty, and with this advantage, that the deeper it was immersed the more effective it became, and the only difference in a screw-steamer's speed on a long voyage is that simply due to the different measures of displacement of the vessel's body, with fuel in or out.

It was also found to be more economical, first because the slip of the propeller is less than that of the paddle, and consequently the effective power of every pound of coal much greater; and also because greater advantage could be taken of sail power when possible, especially with the wind abeam.

It was long objected that the screw-propeller was unfit for passenger steamers, as the motion of a screw-steamer was so much more unsteady than that of the paddle-steamer, and for a long time this notion so far prevailed as to maintain the position which the paddle-steamer held in all the principal mail lines. This idea was also backed by the Government, who for years would not permit the use of screw-steamers on the mail routes. Under this pressure the steam companies sailing under mail contract still continued to build paddle-steamers.

In 1852 the Cunard Co. built their last wooden steamer, the *Arabia*, 2400 tons and 938 H.P.; in 1855 their first iron steamer, the *Persia*, 350 ft. by 45 ft. by 30 ft., 3766 gross registered tonnage, and 3600 I.H.P. The *Persia* attained an average speed of 13 knots, and proved a successful competitor with the American Collins line of steamers. In 1862, their best paddle-steamer, the *Scotia*, was built; her dimensions were 366 ft. by 47½ ft. by 30½ ft. The average passage was reduced by her to 9 days.

The Government in that year gave way, and permitted the use of the screw-propeller, which is now universal, except for rivers or inland navigation, or short channel routes.

With heavy subsidies the mail lines did not so much feel the want of economy in fuel, but to those lines which opposed them without subsidy, the screw-propeller and its greater economy was the only lever they could depend upon for prosperity. Year by year, as larger and larger screw steamers were built prior to 1862, their speed increased until they were quite a match for the paddle-steamers, when these fell into disuse, and were quickly given up. Several of the last Cunard paddle-steamers had their machinery taken out and were converted into useful sailing-ships. The *Scotia*, converted into a twin-screw, is now a cable steamer in possession of the Telegraph Maintenance Company.

The Collins Line. — We must here briefly allude to the last shadow of opposition offered us in the Atlantic trade by our American cousins. They did not view with content the loss of a trade, which had, at one time, been so completely in their own hands in the old sailing-packet days. In the end of the forties, Mr. Collins, of New York, who had been largely interested in the packets, determined to oppose the Cunard Company on their own ground. He formed an American company, which, after much thought, and enquiry into our shipbuilding and engineering practice, constructed four splendid paddle-steamers, the *Arctic*, *Atlantic*, *Pacific*, and *Baltic*. These were well designed upon the famous clipper lines, and larger and more powerful in every way than the Cunard boats then in existence, or building, which the *Asia* and *Africa* then were, and their proposed dimensions and power well known to Collins.

It need hardly be said that they were successful in beating the Cunarders. The older boats were much inferior to them, and the new *Asia* and *Africa* barely maintained their own. On the 20th of May 1851, the whole of Liverpool was thrown into excitement upon learning that the *Pacific* had reached Holyhead from New York in 9 days 19 hours and 25 minutes, then an unprecedented passage. And so once more our American cousins had lowered the British flag and beaten the record. This successful opposition lasted a few years, but it was carried on at such a cost that it became its own Nemesis, and was eventually terminated in 1858. The terrible losses of the *Arctic* and *Pacific*, with many lives, and the success of the new Cunard iron steamship, *Persia*, succeeded in turning the tide once more in favour of Great Britain.

To this end, perhaps, another cause had a determining effect. The American packet owners, finding their trade gradually slipping out of their hands, raised an outcry against the employment of steam, and little thinking how futile was such an opposition, prevailed upon the American Government to withdraw its mail subsidy from their own steamers, which left the field clear for their British opponents. This is another clear instance of the futility of opposing scientific progress. The immediate effect was the investment of American money in many lines of steamers sailing under the English flag, which redounded to the profit of British masters and crews, as well as that of the steamship managers in Britain, and gave an immense spurt to her nominal tonnage. This has been largely accentuated since the Civil War in America, and its subsequent adoption of highly protective legislation.

The Collins opposition had had one considerable effect upon the rate of freight in favour of the merchants and traders, for before the opposition the Cunard Company were getting £7 10s. per ton for fine goods, and two years after it fell to £4.

The Advance of Steam steadily Progressive.—We have treated thus fully with the Cunard Line and Collins Line steamers because it was on the Atlantic only that our ships and steamers had found any real opposition. From the date of the abrogation of the Navigation Acts of this country, the advance in steam became so imminent that it need not be treated of further as a separate branch of the Marine. It will also be seen that that advance has been the one great cause of the present eminence of this country in the maritime progress of the world, of which proof will be found in the chapter on statistics.

CHAPTER X.

DEVELOPMENT OF FREE TRADE.

CONTENTS.—New departure under free trade—Mr. Richard Green and the Americans—Iron and Steam—Goldfields of California and Australia—Increase of shipping—Speed of American ships—China trade—British tonnage laws—Mr. Moorsom's plan of measurement becomes the basis of legislation in 1854—Improvement in ships—Parliament relieves burdens upon shipping—Effect on British seamen—Coasting trade thrown open, 1854—American coasting trade—Shipping laws consolidated, 1854—Apprentices—Russian war—High freights—Indian mutiny—Glut of shipping in Eastern seas—Increase of foreign shipping in British ports—American civil war—Its consequences—Drop in American shipping in British ports—Competition in the China trade—*Thermopylæ* and *Sir Lancelot*—French bounties—Conclusion.

New Departure under Free Trade.—We now enter upon a new departure for the British shipowner. The Free Trade principles of the Lancashire manufacturers had been triumphant. Freed from the Corn Laws they hoped to reduce wages. Freed from the Navigation Laws they hoped for increased and cheap transport for their wares. The shipowner, despondent at being deprived of his privileges, sought relief by agitating for the reduction of all taxes upon shipping and relief from all imposed burdens. Foreign competition was pressing upon him in every direction; but there was still some pluck left, and all did not despond. Although American clippers were stealing into all our valuable trades, the British shipbuilder determined to do his best to compete.

Mr. Richard Green and the Americans.—There is a story told of Mr. Richard Green, the eminent shipbuilder, of Blackwall, and owner of some of the finest ships in the Eastern trades, who, being present at a public dinner in 1850, and having to reply to a speech by the Secretary of the American Legation, said: "We have heard a great deal to-night about the dreary prospects of British shipping, and we hear, too, from another quarter much about the British lion and the American eagle, and the way in which they are going to lie down together. Now, I don't know anything at all about that, but this I do know, that we British shipowners are at last sitting down to play a fair and open game with the Americans, and, by Jove, we'll trump them." And he did trump them; for he shortly after built the *Challenger* to match the American ship *Challenge*, which had been carrying all before her in the China trade, and thoroughly eclipsed her.

Iron and Steam.—But all our shipbuilders were not so buoyant as Mr. Green, who was a builder as well as an owner of ships. For some years prior to 1850 our shipbuilders seemed to be at their last gasp. Wood shipbuilding in Britain was fast disappearing, and our builders of wood ships, unable to compete with the cheaper ships of the colonies, the United States, and the Baltic, were failing everywhere. This despondency did not last long, for with true British foresight, they turned their attention to iron as a material for shipbuilding, and especially for steamships, which, aided by the success of the screw as a propeller, soon found ample employment for them, and the ruined yards of the Tyne, the Wear, and the Tees, which had suffered most, sprang into new life at the sound of the rivetting hammer on their banks. Thus, when all seems lost, Providence supplies compensations.

Gold Fields of California and Australia.—The opening of the gold fields in California, and its cession to America in 1850, and the discovery of gold in Victoria the year after, created an immense demand for shipping.

Increase in Shipping.—The rush from the Eastern States to California found an opening for the American ships which were now being beaten off the Atlantic by our steamers; as there were no railways across the American continent within hundreds of miles of California, passengers and goods had to be transported thither by way of Cape Horn, and American shipping reaped a fine harvest.

Speed of American Ships.—On our side, the rush to Victoria employed every ton of spare shipping that could be found, and freights increased enormously. As much as £7 per ton was paid from London to Melbourne, and the demand for ships was not easily satisfied. London and Liverpool vied with each other for the greatest share of the immense emigration going on. The former transferred the most of the fine passenger ships which had been employed in the Indian trade, and the latter purchased some very fine American vessels. The fastest ships got the pick of the passengers, and the excitement in Liverpool was intense, when the news came home that the American built ship *Marco Polo* had made the voyage to Melbourne in 75 days, a feat unparalleled in those days. The London ships all made long passages, their average in 1852 being 123 days as against Liverpool's 110½. In

1854, the Americans sent across two splendid ships, the *Red Jacket* and the *Lightning*, built by the famous Donald McKay, of New York. The latter ship made still quicker passages—in 65 and 63 days out to Melbourne, and home in 64.

From the first settlement of the British American Colonies down to the War of Independence, their trade with Britain was carried on with freedom of intercourse as between the two countries, and upon a footing of equality; but their trade with other colonies, whether of Britain or of Spain, was rigidly restrained by the navigation laws of both countries, and their ships were much molested by the English and Spanish cruisers exercising the right of search. Many of these colonies, both British and Spanish, were excellent markets for the fish and agricultural produce of the English American Colonies, but they could not lawfully trade with them. To get over this difficulty, the American shipowners chose to risk their vessels in carrying on a clandestine trade, rather than lose it. In such a business good sailing qualities were necessary, and it gave rise to the building of those "Baltimore Schooners" which afterwards became so celebrated for their speed and consequent freedom from capture when employed in the smuggling business.

Necessity is the mother of invention, and it was the necessity of their position which compelled the Americans to use their inventive powers in shipbuilding, and taught them those principles in the art which, many years after, placed and kept them at the head of the field in the ocean races.

At that time, for ourselves, there was no such necessity. Protected by stringent laws, we feared no rivals, and there was no stimulus for improvement. Embroiled in war, as we almost constantly were during the eighteenth century, our merchant's fleets sailed under convoy, when the slowest ship ruled the race, and there was little inducement to build fast ones.

The day of competition and ocean racing had not then begun, but when it did the advantage was with our rivals. The lines of the Baltimore clippers told a tale, and the English ships were nowhere in the race.

China Trade.—In the China trade the same thing was occurring. From the time of America's independence she had imported her own teas from China. Tea is a delicate article to transport, and loses fast in flavour and quality in a ship's hold. To meet this contingency, the Americans began, in 1842, to build at New York those clipper ships which were to become so famous. In 1844, John W. Griffiths designed the *Sea Witch* ($170'\cdot3'' \times 33'\cdot11'' \times 19'$), 907 tons register, and carrying a China cargo of 1100 tons. With her the long sharp bow and fuller after-end came into permanent use the world over for fast ships of the merchant service.

After the China trade was thrown open in 1833 the tea trade fell into the hands of the merchants in China, many of whom had been formerly connected with the East India Company, such as Jardine, Matheson & Co., the Dents, &c. There were many good ships in the trade, notably the *John o' Gaunt, Euphrates, Foam,* and others, but they could not compare with the American ships for speed.

No sooner was trade open in this country than the Americans took advantage of it, and they were peculiarly well situated to do so. The ships from New York to San Francisco had mostly had to go back in ballast, but now many of these vessels ran on from Frisco to China, and competed with our ships in the carriage of teas to England. For years our merchants had given a premium to the first ship home in the fall of the year with the new season's teas, and the Americans now entered the race. With such vessels as the Americans had built, our ships of that day could not compete, but such men as the partners of Jardine, Matheson & Co., were equal to the occasion.

That firm, determining not to be outdone, ordered Messrs. Hall, of Aberdeen, to build the *Stornoway,* and the *Chrysolite* followed. These vessels were constructed more or less upon the new wave-line principle, but although very fast vessels, did not succeed in beating the Americans. In 1853 the race was run by the following ships:—

Canton to Deal, American ship	*Challenge,*	105	days.
” ” ”	*Surprise,*	106	”
Canton to Liverpool, British ship,	*Chrysolite,*	106	”
” Deal ”	*Stornoway,*	109	”
” ” ”	*Challenge,*	113	”
Shanghai to Deal, American ship,	*Nightingale,*	110	”

The Americans had still the best of it for a few years, and it was not until the *Lord of the Isles,* built by Scott & Co., of Greenock, and commanded by Captain Maxton, beat two of the fastest American clippers in 1856, that British fame became re-established. The character of the American ships had however been failing, notwithstanding their speed; for they were weakly constructed, and damaged their cargoes badly, which the better built English ships did not do.

British Tonnage Laws.—The tonnage laws of Great Britain, based upon false principles, had given rise to an unwholesome, slow and feeble type of ship, as only length and breadth to the exclusion of depth entered into the calculation for tonnage. The

Americans, bound by no such absurd rules, and with freedom to build as science dictated, outstripped us with vessels of greater burthen, more beam, and finer lines.

As early as 1821 a Commission was appointed to inquire into the tonnage laws, and again another in 1833, both of which reported upon them, recommending a system of internal measurement. Based upon these recommendations the Act 5 and 6 William IV. c. 56, was passed, but the system adopted was imperfect, found easy of evasion, and incapable of yielding just and satisfactory results. A third Commission was appointed in 1849, which issued a report in 1850 in favour of external measurement, but so little satisfaction did this afford that it was allowed to remain a dead letter.

Moorsom's Plan of Measurement.—Mr. George Moorsom, a member and honorary secretary of the late Commission, aided by the great practical skill of Mr. Joseph Horatio Ritchie, one of the surveyors to Lloyd's Registry of Shipping, perfected a plan of internal measurement which was received with general approbation, and became the basis of a new law embraced in the Act 17 and 18 Vict. c. 104. This, with some amendments in matters of detail, has since controlled the measurement of British ships for tonnage, and has given scope for the introduction of a superior class of vessel, of greater speed, stability, and carrying capacity.

Improvement in Ships.—It is a curious fact that on comparison of some of the vessels built under the new law with a fair average number of those built under the old law the actual tonnage was not seriously affected; in fact the new measurement was found to be slightly in favour of the shipowner in regard to carrying capacity. The great benefit derived was from the fact that it gave a greater elasticity to the builder in regard to design and dimensions, and the result was an infinitely better and more seaworthy type of ship.

Parliament relieves Burdens upon Shipping. Effect on British Seamen.—In 1853 an Act was passed relieving the shipowner from further burdens by modifying light dues and other dues on shipping which seemed to press heavily upon him in comparison with foreigners; it also repealed all the restrictions as to British masters and seamen permitting the employment of foreigners indiscriminately, and admitting them to equal rights with the British seamen of all classes. Thus were the interests of the British seaman sacrificed to those of the shipowner, the evil effect of which has been clearly shown by the current of events in the subsequent years.

Coasting Trade thrown Open, 1854. American Coasting Trade.—In 1854 the Act 17 and 18 Vict. c. 5, repealed the last fragment of protection, and threw open our coasting, as well as our foreign trade, to the world. To accomplish this the argument used by the Free Traders of the Manchester school was that when other nations saw the immense benefit which we, as a nation, should derive from this act of generosity, they would become generous and reciprocate; especially would this be the case with the United States of America. To this end negotiations were entered upon, and our Free Traders were beguiled with soft speeches and fair promises, until our legislation was completed. The Americans indeed opened their ports to foreign trade, but when it came to the American coasting trade, they refused to accede to their wishes, and replied by declaring that the long sea voyage around Cape Horn from the east to the west of America was included in their coasting trade, thereby shutting out our ships from participating in a trade which was a mine of gold to American shipowners, and became an immense aid in their competition with us in the China trade in after years. So much for the vain dream of reciprocity! This action of the Americans was a bitter pill for our Free Traders to swallow.

Shipping Laws Consolidated.—In this same year the Merchant Shipping Acts were consolidated into one, by the Act 17 & 18 Vict. c. 104, by which the former Acts were not only consolidated but entirely recast; and the laws of registry and measurement of tonnage of British ships, and the law relating to wrecks and shipowners' liabilities, were revised.

It also provided summary remedies for the recovery of wages; for the punishment of breaches of discipline on board ship, &c.

Apprentices.—At the time of the passing of this Act considerable alarm was felt in many quarters at the extraordinary falling off in the number of apprentices, and the consequent education of seaman. A proposition was made, that a clause should be inserted in the Act "Making it once more compulsory upon shipowners to carry a certain number of apprentices;" but the shipowners, unable to see *the justice or propriety of such a course*, made such strong protestations against it, that it was abandoned.

Russian War: High Freights.—The outbreak of the Russian war in the autumn of 1854 created a heavy demand for transport from the French as well as ourselves, especially for steamers. Our shipbuilders were fully employed at very high prices, but after the landing of the troops in the Crimea the demand for sailing ships ceased, and the glut in the Australian market threw a large amount of sailing tonnage out of employment. Steamers were, however, in full demand, and transport freights high in consequence. Amongst the sailing-ship owners who had bought

Indian Mutiny. Glut of Shipping in the East. Foreign Ships in British Ports.—Through 1855 and 1856 freights were fairly well maintained, but the cessation of the war in 1856 threw all the vessels which had been engaged in transport into the market, and the Indian Mutiny, which broke out in 1857, completely paralysed trade in India. This latter had the effect of creating a momentary demand for transport of troops and stores to India, but the ships were only engaged for the voyage out, and, this work finished, hundreds of thousands of tons of shipping found themselves in Indian and other ports without employment. This continued for months, and shipowners were in despair. Foreign shipping in British ports had increased from 30 per cent. in 1845, to 35 per cent. in 1850, and to 41 per cent. in 1855.

The old discussion upon Protection *versus* Free Trade broke out virulently, and continued almost until the American war in 1860 put a stop to it. The Rubicon once passed cannot be repassed, and Protection has passed away perhaps for ever for this country—that is for food and freight.

American Civil War.—In 1860 broke out the disastrous Civil War in America, which cost the States £600,000,000 in money, and thousands of valuable lives. No doubt great principles were at stake; and this war is only an example of the fact that when the time comes, and human thought and intelligence demand it, nothing can prevent institutions which have passed their period of usefulness, and are not in accordance with the progress of the times, from being swept away for ever, no matter at what cost. Such was American slavery.

Its Consequences.—The effect of the war was to break the back of the American shipping trade, as an opponent to us, and it no longer affects the progress of our own.

Drop in American Shipping in British Ports.—There can, however, be no doubt but that the cheapness with which we can produce iron ships and engines has been a great factor in our present success. After the war, the Americans in their distress, and confident in their internal resources, flew to protection of their manufacturing interests, and laid heavy duties upon those of other countries, including our own. Unable to build ships and engines cheaply themselves, they refused to take what we could so well have supplied, and the consequence is that the American foreign carrying trade between Europe and the States is largely done in British ships and under the British flag. Showing how large a factor the American shipping had been in our foreign clearances, they immediately fell from 43 per cent. in 1860, down to 33 per cent. in 1865, to 28 per cent. in 1885, and in 1888 were only 26½ per cent., 1½ per cent. more than they were in 1815.

Competition in the China Trade. "Thermopylæ" and "Sir Lancelot."—From that day our progress has been by leaps and bounds. Only one thing more will be referred to in connection with sailing ships from 1860 onwards, and that is, that we did not forget the lessons in shipbuilding which had been forced upon us by so much opposition and many reverses. The China competition was kept up by amicable rivalry amongst our own owners and merchants, and a splendid fleet of clippers were produced one after the other, such as the *Thermopylæ* and the *Sir Lancelot*, two of the fastest vessels, perhaps, ever built. The former, designed by the late well-known and much-respected Secretary of Lloyd's Registry, Bernard Waymouth, and built by Hood, of Aberdeen, for Messrs. George Thompson & Sons; and the latter by Messrs. Robert Steele & Co., of Greenock, for the late Mr. John McCunn, of Greenock. In the race of 1869 the *Thermopylæ* was the first ship home, making the passage in ninety-one days, followed by the *Sir Lancelot*, which sailed a few days later, but performed the passage in eighty-nine days. The opening of the Suez Canal a few days later put a stop to this interesting race. Out of a long list of these clippers only four remain: the *Thermopylæ, Sir Lancelot, Titania,* and *Leander*.

French Bounties.—The only scare we have of late years had, was when the French granted bounties to their builders and owners; but we need not have alarmed ourselves, as the object has not been attained, and the effort to sustain and encourage French shipping by such means has fallen flat and profitless—it has not injured us in the least.

American foreign tonnage has fallen off ever since 1860, and in 1880 it was not much more than half what it was in 1860.

In connection with our Mercantile Marine, difficulties and opposition have beset us in many ways.

Conclusions.—But for the hostility and cruelties of Spain we should never have reared the ships and the men which helped to preserve us as a nation by defeating the Spanish Armada; but for the opposition and insolence of the Dutch we might never have been so self-dependent in character and so successful as seamen as we have been; but for the rivalry of America, with her forests of building timber and splendid spars at her back, and the progress in the art of shipbuilding which necessity taught her, and then made her such a dangerous rival to ourselves on the ocean, we might still have been building tea-boxes, and floating over the ocean with the same tortoise-like speed. Competition has been our salvation and the cause of all our later successes.

CHAPTER XI.

SHIPPING LEGISLATION, 1862 TO 1875.

CONTENTS.—Shipping legislation, 1862—Engineers' examinations—American blockade—Origin of the Suez Canal—Canal condemned by the English—Increase of steam trade to India through the Canal—Mr. Plimsoll and loss of life at sea—Mr. Fortescue's Act, 1871—Marine department of Board of Trade invested with full control of British shipping—Mr. Plimsoll's book—Lord Carlingford's Bill—Ships sold to foreigners—Royal Commission, 1873—Mr. Plimsoll's Bill, 1874—Report of the Commissioners—Sir Charles Adderley's Bill, 1875—Mr. Plimsoll's conduct—Painful incident in the House—"Stop-Gap" Act, 1875—Excitement amongst shipowners.

Shipping Legislation, 1862.—The consolidation of the Shipping Acts having been completed in 1854, there was for some years a period of rest from shipping legislation. The war with Russia from 1854 to 1857, succeeded by the Indian Mutiny in the latter year, withdrew public attention from all other subjects. Shipping of all classes was remunerative, and as long as this is the case, grievances or difficulties, from which relief is sought by legislation, remain in abeyance. The first appearance of renewed legislation is found in the Act 25 and 26 Vict. c. 63, which instituted examinations for engineers, made further provision for wreck inquiries, and in the power of local boards, defined the master's powers in connection with the misconduct of passengers and others on board ship, and issued "Rules for the prevention of collisions at sea," under the joint recommendation of the Admiralty and the Board of Trade, which, by this Act, was henceforth to be associated with the Admiralty in framing or altering the said Rules.

During the dozen years prior to this Act, a very considerable increase in the steam tonnage of the kingdom had taken place, as also in the size and power of the marine engines employed, and it had become a question as to whether it would not be prudent to inquire into the experience and capacity of the engineers employed on board steamers going on foreign voyages. Prior to this there was no guarantee that the men in charge of marine engines had any experience as tradesmen, many of them having been bred from the ordinary firemen. Such men answered the purpose well enough in coasting or home trade steamers, which, in case of accident, were not far from engineering assistance, but as the voyages became extended, and the engine driver likely to be thrown more upon his own resources and tradesman-like ability for repairs, &c., it required persons of a more intimate acquaintance with the construction of machinery and the theory of steam power.

Engineers' Examinations.—It was therefore enacted that in future all engineers, prior to being placed in charge of marine steam machinery, should prove their capability and experience by examination. The certificates to be granted were of two classes. The second class certificate enabled an engineer to take charge of machinery up to one hundred horse-power, and the candidate was required to show that he had either served a full apprenticeship in a factory, or three years in a factory and one year at sea. The first class was for those who had served one year at sea in possession of a second class certificate, and were entitled, after passing a second examination, to take charge of machinery of any power.

All those who had already served at sea were entitled to certificates of service for the capacity in which they were serving at the time of the passing of the Act.

This legislation was very beneficial to the engineers, and gave them a secure position as members of the crew of a steamship, which they had not hitherto possessed.

American Blockade.—The course of the civil war in America, and the consequent destruction of its foreign shipping trade, created a largely increased demand for British shipping, especially steamers, and with it increased employment for engineers; consequently, their wages ruled very high in contrast with those of the navigating officers, except masters; which disparity has continued to the present day. Large numbers of British steamers were employed in running the blockade of the southern American ports; those who were fortunate were able to realise very handsome remuneration, in some cases sufficient to lay the foundation of independent fortunes.

Origin of the Suez Canal.—The opening of the Suez Canal for traffic created another new era for steam shipping. The steam trade to India or Australia, *viâ* the Cape of Good Hope, had not, as yet, been very successful, but the opening of the Canal soon told a tale.

One of the ambitious dreams of the French General, Napoleon Bonaparte, was the acquisition of Egypt, and through it to cut a highway for his fleets to India, which he coveted beyond all earthly possessions. He had heard of the old canal which is said to have been commenced by Pharoah Necho and completed afterwards by Darius, which was quite sufficient to suggest to his daring brain the feasibility of a ship canal joining the Mediterranean with the Red Sea. Strabo, writing in the time of the Roman Emperor Tiberius, speaks of a canal uniting the Nile with the Red Sea, and relates "that an East India fleet sailed from Alexandria up the Nile and thence through the canal into the Red Sea, and so on to India."

Napoleon's projects were defeated by England's wariness; the loss of his fleet, which was shattered by Nelson at the battle of the Nile, and the defeat of his army by Abercromby, put an end to his hopes in that direction, and he was obliged to make an inglorious flight to the shores of France.

Suez Canal condemned by the English.—After the close of the war by Napoleon's last defeat at Waterloo, the idea of a canal was a favourite theme with French engineers, and many schemes were proposed for its construction. The discussion had so far advanced in 1847 that a Commission was jointly sent by France, England, and Austria to test its feasibility and report. On this Commission England was represented by the eminent engineer, Robert Stephenson, who reported against it, giving it as his opinion that "it was impossible to make a really practicable ship canal." As an alternative, he planned a railway from Alexandria to Suez *viâ* Cairo, which was formed and opened for traffic in 1858. The French never approved of this, and were jealous of English influence in Egypt. M. Talabot, the French Commissioner, designed a scheme for a canal, but while this was being considered another Frenchman, who was in the diplomatic service in Egypt, and who has since become famous as Ferdinand de Lesseps, made use of his position and obtained from the Khedive the exclusive privilege of forming one. A French company and the Egyptian ruler found the money, the work was proceeded with, and after ten years of arduous toil the canal was opened for traffic.

Increase of Steam Trade to India through the Canal.— Although the English had looked with no favourable eye upon this canal, it was no sooner opened than they took advantage of it, and have been by far its largest customers from that day to the present. Our steamship owners at once entered into competition with the sailing ships for the Indian carrying trade, but steamers which had been very suitable for the Mediterranean or the Atlantic trades, were quite unfitted for the tropics, and they were not so favourably received in Indian ports as they might have been. The sudden reduction in the time occupied between, say, Bombay and London, disarranged the course of trade, and the route was not at first favoured by the Indian shippers. It often happened that the merchants preferred to pay a higher freight, *viâ* the Cape, in a sailing ship taking 90 days on the passage, than to a Canal steamer which could complete the journey in 30. But the steamship owner struggled on, and all these difficulties were soon overcome. He had to build vessels suitable to the trade, and shipbuilding had such a spurt as had never been seen before. The price of material and wages in 1872-73-74 went up in a most unprecedented manner. The price of pig iron and coal trebled in value, and the excitement was enormous. It can hardly ever again be paralleled. This was, however, due to more causes than the opening of the Suez Canal, and to none perhaps more than the operation of the Limited Liability Acts of 1862 and onwards.

Mr. Plimsoll and Loss of Life at Sea.—In 1868 attempt was made to codify the Merchant Law, and to bring into one all the Statute Law in any way affecting ships and mariners. It proved a most onerous task, and occupied the successive Governments until 1875, when it was finally withdrawn, in consequence of want of time and the difficulties besetting it in the opposition of interested parties. About this time, also, Mr. Plimsoll commenced his advocacy of the cause of the British seaman against what he called the mercenary and murderous greed of the shipowner in sending overladen and rotten ships to sea, and thereby causing a criminal loss of life.

If the shipowners were to blame in this matter, the shipmasters were to blame equally with them, for not understanding their responsibility and acting up to it. The master ought to know when his ship is overladen, and if such a thing is attempted and forced against his judgment, it is his duty to protest, and if masters would only have the courage of their convictions, no shipowner could dare persistently to act against it. For sending a rotten ship to sea no excuse can be found.

Mr. Fortescue's Act, 1871.—In 1871 Mr. Plimsoll brought forward a Bill for compulsory survey of all ships and a universal compulsory load-line, but on the promise of the Government to include his clauses in a new Bill it was withdrawn. Finding that it would be impossible, in the face of a strong opposition on many points which the Government desired to become law, to pass the Bill that session, Mr. Fortescue brought in a short Bill, now known as the Merchant Shipping Act, 1871 (34 and 35 Vict. c. 110), and included in it a clause giving seamen charged with desertion a right to a survey, but Mr. Plimsoll's clauses were modified by confining it to cases where the complaint was made by at least one-fourth of the crew, or at least to five, and to cases where the complaint had been made by them before quitting the ship.

This did not satisfy Mr. Plimsoll, who continued his agitation re loss of life by culpable shipwreck, and poor Jack was, by a sentimental following, raised almost to the position of a martyr.

The Act of 1871 also made it a misdemeanour in any person to send an unseaworthy ship to sea, and made it incumbent upon the masters of vessels, which happened to get into collision, to make known the names of their ships to each other, and also their ports of registry.

British Shipping placed under the Control of the Board of Trade.—In the next year Parliament extended the power of the Marine Department of the Board of Trade, by placing under its control the measurement and registry of ships, which duty had hitherto been performed by the Commissioners of Customs and their officials. This was done by the Act 35 and 36 Vict. c. 73 of 1872, which also transferred to the Board the powers formerly wielded by the Emigration Commissioners under the several Passengers Acts; and the power of a principal Secretary of State under the Passengers Act Amendment Act of 1863. These transfers fully completed the power of the Board of Trade over all classes of merchant vessels, and put into its hands the administration of all the Statute Law controlling them.

Mr. Plimsoll's Book.—As already stated, Mr. Plimsoll still kept up his agitation against "rotten and overladen" ships, and in this year (1872) published his celebrated impeachment of the British shipowner, producing a most astounding array of facts and figures to prove his contention, and, doubtless, it looked very bad for some of the individual shipowners whom he arraigned. A generous and sympathetic public, worked upon by his pleadings, supplied the funds wherewith to carry on the war, and keep up a strict surveillance upon rotten and unseaworthy ships, and the "nefarious" shipowner, in aid of the life of poor Jack.

Lord Carlingford's Bill.—Unable to stem the tide of sentiment, Lord Carlingford, the President of the Board of Trade, brought in a Bill in 1873 * to increase the power of the Board over unseaworthy ships, and strengthen the Act of 1871. Mr. Plimsoll's spies were continually bringing what they deemed unsafe ships under the notice of the Board, and it was thought prudent to appoint Government surveyors for the purpose of watching ships, rather than to leave it in such hands. The Board of Trade had given Mr. Plimsoll every assistance, but with what

---

* Eventually passed as 36 and 37 Vict. c. 85.

result? Of the cases of unseaworthiness which he presented to the Board not one-fifth were worthy of detention; in some few beyond this very slight repairs were needed and readily made; in more than one-half the charge was entirely groundless. In the next year or two the Board's officers were not idle, but of all the vessels detained by them only three per cent. were proved seaworthy. Instead of being content to believe that the Government would use every legitimate endeavour to attain the end he worked for, Mr. Plimsoll continued his agitation as if nothing would satisfy him but to get a rope around the necks of British shipowners. Carried away by extreme fanaticism, he condemned them as a class and insulted them in every possible way.

Ships sold to Foreigners.—By the end of 1874, 440 vessels had been surveyed; of these only 17 were steam vessels; 404 were pronounced unseaworthy without repair, 14 were seaworthy, and the remainder pending result of survey. Only 25 were condemned to be broken up. The effect, however, was so great upon the shipowners that, from January 1873, to the middle of 1875, 875 ships (principally wooden vessels) were transferred to foreign flags, not necessarily because they were unseaworthy, but to free the owners from the harassing measures pursued by Mr. Plimsoll. It destroyed the fleet of timber ships which had been used in the St. Lawrence and American trades, and the timber carrying business fell into the hands of foreigners who were not hampered by such strict regulations.

Royal Commission, 1873.—With a view to allay the excitement of the nation, and to ascertain the truth in regard to the condition of our merchant ships, and the conduct of owners in regard to their seaworthiness, a Royal Commission was issued on the 29th March, 1873, to twelve noblemen and gentlemen, who were instructed "to make inquiry with regard to the alleged unseaworthiness of British registered ships; whether arising from overloading, deck-loading, defective construction, form, equipment, machinery, age, or improper stowage; and also to inquire into the present system of marine insurance, the state of the law as to the liability of shipowners for injury to those whom they employ; and the alleged practice of undermanning ships; and also to suggest any amendments in the law which might remedy, or lessen, such evils as may be found to have arisen from the matters aforesaid." This Commission was presided over by the Right Honourable the Duke of Somerset, K.G., and on it sat H.R.H. the Duke of Edinburgh, R.N., K.G., &c., and Admiral Sir James Hope, R.N., G.C.B., representing the Navy; the Court of Admiralty was represented by H. C. Rothery, Esq., and the rest represented the Government and all the other authoritative bodies connected with shipping, except the shipowners themselves. Of this the shipowners bitterly complained; but as it was a question between Mr. Plimsoll and his party, who were numerous throughout the country, and the shipowners, it was perhaps better that it was so, especially as ample opportunity was given to both sides to bring forward evidence in support of their contentions, as well as rebutting evidence where necessary. All they lost was the power of cross-examining witnesses, which could have hardly been afforded them unless the same had been conceded to Mr. Plimsoll. The well-known characters of the members of the Commission was quite a sufficient guarantee of impartiality, and this was justified by the result.

After hearing a large number of witnesses, during almost continuous sittings from March to November, the work was still incomplete, but, with a view to allaying suspense, the Commissioners issued an interim report. Whilst giving Mr. Plimsoll credit for having called attention to the loss of life which occurs in the mercantile marine from the culpable neglect of shipowners, as well as from other preventible causes, the Commissioners aver that some of his statements were exaggerated, and that many of his imputations on the Board of Trade, for complicity with shipowners, were not borne out by the evidence brought before them. In the meantime they advised that great caution should be exercised in regard to legislation, until experience had been gained from the great powers already granted to the Board of Trade for the supervision, and, if necessary, the stoppage of unseaworthy or overladen vessels. In conclusion, they hoped to complete their work and present a full report during the ensuing session of Parliament.

Mr. Plimsoll's Bill, 1874.—Mr. Plimsoll, not satisfied with this progress, in the next session (1874) brought in a Bill endeavouring to force the Government into the survey of every vessel loading or discharging in the United Kingdom. This the Government resisted, more especially on the plea that it was unadvisable to relieve the owners and masters of all responsibility, which would be the effect of such legislation as was demanded by Mr. Plimsoll. His Bill was thrown out, the Government at the same time promising to legislate fully upon receipt of the Report of the Royal Commission.

Report of the Commissioners.—This Report, which was published in July 1874, was a very long one, very exhaustive yet moderate in tone. It adhered to the principle that the shipowner should not be relieved from any responsibility in regard to the seaworthiness, or lading, of his ship; but that, as unseaworthiness and overloading in some cases had been proved, a supervision by authority should be exercised, and it was thought that the power now in the hand of the Board of Trade was sufficient for the purpose. It entered upon many points too tedious to detail, and made representations with regard to safety of life, which have since become the subject of legislation. One point, however, affecting our seamen they considered established, and that was, that by far the larger proportion of loss arose from their neglect or bad navigation. As a remedy for this, they suggest improvements in the mode of master's depositions as to wreck, collisions, &c., and in inquiries into such casualties.

Sir Charles Adderley's Bill, 1875.—In February 1875, the President of the Board of Trade brought in a Bill to amend the Shipping Acts, which embodied many of the recommendations of the Royal Commission, and would have dealt fairly with most of the questions had it been carried into law. Mr. Plimsoll, not satisfied with this, reintroduced his own Bill, which he was eventually persuaded to withdraw, upon the plea that he could move his own special clauses as amendments.

Mr. Plimsoll's Conduct. Painful Incident in the House. —There was evidently a good deal of quiet opposition to the Government Bill, which was piloted by Sir Charles Adderley, and it is probable the Government was not over anxious about its welfare. Most of the session passed away, and when the business before the House was dealt with in the end of July, the Government, finding it impossible to deal with the Shipping Bill in reasonable time, withdrew it on the 22nd of that month. This was hailed by Mr. Plimsoll and his friends with a storm of indignation, and led to a most unfortunate scene in the House of Commons, in which Mr. Plimsoll completely lost his head, and made use of such violent language that he was called to order by the Speaker, but refused to withdraw the obnoxious expressions. He was then reprimanded by the House and withdrew.

This was a most painful incident, and clearly showed Mr. Plimsoll's want of tact and discrimination. It was a great pity that he could not endure opposition more patiently, for, after all, he had something of righteousness in his cause, and was supported by the strong feelings of a numerous body throughout the country. The action of the Government in dropping the Bill was severely criticised outside the House of Commons as well as inside, and this was so much felt that the Prime Minister, Mr. Disraeli, in an after-dinner speech at the Mansion House, thought it best to defend his conduct. Mr. Disraeli explained that, for some reason for which he could not account, the Bill did not make way, "although," he said, "there was no Bill to which individually, representing the Government, he more adhered," but when on the 22nd of July "there were found on the paper 178 *amendments* to that Bill, 140 of which were presented by the Opposition . . . . he felt it was his duty to recommend that it should not be proceeded with!"

"**Stop-gap**" **Act, 1875.**—Although that Bill was withdrawn, a short Bill was brought in of only two clauses to increase the power of the Board of Trade in regard to the appointment of surveyors, &c., and to enable them to stop ships upon the complaint of one-fourth of the crew as to defective condition. This Bill was passed in a very few days, although several clauses relating to grain cargoes, marking deck- and load-lines on vessels, imported from the dropped Bill were added to it in Committee. This Bill then became the Act 38 and 39 Vict. c. 88, which has been termed the "Stop-gap" Act, as its powers only ran for twelve months to tide over the time until the conclusion of the next session. As it conferred much stronger power on the Board of Trade with regard to the stoppage of vessels presumedly unseaworthy, it did not at all meet the views of the shipowners. A sop was, however, thrown to them by giving them power to prosecute the Board of Trade through its principal secretary for improper detention of vessels by its officers.

Excitement among Shipowners.—This course of legislative action and the continued excitement relative to loss of life at sea, at length thoroughly roused the feelings of the shipowners, who deemed it an unwarrantable interference with shipping business. The result was a mass meeting of shipowners from all parts of the kingdom, which was held in London on the 2nd of February, 1876, whereat strong resolutions were passed protesting against such legislation, and especially of the action of the Board of Trade surveyors under their new powers, as detrimental to the British shipping trade, and as affording an open door to the competition of foreigners who were not hampered by such surveillance and restrictions. The feeling of the meeting was that the large body of shipowners who conducted their business properly and honestly were being hampered and punished for a *small body* of *reckless*, if not *dishonest*, shipowners. "Let the responsibilities of shipowners," said Lord Eslington, the chairman of the meeting, "be clearly defined. If any man sent a ship to sea in an unseaworthy condition—that was a crime and ought to be punished; then make the punishment certain and severe, but take care to make that man only responsible for acts over which he had control." Another speaker complained that no less than forty-one Acts bearing upon the merchant service had been passed since 1849— that such legislation kept shipowners upon the tenterhooks of suspense not knowing what was next to happen. General reference was made to the decrease in number and deterioration in the quality of British seamen, as a cause of loss at sea.

Finally it was resolved to request an interview with the Prime Minister prior to the meeting of Parliament, to enable them to state their feelings more fully on the question, with a view to relief from further harassment, and to appoint a deputation to meet him. This deputation was received by Mr. Disraeli a few days after, to whom they were introduced by Mr. Goschen, M.P., who, while deprecating anything like special pleading for shipowners, said that he, to some extent, sympathised with them on the ground of the "state of uncertainty which had for some time past materially interfered with that great trade, and if Government with the aid of the legislature could complete the work of Merchant Shipping Legislation a great advantage would be gained."

Lord Eslington, in stating the case for shipowners, referred to the series of resolutions, and said that "the recent changes in legislation had been most inconvenient and harassing to shipowners—that it had been fragmentary and ill-considered—but the shipowners were willing to accord their support to any well-considered measure for saving life at sea.

"That there should be local appeal against arbitrary decisions of the Board of Trade surveyors in the various ports.

"That they entered 'a protest against Clause 4 of the Act of 1875 (as to unseaworthy ships), which imposes on shipowners a responsibility hitherto unknown in the jurisprudence of the country.'

"That a large proportion of casualties, &c., were caused by the inefficiency, intemperance, and negligence, or insubordination of crews."

Also "a protest against section 2 of the same Act which permitted a ship to be detained upon complaint of one-fourth of the crew."

And "against a hard-and-fast load-line."

"The shipowners," he said, "were desirous to give their best assistance to the Government in passing necessary legislation, but they trusted that they would have means afforded them of making known their opinions."

The Prime Minister assured them the Government had no desire to do anything which would militate against so vast and important an interest, and that what had been done seemed necessary. He reminded them that the Merchant Shipping Act would have been consolidated any time within the past seven years had it not been for the opposition raised not only by shipowners, but in many other quarters. That he would take care that their resolutions had the careful consideration of the Government prior to any future legislation, but that he could not promise to deal with the Merchant Shipping Acts, as a whole as it would take up too much time, to the detriment of other important matters.

In one point alone did the shipowners make their influence felt. Courts of appeal were appointed to deal with surveys. On the other points there was no withdrawal, as will be seen in what follows.

CHAPTER XII.

LOCKSLEY HALL CASE.—SHIPMASTERS' SOCIETIES.— LOADING OF SHIPS.

CONTENTS.—Further legislation, 1876—Wreck Commissioner—*Locksley Hall* case—Unjust sentence on Captain Barker—Shipmasters and the Prime Minister—Formation of Shipmasters' Society of London—Court of Appeal for inquiry into shipping casualties—Serious losses at sea—Stowage of grain cargoes—Mr. Martell's Paper on Losses at Sea—Port of Montreal—Capsizing of the *Daphné*—Inquiry by Sir E. Reed and his report—Detention of overladen ships—Load-line Committee—Royal Commission of 1884 on loss of life at sea—Wreck reports.

Further Legislation, 1876.—In 1876 an Act, 39 and 40 Vict. c. 80, was passed, making the sending of an unseaworthy ship to sea a misdemeanour, with further stringent regulations as to surveys, and appointing courts of appeal to decide cases; making the rules as to overloading applicable to foreign ships loading in British ports; regulating the carriage of grain and deck loads of timber; and insisting upon a maximum load draft being marked on the vessel by the owner; appointing a wreck commissioner, or commissioners, not exceeding three, and determining their duties as to inquiries into shipping casualties, &c.; enforcing the registration of the managing owner; or, if no such owner, a ship's husband, or other person having the management of the ship, with his address in the United Kingdom. This Act repealed certain sections of the Acts of 1854, 1871, 1873, and the whole of the Act of 1875 bearing upon these subjects.

Wreck Commissioner.—The appointment of a judge in the capacity of a wreck commissioner was a new departure. At first it was contemplated to appoint three such commissioners for the North and South of England and Scotland; power was moreover given to appoint one for Ireland, if found necessary, and these appointments were placed in the hands of the Lord Chancellor. Shortly after the passing of the Act, the first commissioner of wrecks was appointed by the nomination of Mr. H. C. Rothery, Q.C., an experienced Admiralty Court lawyer. Although local magistrates might still be called upon to act upon courts of inquiry, the creation of this office dispensed with their services to a large extent.

Locksley Hall Case—Unjust Sentence on Capt. Barnes.—A circumstance occurred this year which must now be referred to, as it clearly displays the effect of an abnormal sentimentality upon the minds not only of the public who sympathised with Mr. Plimsoll, but upon the minds of magistrates in their administration of the law, in regard to shipmasters and their treatment of seamen who were guilty of insubordination. Captain Barnes, of the ship *Locksley Hall*, brought a seaman named Allen before Mr. Paget, at the Thames Police Court, and charged him with assaulting the chief officer on the high seas, and gross and continued insubordination and refusal of duty. The seaman, on the other hand, brought a charge against the captain for illegal assault by placing him in irons. The magistrate admitted that the captain's case was fully proved, but in passing judgment said " he had taken into consideration what Allen had *already suffered* " (by having been confined in irons on board). " For the refusal of duty he inflicted a nominal punishment of one day's imprisonment, and for the assault another day's imprisonment." The " quality of mercy " was surely strained in this case, for the punishment provided by the Act was imprisonment for any period not exceeding twelve weeks, and also at the discretion of the court to forfeit, for every twenty-four hours of such disobedience or neglect, a sum of six days' pay. But on the other side there was no straining of mercy; for the admitted placing of the man in irons, the captain was condemned, ostensibly under the common law procedure, to be imprisoned for twenty-one days without the option of a fine. This sentence was so unjust—so contrary to law—that it raised a storm of indignation throughout the shipping world of London.

Shipmasters and the Prime Minister.—A strong deputation waited on the Prime Minister and laid before him an unanimous protest against such injustice. There was no doubt that the magistrate erred in his law as egregiously as he did in his sympathy for such a case as Allen's was proved to have been. The result of the appeal was the Home Secretary's intervention, and the release of Captain Barnes. The judgment could not be sustained. To sustain such a judgment would imperil the necessary discipline of a ship *in toto*. The power to maintain discipline and exact obedience to his orders has been placed in the master's hands by the Law of the Sea from the days of the Rhodians downwards, and anything which has a tendency to weaken it would react most injuriously upon the master's power to exact obedience to lawful commands, and performance of duty by the crew in the prosecution of a voyage. Such a reading of the law as was given by the Thames police magistrate in Captain Barnes' case would render it impossible for shipmasters to use the commonest restraint on any member of a crew guilty of mutinous conduct or assault. In the excitement of the moment a deputation of shipmasters and others again waited upon the Prime Minister, Mr. Disraeli, and craved an alteration of the law to prevent the recurrence of such a judgment, and to establish the authority of the masters. The Prime Minister, in reply, told them "that the law gave the shipmaster full power on board his ship at sea. What could they want more?" He moreover explained that in Captain Barnes' case it was not the law that was at fault, but the judge, and expressed his disapproval of Mr. Paget's judgment. "An error had been committed, and would be remedied." And so it was—by Captain Barnes' release and Mr. Paget's subsequent removal from the Thames Street Police Court. All power is in the hand of the master, but he must use it wisely and with discretion.

Formation of the Shipmasters' Society of London.—The strong feeling in the shipping world caused by the *Locksley Hall* case found its expression in several meetings of both shipowners and shipmasters, notably in London, where a society of shipmasters, supported by the shipowners, was formed for mutual defence against unjust legislation and legislative action. A Shipmasters' Society had been in existence since 1857, whose headquarters were at Liverpool. This society was incorporated in 1862 by Act of Parliament as the "Mercantile Marine Service Association," and it ought to have been one great and undivided society of shipmasters for Great Britain and Ireland as was at first intended, but unfortunately dissensions arose at the very outset between the London, Southampton and Liverpool branches of the proposed Society, with the result that a most uncompromising split occurred. The London and Southampton Societies died a natural death in a year or two, whilst Liverpool proceeded quietly on its course and formed a national society sanctioned by Parliament.

The re-awakening in London to the absolute need of such a society resulted in the formation of the "Shipmasters' Society," now in active life. The general objects of the society are, the mutual protection and advancement of the general interests of the members, and to assist in defraying legal expenses which may be incurred in defending the interests of members who may be brought before a Court of Inquiry, and may appear to the committee of management to require such aid. There are several other societies representing other districts of the kingdom which have been formed for the same purpose.

Four of these societies, viz., the Mercantile Marine Service Association, the Scottish Shipmasters' Association, the Shipmasters' Society, and the British Shipmasters' Protection Society (North-east Coast), are now joined together, for consultative, legal, and other purposes, in a federation, which is governed by a council elected by the several societies. Its business is principally to watch legislation which may have a tendency to injure the position of shipmasters and officers, and to promote such as may be for their benefit.

Court of Appeal for Inquiry into Shipping Casualties.—The circumstances of the *Locksley Hall* case, and the excitement attending it, had the effect of making shipmasters and their friends review their position in connection with the legislation of the past twenty-five years, and especially in regard to the proceedings and procedure of Courts of Inquiry—their constitution and the want of a Court of Appeal in doubtful cases. This want became so apparent as time passed on that in 1879 the Government brought in and passed an Act, 42 & 43 Vict., c. 72, which created a Court of Appeal for the re-hearing of any case in which " new and important evidence which could not be produced at the investigation has been discovered, or if for any other reason there has been in their (the Board of Trade's) opinion ground for suspecting a miscarriage of justice." This was a measure of justice, but it stopped short of what was actually required, which was put off for a more convenient season.

In compliance with the requirements of this Act, the Lord Chancellor made new rules as to assessors on Courts of Inquiry, which placed their appointment in the hand of the Home Secretary. These rules also ordained that where the certificate of any officer was in question there should not be less than two assessors having experience in the merchant service; and in the case of an engineer, one at least was to be an engineer holding a first-class certificate and of at least five years' sea service. In 1880 new rules were added, principally applying to the re-hearing of cases in Courts of Appeal.

Serious Losses at Sea.—Stowage of Grain.—Mr. Martell's paper on Losses at Sea.—In addition to the discussion as to seaworthy ships, another feature leading to unseaworthiness was now seriously exercising the minds of owners and others connected with merchant shipping, and that was the very serious number of vessels (principally steamships) which, grain-laden, were lost and missing. As, in most of these cases, the crews disappeared with the ships, it was very difficult to obtain evidence as to the momentary causes. In a most valuable paper addressed to the Institution of Naval Architects in April, 1880, Mr. Martell, the Senior Surveyor to Lloyds, discussed the probable causes. *Inter aliâ*, the "want of proper care in loading," and a "want of initial stability" in certain classes of vessels, were prominently adduced. The latter was a question for Lloyds and naval architects to deal with; the former could only be properly dealt with by legislation. Accordingly, the Government introduced and passed the Act, 43 & 44 Vict. c. 43, in which stringent rules were laid down in reference to the stowage of grain cargoes, under heavy penalties. Beyond the two causes stated above, Mr. Martell, while laying no undue blame on either, referred to acts of management as being partially responsible for bad stowage. First, the hasty despatch required by owners. "The greater original cost, and the expenses in working steamers, as compared with sailing ships, have also made rapid despatch in port a question of greater importance; the consequence of this has been that too little attention has been given to the stowage of cargoes," &c. &c. Secondly, of the masters, after giving credit for increased education and intelligence, he says, "When we come to consider other causes of loss arising from overloading and improper stowage, it will be *impossible to acquit shipmasters of all blame;* but it must be remembered of them that, whatever their faults of omission, or of commission, *they always risk, and too often have to pay the penalty with, their lives* for their mistakes, whether they arise from ignorance or inadvertence."

Port of Montreal.—As a proof of recklessness or carelessness, he refers to what had occurred at Montreal, than which port none had suffered so many losses of grain-laden ships prior to 1873. The Port Warden of that port was charged with seeing all grain ships properly laden under certain rules laid down by the port authorities. The fine upon any shipmaster for non-compliance was $40. "This fine was so ridiculously low that the shipmasters paid it as a matter of course, loaded their ships as they liked, and numerous losses used to ensue." In that year the fine was raised to $800 for evading the Port Warden's regulations, and since that time *not a single grain-laden vessel* from the Port of Montreal has foundered at sea. This story tells its own tale and teaches its own lesson to shipmasters. Whatever they may choose to risk for themselves, they have *no right to imperil the lives of their crews.* How many lives have they sacrificed, as well as committed moral suicide themselves, to satisfy the greed of unscrupulous owners? A small fine was paid with a light heart, but when it was made heavy enough to make it no longer worth while to risk it, the evil was cured.

Capsizing of the "Daphne."—Inquiry by Sir Edward Reed and his Report.—The capsizing of the *Daphne* S.S., in course of her launch upon the Clyde on Friday, July the 4th, 1883, accentuated the fears in regard to the stability of vessels generally. The Home Secretary appointed a Commission of Inquiry into the circumstances of the *Daphne's* disaster, which was presided over by Sir Edward Reed, the eminent naval architect. Its cause and the general question of stability were exhaustively treated. The Report is too long to be dealt with here, but Sir Edward's concluding remark may very well find a place as interesting to shipmasters and officers. He says, "I venture to add (in view of the relation of this case to the general question of stability) that with the large number of ships afloat possessing so little stability as to make their safety at sea dependent upon the judicious stowage of cargo, arrangement of coal and use of water ballast, it would appear to be high time that some knowledge of the elements of a ship's stability was imparted to the officers of the Mercantile Marine, and required of them by the Board of Trade examiners. I must be excused for further adding that the recent legislation of Parliament has, in my opinion, been *much less efficient* in preserving life and property at sea *than it might have been* had the Board of Trade *understood and recognised* the very large extent to which this question of stability of necessity enters into the design, construction, stowage, load line, freeboard, and almost every other subject with which the Board has to deal in regulating merchant shipping matters."

Detention of Overladen Ships—Load-line Committee.—The course of legislation had made it incumbent upon the Government officers to prevent overladen ships from proceeding to sea, but an absolute answer as to what was an overladen ship never having been given, left the question surrounded by difficulties. The various types of vessels that had sprung into existence, especially steamers, filled the judgment as to the meaning of the term "overladen" with ambiguity. With a view to the solution of the question a Departmental Committee was appointed by the Board of Trade in January 1884, which consisted of thirteen of the most eminent Government officials, professors of naval architecture, and practical shipbuilders, to consider "Whether it is now practicable to frame any general rules concerning freeboard which will prevent dangerous overloading without unduly interfering with trade," &c. &c. This committee has usually been termed "The Load-line Committee."

With a view to meet the question Lloyds' Committee had worked out for themselves a set of freeboard tables which they considered would fully answer the purpose, without undue pressure upon any class of vessel. The Board of Trade also presented their ideas upon the subject, and the result was a difference of opinion.

After a long and patient inquiry, the Committee reported to the President of the Board of Trade, in answer to the questions submitted to them:—

"That, 1. We are of opinion that it is now practicable to frame general rules concerning freeboard, which will prevent dangerous overloading without unduly interfering with the trade.

"2. We have the pleasure to submit herewith tables which we consider should be adopted."

And in the 3rd they expressed an opinion "that they would be applicable to all existing types of cargo vessels, and for some years to come," &c.

The rules submitted were based in principle upon the latest tables of Lloyds' register office, with such limited modifications as were concurred in by that body and the Board of Trade, both being represented on the Committee, whose recommendation was unanimous. At the same time they guarded themselves by saying "that if rigidly applied to some cases that might arise" (such as new types not at present in existence, or perhaps not contemplated in Lloyds' and other classifications, which would have to be dealt with on their own merits), "injustice might be done." By the legislation which followed such cases are left to the discretion of the Board of Trade.

Royal Commission of 1884 on Loss of Life at Sea.—Although the labours of this Committee settled fairly the question of a load-line there were many others in connection with unseaworthy ships still unsettled, and these were referred to a Royal Commission granted in the end of 1884 "To inquire into the extent and cause of the loss of ships and lives at sea since the Report of the Royal Commission on Unseaworthy Ships, and to report on the remedies for such losses, having special but not exclusive regard to the following subjects," viz.:—

"The laws concerning marine insurance and the liability of shipowners;

"The functions and administration of the Marine Department of the Board of Trade;

"The functions of the Courts before whom wreck inquiries are conducted;

"The condition and efficiency of merchant officers and seamen, and the best means of improving the same."

Wreck Reports.—The gravity of the circumstances connected with the increase of casualties, especially in steamships, rendered such an inquiry absolutely necessary. The Wreck Report for 1883–84 showed a steady annual rise in serious casualties to steamships, from 406 in 1877–78 to 656 in 1883–84, or more than 50 per cent. The loss of life in 1883–84 was 2245, which was less than the loss on the preceding year, but above the average of the past seven years. The number of missing ships was 121; of which 109 were sailing vessels with 1044 lives, and 12 steamers with 238 lives; together making more than one-half of the total loss of life. The serious part of this loss was that of the increase of classed vessels. Of the number of lives lost in ships and steamers 197 were those of passengers.*

* "Report to the President of the Board of Trade on Wreck Abstracts for 1883–4," dated October, 1885, by Mr. Thomas Gray, assistant secretary.

CHAPTER XIII.

SHIPPING LEGISLATION, 1884-1894.

CONTENTS.—Mr. Chamberlain's Bill—Opposition of the shipowners—Depression in shipping, 1885—Full report of the Commission in 1887—The effects of late legislation described—Its apparent inutility in preventing loss of life—Papers by Professors Elgar and Jenkins—False competition and careless stowage—Amount of shipping legislation.

Mr. Chamberlain's Bill.—In 1884 Mr. Chamberlain brought into the House of Commons a very comprehensive Bill dealing with Insurances (with a view to prevent over-insurance, &c.), contracts between shipowners and seamen (making shipowners responsible to the crew for the ship's seaworthiness, and extending the Employers' Liability Act to seamen), Joint Stock Companies and Criminal Law, amendment of the procedure for detention of unseaworthy ships, tonnage measurement, with the view of amending certain anomalies which had crept into legislation, defining the mode of ascertaining net register tonnage, &c.

Opposition of the Shipowners.—During the winter recess Mr. Chamberlain had attended several meetings advocating the principles of the proposed measure with a view to saving life at sea, he being impressed, from his experience as President of the Board of Trade, with the opinion that much of the loss which had been occurring with large increase from year to year was preventible, and that erroneous principles of sea insurance existed which permitted of an absolute profit being made by the loss of a vessel insured beyond a value which would fairly recoup the owners for their loss. At some of these meetings he met with indignant opposition from the shipowners. On the introduction of the Bill, Mr. A. B. Forwood, of Liverpool, wrote a very strong letter to the *Nautical Magazine*, impugning the premises upon which Mr. Chamberlain relied, especially in regard to insurances; and after making some remarks upon surveys, shipping courts, and the Plimsoll mark (as then carried out), he winds up by a strong indictment of British shipmasters and officers. "I have had," he said, "twenty-five years' experience as a managing owner of many thousand tons of steam shipping, and also as an underwriter, and

I unhesitatingly say that far more losses occur from the fault of our Board of Trade certificated officers and engineers and the State-pampered seamen of to-day, than from any other cause or causes." "Insobriety stands," he continues, "as owners too well know, in the forefront as the cause of disaster, yet nothing is more difficult of legal proof; but when brought home the culprit's certificate should be cancelled. Reprimands and suspensions do not meet the gravity of the offence."

The Bill got, however, little further than the second reading, and eventually was dropped for want of time to carry it through. Many portions of it were dealt with in the following years, but little alteration in the mode of insurance has been achieved; neither has the Employers' Liability Act been extended to seamen.

Such a state of matters as was disclosed by the late Wreck Reports in connection with the abnormal loss of life, and the continued excitement maintained by the seamen's trade unions and their political supporters, determined the Government to appoint the Royal Commission to inquire into the causes of such losses, and to report upon the best means to attain "the saving of life at sea," referred to above.

Depression of Trade in 1885.—The beginning of 1885 found the shipping trade in a state of great depression, and the amount of tonnage building had dropped to about one-half of what it had been in 1883; perhaps it was not so much depression as a return to a normal state, after the excitement of 1882–3. There was one noticeable feature in that excitement which led to the building of at least-one-fourth more tonnage than even in the years 1873–4, and more than has been quite reached since, and that was, the elevation of prices either of ships or material did not reach anything like the point of those years, the manufactories of both iron and steel being better able to meet the demand upon their resources. The labour market was the one most benefitted. Freights had gone up to a small extent, but now had fallen lower than ever. The volume of trade was little, if at all, diminished, but prices were less in every direction.

Full Report of the Commission in 1887.—At the end of 1885 the Royal Commission on the Saving of Life at Sea issued a *résumé* of the evidence taken throughout the session, but without making any recommendation, as the inquiry was not finished. Parliament having been dissolved in November, and the old Commission superseded by a new one, under the chairmanship of Mr. Shaw Lefevre, in the beginning of the session of 1886, its labours were continued until 1887, in which year, on the 27th of August, its full Report was issued.

The Effects of late Legislation described.—After reviewing the legislation of late years, the Commissioners said: "When we look at the general results of the legislation thus referred to, upon the loss of life and property at sea in British vessels, it is most *unsatisfactory* to find no sensible effect has been produced in reduction of their loss."

Its apparent Inutility in preventing Loss of Life.— "From the returns laid before this Commission by the Board of Trade, the substantial accuracy of which has not been questioned, it appears that from 1874 to 1883 inclusively, there was a marked increase in the losses of British ships, and of the lives of those employed in them. . . . . The most serious losses occurred in respect of vessels (excluding fishing vessels) reported as missing. No less than 699 vessels, with 8475 hands on board, were reported as missing during this period of nine years, the cause of whose loss was unknown."

Mr. Thomas Gray and the shipowners differed as to the number of seamen employed and consequently as to the average percentage of loss; "but," says the Report, "whichever method of comparison be taken, the proportion of deaths from drowning of seamen was very high, and had undoubtedly increased during the period under consideration—viz., from 1 in 81 in 1875, to 1 in 56 in 1883." . . .

To outside observers there is no reason to suppose that Mr. Gray was actuated by malice towards the shipowners, and that he wished to exaggerate the truth; whereas it is very evident from the course of the evidence that, by every device possible, they endeavoured to minimise the truth, and to show that the ordinary perils of the sea alone were responsible for the loss, and not, as was alleged, from preventible causes.

"It should be borne in mind," continues the Report, "in considering this subject, that besides the lives actually lost at sea, very many more have been endangered, and only preserved by the means of safety so largely provided by Government aid and by private philanthropic effort."

"From the tables prepared by the Board of Trade for nine years ending June 30, 1883, no less than 96,494 lives were saved at home and abroad, chiefly by lifeboats, rocket apparatus, ships' boats, &c.

"The statistics above referred to were the latest available in the earlier inquiries of the Commission in 1885. Since then the statistics of three additional years have been obtained." . . . . Loss of life fell from 2019 in 1883 to 1181 in 1884—1190 in 1885 and 1067 in 1886—a reduction of 42 % in those three years from the average for the previous three years. . . . . Mr. Gray referring to this diminution, says, "he believes there have been three operating causes. In the first place there has been, on the whole, comparatively favourable weather; in the second place there has been a marked, almost a general, decrease in the value of ships in policies of insurance; and in the third place, the attention bestowed on the depth of loading and the general seaworthiness of ships has had effect."

The Commission did not coincide entirely in Mr. Gray's views, but came to the conclusion that, "To whatever cause this diminution of loss of life during the years 1884–86 may be due, it cannot be contended that it was in any way the result of the legislation of 1875-6; and the fact remains indisputable that, in spite of all the provisions made by Parliament, and the great increase of the staff of the Board of Trade, entailing a very large charge upon the country, there was not only no diminution in the loss of life at sea in merchant vessels in the years following upon this legislation, and up to the year 1883, but a considerable increase." . . . .

In considering this conclusion of the Commissioners, it must not be forgotten that the aim of Mr. Plimsoll, and those who supported him, was to bring every ship of whatever class or description under the notice of a Board of Trade surveyor prior to sailing. On the other hand, the immense cost of such close surveys must not be lost sight of; it had been shown that the annual charge for surveyors had risen from about £12,000 per annum to over £50,000, and the question for the Commission was, Had the country received value for the increase? And was it right that that should to any great extent be added to? Although the action of increased strictness in survey had not been able to prevent an actual increase of loss, yet, without it, might not the loss have been a great deal more?

"The action of the surveyors," says the Report, "led to the breaking up of a considerable number of vessels of the lowest grade, ... and if these vessels had not been interfered with, it might have been that the loss of life would have been greater even than it proved to be. . . . . On the other hand, it is equally clear that the surveyors of the Board of Trade were unable to prevent a large number from going to sea in a state which undoubtedly contributed to, if it was not the immediate cause of, disaster and loss."

In connection with Mr. Chamberlain's proposed Bill, Mr. Forwood's letter to the *Nautical Magazine* has been quoted. The line of argument he adopts with regard to British shipmasters and officers was persistently followed by many of the shipowning witnesses, and with such full effect that the Commissioners came to the conclusion that, "Of all the vessels lost by strandings and by collisions, it is undoubtedly the fact that a very great number of losses were due to the misconduct, or neglect, or error of judgment, of the officers or persons in charge of the ships; and we are satisfied that in a large proportion of these cases the loss was due *not to mere error* of judgment, but to the *neglect* by the master or officers of the *most ordinary rules and precautions of navigation*. We notice habitual neglect of the use of the lead, and omission to slacken speed in fog. We think, however, owners may do much to prevent this class of accident by a careful selection of officers, and by insisting on the strict observance of recognised rules and precautions, especially as masters undoubtedly feel the *pressure of the demand for quick passages!* We also think that the neglect of the lead is sometimes attributable to an *insufficient number of hands* in the watches, and that this also sometimes affects the character of the steering and look-out, and has thus a bearing upon both strandings and collisions."

The Report goes on to state the difficulty of bringing home responsibility to shipowners, and that "the very important provision of the Act of 1876, which made it a misdemeanor for the owner or manager to send a ship to sea in an unseaworthy condition, in consequence of the legal and other difficulties attending its enforcement, have been such that it has almost become a dead letter." .... "The alternative procedu reprovided by the Acts of 1875–6, viz., that by which the Board of Trade is empowered to detain vessels which are unseaworthy, and to prevent them from going to sea, is attended with the utmost difficulty, and in practice has proved inefficacious." Mr. Gray, in his evidence, went very largely into the reasons for that failure, and the Commissioners conclude that they "do not see that any good results can be got from the extension of the system of surveys and from the increase of power of detention. . . . . It would almost necessarily result either in the surveys becoming mere formalities, as in the case of France, or in the management of ships and everything connected with them being transferred from the owners to Government officials. . . . . It would tend still more to level down, than to level up, the average condition of vessels, &c."

The only alternative policy is to make shipowners more directly responsible in their civil relations to underwriters, charterers, and the officers and men employed in the vessels; and on these points they make some recommendations.

In regard to the condition and efficiency of officers and men, they were "unable to come to the conclusion that there was any just foundation for the allegations that British seamen have deteriorated in quality," and "in view of the facts of the case," they say, "we are unable to advise any interference by law with the employment of foreign seamen," stating further, "it is almost universally admitted by the witnesses that these men from the north of Europe are excellent seamen." They do not recommend reverting to the system of compulsory apprenticeship, which "system had to be abandoned in 1849 owing to the abuses it had given rise to," and say "that in the present day there would be far greater difficulty in re-establishing such a system."

They recommended "that a simple professional examination should be required for the ratings of carpenter and boatswain," and "that seamen with the rating of A.B. should be required to have continuous records of their services."

To any one who has the leisure to do it, a perusal of the evidence and full report will be instructive, but the meagreness of the result of two years and a half inquiry will undoubtedly be apparent. The great decrease in loss of life in the three years 1884–6 must have been due to some cause, but to what cause the Commission seemed unable, or unwilling, to attribute it. The result of all such inquiries, notwithstanding the evidence brought forward, seems to be a miserable and unsatisfactory compromise of the truth. Nevertheless, some good resulted, for it set many of our shipping authorities, naval architects, and others upon the alert.

Papers by Professors Elgar and Jenkins.—In the autumn of 1886, at the meeting of the Naval Architects at Liverpool, during the Liverpool Exhibition, Professor Elgar presented a most valuable paper on "Losses at Sea in 1881 to 1885," in which he treated the question very exhaustively, and accompanied it by a set of admirable tables and drawings. A reference to these tables shows that a very large number of the vessels which disappeared were by no means old vessels, but of most modern build and type; also that by far the larger number were either coal or grain laden, and the conclusion arrived at was that they foundered from shifting their cargoes, or, especially in steamers of the then fashionable narrow-beamed three-decked type, from absolute want of stability.

This paper was followed in the spring of 1887 by another paper, contributed by the late Professor Jenkins, "On the Shifting of Cargoes," in which he treated the action of various cargoes under stress of weather and rolling and heeling motions of the ship, and what would undoubtedly take place under various degrees of shifting whether of coal or divers kinds of grain. "Notwithstanding the enforcement of the stringent regulations (of the Grain Acts of 1876 and 1880) . . . . the annual loss of life continues to be very large. During the three years ending 1877, 93 grain-laden British vessels foundered or were missing, the number of lives lost being 833. In the next three years the number of vessels so lost rose to 111 and the lives to 946; but in the next triennial period, during the whole of which the Carriage of Grain Cargoes Act (1880) was in force, the numbers were reduced to 74 ships and 854 lives." The Professor then goes on to show that notwithstanding all the precautions taken, grain laden in bulk is a dangerous cargo.

False Competition and Careless Stowage.—He touches also on coal-laden ships. "Vessels carrying cargoes of coal are subject to no restrictions as to stowage similar to those enforced in the grain trade. . . . . Statistics appear to show that they need it quite as much. During the three years ending 1877, 200 coal-laden British vessels foundered or were missing, and with them were lost 991 lives. During the three following years the numbers of vessels so lost fell to 184 and the lives to 912; but in the triennial period ending 1883 the number of vessels rose to 314, and the lives reached the melancholy total of 1849, or more than twice as many as were lost during the same period from grain-laden vessels. . . . . The subject," he says in concluding a most interesting paper, "is one that has no doubt received the attention of the Royal Commission now sitting on 'Loss of Life at Sea;' and it is to be hoped that that body will not fail to recommend some plan under which the annual loss of life resulting from the shifting of cargoes will become much reduced." This hope was never fulfilled, and the stowage of coal cargoes remains in a most disgraceful state for want of even the very common precaution of trimming properly. The coal is literally poured into the ships from shoots and staithes, and the moment the lading is finished the vessel is hustled off to sea, neither the owner, master, or charterer taking the least care of proper trimming or stowage, each party trying to throw the blame on the other, and so between them valuable lives are lost, the master too often sacrificing his own with those of the crew. As Admiral De Horsey remarked, "With unskilled stevedores, and *fully insured* ships and cargoes, *the safety* of the ship appears to be a matter of very *secondary importance*," and there can be no doubt that morally the possibility of full insurance of ship and cargo is, notwithstanding all the owners may say against it, a very important and undeniable cause of loss. The false competition of managing owners makes it imperative to save expense in the treatment and loading of cargoes, and although their great outcry is for *seamen* to command their ships, seamen are useless to prevent this dangerous practice of taking ships to sea improperly stowed, and all their experience stands for nought as against this cruel saving of expense.

The recommendations of the Commission on many points has been a dead letter, the general outcome of their inquiry being the "Life-Saving Appliances Act of 1888," which does not touch the root of the evil, but only makes provisions for the saving of life when accidents do occur.

In 1888 an attempt was made to extend the Liability of Employers Acts to seamen. In the Bill introduced into Parliament in that year Clause 14 extended the liability not only to the owners, but to the masters also. The manifest injustice of this aroused strong feeling throughout the profession, and the shipmasters' societies made such valid representations to the Government that there is no doubt the Bill would have been altered. The Bill, however, was dropped for want of time to carry it through in that session, and it has not since been revived.

Amount of Shipping Legislation.—The extraordinary amount of legislation relative to the affairs of the merchant service which had taken place in the past half-century now rendered the codification of the Mercantile Marine Laws a matter of absolute necessity. There were no less than eighty-one separate Acts referring to merchant ships entered in the Statutes in fifty-four years, *i.e.*, from 1840 to 1894, which made it difficult to ascertain what the law really was. In 1894 the Government set about this work, and by avoiding anything like new legislation or the introduction of such controversial matter as had wrecked the attempts of former Governments, it succeeded in passing the grand Act (57 & 58 Vict. c. 60) of that year. By it all the former Shipping Acts were repealed, and with a few minor exceptions it contains the whole law of merchant shipping and its *personnel*. The subject is one which touches so many interests that it is doubtful how long it will remain the single and undivided code; already there are Bills before Parliament introduced by the separate interests, owners, officers and seamen, but they are all of so controversial a nature that it is difficult to say whether all, or any, will become law.

This brings to an end the history of the legislation affecting the Mercantile Marine and its varied interests, a history of which no British sailor ought to be ignorant. The material progress of the marine in wealth and volume has not been included in these last chapters, as it was thought best to give it a place by itself in the concluding portion, which will be found in the chapter on Statistics.

CHAPTER XIV.

STATISTICS OF SHIPPING.

CONTENTS.—Board of Trade returns—British tonnage—Its increase compared with foreign—Steam tonnage—Fluctuation in shipbuilding—Gradual increase in number of ships since 1865—Increase in size of ships and decrease in crews—Large vessels in 1850 and 1884—Shipbuilding in 1895—Comparison of the largest steamers in existence—North German Lloyds' new steamer—Increased competition in building in foreign countries—Causes of British success—Speculation—Improvement in economy of engines—Principal sources of foreign opposition in shipping.

Board of Trade Returns.—For some years the Board of Trade has compiled from the returns of custom-houses and other sources in the various countries of Europe, our Colonies, the United States of America, &c., very elaborate statistics of the shipping of the world, which are year by year laid before Parliament. Without such returns it would be impossible to gauge the progress of British shipping, or form an estimate of the commerce of the world, and thereby obtain a satisfactory knowledge of our own progress as compared with that of other nations.

Sufficiently meagre at first, these returns have improved year by year until they have obtained a considerable degree of completeness, and could we obtain from foreign countries full and *regular* returns, there would be little left to be desired. Since 1870 complete returns of tonnage owned, and of port entries and clearances, have been received from Norway, Sweden, Denmark, the German Empire, France, Holland, Belgium, Austria-Hungary, Italy, and the United States of America. From Russia, Finland and Greece they have been irregular, but sufficient to afford an approximate yearly estimate. From Portugal the returns of entries and clearances only have been obtained, and from Spain none whatever.

During the past fifteen years China and Japan have acquired fleets of ships built in Europe, and are now constructing warships and mercantile steamers on European models themselves. From those countries we have returns since 1880.

British Tonnage; its increase compared with Foreign.—From the Progressive Tables relating to British and Foreign Shipping, presented to Parliament on the 17th day of June, 1895, the increase of the merchant navy of the British Empire appears to have been continuous from 1840 to 1885, during which period the tonnage was very nearly trebled, having amounted in the former year to 3,311,538 tons, and in the latter to 9,323,615 tons. Between 1885 and 1888 there was a serious lull in shipbuilding, and the registered tonnage had lost about 200,000 tons in 1887. From that date forwards the addition of tonnage has been progressive, and the amount possessed by the Empire in 1894 was 10,512,272 tons.* This increase is more than accounted for by large additions to the steamers of the Empire, amounting during the seven years to no less than 1,967,334 tons, the total amount of steam tonnage being 6,377,337 tons, which, if we omit the coasting, river, and lake steamers of the United States of America (seeing that no competition exists between these steamers and those of other countries), is very nearly twice as great as the steam tonnage of all the rest of the world.

The drop in British tonnage, 1885 to 1888, had its counterpart in all the other maritime countries, except in regard to the coasting trade of the United States of America, the two German ports of Hamburg and Bremen, China and Japan, the tonnage of these countries having increased continuously, apparently not experiencing the glut in shipping reached everywhere else.

The great increase of foreign shipping in British ports from 1815 to 1860 has already been referred to. This will now be further illustrated. In 1840, whilst the navigation laws were in full force, the foreign entries in British ports were 31·25 % of the whole entries, leaving 68·75 for British vessels. In 1850, when Free Trade had just begun its course, the foreign entries amounted to 34·9 %, and after a further ten years, in 1860, to 43·65 %. Up to that year the United States had been one of our most serious competitors. In 1840 the proportion of vessels entering British ports flying the American flag as compared with the British was 15·89 %, and about the same in 1850; in 1860 it amounted to 21·43 %, or 31·35 % of the total foreign entries. From that period the proportion dropped to 5 % in 1870, 2·43 % in 1880, and ·54% in 1890, or practically *nil* for all competitive purposes.† At the same time foreign entries dropped

---

* The tons referred to in these returns are the registered tons—gross tonnage would largely add to this amount.

† As an illustration of this, in 1855 American vessels carried 76·6 per cent. of their foreign trade. In 1885 they carried less than 10 per cent., and in that year not a single American vessel left New York loaded with

from 43·65 in 1860 to 31·58 % in 1870 and 28·23 % in 1880. During the past five years it has been about 27 %, at which it seems stationary.

To take another view of British commerce, reference is now made to the shipping entries in the ports of the principal European countries and the United States. In all these countries the progress of British commerce is more than satisfactory; in Russia in Europe British shipping entries increased in the years between 1880 and 1893 (the last year of completed returns), from 40 % to 53·8 %; in Norway, from 11·8 % to 13 %; in Sweden, from 13·5 % to 20 %; in Germany, with slight fluctuations it has been 38%; in France, from 40 % to 46·7 %; in Italy, from 34·3 % to 44·8 %, and in the United States it has been fairly regular from 51 % to 52 %; in Holland, the same at about 50 %; Portugal is the only country in which there is a falling off in British shipping entries, viz.: from 63 % to 50 %. The foregoing items are sufficient to show the enormous preponderance of British shipping in the ports of the world, and there is little doubt but that in those countries from which the information received is slight and irregular, it would be found greater still.

Steam Tonnage.—When reference is made to the steamship commerce of the world, some curious facts are discovered. In ports of the United Kingdom the entries of British steamers stood at 1,800,000 tons in 1850; in 1893 they were 49,893,628 tons, an increase of more than 1,000,000 tons per annum. Foreign steamship entries in 1850 were 406,892 tons; in 1893, 13,776,504, or an average increase of 310,921 tons per annum. Although the increase in British steam tonnage entries is so much greater than that of foreign, the absolute percentage is slightly reduced from 81·5 % in 1850, or 88·5 % in 1870 (when it was highest) to 78 % in 1892 (when it was lowest), that year being the highest for foreign steam entries with 22 %. In 1893 the British steam entries were 49,893,628 tons, or 78·4 %, and foreign, 13,776,504 tons, with 21·6 per cent. In 1894 they were respectively 54,413,130 tons, or 78·7 %, and 14,745,515, or 21·3 %, the increase in the total steamship entries in the United Kingdom being no less than 5,488,513 tons in the year 1894.

In Russia the percentage of British steamship entries in 1893 was 58·6; in Holland, 51·8; in Portugal, 52; in the United States, 55·9; in Germany, 41·1; in Italy, 45; in Sweden, 26·3; and in Norway, 20·8; but when the actual tonnage is taken into consideration it will be found that more than one-half of the steam commerce of the world is under the British flag.

grain, although 1098 steamers and 93 sailing ships cleared from that port during the year, principally British.

The steam tonnage owned by the British Empire in 1880 was 2,949,282 registered tons; that of all other foreign nations, 1,263,930 (omitting American coasting and inland vessels, which are strictly protected); in 1893 it was 6,149,188 and 3,164,131 tons respectively. From this it will be seen that while the increase in foreign steam merchant navies has been 1,901,201 tons in the thirteen years, that of the British Empire has been 3,199,906 tons.

We now return for a moment to the total tonnage of the world, sail and steam combined. The total British tonnage in 1880 was 8,447,171, and in 1893 10,365,567. That of foreign countries from which we have regular returns, in 1880—again omitting the enrolled coasting fleet of the United States, but allowing the approximate tonnage of 1,000,000 tons for those countries giving no regular returns, judged from what is to be found in odd years—was 8,569,516, or slightly more than the British; in 1893 it was about 8,632,616, showing very little increase. Now whilst all other countries had increased their steam fleets more or less, the increase of actual tonnage in any of them was but small; in several there was an actual decrease. The most notable increase was in the tonnage of the German Empire, amounting to 340,533 tons, but still more notable is the increase in the steam fleets of Hamburg and Bremen—the former having 473,984 in 1894, more than five times the amount it possessed in 1880, very closely approaching the total steam tonnage owned by the French, which for several years has averaged 500,000 tons. Hamburg and Bremen possess 1,091,438 tons of shipping between them, or about one-twentieth of the whole world. These two cities are our severest competitors in the long steam routes of the world. Norway, Sweden, Denmark, China and Japan have gained, but in Italy, France, Austria-Hungary and the United States tonnage has declined—the latter most seriously, but her loss is compensated for by a large increase in her protected coasting trade. The tonnage of Greece has improved since 1880, and it may be presumed that of Russia also, at least of steam tonnage, to which she has lately added largely. The steam tonnage of China is very regularly increasing, but still more that of Japan, a wonderful country, as she of late has proved herself in her struggle with China.

From the foregoing figures we arrive at the conclusion that during the past fifteen years there has been added nearly 25 per cent. to British tonnage, whilst all the rest of the world has *collectively* been at a standstill.

Fluctuation in Shipbuilding.—So far then as the nominal amount of tonnage shows the progress of British shipping we ought as a nation to feel very proud of the position we occupy at the head of the world of commerce. As a shipbuilding nation our position is more remarkable still; in forty years the average annual additions to tonnage have more than trebled. In 1854 the amount of tonnage built was about a quarter of a million tons, whilst in that year the United States of America built over half a million tons, a higher limit than they have since reached. Since 1854 there have occurred four well-marked cycles in British shipbuilding; and singularly enough the same thing has occurred in America, but with increasingly different results. In 1864 we reached the first summit with 460,833 tons; a sudden drop occurred three years after to 305,979 tons. In that year also the United States reached its summit with 415,741 tons, dropping gradually year by year, until in 1872 it was only 209,052. The United Kingdom, on the other hand, went on increasing its output, until in 1874 it reached the second summit of 603,867 tons. In the same year America made also another spurt with 432,725 tons, and this increase was absorbed entirely by its coasting and inland trade. The over-sea trade had been ruined by the Civil War, and in the years succeeding the war she sold no less than 800,000 tons of her foreign-going ships to foreigners. In 1883 we reached another summit with 892,216 tons, and in 1889 another with 854,799 tons. In 1874 a great plethora of tonnage was created, and this was felt by the sudden drop in the output two years after to 378,020, not two-thirds of that of 1874. In 1883 the highest point was reached, and so great had been the effort and excitement that in two years it fell to only about one-third of the amount, showing that the output had been considerably overdone, and yet for the four years, 1889-92, there was added new tonnage to the amount of over 800,000 per annum. Where it all finds employment is one of the marvels of this age of iron and steam.

Gradual Decrease in Number of Ships since 1865.—There is another statistical view of shipping and tonnage which must not be overlooked. In the discussion of the foregoing figures, it must be remembered that tonnage alone has been dealt with; we must now refer to the number of ships in relation to tonnage, and we shall find this part of the discussion of more interest to sailors as affecting their employment, for this is regulated more by the number than the tonnage of the ships, especially as regards masters and officers.

Increase in Size of Ships and Decrease in Crews.—In 1815, at the close of the French and American wars, we possessed 21,869 ships, of 2,477,831 tons (of these about a dozen were small steamers), and 163,817 men, the average size of ship being 113 tons, and the average number of men 6·6 to every hundred tons. In the twenty following years this number absolutely decreased, and in 1835 we had only 20,300 ships of 2,360,303 tons, and 144,978 men, a reduction of 1569 ships, 117,528 tons, and 18,844 men; and the curious fact is also seen that the American shipping decreased in the same, if not greater proportion, whilst the shipping of the British plantations increased from 203,445 tons to 423,458 tons, or more than double. As Australia was still in its very infancy, this shows the great prosperity our North American colonies enjoyed on the accession of peace, which also made room for the 18,000 seamen we could not employ at home. In that period the average size of ship had increased to 116 tons, and the average number of men to every hundred tons was reduced to 6·2.*

In the next twenty years—1835 to 1855—we find an increase of 9648 ships and 1,989,031 tons (rather better than 80 per cent.), and 71,395 men, about 50 per cent. more than in 1835, which gives in 1855 29,948 ships of 4,349,334 tons, and 216,368 men. In this same period American shipping had quadrupled, and then stood nearly level with our own; that of our colonies had again more than doubled—now exceeding 900,000 tons. British ships averaged 145 tons, with 4·95 men to every hundred tons.

In 1865 the number of ships was 21,626, of 5,408,451 tons, and 197,643 men; which gives an average of 250 tons a ship, and 3·65 men for every hundred tons.

In 1875 there were 20,191 ships, of 5,891,692 tons, and 199,667 men, the ships averaging 292 tons, and the number of men 3·4 for every hundred tons.

In 1885 there were 18,791 ships, of 7,209,163 tons, and 198,781 men, the ships averaging 377 tons, and the number of men 2·75 per hundred tons.

* A very interesting statement is to be found in Lloyds' Annals, relative to the tonnage of the United Kingdom in 1830. It gives the number of ships and their tonnage, classified as under:—

50 tons and under	.	.	6452	vessels
50 ,, to 100 tons	.	.	5212	,,
100 ,, to 300 ,,	.	.	5890	,,
300 ,, to 500 ,,	.	.	1298	,,
500 ,, to 800 ,,	.	.	110	,,
800 ,, to 1000 ,,	.	.	15	,,
1200 ,, and upwards	.	.	43	,,
Total	.	.	19,110	

As this total is only a trifle under the Government returns, it may be taken as correct. The 43 ships of 1200 tons and upwards may be taken, with few exceptions, if any, as belonging to, or chartered by, the East India Company.

In 1894 there were 16,547 ships, of 8,716,285 tons, and about 224,000 men, of whom 26,175 were Lascars; which gives the average size of ship at 527 tons nearly, and 2·56 men per hundred tons.

The foregoing statistics and the averages calculated from them refer to net register tonnage of the total number of British ships, including coasting and home trade vessels.

Another view may now be taken, in which the foreign-going ships and those partly engaged in the foreign trade may be considered to represent the number of vessels requiring certificated masters and officers. In 1849 there were 8611 of these ships, of which 8509 were sailing vessels and 102 were steamers. The ships averaged 273 tons, with 4·5 men to every 100 tons. The steamers averaged 531 tons, with 7·38 men to every 100 tons.

In 1865 the foreign-going ships, &c., had increased to 9914, of which 9047 were sailing ships and 497 steamers. The sailing ships averaged 432 tons, with 3 men to every 100 tons; and the steamers 653 tons, with 5·4 men to every 100 tons.

In 1894 our foreign and partly foreign-going ships had decreased to 6030, of which 2091 were sailing vessels and 3939 were steamers. The sailing ships averaged 1109 tons, with 1·7 men nearly to every 100 tons; and the steamers 1,400 tons, with 2·25 men to every 100 tons.

If we take the foreign-going ships alone, we shall have sailing ships, averaging nearly 1,240 tons, with 1·6 men to every 100 tons, and steamers 1,462 tons, with 2.24 men to every 100 tons.*

It will be evident from the foregoing figures that one of the most remarkable features is the increase of the size of the vessels since 1865, the ships now averaging three times the size they did at that time. On the other side we have a decrease of fully 39 % in the number of ships, and so employing an equivalently less number of masters and officers. No wonder the masters have felt the severity of the times as compared with a generation back. The striking increase in the generation before gave employment to masters and officers as fast as they could be bred ; but now the reverse is the case. In the past thirty years more than 100 masters have been thrown out of employment every year in consequence of the reduction in the number of vessels; this more especially applies to the masters of sailing vessels, who are 7823 fewer than they were in 1865, so that an average of 260 must

---

* The average number of hands in steamers includes the crews of the large passenger steamers with their numerous stewards and servants, all of whom count. As a fact there are many cargo steamers sailing on long voyages with less than *one man* for every 100 tons gross, seamen and engineers all told.

have lost employment every year. The effect of this will be referred to later on.

Large Vessels in 1850 and 1884.—Although the means of employment have decreased so largely, the responsibility of masters has largely increased, In 1850 there was not a vessel on the register of 2000 tons. In 1884 there were afloat or building 138 vessels of over 4000 tons; one, the *Great Eastern* (now no more, having been broken up), of 18,915 tons; the *City of Rome* 8141 tons; the *Etruria* and *Umbria*, 7718 tons; the *Servia*, *Oregon* (since lost) and *Aurania*, each over 7000 tons; 31 over 5000 tons, &c.

Shipbuilding in 1895.—The shipbuilding returns for 1895, compiled by *Lloyds' Register*, show that the total output from the shipyards of the United Kingdom during the year was 638 vessels, of 1,099,078 tons, consisting of the following classes:—

Merchant and other vessels, steam	526.	904,991	gross.
sail	53	45,976	,,
Warships, steam—			
At Government yards	8	70,370	D.S.
At private yards	51	77,741	
Total	638	1,099,078	tons.

The output of the year in the United Kingdom is less than that of 1894 by over 95,000 tons, but the proportion of steam tonnage to the total launched has been much higher. In 1892, sailing tonnage formed no less than 24 % of the output; in 1893, 14 %; in 1894, 8 %; and in 1895 it has formed less than 5 %. The warship tonnage launched in 1895 has exceeded that launched in 1894 by upwards of 115,000 tons displacement. If these figures be included in the comparison, the output of 1895 has exceeded that of 1894 by 20,000 tons. The increase of the merchant tonnage of the United Kingdom, after accounting for purchases and sales abroad and losses by wreck, is 129,000 tons, produced by an increase of steam tonnage, and a decrease of sailing tonnage of 108,000. The net increase of the United Kingdom, compared with the total output of new tonnage, is unusually small, and this is accounted for by the larger number of sales and of building orders from abroad.

Comparison of the largest Steamers in existence.—The largest steamers which have been launched in the United Kingdom during 1895 are the following:—

Georgic	10,077	gross tonnage.
Armenian	8,765	,,
Cestrian	8,765	,,
Victorian	8,677	,,
American	8,196	,,

The largest sailing vessel is the *Iranian*, 2958 tons gross. In the United States of America the s.s. *St. Paul* and *St. Louis*, of 11,629 tons, have been launched, but no other steamer over 6500 tons is included in the returns from abroad. Germany has launched the five-masted barque, *Potosi*, 4027 tons; and France the four-masted barque, *Wulfrau Puget*, 3062 tons. The total output for the world of merchant tonnage is computed at 1,218,000 tons, and deducting losses, &c., the net increase is 518,000 tons, produced by the growth of steam tonnage, overbalancing a net reduction of 306,000 tons of sailing vessels.

According to *Lloyds' Register* for 1895-6, the United Kingdom possessed 114 steamers of 5000 tons and over; Germany, 12; Spain, 4; Russia, 3; Holland and Belgium, 3; France, 1; and America, 2, to which she has added 2 more. Of steamships over 8000 tons, the United Kingdom possesses 16; America, 4; Germany, 2; and France, 1. The two largest steamships now afloat are the Cunard steamers, *Lucania* and *Campania*, of 12,950 tons each, and the Americans have the two next, the *St. Louis* and the *St. Paul*, of 11,629 tons each. The American steamers, *New York* and *Paris*, transferred from the British register, are of 10,508 tons. Then come the White Star British steamers, *Teutonic* and *Majestic*, of 9984 and 9965 tons respectively. These vessels are all twin screws, and have a speed of 20 knots or over, but the *Lucania* and *Campania* broke the record with voyages completed at 21 knots and over.

North German Lloyd's new Steamers.—The North German Lloyd is generally supposed to be taking a leap in the dark by entrusting the construction of their new 22-knotter to a firm which previously has built nothing bigger than torpedo boats. A demand for high speed and a desire to foster home industries have, no doubt, prompted the company to fix on Elbing for the building of a ship which is to put the Cunard and White Star Lines in the shade.

Increased Competition in Building in Foreign Countries. —This is mentioned to show the gradually increasing competition of foreigners in the building of large steamers, for which they have hitherto been dependent mainly on British shipbuilders, and it does not require much argument to show that as more and more capital is invested in tools and plant in foreign countries, and the cost of production more equalised, the greater will that competition become, and the less able shall we, as a country, be to maintain our present superiority in tonnage and our position as the carriers of the world.

Causes of British success.—It has been said that you can make figures prove anything, but it requires no unreasonable stretch in this case to show that our position in the over-sea carrying trades of the world is a very proud one.

The out-and out free trader still imagines that free trade has done all this for us (and, strange to say, when we remember the opposition free trade received at his hands forty years ago, our shipowner has become in many, if not all, cases our most out-and-out free trader); but, in following our history, other circumstances seem to have had quite as powerful an influence in placing us in our present position as free trade itself—in fact, these have become so intimately woven together with it that it is difficult to separate them. The American War occurred almost simultaneously with the transition from sail to steam, and from wood to iron in the construction of ships. As long as we were confined to timber for their construction, America and the Baltic countries could beat us; but when our Watt, our Symington, and our Napier had shown us the road to steam power, and our Trevethick, our Dickenson, and our Laird had demonstrated the possibility of using iron as a material for our hulls, we began a race which, aided by a plentiful store of cheap iron, coal, and labour, ended in more than victory, and must have done so, all other circumstances notwithstanding.

The American War, ending in the destruction of America's fine fleets of wooden vessels, accentuated the position, but did not create it; and free trade did not do much for us, except open a door for unlimited competition, prior to that war. One thing we know—America had tried to compete with us for the steam trade between the two countries and signally failed. Again, America's protective policy, produced by the determination to foster her internal resources, caused her refusal to purchase the ships and steamers we could have supplied her with so cheaply, and left the field still more open to us.

May we not conclude then that our remarkable facilities for the production of cheap steamers and ships of the modern type have done more for us than all the other fortuitous circumstances put together, and as long as we can maintain this cheapness of production the pre-eminence must remain with us, and our position as the great carriers of the world be secure? Were it not for the intense fluctuations caused by over-production on the one hand, and ruinous depression on the other, British shipping would be a secure and valuable property.

Speculation.—The slightest lift in freights seems to create a speculation in shipbuilding, and a corresponding increase in tonnage, which is thoroughly unwarranted by the real necessities of trade, however much it may be by a desire to conduct it economically. The progress of science, and in the arts of shipbuilding and engineering, have made such wonderful strides not only in economy of construction, but also in the cost of working steamers, that the new vessels are completely superseding the older, and can really make a fair living at freights, which it is beyond the power of the older vessels to do. Hence the desire to build vessels of the newer type beyond the actual tonnage wants of the day.

Improvement in Economy of Engines.—Of vessels with the old-fashioned direct acting engines, burning at the rate of three to four pounds of coal per indicated horse power per hour, very few are left. The highest steam pressure employed in these seldom exceeded 30 pounds per square inch.

When we consider that the compound engine was only introduced into commercial steamers generally about 1870, it follows that the whole commercial steam fleets of the world have been revolutionised within the past twenty-five years. First, by compound two-cylinder engines with pressures ranging from 60 to 90 pounds, replacing the old direct expansion engines, which in their turn are being fast superseded by triple and quadruple cylinder expansion engines with pressures ranging from 140 to 180 pounds. The most favoured ones at present being triple expansion cylinders on three cranks with about 160 to 200 pounds pressure. There is no doubt but that the three cranked engine can give many points to the two cranked engine, and that the only improvement in using higher pressures as far as the cylinders are concerned, will be attained by placing three small high pressure cylinders over the present three cranked engines, which has been done in a few instances.

We have now to add the system of forced draught, with or without superheated air, as a further economiser. By this means the boiler power is said to be obtained with little more than half the firegrate and heating surface otherwise necessary, and the saving of room is so great that owners can afford to give up the 32 per cent. reduction from the gross for net register tonnage, and be content with the allowance of the actual engine and boiler space occupied, plus (in the case of screw steamers) three-fourths of that space, according to the Shipping Acts.

Every improvement makes a percentage of improved profit in the owner's favour, and the rate at which cargoes can now be moved about the world is astonishing to us of the older *régime*. A ton weight of cargo can be taken to or from Bombay, in a modern cargo steamer, at a cost of less than five shillings per ton for fuel, crew, and stores, at the average cost of fuel, wages, and victualling on such a voyage.

Principal Sources of Foreign Opposition in Shipping.— In considering our present position we must not overlook the foreign competition which some of our friends look upon with so much dread. Referring to the statistics it does not seem as if we had much to fear, tonnage alone considered.

Take the German Empire, usually thought to be one of our most prominent opponents, and we do not find that its tonnage has increased so very largely in the past fourteen years, as that increase has only been 340,533 tons, as compared with the United Kingdom's increase of 2,381,668 tons in the same period. What we do find is that the German ports of Hamburg and Bremen have increased their fleets by 636,950 tons, whilst the other ports of the Empire have lost proportionately.

The greatest opposition then we have to encounter from the Germans is in the increase of the fleets of mail steamers running across the Atlantic and to the Eastern seas from these two German ports, which steamers, principally, and until of late years, built in the United Kingdom, compare very favourably with our own.

The steady stream of emigration from Germany to the United States, and elsewhere, accounts in great measure for the production of these fleets, and it would have been more than human if such a country as Germany had neglected such an opportunity, and permitted their people to be dependent upon British lines of transit in their exodus from the Fatherland, as they formerly, to a great extent, were.

In the same way and upon the same lines we have opposition by the French, but this is not an increasing quantum, although largely bounty-fed.

Russia also runs its lines of steamers to the East *viâ* the Suez Canal, but they can scarcely be called competitors, as they are entirely the creation of the State, and would not live for a year if left simply to commercial resources.

The Italians also have made desperate efforts to maintain oversea trades, but, if we may judge from the persistent decrease in Italian tonnage, with very poor results.

Then again we hear of Norwegian and other Northern opposition. We are told that our timber trade has fallen into their hands, and, perhaps, the rough timber trade did for a time, when they purchased our used-up fleet of timber ships—legislated out of our hands by our prudent precautions against loss of life, which had become serious in these fleets. But what proof have we that this opposition is very serious after all? Norwegian tonnage in 1894 was only some 270,000 tons in excess of what it was in 1875, and we have also this fact apparent, that a great portion of the timber which used to be sawn in this country is now sawn, and to a certain extent worked, where it is grown, into such portable stuff that it is brought to this country in steamers mainly our own. Our saw-millers and joiners have suffered from this change more than our shipowners.

There is one branch in which the Norwegians have succeeded in great measure in supplanting us, and that is in the trade between the United States and the West Indies, where at one time a goodly number of British steamers were employed; and one reason given for this success is the fact that the Norwegian crews are more docile, and stick better to their ships when employed so far from home than the British, and being more thrifty are able to save more money to take back to their own homes out of less wages! Certain it is that at the end of 1889 there were about 30 steamers belonging to Norway so employed, and since that time many others have been built in this country for Bergen owners for the same trade.

All things considered there is not much reason to complain. The bulk of the carrying trade of the world is still in our hands, and we are far more indebted to our constant periods of over-building than to outside opposition for our periodical measures of unsuccessful trading. All the world's trade is not ours, and we cannot expect that it should be.

PART II.

THE PERSONNEL OF THE MERCANTILE MARINE.

CHAPTER I.

SHIPOWNERS.

CONTENTS.—Shipowners—Tenure of shipping property—Sixty-fourths—Different kinds of companies—Limited Liability Acts—Mr. Thomas Gray's opinion of them—Reasons for adoption by ship managers.

HAVING dealt with the general history of the Mercantile Marine, a description of the persons connected with it, their position, duty, and powers, will appropriately follow.

The **Personnel** may be divided into two principal classes: the one being the owners of ships, and the other those who navigate them, who are usually termed **Mariners**.

Shipowners.—The shipowner is one who invests his capital in ships with a view to profit, whether he has any knowledge—that is, technical knowledge—of ships or not, or of the business connected with their management. There are two modes recognised by law by which such investments may be attained; either by investing in shares in vessels managed by private individuals, or by investing in a joint-stock company holding property in, or in owning, ships.

Tenure of Shipping Property; sixty-fourths.—The former mode of holding individual property in ships has been rigidly regulated by law. For the purpose of defining or registering such property a ship is divided into 64 parts or shares. If a ship belong to one individual, he is registered as the owner of 64-64th shares; but if there be a number of co-owners, each is registered as the owner of so many 64ths, according to the value of the interest held. Until 1880 there could not have been more than 32 persons registered as owners in any one ship, but in that year the number was extended to 64. For the encouragement of small investors, a number of persons, not exceeding five, may be registered as joint owners of a 64th share, but such joint owners are deemed one person, and the property must be dealt with as a whole, and not in severalty (57 & 58 Vict., cap. 60, sec. 5).

The power to hold such 64th shares is strictly confined to British subjects, or to foreigners who have been duly naturalised according to law, and shall have taken an oath of allegiance to the British Crown and Constitution. Either must reside within the British dominions, or be a partner in a firm carrying on business within them; for instance, an Englishman resident in Paris, with no business in the British dominions, cannot own a British ship under this law (57 & 58 Vict., cap. 60, sec. 1).

The responsibility of the management of ships so registered rests upon the combined owners, but for convenience it has been the practice for them to appoint one of their number as **managing owner**, or ship's husband, who can only be displaced by the vote of a majority of 64th shareholders, by whomsoever held. The managing owner must be registered at the registry office in which the ship is registered, and he is, in law, held responsible for all acts of management. If one of the co-owners be not appointed, then some other person must be registered as manager, and he will be subject to the same liabilities as if he were the managing owner. If this is not done, the co-owners are liable in proportion to their interest in the ship to a fine, not exceeding in the whole, of one hundred pounds each time the ship leaves any port in the United Kingdom (57 & 58 Vict., cap. 60, sec. 59).

Under this tenure a shipowner's liability is *not limited*, but the managing owner remains, to a certain extent, under the control of his co-owners, and he can only contract debt on their behalf to the extent of necessary repairs, or the outfit necessary for a proposed voyage. He cannot perform any work upon the ship which may be held to be a new construction, alteration, or addition, without the several consent of the registered owners. Moreover, he cannot deal with the property of a minority of co-owners against their consent. For instance, if he proposes to send the vessel upon a voyage of which they disapprove, the court may be instanced to compel him to find security against loss on such a voyage.

Different kinds of Companies.—On the other hand, "a corporation" (such as a joint-stock company) "may be registered as owner by its corporate name" (57 and 58 Vict., cap. 60, sec. 5 [v]); but an officer of the company must be authorised, under the common seal of the company or corporation, to perform the registration and all other acts required by the Merchant Shipping Act.

In connection with shipping, bodies corporate may be included under two general heads, viz. :

First, those companies which are incorporated, and hold their rights and privileges under Royal charters, or by special Acts of Parliament.

Second, those companies which are incorporated under the Joint Stock Companies Act of 1837, or the Joint-Stock Companies Act of 1862, &c., commonly called the Limited Liability Acts.

Instances of the first date back to the sixteenth century, and are exemplified in the charters granted to the Russian, Levant, East India, Hudson's Bay, and other trading Companies which carried on the greater part of the British foreign trade for over two centuries. All these have passed out of existence as trading companies except the Hudson's Bay Company, which still owns a few ships. They have been succeeded by the great chartered Steam Ship Companies of modern days, many of which have become enormous establishments, owning splendid fleets of immense tonnage, such as the Peninsular and Oriental Company, the Royal Mail, the Pacific Steam Navigation Company, and others.

Of the second there are many gradations, ranging from fleets as large and important as those of the Chartered Companies, as, for example, the Cunard S. S. Co., (Ld.), (formerly a private company), the British India S. N. Co. (Ld.), the Union Steamship Co., &c., down to single ship companies of all sizes.

Limited Liability Acts.—Under the Joint-Stock Companies Act 1862, &c., a company may be limited or unlimited, but there is no restriction as to the nationality of the shareholders, and the company may consist for the most part, if not entirely, of foreigners. Any person may form a British company, and hold British ships as the property of the said company, bounded only by the restriction that the office of the company must be within the British dominions.

Some Single-ship Joint-Stock Companies are carried on under the unlimited powers of the Acts, these having been formed for the express purpose of the admission of foreign shareholders. By far the greater number, however, are enrolled under the limited liability principle, and these are largely increasing, as they afford the best field for speculative ship managers.

It is very doubtful whether the Limited Liability Acts were originally intended to apply to individual ships, and it appears that about fourteen years elapsed after the passing of these Acts before they were so applied; and, seemingly, the vast changes in ship-owning and management brought about by it were not contemplated by the legislature, or intended in any sense to override the old method of holding ships in sixty-fourths.

Mr. Thomas Gray's opinion on the Limited Liability Acts.—Mr. Thomas Gray, the Assistant Secretary of the Marine Department of the Board of Trade, gave some remarkable evidence of what he deemed the evils of the system, and the reckless speculation and mismanagement to which it gave rise. He attributed the invention to one of the largest shipowners of Liverpool, who adopted the system with a view to escape the legal liability of one ship belonging to a shipowner being seized to answer for the default, by damage or otherwise, caused by another ship belonging to the same owner. Each individual ship belonging to a separate Company, although under the same actual management, could not be so attacked; and so by separating the interests involved the shipowner escaped this liability.

Reasons for Adoption by Ship-managers.—The possibility of owning ships in this manner attracted the attention of the speculative ship-manager, and it was soon brought into use, as it afforded a much larger distribution of shares—to him a £10 shareholder was as good as a £1000 one, as long as he could get enough of them.

The reasons for a ship-manager preferring to form a company even for the holding of a single ship are obvious:

First, a speculative investor is much more easily induced to take a share or shares when liability is limited to the sum mentioned.

A *second* reason is, that a foreigner may be a shareholder in a company, and advantage has been largely taken of this loophole by the modern ship-manager to strengthen his own particular connection in foreign countries.

A *third* is, that the ship-manager, who wishes to possess undivided or autocratic power, can so manipulate the Articles of Association that he obtains the indefeasible right to manage the ship just as he pleases, and very possibly succeeds in placing himself above all responsibility to his shareholders, except the paying of such dividends as may accrue, and sometimes even so far as to prevent the shareholder withdrawing his capital out of the company for ever.

The result of the law as it stands is, that it lands us in the curiously anomalous position of having two exceedingly diverse modes of holding property in ships called British; by the one it rigidly restricts ownership to British subjects, and, by the other it throws it open to the world. Each system has its advocates, but probably in a few years the private shipowner will be a thing of the past—the company system will have obliterated him.

The management of ship companies under limited liability is

so generally lucrative without entailing personal responsibility, that it is not to be wondered at that so many have entered upon it, and thereby created a competition which has proved well-nigh fatal and forced freights down to such a low ebb as to make it almost impossible to provide for the due depreciation of shipping property, which takes place rapidly, and the consequent loss of capital.

CHAPTER II.

THE MARINERS, OR THE EMPLOYED.

CONTENTS.—The Mariners—Master Mariner—The Mates—Their qualifications—Petty Officers, &c.—Able Seamen—Apprentices—Engineers and Firemen—Cooks, Stewards, &c.

The Mariners.—The terms mariners, sailors, or seamen, have been indifferently applied to those who make up the navigating crew of a ship; but by way of distinction the term "seaman" has been used as meaning more than mariner or sailor and as signifying a "*skilful* or *experienced* mariner."

Master Mariner.—The head or chief mariner in each ship is termed the master mariner, and, in law, he holds a special place as distinguished from all the others. By courtesy, when addressed he is styled "Captain," but legally, the "Master." He must be an experienced seaman and navigator, appointed by the owner to take charge of and navigate his vessel, and to perform all the duties required for its profitable employment, conduct, and safety. The law gives him almost unlimited power and authority over the crew, and at the same time places upon him many responsibilities, with regard to his ship and them. He must be 21 years of age, and have served six years at sea, one of which must have been passed as a mate in charge of a watch, and in possession of a first mate's certificate; he must also have passed an examination by the Board of Trade and obtained a Certificate as an Ordinary, or Extra, Master, to qualify him for an appointment as Master by the owner of any foreign-going vessel under the British Flag.

In the Home Trade the Master does not require a certificate unless the vessel is licensed to carry passengers, in which case the master must possess a Home Trade certificate, unless he possesses a foreign-going one. If an officer proceeds to sea as master without a certificate of the rank in which he is employed, both he and the owner are liable to forfeit £50 (57 & 58 Vict. c. 60, s. 92 [2]).

The Mates.—Their Qualifications.—The first mate is the next officer in command; he must be at least nineteen years of age, and have served five years at sea, one of which must have been as second mate, or as a junior mate in charge of a watch, in possession of a second mate's certificate, for twelve months at sea.

The **second mate** ranks next, and must be seventeen years of age, and have served four years at sea, as an apprentice or before the mast as a seaman, and produce certificates from his employers for good conduct and sobriety, especial stress being laid upon the latter. Since the increase of steam shipping the regulations require that at least one year of the four must have been passed in a square rigged sailing ship,* if the future service is to be in sailing vessels.

The law has nothing to say to a sailor in respect of the manner of his education; this is left entirely to individual effort; but a certificate applies to sailing vessels as well as steamers, and therefore a certain amount of sailing ship experience is required. There are, however, exceptional certificates applying to steamers only, for those who have had no sailing ship experience, and wish to apply for them, which we believe is rarely the case.

The number of mates carried in any ship is dependent upon the will of the owner. The law would perhaps insist upon one only; for, although, by the granting of two classes of certificates (first and second) two are contemplated,† yet this is not compulsory. A ship of any size may therefore proceed to sea with only a certificated master, and a single mate, and there are many instances in which sailing vessels and steamers do so.

In the better class of vessels, especially steamers, as many as four, five, or even six mates are carried, and in that case the first and second mates must possess certificates of competency as such. Practically in all the mail lines these officers are required to have masters' certificates, and the third, &c., certificates as chief or second officers. It is not the custom for these vessels to carry apprentices; they are dependent upon those trained in sailing ships for their officers.

Petty Officers, &c.—In these liners there are to be found, in addition to the mates, a number of petty officers, such as the **boatswain** and **his mates, carpenters** and **sailmakers**; besides these the active part of the crew consists of **quartermasters** (experienced seamen whose chief duty is to steer, &c.), **able seamen, ordinary seamen** and **boys**.

As very few of our modern sailing ships are engaged in passenger trades their crews usually consist of the master, two, and

---

* See *Board of Trade Regulations* for the examination of Masters and Mates, &c.

† See *Merchant Shipping Act*, 1894, sec. 92.

occasionally three, mates, a carpenter and sailmaker, able and ordinary seamen, and sometimes apprentices and boys.

All these petty officers, seamen, &c., are shipped by the master in their several capacities upon such evidence of their knowledge and experience as he is able to obtain from their previous discharges and otherwise. In the eye of the law they are all simply seamen.

Able Seamen.—An able seaman, to *entitle* him to that rating, should be able to hand (that is, to take in and secure) the sails and reef them, and steer; also to be able to take accurate soundings with the hand and deep sea leads, &c., and to perform all the handicraft work connected with the ship's standing and running rigging, sails, &c. As such duties cannot be performed without previous experience, the Merchant Shipping Act of 1894 enacts that "a seaman shall not be *entitled* to the rating of A.B. unless he has served at sea for four years before the mast," with conditions as to where those four years have been served, and the Registrar-General of Seamen is to grant a certificate when required to that effect, stating how and where the service has been performed, and the nature of it. This clause has been in existence since 1880, but not being compulsory it has become a dead letter.

Apprentices.—Apprentices to the sea service are still duly provided for by law, which regulates the indenture, and a register of them is kept in the office of the Registrar-General of Shipping, &c., but it has not been compulsory upon shipowners or masters to employ them since the Navigation Laws were repealed. The consequence is that the number of apprentices enrolled annually since 1850 has largely diminished, and it now stands at about 2100 to 2200, which has been the average number enrolled for the past six years.*

Prior to 1850 the Navigation Laws regulated the number of seamen carried in every British vessel, but since that time it has been left entirely with the owner to say what number shall be carried, with only this one restriction, that it shall be stated on the articles what number is to be carried upon the voyage about to be entered upon, and that number must be maintained as a minimum during the voyage.

Engineers and Firemen.—Besides the navigating crew of seamen we have in steam-ships a very different body of hands, viz., the engineers, and firemen, or stokers, whose duty is to attend to the machinery and boilers.

Up to the year 1862 the position of the engineers was simply that of an ordinary member of the crew, similar to that of any

---

* See Appendix D.

other tradesman—*e.g.*, a carpenter or a sailmaker—and their appointment and position was entirely dependent upon the will of the owner, who alone was the judge of their qualification for the work required of them. Their present position is that of engineer officers who, having passed a Board of Trade examination, form a body from whom shipowners must select them for employment. In the disciplinary clauses of the Consolidated Shipping Act of 1894 their position as officers has been for the first time duly recognised.

Stokers and coal trimmers are for the most part bred from shore labourers who must be grown men, the work being unfitted for boys, or very young men. Their ranks are frequently recruited from the able seaman class, who are attracted by the higher wages usually paid to stokers.

Cooks, Stewards, &c.—In addition to these, the working members of the crew, there are numbers of men employed in passenger vessels as stewards and cooks, butchers and bakers, who all count as seamen in making up the gross number on board British ships.

CHAPTER III.

THE DUTIES OF THE PERSONNEL.

CONTENTS.—Early years of commerce—Duty of the shipowner—Master and owner—Effect of rapid communication on master's position—Master's duties—Limitations—Duties of the mates—Relation between masters and officers—Relation between owners and seamen—Result of the abandonment of compulsory apprenticeships—Engines and engine-room crews—Necessity of true discipline.

Early Years of Commerce.—In the early years of British commerce, we find that merchant adventurers equipped their own vessels, and frequently sailed as the masters of them, but as trade grew and its field was more extended by the usual law of the division of labour, it became the custom for the merchant and shipowner to sit at home and entrust the navigation of the vessel and the transaction of business in foreign parts to professional master mariners.

By-and-by the business of the merchant and shipowner were also, to a great extent, separated, and a race of shipowners, who made shipowning their principal, if not sole, business, sprang into existence, and they became the carriers for the merchants over the great water-ways of the world. Many of them were practical shipbuilders or old masters, who understood and supervised the construction of their vessels, and were fully conversant with all their details.

Prior to this century the profits on successful voyages were large, but the dangers of navigation were great; besides the ordinary risk of sea and weather, unknown seas and unsurveyed shores caused frequent losses, which pressed heavily on the fortunes of the shipowner when they occurred, and too often he found himself in like case to the Merchant of Venice, when

> From Tripolis, from Mexico and England,
> From Lisbon, Barbary and India,
> Not one vessel 'scaped the dreadful touch
> Of merchant marring rocks!

Is it not a wonder that men could be found to brave such risks?

But for the love and spirit of adventure, which often reigns supreme in the bosom of mankind, they would not have been. In no race have these qualities existed to a greater extent than in the Anglo-Saxon and his congeners, teaching them to toss aside with light hearts the danger of adventure and the risk of loss, as unconsidered trifles, in comparison with the greater gain and happiness of success.

The practice of Marine insurance, co-eval almost with commerce itself, has, fortunately for the shipowner, enabled him to minimise his risks, but at the sacrifice of some portion of his profit which he imparts to the insurer, who thereby pledges his capital to the shipowner in proportion to the amount of risk undertaken.

Duty of the Shipowner.—The first duty of the shipowner is so to employ his ship that she may return a fair profit to himself and co-owners in proportion to the risk run; and his next is to see that she is staunch and tight, properly fitted and well found for the proposed voyage, and sufficiently manned.

The law formerly interfered very little with the sufficiency of the vessel, this having been left pretty much to his own discretion, and, as a duty to himself and his co-owners which he was not likely to neglect; but there are others interested in this sufficiency —on the one side the insurer, on the other the crew and passengers, if any. For his own sake then the insurer keeps or establishes a surveillance on the ship, and rates his premiums according to her age and condition. Hence the establishment of such bodies as Lloyd's Register of Shipping and others, whose duty it is to survey the vessel at convenient periods, and report to their employers, the underwriters or insurers. Such surveys are a matter of arrangement between the parties, and are not in any way compulsory. If the shipowner does not wish his ship insured, he need not have her surveyed. If he does not, the underwriter will not insure, or, if he does, it will be at an excessive premium for a more than ordinary risk, unless, perhaps, the character of the shipowner as a careful man is well established.

Now, these surveys are also a guarantee of the soundness of the ship to the crew who are to sail in her, as well as the passengers and shippers of goods. The crew could probably judge for themselves of the vessel's upper works, rigging, &c., but of hidden defects or soundness of the hull they cannot judge, and for these they trust the professional surveyor.

Master and Owner.—The owner's next duty is to select the most experienced and trustworthy master he can find to take charge of his ship. The master, once appointed, becomes the trusted agent and coadjutor of the owner, who should fully instruct him as to the conduct of the ship's business, and it is the master's duty to obey these instructions to the letter. When out of the owner's reach and sight, he becomes his *alter ego*, and, failing instruction, must act upon his own responsibility, and as experience may teach him to be for the best welfare of the property and people under his control; and he is bound to do honourably whatever he thinks his owner would himself do were he present, always remembering to act within the law, which places upon him the responsibility of the safe conduct and navigation of the vessel.

Effect of Rapid Communication on Master's Position.— Up to the middle of this century, and before the quick transit of correspondence by mail and telegraph, the owner at home knew very little as to what his ship, on an eastern or other long voyage, was doing until her return home. In the foreign port the ship's business was entirely under the master's control; the agents presented to him such freights or passengers as were forthcoming, but the final aye or nay, as to rates of freights and passage money, rested with him. Such a state of matters demanded the utmost confidence between the shipowner and the master, and all law regulating their proceedings was based upon these confidential relations.

But the last fifty years have made vast changes in such relations. The speed with which messages are now flashed around the world enables the owner to conduct his business almost from his own office-chair, and has rendered the necessity for the master's interference in the general business of the ship and her freightage gradually less and less. This has correspondingly changed the master's position and reduced his power as well as his responsibility, transferring it to the agents in foreign ports, with whom the owner can be, if necessary, in daily communication. Seeing that this is the case there ought always to be a clear understanding between the owner and the master as to the power to be placed in the agent's hands in the transaction of ship's business, chartering, &c., and equivalent responsibility withdrawn or attached. The want of such an understanding leads to frequent difficulties. Not having been instructed to the contrary by his employer, the master naturally thinks that the power and responsibility remain with himself, and, legally, he is right. If the owner authorises an agent in a proper and sufficient manner, the master must obey him as if he were the owner himself at that port; but, on the other hand, it is only right that the master should be acquainted with the authorisation and its sufficiency. This done, the master is relieved of the responsibility. In such a position there is often a lingering feeling in the master's mind that he is still required to see that even the agent is acting fairly and honestly for the good of the ship, in the fear that, if things do not turn out well, he may be blamed for it. It is not so, but that, the owner having appointed the agent, the responsibility as to the agent's good faith rests entirely with himself, and he has then no right whatever to throw responsibility for any failure which transpires upon the master.

Again, with regard to the care and stowage of cargoes, heavy responsibility rests upon the master. As long as the reception of cargo and its stowage is in the hands of the officers and crew this is very properly so; but cargoes are now more frequently stowed by stevedores and their gangs. When these are employed by the owner, or the captain on his behalf, the responsibility remains; but how often is it that we see the owner handing, by his charter, the stowage of the cargo to the charterer and his stevedores, who rush the cargo into the ship and stow it in such a manner as it would be next to impossible for the master to control.

Master's Duties—Limitations.—The master being appointed, his first duty is to make himself acquainted with the state of the ship and her outfit, and to see that it is in every respect seaworthy. If he finds that this is not the case in any respect, it is his duty to report the same to the owner or ship's husband with the view of having it rectified. If it is not then done, and he takes the ship to sea with any known defect, he is in law held responsible. It will not do for him to attempt to shift the responsibility upon the owner, on the plea that the owner would not sanction or neglected the necessary repair. He has no right to risk the lives of the crew, or the safety of the vessel, under such conditions. The shirking of responsibility in such matters has cost many a master his certificate—the records of the Courts of Inquiry will afford ample proof of this. Neither will it do for him to shelter himself under the plea, that he will offend the owner and perhaps be dismissed. The owner has no right to demand, or the master to perform, an act which he knows to be fraught with danger to the ship or the lives of those on board. Irresponsible masters have gone a long way to make what Mr. Plimsoll has called "the greedy bad owner." An owner who is worth any consideration would rather retain a master who knows his responsibility, and has the courage of his opinions as well as the ability to state them candidly, than dismiss him on such a plea. A master is bound to respect and obey his owner's wishes or commands *within the limit* of the law, but not *beyond*: he has responsibilities to others besides his owner.

He must remember that he is also the Agent of the owners of the cargo placed on board his ship for safe transit from place to place, and that in case of accident by stranding, collision, or otherwise, he is bound to protect all the interests involved without distinction. For the assistance of shipmasters in distress of any kind the underwriters of Lloyds appoint Agents all over the world in all the principal ports, to whom the master may apply for assistance and advice, and masters are advised by Lloyds' Committee to take advantage of their assistance. On the other hand, the masters must not give up the power of action into the hands of Lloyds' Agents, and thereby think they are divesting themselves of responsibility. What they should do is this—as it is supposed that Lloyds' Agents are better acquainted with the port and its facilities—the power of performing repairs and its cost — the master should apply for all the assistance which can be afforded by such knowledge, but keep the power of determining the best and cheapest mode of carrying out such repairs, guided by his own experience, in his own hands. Failing to do this many a Master has been run into expenses oftentimes unreasonable and probably unnecessary for which owners or underwriters have to pay.

At sea the duty appertaining to the master is the safe navigation of his ship and the governance of the crew; and his chief concern should be to see that the duties of each and all are so carefully carried on that the voyage may be performed with all due speed and safety. To this end he must see that the officer in charge of the deck keeps a sufficient look out and is never absent from his post unless relieved by himself or another officer; that every precaution is taken against danger to the safety of the vessel, or the lives of his crew and passengers; that the boats are properly fitted with everything ready in them for lowering in case of accident; that all the sanitary arrangements are complete, and cleanliness preserved in every part of the ship. Many of these things are now regulated by authority of Parliament, and the master should make himself fully acquainted with all its requirements. No master can now plead ignorance of what such duties are, for there are now so many works on Navigation, Insurances, Charter parties, Stowage, &c. &c., that "he who runs may read," and there is no room or excuse left for ignorance. The shipmaster must read if he does not intend to be left behind in the race. In the good old days a man's knowledge was ground out of experience, but everything travels too fast for this in modern times, and unless the sailor as well as the landsman makes use of the experience of others who have gone before by reading and study he will never succeed.

Duties of the Mates.—In former days the Master was very usually allowed to select his own officers, the owner judging rightly that, as the whole responsibility rested upon the Master, he was the fittest person to select his own assistants; but now owners generally exercise this patronage themselves.

The mate or mates, having been appointed, it is their duty to carry out the master's orders, and assist him to the utmost of their ability in the duties of the ship. One of their first aims should be to make themselves acquainted with her from truck to keelson, not leaving such knowledge to blind chance or until some urgent duty demands it. In their ordinary duties the law places upon them serious responsibility, and especially when not relieved by the presence of a senior officer. They should never forget that at sea they are equally responsible with the master for the safety of the ship as well as for its good conduct, which will generally depend upon their mutual sympathy and support.

As to the number of mates to be carried in any ship there is no direct legislation beyond what has been stated,* but common-sense teaches that the number should be regulated by the size of the vessel, or the length of the voyage, its nature and difficulty. The strict adherence to the old trading sailing ship fashion of carrying only two mates, and its system of watch and watch for any length of voyage in the large ships and steamers of the present day, is simply monstrous, and to it may be attributed a vast number of the collisions now continually occurring. One excuse put forward for its continuance is, that it is not lawful for any one but a chief or second mate of a ship to have charge of a watch under way. This is an absurd fallacy. There may be any number of persons holding chief and second mates' certificates in a ship, and each is thereby qualified to take such charge. In law it matters nothing as to the series on the articles—this only shows the seniority of appointment by the owner in the ship; the possession of the certificate is the legal qualification as to capacity to perform the duty. If not, of what value is it? To put a junior officer, who has no certificate, in charge of the deck, and the navigation of the ship, would possibly be an illegal thing which must be avoided.

Relation between Masters and Officers.—For the satisfactory working of the ship and creditable performance of duty, the relation between Master and Officer should be one of kindliness and sympathy. It should be the Master's pleasure, as well as duty, to make his officers his fellow-labourers in the navigation of the ship, instructing them where they are weak and giving them as much time for self-improvement as possible, as well as hints as to how this is to be accomplished. On duty, the officer should treat his commander with a distant respectfulness, evincing a desire to perform his duties cheerfully as well as carefully. The master, on his part, should have respect for his officers,

* See p. 147.

shunning harshness on the one hand, as he would familiarity on the other, yet issuing his orders with strict firmness. Should there be occasion to find fault with any slips of duty, let it be done privately : a reproof so administered has treble weight. A master who habitually rebukes his officers publicly before the crew, destroys all self-respect in the officer and all obedient respect in the crew.

With regard to their duties, the necessity of realising a sense of their responsibility cannot be too often and too earnestly impressed upon the officers. Anything like drifting into carelessness or lukewarmness in their duties must lead to difficulties. In charge of a ship under way they must necessarily frequently be called upon to exercise their own judgment. If caught in a sudden danger it is their duty to endeavour to place the ship in safety if possible, and not to wait for the master if he is not present. Many an accident has occurred through an officer leaving the bridge to call the master. That duty ought to be performed by some one else in the watch ; at all events the officer should not quit his post until the source of danger is removed. It is well known that many masters are very jealous of having the course altered by an officer. This, if insisted upon too urgently, will probably lead to difficulty, which, in fact, is too often the case. Such an instance may be given. A steamer was once run ashore upon a well-known coast on a very fine night. The officer of the watch had seen the land for some time, the ship evidently closing in with it, and yet he did nothing for her safety upon the plea that "if the captain set a course which put the ship on shore, it was no business of his"! One can easily imagine the kind of relationship existing between that master and officer, and what a want of true sympathy there was, to say the least of it. It is to be hoped there are not many such afloat! Officers who would learn to command must first learn how to obey!

Relation between Owners and Seamen.—The relation between the owner and the seaman is not an intimate one, and is, from the nature of the employment, an entirely different one from that existing between an employer on shore and his labourers, whether skilled or unskilled. There, should dissatisfaction arise between the parties it is easily solved ; the employer can dismiss, the labourer can leave, and this condition of matters admits of an easy adjustment of labour, and the fulfilment of its terms on both sides. Not so with the sailor and his employer. The conditions of a voyage do not admit of it, especially a long voyage. This necessitates an agreement for an absolute period, which cannot be rescinded on either side until its purpose is fulfilled. The form of this agreement is provided for by statute, and must be entered into on behalf of the owner by the master, who makes and signs the agreement with the crew, whereby the owner—the real employer—is bound to his part of the contract—viz., the payment of the stipulated wages of, and the providing a sufficiency of proper food and accommodation for, the crew. The terms of the contract should be fully set forth in this agreement and understood by the parties before signing.

Herein, then, the master is in a very peculiar relation to his crew. He is not the actual employer, but he is the intermediary between the employer and the employed, and, what is more important still, he is a kind of trustee for the law, which invests him with important, nay, almost unlimited, power, which it demands he shall exercise with punctilious care.

Both owner and master should faithfully carry out their portion of the contract. Life at sea has sufficient hardship in itself, and once at sea the seamen are so completely in their power, that it is only a reasonable duty that they should care for their men's comfort and welfare as far as possible, and feed and use them well.

On the seaman's side of the contract, both law and reason teach that, in return for pay and food, he should render a willing and obedient service, performing his duty to the best of his ability and with alacrity.

Leaving out of sight the higher classes of seamen and petty officers required in the larger and more important vessels, we may here confine our remarks to the seamen required in all vessels—viz., the able and ordinary seamen, apprentices, and boys.

From being so classified, it would be very naturally supposed that there would be some standard of capability for the higher grades easily applicable, but such a standard has never been legally attempted. It has been mooted more than once, and there is no good reason why some kind of examination should not be enacted and enforced.

Result of the Abandonment of Compulsory Apprenticeships.—Prior to 1854, almost every seaman served an apprenticeship of five—some even seven—years, and after that, would have to pass some time as ordinary seaman before he was able to ship as an able seaman, which was in itself a guarantee of fitness and experience.

As we have shown in our historical chapters, the manufacture of seamen had been encouraged by legislation, but sumptuary laws when driven to extremes do more harm than good. The attempt to force *compulsory apprenticeship* in 1844 eventuated in the ruin of the system; for what a man has forced upon him visibly, he at once considers a tax to be got rid of at the earliest opportunity. The apprentice had been borne as a necessary adjunct to the Mercantile Marine by the British shipowner until the law said "*you must*" have him, and then he became an eyesore and a plague to be got rid of. With the riddance commenced the decadence of the qualities formerly characterising the British sailor, for whom no true school was then left. Henceforth he had to pick up his knowledge as best he could. The consequence of this was, that soon all distinction, *quâ* ability, was lost, and the slightest amount of service, after actual boyhood, enabled him, especially in times of pressure from sudden increase in shipping, to obtain an equal rating with the best men in the ship, breaking down in the well-trained seaman everything like technical pride in his calling. Of what use was it to him to be a better man than others? It gave him no better standing—no better pay, and he found himself with the heaviest share of the work to be performed, whilst the ignorant lout stood idly by only fit to pull and haul or sweep the decks.

Indifference and sullen carelessness was the result; many of the best men fell out of the ranks, finding other employment—on shore, anywhere rather than put up with such a position, and the ignorant *residuum* remained behind for the use of the British shipowner, to the delight of the boarding-house keeper, to whom all are fish for his net, as long as they get the same pay for him to work upon, and to ease the red-tape shipping master, who is saved the bother of distinctions or qualifications, and who is only pleased and happy when all are starred "A.B." and "V.G." alike. It saves trouble in securing the next ship, whose unfortunate master only finds the difference when too late.

The issue of such a state of matters is, that, from 1854, the character which the British sailor formerly possessed for good seamanship—readiness to perform his duty and rollicking good nature, mixed with a righteous pride in his calling—has not only become seriously tainted, but in danger of being lost altogether. In fact, if it had not been for the employment of a considerable number of well-trained foreign seamen, the decreasing yearly amount of sailing tonnage would have only been exceeded by the decreasing power of manning them with home-grown seamen.

There are doubtless still a goodly number of British seamen; but not anything like the number required, and such as these find no difficulty in securing employment as quarter-masters, &c., in the best classes of steamships, leaving very few for our sailing fleet.

In 1876, it was found that things were going from bad to worse, and it appeared to many that the only way to meet the difficulty was to restore the system of compulsory apprenticeship; but the continued opposition of the shipowners prevented it, and it appears that the Government in 1880 passed the Act 43 & 44 Vict. cap. 16, sec. 7, referring to the qualification of an A.B. as an attempt to solve the difficulty, supposing that a servitude of some sort for four years is long enough to teach a seaman his duties.

The clause has been in existence for over fifteen years—and with what result? Simply *nil!* Few shipmasters are aware of its existence! It is contained in an Act that was compulsory throughout in regard to payment of wages and other things; but this clause was framed as if it were not intended to be carried out. It did not prevent a seaman from obtaining the rating of A.B. until he had served the prescribed period, but only affirmed that he should not be *entitled* to it; and then loaded the certificate required to substantiate his claim with a tax which no one would pay—certainly not the seaman, if he could help it.

To have made the clause of any effect, it should have been compulsory, and shipping masters should have been charged with its enforcement. With regard to the manning of ships it could have had no bad effect, and it would have had a wonderfully good effect upon the really good men. It would have made the *really able seamen* no fewer than they are, or were, since 1854. In the existing crews we have only the really proportionate number of A.B.'s that there are in existence; the remainder are made up of incompetent sailors and loafers. If the clause had been enforced, we should have had the same proportion of *competent* A.B.'s that we now have, very probably more; but the remainder of the crew would have been shipped in their proper places as ordinary seamen, or boys. The crews would have been quite as serviceable and valuable as they now are to every one except crimps and boarding-house keepers.

As things are, the fulfilment of the proper relation between master and crew is infinitely more difficult than in times past when seamen were really professionally educated. Ignorance, laziness, badly performed work in the man (for it is an axiom that a half or badly bred workman can never make a good one), begets suspicion, then anger, then harshness in the officer, who has not learnt fully to control himself, ending frequently in unseemly quarrels, which lower the officer, and do no good to the man.

Engineers and the Engine-room Crews.—During the past fifty years steam power has gradually increased, until now it has become, as the motive power, the most important factor in the economy of the Mercantile Marine, as well as of the navies of the world, and the calling of an engineer has risen with it in corresponding importance.

The engineer receives the first part of his education as a landsman, and for the first four or five years of his life pursues his calling in an engine shop or factory. These years are to him an education, and if he has taken advantage of all the means at his disposal, he may be highly trained in his business, theoretically as well as practically; certainly in these days he has to pass a very thorough examination before he is allowed to take charge of the valuable machinery under his control, and must prove himself a competent man.

His work on board is of a nature entirely different from that of a seaman. Lying for the most part below the deck, it does not partake in any degree of seamanship, and yet the master, who formerly controlled his ship by her sails, is now dependent upon the engineer for his motive power. The value of a good engineer is untold. As long as things go smoothly in the engine-room, his task is not a difficult one; but there are times when every nerve is strained, and his powers put to a severe test. A successful voyage is greatly dependent upon his care and attention; and it is equally within his power to mar it, if careless and inattentive.

Both owner and master should not forget that his position is not one of entire ease and comfort. Working in a hot engine-room, often rendered doubly uncomfortable by imperfect ventilation, in the midst of oil and coal dust, and having under him a rough and, too often, untractable crew—rougher even than the ordinary run of deck hands—his temper is frequently tried to the utmost. Every consideration then should be given to him, and his comfort as far as possible attended to. We may then expect that he will do his duty, and assist the master in maintaining the discipline of the ship to the utmost.

The master of a steamship is placed then in the position of having two distinct classes of workers under his command, whose duties march steadily alongside of each other, but can never clash, at least as long as reason and common-sense prevail. Their relation to each other, for the good of all, should be one of mutual sympathy and support, and in the majority of cases such a relation prevails; but, like many other relations in this world, it is entirely dependent upon the men themselves, and upon the extent to which they have learnt the useful lesson of keeping themselves under control.

The only thing which will disturb such a relation are prejudices arising from differences of education, backed by uncontrolled temper.

The healthy life of a ship results from that true discipline in which the parts are duly subordinated in their working to each other. The eye cannot say to the hand, "I have no need of thee"—nor can the foot say to the hand, "I have no need of thee." Or, as in a good watch where each part, duly fitted into its proper place and working smoothly, results in perfect time, the mainspring cannot perform its work without the balance, and the balance without the mainspring is useless.

True discipline is that state in which each man does his duty with a single eye and an honest heart in the manner which his conscience tells him is right, if he will only listen to its teaching.

If the co-relation of the parts of the living watch is not perfect it must be caused by bad adjustment, and the causes of bad adjustment are ignorance, false pride, selfishness. These can only be corrected by education, a sense of duty bred of true humility, and a due regard for the wants and feelings of others.

The want of true discipline, when it occurs, is the result of mistakes on all sides—masters, officers of both kinds, crews, and even the owner—very unfortunate mistakes indeed.

Let us not forget that true discipline is not anywhere the result of a blind obedience, much less is it the result of misapplied force; club law—the word and the blow, the rugged oath or sneering curse—may have seemingly attained their object in bygone days, but it is to be hoped never will more.

> Who overcomes
> By force hath overcome but half his foe.

Moral discipline alone must be the ruling power; in most difficult positions it will never be found to fail.

In every ship there must be a head, and that head the law finds in the Master, to whom it places all others in subordination, whatever may be his position, and to him it expects obedience.

CHAPTER IV.

THE PRESENT POSITION OF THE PERSONNEL.

CONTENTS.—The Mercantile Marine service not a homogeneous one—Its division into classes—The shipowner—Company directors—Private ship managers—Effect of high competition on shipbuilding and owning—Merchants and shippers—Home trade—Shipmasters—Their responsibility—Their position decaying—Number of certificated masters unknown—Annual passes in the various grades—Competition of aliens—Reasons for employing foreigners—First mate, his duties and position—Junior officers—Ocean tramps—Want of consideration in masters—Seamanship less required than formerly—Engineers, their improved position and education—Remuneration—Experience valuable both at sea and on shore—Advantages of engineers greater than those of sailors.

The Mercantile Marine service not a homogeneous one.—There are many persons, especially among our navigating officers, who have a desire to look upon the British Mercantile Marine as a service, and to speak of it as such in the same sense as the navy is a service—a homogeneous service—but this it is not, and cannot be from the nature of its details.

Indeed it is a service of services. Every separate line of ships owned and managed by its own company of shareholders and their directors or ship managers is, to all intents and purposes, a separate and distinct service, having each its own regulations of internal duty, working and promotion. The ideas of management, routine, &c., are as varied as the companies which own the lines, and, unless very exceptionally, an officer who had filled a rank in the one would not be accepted and appointed to the same rank in another (especially in the higher grades), without a probationary service in a lower grade. In fact, the employment in some services is a distinct bar to employment elsewhere, in consequence of the difference of education and routine.

The only sense then in which our Mercantile Marine can be deemed a service arises from the fact that all its officers must pass the same examination, and receive their passports to service as masters and officers from the Board of Trade, no matter in what or whose employment they may serve; but beyond this, what might be said of one branch of the service would be utterly inapplicable to another, and the variations in education and social position of its members are more wide-spread than in that of any other profession, and make it difficult to legislate for it or even fairly to describe it.

To enable us to form some estimate, under such conditions, of the present position of the various branches of our *personnel*, we must make a kind of classification, and see how its elements are affected in each of the classes.

Its division into two classes.—In the first place the marine is naturally divided into two great classes—the steam fleet, and the sailing fleet. The difference of organisation in these two classes is very great; and this not only in their management, but also in their internal economy. These again may be subdivided according to the nature of their employment.

Of the steam fleet, we may place in the first class all the great lines of mail and passenger steamers, which are now the principal means of communication between Great Britain and the far-off places of the world. In the second class we place all the general cargo steamers, known as tramps, which are employed almost solely in transferring earth's products from one soil to another, and in the exportation of the coarser manufactures of various lands. Third and lastly, the home trade steamers, which includes those trading to the coast of Europe contained between the Elbe on the east and Brest on the west, as well as our own coasts.

Sailing vessels may also be similarly divided, as we have still some considerable lines of passenger ships employed in the Eastern and Southern trades, especially that of our Australasian Colonies; but for the most part they divide with steamers of the second class the rough carrying trade of the world.

The Shipowner.—In former days shipowning was a much more personal matter than it has become under the new influences we have already considered. He was veritably *shipowner*, as well as manager, and was largely interested in the *success* of the property under his control, holding, if not all, by far the greatest individual share in his vessels, and he very seldom attempted the business of a shipbroker. His remuneration for transacting the business of his ships, when he had others associated with him as co-owners, was in most cases only sufficient to cover his actual outgoings of management, and he looked upon the investment made by his friends in his ships more as a collateral advantage in the building up of his own influence and fortunes, than as a means of large management returns by way of commissions on freight earned. His vessels, as well as his officers and crews, were to him matters of personal interest, and when they were in the home ports claimed his personal attention and supervision. "All respectable ship-owners," says Mr. Lindsay in his "History of Shipping," "not only attended to the seaworthiness and proper equipment of their ships, but were wont in person—when they had time" he naïvely adds—"to inspect the forecastle; to see it properly cleaned and white-washed, or painted, and furnished with every reasonable convenience." That is to say, that they not only had a sound knowledge of their masters and officers, and generally of their crews and their capabilities, but also an intimate knowledge of their ships, and all their intricate fittings. Many of them had themselves been masters, and knew their business thoroughly, and were not dependent upon a surveyor from Lloyd's to tell them what their ships needed.

Company Directors.—In the present day of large establishments we find that with few exceptions steamships of the first class are in the hands of joint stock companies, whose directors and managers are able and capable men, who have an intimate and careful knowledge of their ships as to their capacity for performing what is necessary and suitable to the particular line, or trade, in which they are employed, from a profitable or commercial point of view, but who cannot have the same intimate knowledge of their officers or of the details of each ship as is possible, and customary, with private shipowners. Like great generals, the main points of action are under their control, but for general detail work they must trust to their subordinates. As the business connected with such large fleets is of a highly technical character, the directors are assisted by persons bred to the work of each department, such as marine superintendents, who are usually old experienced masters; superintendent engineers; and even, in some cases, naval architects to design vessels most suited to the particular trade and regulate their internal economy. Besides these, there is usually a large staff of departmental shore officials to superintend the forwarding and shipping of cargo, supplying the necessary outfit and provision for passengers and all other things required for the voyage. The whole forms quite an *imperium in imperio*, and the chairman of such a company is a little king in responsibility as well as authority. The directors are usually highly paid for their services, but they are not subjected to the temptations of the combined ship manager and broker, as commissions on work done would not, or certainly ought not, to be recognised in such companies. Their interest lies in maintaining their position as able managers and financiers, and so rendering themselves, as it were, necessary to the well-being of the shareholders in their companies by whom they are chosen.

It is to their interest to obtain, and retain the services of the most able and efficient masters and officers, as well as by sympathy and support as by fair remuneration for good work done; and in the large companies such a feeling and intention towards masters and officers is fairly carried out.

Private Ship Managers.—The second class of steamers are very variously owned; some by private shipowners on the sixty-fourth principle; some by companies having directors and managers; but a very large proportion in single ship companies under individual managers—who have been bred as shipbrokers, and have little or no real maritime experience beyond that relating to freights and brokerage. Their attraction for shipowning is the large emolument derivable from the commissions upon freight earned, which according to the generally received practice is calculated upon the gross freight, as brokerage usually is. Too frequently their own interest in the absolute property is of the smallest. Their whole effort is to make the largest commissions possible for themselves, and sail their ships on the cheapest possible terms.

Effect of high Competition in Shipbuilding and Owning. —To this class of owner and the speculative shipbuilder must be attributed the frightful competition and continued overbuilding of late years. Its effect upon the shareholders in these limited ship companies is frequently disastrous, but if the public cannot take care of themselves in such matters, nothing that can here be said will have any effect upon them. Gulled by plausible prospectuses, their desire for abnormal interest on the capital resulting from often hard-earned savings, they give themselves up, without sufficiently close inquiry, an easy prey to reckless speculators.

The effect upon the shipbuilding classes is quite as bad, and gives rise to periodic states of violent demand for their labour one day, and half-employment and semi-starvation the next.

As the Secretary of the Iron Shipbuilders and Boilermakers' Society is reported to have said some time ago: "How much better would it be for employers, and how much happier for the employed, if the natural requirements of the shipping trade—the necessary amount to replace losses and meet the natural increment of trade —could be more accurately gauged and spread more evenly over time than at present!"

How much better would it not indeed be for everybody! We should not then see periodically so many thousands of tons of shipping lying idle in our ports and the capital lying idle and wasted, or vessels run at a loss by the speculative ship manager for the sake of his own commission upon gross freight, which leaves him still a handsome profit, to the disadvantage of the long-suffering shareholder.

Merchants and Shippers.—Merchants and shippers can look upon this state of matters with complacency, as it keeps freights down to the lowest possible ebb, but the unfortunate shareholders suffer without the slightest chance of relief, except by an expensive lawsuit, which, after all, their own Articles of Association may bar, as witness the letters which appear constantly in the public press from such shareholders asking editorial advice under such circumstances. And for every letter that appears, how many persons are there that suffer in silence?

Home Trade.—In the home trade the shipowners are generally men who have their ships under their own eyes, and have a steady personal influence upon and interest in their crews. Employers and employed grow up, live in intimate relationship with, and respect each other. Here there is no opening for the purely speculative shipowner—trade wants are known and gauged accurately; and although there is now and again a little acrimonious competition carried on, it is usually caused by the efforts of certain shippers to cheapen freights. It soon dies a natural death and the survivor is left in peace.

In sailing ships the owners and managers are usually of the older type, although the limited company system is applied to them occasionally. Amongst them will be found many who have had a practical knowledge of sea life, and are able better to understand and appreciate their masters and crews than the shipbroker-manager who has had no experience of ships or seamen beyond what can be learnt over an office counter.

Shipmasters.—The position of the masters in our first-class steamers is an honourable as well as a most responsible one, and what was said by a writer in the *Mercantile Marine Magazine* some years ago may be repeated: "In our first-class ships they are generally speaking as fine a set of men in respect to ability, discretion, and gentlemanly bearing, as can be furnished by any profession."

As compared with the masters of the old passenger ships of fifty years ago, their position is not so independent a one; nor is their remuneration at all so good as it was or as it might be, considering the length of time they have to serve before reaching a command, and the high responsibility when that command is reached.

Our high-pitched competition and the struggles of directors to maintain dividends for their shareholders has seriously affected them, and occasion has been taken in many of our first-class ships to reduce salaries rather than increase them, although the value and earnings of the vessels entrusted to them has increased from five- to ten-fold.

In evidence of this, a writer in *Scribner's Magazine* for the month of May 1891, when describing the *personnel* of a first-class Atlantic liner, after tracing the rise and progress of the officers of such vessels, says:—" And with this hardly earned promotion do not come as in other professions ease, comfort, and proper recompense for duty well done, but heavier responsibilities, harder work, and greater self-sacrifice. What is worse—and this to the shame of the great steam-ship corporations—these gallant men, even at their prime, receive the most inadequate pecuniary recognition for the burden imposed, for the mental and physical qualities exercised, for the experience brought to bear; in no other trade or profession is equal ability so badly paid!" This may be thought an extreme view of the case, but it is one deliberately issued to the reading public on both sides of the Atlantic, and has some ground to rest upon.

Their Responsibility.—The responsibility resting upon the shoulders of the masters of these vessels is very great. Look at the lives and property contained in an *Orient*, an *Arcadia*, or a *Jumna*, starting from our docks, and proceeding on her voyage to the Antipodes or the Far East, with their hundreds of passengers and many thousand tons of valuable merchandise on board. The care of so many souls is a responsibility sufficient to make any man sober and thoughtful—sufficient to imbue a man with an unbounded watchfulness and care that should never desert him, or permit him to neglect every known precaution against danger.

That our mail-steamer commanders are, on the whole, a clever, self-reliant, and wary set of men is perfectly patent from the comparative freedom from loss in our mail services. Whether they are as perfect seamen as were our first-class masters fifty years ago may be debated; but that they are as perfect navigators, and as well fitted to meet the present circumstances of navigation, cannot be denied.

Among the masters serving in the second-class of steamers, now very commonly called "Ocean Tramps," will be found many well-educated men, quite as capable as seamen and of as gentlemanly bearing as those in the first-class steamers; but unfortunately this is not always the case. Where it is not so, it is due to defective education arising from want of early opportunity. If a master is little better educated than the men under his command, it is very unlikely he will ever rise far above them, either in manners or mental capacity.

Position Decaying.—In point of fact, the position and independence of the ordinary steam shipmaster has been gradually, but surely, decaying. There are many reasons for this. One of the first and most overwhelming is the number of men holding masters' certificates. This has made the competition for employment very severe in "tramp" steamers and rendered the position a most precarious one. The unhealthy competition in these ships forces managers to cut down salaries in every possible direction; consequently the cheapest man is the best.

Number of Certificated Masters Unknown.—Another is the low standard of education, the ease with which a man of very moderate knowledge can be crammed for the Board of Trade Examinations, and the short period of service required for a master's certificate have enabled the Board of Trade to pass *competent* masters *without number.* This is said advisedly, for the authorities have not the slightest idea how many there are in existence. The number of masters and mates in possession of foreign-going certificates is unknown.

Annual Passes in the Various Grades.—The Registrar-General of Shipping and Seamen reports that the department has no means of knowing the number of certificates extant; all that is known is that about 800 masters, 800 mates, and 1000 second mates receive certificates every year. This must be a great many more than are required to fill up the waste caused by death or superannuation, especially when we take into account that *the ships are annually decreasing in numbers.* A great number are serving as officers, and many must be driven into a forced retirement or to find a living in other ways.

This must have a depressing effect upon the masters, especially upon the older ones, for the superabundant supply of younger men coming forward qualified by Government as masters, ready and willing to take the lowest pay for the sake of getting a command, forces many of the older men to accept an utterly inadequate salary or they are shunted into poverty and oblivion while yet fit for honest work. Of course this is not the case in first-class ships where it is of the highest importance that the masters shall be men of trained experience, and are retained as long as it is possible on account of the prestige they have acquired in working their way up from the lower grades by painfully slow degrees.

Referring to such a state of matters the annual Report of the Mercantile Marine Service Association for 1896 says: "The result of this deplorable state of things was that a considerable number of middle-aged officers were displaced and were unable again to secure employment through the demand for young men to fill their places."

Competition of Aliens.—There is another cause which seriously affects the position of British shipmasters, and that is the competition brought about by the admission of aliens to the same privileges as themselves. In this the interest of the British mariner was wholly lost sight of in that of the shipowner, to the great loss of the nation as a whole.

As the Regulations now stand, an alien who has served as an apprentice, mate or master in the ships of his own country for the prescribed period may, upon proof of such service satisfactory to the Board of Trade, apply for examination, and, if he passes successfully, be passed into the ranks of the British officers, without ever pretending to become a naturalised subject.

Reasons for Employing Foreigners.—The number of such foreign masters and officers in existence, it is impossible to discover, being, as is the number of British shipmasters themselves, an unknown quantity.* It seems strange that a British owner should or would prefer a foreigner to his own countryman as a master or officer, and there can only be two reasons for such preference; either the foreigner is *better* or he is *cheaper*—it may be both. Ask the shipowner for his reason, and his reply is, that "he is a better shipmaster" and understands his business; is more attentive, more docile, and altogether *better educated* and *better mannered!* Is this true? It is not universally true. For the reason that this competition does not take place in the higher classes of British ships, but principally in the lower classes of tramp steamers and sailing ships, in which many of our own shipmasters cannot be called educated men, and this mainly because the nation has taken no care for his education. This is not the case with the foreigner. He at all events must be pretty well master of two languages, and able to speak and write them intelligently, before he can get an English certificate. However, whatever truth there be in the shipowner's assertion, it is within the power of British officers to correct it by attending to their education and so falsifying it.

First Mate, his Duties and Position.—The chief officer or first mate of a first-class steamship holds an appointment of great responsibility. He is the chief executive officer, upon whom the care of the ship mainly devolves. From daylight until dark his duties keep him on the alert. He regulates the work of the crew and appoints them to their several stations; sees that everything about the ship is kept in proper working order, especially the boats and their gear, and all life-saving apparatus, in case of accident; that all the safeguards against fires, such as pumps, hoses, and fire-buckets are kept in their appointed places and ready for any emergency; he is also responsible for the reception of all stores and their proper expenditure, as also for

* Since this was written the Board of Trade have reported to the Manning Committee that the percentage of foreigners obtaining certificates are: as masters, 4 per cent.; mates, 3 per cent.; engineers, 2 per cent.

the shipping and delivery of all cargo. All the other officers, petty officers, and the crew, and everything connected with their duties are under his immediate control. As far as the navigation of the ship is concerned it is his duty to see that the ship's log is properly kept and carefully written day by day. A personal knowledge of every part of the ship is incumbent upon him, and he is specially charged with its cleanliness and sanitary arrangements.

Junior Officers.—The second officer usually assists the Master in the navigation of the ship, care of the chronometers, &c., besides keeping his usual watch. He also has charge of the holds and cargo. The junior officers have their fixed duties in assisting the chief and second officers. In these ships three watches are usually kept. As it is not usual for these ships to carry either midshipmen or apprentices, no one is employed as a junior officer until he has served for and obtained a second mate's certificate, by service elsewhere.

The position of the officers in these ships is as good as it is possible to be. They are fairly well paid compared with the officers in tramp steamers, but although on the whole they have in many respects advantages over the officers in the general carrying trade, there are some drawbacks, and perhaps the greatest is the slowness of promotion, so that an officer finds himself approaching middle life before he can command an income commensurate with those of many other professions. There are not many fortunes made in these days by merchant captains, and no retiring allowance can be counted upon. It is, however, only fair to say that old and deserving servants are not entirely forgotten by the best companies.

Ocean Tramps.—In the ordinary cargo or "tramp" steamer the position of the officers is a much less desirable one, and involves a much rougher and more toilsome life. These vessels are now sailed with such sparse crews that it is impossible that all the duties of navigation can be properly or safely performed, and moreover, it entails upon the mates an amount of absolute menial labour hardly consistent with their supposed education and responsibilities, leaving them spare time for little else than the necessary rest, and often not enough of that. It is now common for steamers carrying 4000 tons and upwards, to make a voyage to the other side of the world with three deck hands in a watch—not sufficient for a relief to the wheel and look-out. With these few hands it is expected that the hull of the vessels of iron or steel shall be kept in proper order, well attended to, and kept free from rust by scraping and painting. In this case an officer can be little better off than a common seaman and his work no better than that of "a foreman labourer." That an officer should be obliged to leave the bridge at all hours day or night, when a fore-and-after has to be set, or the holds prepared for cargo when under weigh, not only imperils the safety of the ship and all belonging to her, besides making her a danger to other vessels, but it is utterly unfair to any man bred to be, or having the qualification of, an officer.

Want of Consideration in Masters.—Again, in these craft the Masters do not as a rule seem to give the officers any share in the navigation of the vessel beyond watching the courses steered and keeping a look-out. Does this arise from ignorance or jealousy? Too often both combined. The ignorance of many masters, and a deplorable want of sympathy with their officers, or a right appreciation of their responsibilities, is too frequently the cause. Under such circumstances, of what use is it for junior officers to pass an examination in a knowledge of matters which they have not the slightest chance of putting into practice at sea, until they are fortunate enough to obtain a command, when with difficult and inexperienced steps, they have to begin to trace a way for themselves in navigation and maritime procedure?

Seamanship less required than formerly.—In sailing ships the position of masters and officers is still a much more independent one, and in many senses more preferable to the thorough seaman than that in tramp steamers. There is more opportunity for the display of the good old-fashioned quality of self-reliance in sailing vessels, and the officers must be practical and experienced seamen; and yet, in the modern ship, daily life does not bring the experience of former days. Rope rigging is unknown, and the continual oversight which it necessitated to keep it in order almost unnecessary; wire rigging is better able to look after itself. Studding-sails have disappeared, and with them, their booms. There are, no doubt, plenty of officers now at sea who have never handled one. The rig of ships, even the largest, is confined to what is termed plain sail, and is, therefore, much more simple to handle. With masts and yards (except the lighter ones) of iron and wire rigged, an officer has little opportunity of experience in sending them up and down; even royal masts and yards stay where they were placed by the building yard riggers until perchance they blow away. Sailor "pigeon" is now best learnt in the rigging loft, and at the rigging shears. Sails are of a very different cut from those of byegone days—broad and shallow—on yards doubled on each mast; they are much easier handled than the taut topsails with their four reefs, and the deep topgallant sails of our old Indiamen. Our officers are confessedly not such seamen as they were, but at the same time there is not the necessity that they should be.

Engineers: their Improved Position and Education.—The immense strides towards perfection in marine machinery in the last forty years, not only in the practice, but in the theory of construction, have been equalled by the improvement in the men, who work and control that machinery afloat. In our first-class steamers the engineers have, from the first, been picked men, albeit some of them of forty years ago would now be termed illiterate—good practical men of their day, but not as well up in the theory as the practice of their calling. In those days rule of thumb held sway to a large extent in engineering practice, as well in the shops as the ships; better, therefore, could hardly have been expected, and the general run of the engineers in the comparatively small number of trading steamers were an exceedingly home-spun race. A very large number had not served an apprenticeship in the trade, but were engine drivers raised from the shovel—many of them good, steady fellows, who handled well the slow-going machinery of the times with its low pressures—most of them a good deal better drivers than a chance engineer out of a shop put in charge of machinery afloat, with little or no sea-going experience, as was often enough the case. But this is now all changed. The very strides in engineering has compelled better education, and the Act of 1862 introduced men of a very different school; by slow degrees, certainly, but very effectually. The examinations then instituted have been of real value to this branch of the Mercantile Marine, and there can be no hesitation in saying that the bulk of the young engineers coming into the Service are a better educated race than many of those aspiring to be officers in the sailing branch of the Service; this applies not only technically, but even in the general groundwork of an English education, unless those officers are amongst those few whose parents have been able to impart a liberal education to them before going on board ship: and these we know are only the few.

Remuneration—Experience Valuable both at Sea and on Shore.—The remuneration of the engineers is greatly superior to that of the deck officers, as the traditions of their calling have been much in their favour, the competition for employment not having been so severe as that of the sailor. In fact the pay of a chief engineer nearly approaches, in some instances it has exceeded, that of the master; and that of junior engineers far exceeds that of the mates in ordinary steamers. Engineers also have another advantage over the deck officers. Once a sailor, always a sailor—his education fits him for little else; but an engineer, besides his sea-going qualifications has a profession to fall back upon on shore, in which his sea-going experience will stand him in good stead. This makes him more independent and prevents undue competition. Altogether he is a less helpless being than the sailor out of employment.

Advantages of Engineers greater than those of Sailors.—There is another point in favour of the engineers. Their technical training in the factory and experience in fitting up machinery on board new steamers in the building-yard give them a knowledge of the construction of ships and machinery which few deck officers possess; consequently they are now more frequently employed as general superintendents in assisting the owners in looking after and keeping in repair their fleets of steamers, than old and experienced shipmasters, who in the days of sailing ships were entrusted with such duties, but who have not now a sufficiently technical knowledge of iron work and machinery in modern steamers. In fact, so much does this want of that sort of technical training in deck officers influence the minds of many owners, especially tramp owners, that one of them stated to the writer not long ago, "that he expected the time would shortly arrive when the engineer would be the head of the ship and the present master a mere pilot under him!" However, it's a long cry to Loch Awe! Many things must be changed before that can come to pass—indeed a wholesale change in the law itself—but when owners begin to talk in this way, it is time for shipmasters to take warning! The *esprit de corps* which buoys up the engineers and makes them combine to assert their rights is yet lacking in the sailor officer, whose position will surely still further decay until he in some way follows suit. It is the sailor's education which is at fault.

PART III.

EDUCATION IN THE MERCANTILE MARINE.

CHAPTER I.

BACKWARD STATE OF EDUCATION.

CONTENTS.—Deficiency of education in the early part of the century—Recommendation of the Royal Commission *re* Nautical Schools—Apprentice system as a means of education—Its failure—What has the Board of Trade done to promote education ?—Action through Board of Education's Science and Art Department—Grants to nautical schools—Alteration in 1862 fatal to nautical education—Schools in connection with South Kensington—Results of their teaching—Honours examinations—Another change in 1892; consequent falling off in scholars—Divergence of Board of Trade and South Kensington examinations—Why has the Government not done more for nautical education ?—Mr. Bolam's evidence.

Deficiency of Education in the early part of the Century.—An attentive reader of the foregoing chapters on the History of the Mercantile Marine, especially those pertaining to the third and fourth decades of this century, must have been struck by the fact, that, by common consent, the education of our Shipmasters and Officers, with some notable exceptions, was then in a deplorable state of backwardness and inefficiency, quite unbecoming so important a class of the greatest maritime nation in the world. It will also be admitted that, as a nation, we had fallen far behind other European nations, our nearest competitors in the commerce of the world, in fostering and encouraging the education of our mariners. It will further have been seen how the nation, in response to the recommendations of numerous Royal Commissions and Select Committees, had endeavoured to remedy a state of affairs so little creditable to it ; how the officers had been subjected to examinations intended to prove their efficiency as navigators; how, in fact, all the recommendations for the benefit of our officers and seamen, and for the safety of life and property at sea, had received more or less effective treatment by legislative action, except on one point which was, in the language of the *Report of the Royal Commission of* 1836—

"The establishment of cheap **nautical schools**, either in ships adapted to the purpose or in appropriate buildings on shore, in which the practical duties of seamanship and the elements of navigation should be taught to the young apprentices, who are training up for the sea . . . . and for the purpose of inculcating habits of sobriety, and moral character, all of which are at present neglected."

Recommendation of the Royal Commission *re* **Nautical Schools.**—It will scarcely be denied that the Commissioners looked upon this recommendation as of vital importance in leading up to, and affording the proper means for obtaining, such an education as was deemed necessary for every mercantile marine master or officer, and which was to be proved by examination; such a means of education as could be made available during the period of apprenticeship, or such other term of actual sea service as should be deemed necessary to qualify candidates for promotion as mates and masters, or for the preliminary education of lads intended for a sea life.

It may here be premised that the committees, which, one after another, so strongly advocated such national means of education, never for one moment considered it possible that apprenticeship as a necessary means of training seamen would be abandoned. If they had known what was to follow upon the repeal of all protective navigation laws whereby compulsory apprenticeship was thrown as a sop to the shipowners smarting under the loss of protection, there can be little doubt but that they would have set themselves to legislate for some direct system to take its place, in their anxiety to organise marine education upon a sound basis.

Apprentice System as a means of Education—Its failure.—Now, although the apprentice system, as a means of education in the general handicraft work of the sailor, has been sufficiently effectual, as a means of education in scientific navigation it had failed. It was never shown that our seamen were not skilful as seamen; but it was to their failure in general knowledge and scientific skill as navigators that all the inquiries pointed; such knowledge, taken in its widest sense, as is required to make an intelligent ship-master, and fit him for the ordinary business and amenities of life, as well as the proper control of his crew, and demands the best means for its systematic attainment in the form of schools or colleges.

What has the Board of Trade done to promote Education?—Such being the case, the question which requires an answer is,

What has the Marine Department of the Board of Trade done to promote, or encourage, such education?

It may be said that indirectly it has fostered education by insisting upon a certain standard, which must be attained before promotion can take place. But this throws the strain of education upon the examined, gives it no assistance whatever, and is therefore no answer.

No direct answer has been given by the establishment of schools, or school ships, provided by the nation and open to all who apply for instruction. The predominant feeling in the minds of the officials of the Marine Department seems to have been, that it is not the business of the Government to educate officers for the shipowners, upon whom, they say, the responsibility of education should rest. But what is the fact in regard to this? It is notorious that since the shipowners were relieved from maintaining apprentices, and the Government undertook to tell them who were fitted to take charge of their ships, they have taken less and less interest in their education than ever they did. And thus the young sailor is landed on the horns of a dilemma, with no one to lend him a helping hand.

To those who say that the Board of Trade has done nothing for education it may be replied, that, since 1850, the Department has shown some anxiety in regard to education, and it certainly has been very urgent upon the junior officers in many official documents to attend to *their own* education, and upon shipmasters to *assist* them by every means in their power; but to this the shipmaster has turned as deaf an ear as the owner.

Action through Board of Education's Science and Art Department.—In a sense it may be said that the Government has aided in the work of teaching navigation by making grants to teachers through the medium of the Science and Art Department of the Board of Privy Council for Education, which added Navigation and Nautical Astronomy to the subjects in its curriculum.

Apparently the difficulty that presented itself to the Marine Department was that it had no funds for such a purpose as Nautical Schools, and instead of going boldly forward and asking the nation to provide the necessary funds for schools and professors, it fell back upon the General Education Fund, which could only be got at through the Education Board.

Grants to Nautical Schools.—Under the scheme of the Science and Art Department, as it then existed, a grant was given to as many schools in the Kingdom as could show that they were doing a sufficient amount of work to warrant the Department in making a grant. One of the conditions was, that each locality requiring aid should make an effort to maintain a navigation school, although unable to find all the necessary funds, and also that the school should not be carried on for private profit. Wherever this was the case, the Department made up the teacher's salary to £140 per annum, the least grant given being £40.

In this manner some sixteen Navigation schools, with about 3000 students in annual attendance, were maintained, at a cost of about £2500 per annum. To ensure a proper education these grants were to some extent dependent upon the class of certificate held by the teacher, which was a guarantee for competent tuition.

Alteration in 1862 fatal to Nautical Education.—Unfortunately in 1862, when these schools were beginning to take root and good work was being done in them, the Science and Art Department threw overboard the special navigation scheme, and assimilated navigation teaching and grants to the rest of their scheme, in which payment by result of the success of the pupils was instituted. This was done under protest from all the Navigation schools on the ground that the scheme, which was well suited to the fixed landsman, who could attend the full winter's course, was utterly inapplicable to the migratory sailor. Of this protest the Department took no heed, except to relax the period in which the necessary number of lessons had to be taken, and offer four examinations in the year instead of one. Upon this most of the Navigation schools then in existence at once ceased to do anything but *cram* students for the officers' examinations, instituted by the Board of Trade. The Rules of the Science and Art Classes as to the number of attendances and the time within which that number must be taken, rendered them inapplicable to the case of young men at sea, and served to cut away the grants so much as to make them unattractive to teachers, who found their time more remuneratively occupied in *cramming*.

The quarterly examinations failed in their purpose, as a sufficient number of scholars—viz., forty—could not be presented each quarter. At the May examinations, of the number presented, many were pupil teachers and others who took up navigation as part of a mathematical course, with a view to teaching purposes hereafter, and who had been able to pursue its study unintermittingly throughout the usual winter course of six months.

Schools in Connection with South Kensington.—In spite, however, of all difficulties, it will be seen (if reference is made to the work of the classes for 1890-91) that some teachers were willing to take advantage of the aid given. In the Appendix*

* See *Appendix* F.

will be found a list of the schools which proposed to teach navigation, &c., preparatory to the examinations to be held in May 1891, taken from the calendar for that year. Besides the schools named in this list, there were two others which taught navigation, but did not give the number of scholars to be taught—viz.: The Marine School at South Shields, and Science and Art Schools at Great Yarmouth. The presumptive number of scholars in these schools is—in navigation 1116, and in nautical astronomy 492. Of the thirty-five schools enumerated, only three are pure navigation schools, and two are training ships. These contain a very large proportion of the navigation scholars, and nearly all who were to be taught nautical astronomy. The navigation schools taught pure mathematics concurrently with navigation, &c.; the training ships did not. At least, no students were presented in the mathematical classes. The remainder are Board schools, National schools, and others which teach navigation incidentally under the supervision of the local Science and Art Committees.

Perhaps the two most surprising facts to be learnt from an examination of the list of schools are, that Ireland, principally in its fishing villages on the South and West, presents nearly one-third of the total number of navigation scholars, but only twenty-four in nautical astronomy; and that the Metropolis and its suburbs, which has from 300 to 400 Science and Art Classes, does not present a single scholar in navigation in connection with South Kensington.

Results of their Teaching.—To ascertain the result of this teaching we must consult the Report of the Department of Science and Art for the year 1891 published in 1892. From it another table has been prepared showing the number of passes,* and the character of the certificates obtained. The number of papers worked in navigation is stated as 550, but only 544 are accounted for in the return; of these 411 passed in the Advanced and Elementary Stages, and 133 failed. There is no means of discovering from the Report the number presented and passed from each school.

In nautical astronomy 128 papers were worked and of these the result is returned in 126 cases—111 passed and fifteen failed. A glance at the return will show that the passes in the advanced stage are only about one-fourth of the whole, and that seems to apply year after year, showing the small proportion of those who pass beyond the elementary stage. Although we cannot refer to the schools, it may be inferred that the teaching varies very greatly, when the examiner refers to one set of papers as being all "up to the First-class standard," and another batch as being

* See *Appendix* F.

"worthless." It will not be far wide of the mark if it is said that the only part of the teaching in Science and Art classes which will be found to be of much real value to the Mercantile Marine officer is that contained in the four nautical schools of Hull, South Shields, Leith, and Dundee.

Honours—Examinations.—These figures have been discussed with a view to showing that the aid to the education of young sailors is of the smallest conceivable quantity. A very considerable number of the pupils in these classes are not sailors and possibly never intend to be. As an illustration, the Honours List in navigation for 1890 is interesting. One passed with first-class honours; five with second. The first was a Naval schoolmaster, aged thirty-two; of the other five, one was a teacher of navigation, aged forty; another an old shipmaster, aged fifty-seven, also engaged in teaching navigation; and the next an artist, aged twenty-four; the fourth was a pupil-teacher of the Hull Navigation School, aged nineteen; and the last a youthful mariner, aged fifteen, educated at the Marine School, South Shields, the only one likely to be of much value to the Merchant Service. This is not intended as a sample of all the classes, still it may be fairly taken as an indication. As evidence of the value of these classes as Government aid to seamen it is most disappointing. The system of teaching is good as far as it goes; and the system of examination is scientific, trying the general intelligence, as well as the accuracy of those examined.

Another Change in 1892; consequent falling off in Scholars.—In 1892 the system of payment was again changed, and that accorded to the lower elementary standard was altogether withdrawn, on the plea, that "payments are now made to localities under the Local Taxation (Customs and Excise Duties) Act, which payments may, at the *option* of the Town or County Councils, be applied to technical education." This has made the grant earning by teachers more illusory still, and the effect is a reduction of 93 in the papers worked in the year 1893–4; but the proportion of Honours and Advanced Papers increased, which apparently shows a falling off in elementary teaching, the effect of which remains to be seen.

It is only fair to add that under the Organised Science Schools Scheme, certain of the navigation schools are lately dealt with as such, and are paid a capitation grant suited to the migratory habits of the students, who, under the rules, must be *bonâ fide* "seafaring persons." It is to be hoped that this is a move in the right direction, the result of which must, for a few years, be patiently waited for.

Divergence of Board of Trade and South Kensington

Examinations.—There is another point which may be referred to as having defeated the usefulness of the teaching in these classes for nautical purposes, and that is, the Science and Art Examinations, and the Board of Trade Examinations, have never been brought into line—have never had any direct bearing upon each other. The one is an examination in the scientific principles of navigation and the other in the practical art of solving problems by fixed rules; for instance, a second mate might be so crammed with these fixed rules and formulæ as to be able to pass a Board of Trade Examination with accuracy of result, who would be completely stumped by an examination for the elementary stage of navigation and nautical astronomy, although in reality it does not cover much more ground. The one is an examination by scholarly professors for scholars; the other is a rule-of-thumb examination of seamen by seamen, under which seamen can never become scholars.

Why has the Government not done more for Nautical Education?—The result of all this then is that the Government has not proceeded very far in fostering the education of our Mercantile Marine Officers, or with anything like the completeness of many other European nations; and it may well be asked, why not? Is it that our country is so poor that it cannot afford to do what the Swedes, the Danes, the Germans, the French, or the Russians have done for their seamen? Surely not! The country is bound to do something for the education of her sailors; it is nothing less than cruelty to treat them as it has hitherto done—there is no class that has done more for its country than our seamen, and there is no class whom she has treated with such absolutely contemptuous neglect.

Mr. Bolam's Evidence.—As corroborative evidence of the truth of such a statement, if any be necessary, an extract from a letter of Mr. J. Bolam, Principal of the Leith Navigation School, who is *facile princeps* in the question of nautical education, which appears in the *Nautical Magazine* for April, may be quoted. He says, after discussing the new regulations: "The practice of many foreign seafaring nations, and of every professional body in Great Britain (except the Mercantile Marine) is to provide first, abundant and easily accessible means of sound education and training for the members of the profession, because upon that training the 'qualification' depends. Then they fix the examination test, taking care to keep the training standard well ahead of the examination standard.

"Look at the position of the Board of Trade in this matter. Departing from the wiser, but short-lived, ideas of their predecessors in office half a century ago, the parliamentary and permanent heads of the Board of Trade do absolutely nothing to educate and train navigating officers for the merchant service; nor, at the present day, when public bodies are spending huge sums to perfect the technical education and technological training of people in all the industries of the kingdom, except the seafaring profession, does the Board of Trade lift a little finger to influence these public bodies in the direction of giving the sailor officer fair play. . . . . I believe," he continues, "that the navigating officers of Great Britain are the most capable in the world, and in the matter of professional skill and ability are the foremost in the world. But such scientific training as they possess *has been obtained at their own cost*, and in the face of absence of proper provision and other discouragements which would have daunted a race of men less bold and vigorous than they are. And no Government Department would be justified in imposing an exceptionally high standard of compulsory scientific examinations upon its merchant service, whose scientific training the country so shamefully neglects."

CHAPTER II.

GENERAL RESULTS OF THE SYSTEM OF EXAMINATIONS.

CONTENTS.—Results of the voluntary examinations—Lowering of the standard for compulsory examinations—Its effect—Promise of the Board to raise the standard—System of examination productive of cramming—Evil results adverted to in 1870 by a writer to Lloyd's—Board of Trade's recommendation to officers to educate themselves never acted upon—Neglect of the primary sciences in Board of Trade examinations—Comparison with foreign nations—Men of fifty years ago—System rendered shipowners and masters careless of the education of young sailors—Passports to service; their intention—Promotion, an owner's question.

Results of the Voluntary Examinations.—Before proceeding with the general question of education, it will be useful to inquire into the result of the system of Board of Trade examinations as an educative force.

Looking back over the past half-century since the institution of voluntary examinations in 1845, it must be admitted that they were productive of much benefit, not only in proving that there were some masters and mates in the Mercantile Marine who were sufficiently well educated to pass from their quarter-decks to the examination room, and successfully obtain a certificate of competency with little or no assistance from special teaching; but also, the further fact that to a very large majority that was impossible, in the face of the very elementary state of education then, generally, to be found in Mercantile Marine officers.

According to the table in the Appendix,* showing the work of examination done in the various ports, the total number of masters and officers who had passed in the four years and a half ending December 31, 1849, was 2239. Of these 1939 were masters and 300 were mates. Of the masters 1·7 per cent. passed as first-class extra; 18·46 per cent. in the first-class; 60·55 per cent. in the second-class; and 19·24 per cent. in the third-class. The last class was composed chiefly of masters in the home trade,

* See *Appendix* C.

yet in it there were several masters in command of foreign-going ships.

Now, when it is considered that the masters who passed were only about 7 per cent. of the number in existence, who were either able or willing to pass any kind of examination, there is a complete answer to those who deprecated Government interference in the education of the British sailor; and, seeing that a third-class certificate required nothing more than an ordinary knowledge of seamanship, the fixing of a ship's position by dead reckoning, the determination of the latitude by a meridian altitude of the sun, and the ability to work out the tides for any time, or place, from the fixed data of full and change, a very heavy tax was not placed upon the brain-power of our seamen.

Lowering of the Standard for Compulsory Examinations. Its effect.—With such an experience before them, it is not to be wondered at that, when the Board of Trade came to fix the standard of examination and competency under the Compulsory Act of 1850 (with the view of getting as many as possible to pass), the standard of the higher classes of the voluntary examinations was abandoned altogether, and the qualification of masters and mates was reduced to one dead level to meet the state of education rather than to create efficiency. Even with this reduced standard a large number either made no attempt to try for a certificate of competency, or else failed in the attempt, and were content to retain their positions upon "certificates of service." Doubtless many of these were fairly educated, and might have succeeded had they made the attempt, but the element of what may be termed "stage fright" prevented some of the older men from submitting to the test; others were too proud to go to school again after having served for years with credit; and perhaps the elementary parts of the examinations had more deterring influence than the more practical parts of navigation.

Promise of the Board to raise the Standard.—In reducing the standard the Board of Trade deplored what is deemed a necessity, and promised to raise the standard of examination when it could be done *without inconvenience;* but this was really begging the question, and it had the effect of destroying the examinations, as an incitement to education. Judging from this distance of time, it might have been better to have adhered to the former high standard and the three classes, and have allowed all the masters then in existence to remain under certificates of service, in positions they had held for years successfully, rather than have forced them into passing under a lower standard.

The original division of the masters into three classes was well conceived to meet the exigencies of the various classes of ships and voyages and their educational requirements. It was never pretended that a master commanding the smaller craft trading to the Baltic, or the Mediterranean, or even across the Atlantic required to be so well educated as a master of one of the lines of mail steamers, or passenger ships, sailing to the further shores of India, China, or Australia. Foreign nations have such a distinction. The education required in a French *Capitaine de long cours* is a very different thing from that of a *Capitaine de Cabotage*, which latter includes all the European coasts and the Mediterranean. To reduce the requirements for both these ranks to one level had the effect of depressing the one, whilst doing very little to elevate the other.

The System of Examination productive of "Cramming." —The lowering of the standard and the use of stereotyped forms of examination which were calculated to try mere accuracy (a necessary feature), but not general intelligence, soon told its own tale. The effect upon the grade of second mate was very soon visible. The young aspirant, on discovering that no education was required beyond a mere knowledge of figures, troubled himself no more about the matter, until, having put in his four years' time, he went to the nearest "crammer" to be coached for an examination, all the tricks of which the crammer knew beforehand, and this is a rule which has continued to the present day. Any teaching of navigation at sea by masters, with few exceptions, is more honoured in the breach than in the observance. Masters no longer think it their duty. Here's an illustration; a shipmaster being examined before the Manning Committee lately, objected *in toto* to "premiumed apprentices."

Question: "Would not that prevent youths, who wished it, being educated for officers on board ship?"

Reply: "I did not follow you there."

Question: "Suppose you had a son whom you wanted to be educated for an officer on board ship, would you not pay a premium in order that a captain should teach him navigation?"

Reply: (evidently in surprise) "A captain *teach* him navigation?"

Questioner: "I will not ask you anything further about that."

Evil results adverted to in 1870 by a writer to Lloyd's. —As early as 1870 the writer of a letter to Lloyd's "On the Education of the Merchant Service," says, speaking of the result of the system of examinations: "Before its adoption and for *a very short time afterwards*, the parents of young men who had chosen a sea life as a profession, deemed it incumbent on them to provide an education suitable to their children's future advancement, and I have known such young men pass from six to twelve months, or more, at a nautical school, studying algebra, geometry, trigonometry, and a course of navigation, and, in the interval between each voyage, they returned to pursue their studies and perfect themselves in such necessary problems as they had hitherto learnt imperfectly. This, in the main, is wholly altered; the stereotyped form of examination—in seamanship no less than in navigation—is known; why trouble any further in the matter?"

He then goes on to relate the system of cram as it still reigns in the present day; the examination for each grade with its *preceding necessary cram;* the necessity for the mate and the master to commence at the rudiments and *go all over again* as if it were wholly new, and why? Because the mental faculties were never very highly taxed, and the memory cannot retain what was never very deeply impressed upon it; however, the void must be filled, and after an effort the candidate "gets through;" the last ordeal is past and he is a "master ordinary." He contrasts the foreign systems with ours, and shows their superiority.

Board of Trade's Recommendation to Officers to Educate themselves never acted upon.—In their circular of 1850, the Board of Trade issued a strong recommendation to the officers of the Marine *to educate themselves*, and to Masters to *encourage education* in their apprentices. "This," he says, "has never been acted upon to any appreciable extent, and the standard of 'qualification' remains as low as possible."

Neglect of the Primary Sciences in Board of Trade Examinations.—That the standard has, since that day, been raised, to a certain extent, as far as the practice of navigation is concerned, must be admitted; and that examination in several subjects which were in their infancy in 1850 has been added; such as magnetism, and compass deviation, with the modern means and appliances for correction of compass errors caused by the attraction of the iron or steel of which ships are built; the modern intricacies of the rule of the road and the rules for preventing collisions at sea; the handling of steamships, &c., all very important, but appertaining more to the seamanship side of navigation than its literary or scientific treatment. The examinations in navigation simply rest upon the empirical rules of the art, taking no note of any interest or progress in the primary sciences of numbers, algebra, geometry, or trigonometry.

To prove this, reference is made to the Regulations relating to Masters and Mates, 1894, the last issue. In connection with primary education we learn that the candidate "must write a legible hand and spell correctly, and will be required to give in writing definitions of various astronomical and other terms used in navigation (a schedule of which is given). He must have a competent knowledge of the *first five rules of arithmetic*, and the use of logarithms." This instruction contains the whole reference to literary training—what follows, simply referring to the *empirical rules* and *formulæ* of the practice of Navigation, and nothing more.

What the regulations mean by "the first five rules of arithmetic" is not quite certain; neither will the examinations as conducted hitherto throw any light upon it, for all the evidence that can be gathered upon the point goes to show that both these five rules and any test of literary capacity have been ignored by the examiners; the usual course being to begin with examples of multiplying and dividing numbers by means of logarithms, and the examiner passes on to "day works," &c.

Comparison with Foreign Nations.—In the standard of education as proved by examination we are far behind those other European nations whose example we professed to follow, as the table in the Appendix will show.* Does the comparison place much to our credit? The answer is palpable. Out of *thirteen subjects* which contemporary European maritime nations deem necessary to form component parts of a master mariner's education, the Board of Trade deem *five* only necessary, with a sixth—steam—which being voluntary is neglected, only about half a dozen officers yearly presenting themselves for examination in it.

Whatever improvement has taken place since 1850, has simply lengthened the same unscientific groove. All that has been so added has simply rendered the work of the crammer a little more arduous in each grade—a little more difficult of attainment by the candidate—but has not added the slightest incentive to early or primary education. There is no incentive to rise above common mediocrity. The examinations are in the same "barbarous condition" as Sir F. Pollock relates in his *Reminiscences* that he found the law examinations in 1853. "Candidates were either simply passed, or plucked; and there were no means of distinguishing the best from the worst."

Men of fifty years ago.—In the opinion then of many persons capable of judging, the examinations have entirely *failed in becoming an efficient educative force*. To say that no good has been derived would be far from the truth, but there are people who think that the system has done quite enough for the sailor and wants no improvement—that the British shipmaster as the ultimate result of the system is a much better educated man than he was fifty years ago. This is, to some extent, correct, but when we remember the immense strides in education which have taken

* See *Appendix* G.

place in all classes of society, even to the hewers of wood and drawers of water, since then, it is very doubtful whether he has more than held his own. Fifty years ago we could point to men in the Mercantile Marine as clever, as well educated, and as scientific as any men of the present day. Such men are what they are in spite of the system, not in consequence of it, or we should have little to say. The evidences of a want of education are visible in far too many to permit of such a conclusion.

System has rendered Shipowners and Masters careless of the Education of Young Sailors.—The most mischievous part of the system of examination, without any effort to secure sound education, is, that it has tended to burke primary education and to teach both parents and children that no special education is necessary until the certificate to qualify for promotion has to be obtained, and has made shipowners as well as shipmasters careless of any kind of tuition of the young men apprenticed to them.

Passports to Service; their Intention.—Before quitting this subject a word of caution in regard to the passports to promotion, termed certificates of competency, may be given to the young aspirant for honours. Too often it is thought that the passing an examination and obtaining a certificate should lead at once to promotion, and its failure to do so has led to a great deal of dissatisfaction and heartburning. Such a feeling betrays a total misapprehension of the position. The fact is this, the legislature in the endeavour to restrain owners from appointing incompetent men to places of responsibility, says, it is not lawful to appoint such men unless they can show what is deemed to be a sufficient education, and therefore certain lines have been laid down for an examination into that sufficiency; further than that it is not desirable to go, or to pass judgment as to capacity.

Promotion, an Owners' Question.—When a seaman has served a sufficient time in a lower capacity, an opportunity is at once afforded him to show, as far as the regulations are concerned, that he is fitted to proceed to a higher one. This done, the duty of the controlling power ends, and the further judgment as to fitness rests upon the owner who appoints. Hence it will be seen that, as to the choice of employment, the law leaves, with this one restriction, the employer and employed in exactly the same position as they were prior to any legislation on the matter.

CHAPTER III.

OUR YOUNG SAILORS.

CONTENTS.—Attractions to a sea life—The different classes of lads who go to sea—Changes in life at sea—Age of going to sea—Advice to parents—A special education the first necessity for any profession.

Attractions to a Sea Life.—As long as there are ships, be they sailers or steamers, to sail the ocean, there must be seamen to handle them, and navigators to direct them. Hence the necessity for sailors, as men who "go down to the sea in ships" are usually called.

To many of the softer minded people of this world, it is a wonder that any man would ever desire to be a "sailor." They think of the forsaking of home and friends, the many hardships, the terrible risks, the being cut off from the many luxuries and comforts that the well-to-do enjoy on shore, and are astonished at the wilfulness which makes men endure the one and cast aside the other for the sake of a life at sea.

The Different Classes of Lads who go to Sea.—The *love of the sea* seems innate in the British race; descendants of the Northmen and the Anglo-Saxons, their heredity asserts itself. The blood of the Northmen fills their veins and seeks an outlet for their energies upon the ocean—native born shipmen. We find them coming not only from the coasts, but from inland hills and dales, from country valleys where a ship was never seen—gentle and simple all tinged with the same ardour for the sea.

The fairly educated lad born on the sea-coasts sees the mighty ocean spreading out before him, and he longs to see what lies beyond his limited gaze. He sees the ships passing "to and fro" upon that

> . . . . glorious mirror where the
> Almighty form,
> Glasses itself in tempests,

and he is seized with a dread longing to prove it, and them. Perhaps he has learned to steer a tiny boat around the rocky coasts of his "sea-girt home," and the very love of sailing, without ulterior motives of rank or commerce, seems to carry him captive. The passion becomes unconquerable and hurries him away from pulpit, hospital, or bar, to the service of one of which professions he may have been dedicated in a fond father's mind.

The inland boy's longing for the sea is, perhaps, formed in a different manner—the son of an upland farmer or of a village doctor—the love of roaming and adventure has been nurtured in him by reading the exciting tales of the sea by Clark Russell, or the older stories of Marryat, or Chamier; his imagination is filled to the brim with the glories of a sea life, and he longs to throw aside the plough, or his books, and meet his fate upon that ocean which he has only seen in his waking dreams.

Too many of these set out totally unprepared; but, if they are endowed with a fair education, and their enthusiasm is sufficient to overcome unforseen difficulties, and is accompanied by a sense of duty to be performed, they may make good seamen, and, perhaps, cultivated navigators.

Others there are again in middle-class life, who, devoid of any enthusiasm, but hating books, teachers, and all the drudgery of learning, look upon the sea as an open door by which they desire to escape from the restraints of home, school, or college, and throw themselves into its life without one premonitory thought of what such a life entails—a fictitious freedom is their only desire. From this class spring the drones and wasters of the service. Soon becoming disillusionised, and wearying of a life which they find requires as much attention and study as any other, they leave it if possible, or, if they continue in it, do their duty sullenly and reluctantly, never attempting any self-cultivation. Their hatred of books and restraint follows them to the end; they may, after long experience, make what they call "seamen," but never clever shipmasters or navigators. This is the class who sneer at the "educated," and take care to inform you that "books never made a sailor"!

But there is a fourth class of lads who go to sea, brought up in our seaports and fishing villages. Their fathers and grandfathers have probably been sailors before them, and encourage their sons to look forward to a sea life as the fitting field for their energies, taking care to give them an education in some degree fitting for it. These, having put their hands upon the "tiller" seldom turn back, but form the back-bone of our Mercantile Marine. The bulk of these are to be found upon our Eastern coasts, and it is a fact worth noting that it is upon these coasts alone that there is to be found much public enterprise in teaching navigation, &c., and consequently the best schools.

Changes in Life at Sea.—The days of sentiment or even adventure for the merchant sailor are over. The perils of the sea remain to give whatever excitement may be left, but there are no new lands to discover; the face of the world, except in extreme polar regions, is known; the depths of every patch of ocean have been sounded, and nearly all its hidden dangers revealed; and every important region is now within a few hours reach by telegraph. The work of the sailor is more prosaic than of yore, and requires careful and unremitting attention, yet it is a life full of movement and very interesting to observant minds. To those, on the other hand, who follow it with closed and unobservant eyes, it is duller than the dullest factory on shore.

The intervals of ships in port are short, and times of idling, except to those out of employ, shorter still, especially in steamers. On the voyage there are fewer opportunities for reading and study than in the longer and slower voyages of bygone days. Therefore, it is the more necessary that the young sailor should, if possible, enter upon those studies which are necessary to make him a cultivated man, and increase his power of thought and observation before he goes to sea.

Age of going to Sea.—Now one word as to the age at which the young sailor should go to sea—that is, for those who go with a view to rising in the profession. Formerly it was the custom and considered necessary to send boys to sea at a very early age, to harden them into its rough life. Nelson went to sea before he was twelve. Thirteen was the common age in H.M. Navy for a long period; then it was raised to fourteen and now fifteen; and after that some time has to be spent in a training-ship before they actually joined the service afloat. In the merchant-service lads used to be apprenticed at twelve to fourteen, and many a lad has gone to sea at ten: but such a thing is now unheard of. At the present time it is of no advantage to the boys themselves, and in the large sailing ships now in vogue, and steamers especially, they are of no use.

Advice to Parents.—The fact is, no owner cares to take a lad as an apprentice under fifteen years of age, and therefore advantage can be taken by parents who have sons bent upon a sea life to trend their education in a useful direction by affording them instruction suitable to such a life. Taking fifteen as the earliest age at which a boy should go to sea, he has had sufficient time with very ordinary ability and application to conquer all the elements of arithmetic, a fair knowledge of his own language, a competent acquaintance with mathematics, and possibly one or two foreign languages. Many a lad is sent out from the *Worcester* and the

Conway between the ages of fifteen and seventeen well grounded in all these subjects, besides the elements of seamanship and navigation. Now a lad can do all this in a shore school, except perhaps the seamanship, and in the seaports even that might be easily acquired.

Then let this advice be given to parents: If you find in your sons a disposition for a sea life, dedicate them to it by the best preparation possible. Do not put off the evil day, which to some timorous parents it is, and then, when persuasion or dissuasion has failed, let them go hurriedly and ill-prepared in any kind of ship that will take them. Try to discover good owners, and a trustworthy master—there are many such to be found by careful inquiry—and the due preparation having been made, launch them into life with a blessing, remembering that it is not now a life of more than ordinary hardship, and that there is nothing in it, to a well-trained lad, which tends to injure him as a moral being; certainly nothing more than will be found in the heart of our large cities, upon which so many are, of necessity, thrown in their boyhood.

A Special Education the First Necessity for any Profession.—The pressing of this matter of education upon the young who are going to sea, or upon the parents or guardians who are sending them, needs no excuse, for it will assuredly be granted that the first necessity for success in any profession or calling is as thorough an education as possible for it; and, moreover, that such special education to be of the greatest value must be begun early in life and carried systematically forward with growing years.

This is fully admitted in all shore-going professions. Why should it not be also demanded for the sailor? It is the object of the writer to enforce this principle; and having dealt with the past, an attempt will now be made to show what the education of a sailor ought to be, and what may be done to aid and foster it in the future.

CHAPTER IV.

A SEAMAN'S EDUCATION: WHAT IS EMBRACED IN IT.

CONTENTS.—What a seaman's education should be—Changes from sail to steam—Qualifications of a seaman—The science of navigation—What it requires—How to acquire the necessary knowledge—The law silent on this point — Difficulties attending education — Various types of officers.

What a Seaman's Education should be.—It is a self-evident proposition that to enable a man to become a perfect master mariner, education is required upon two separate and distinct lines, viz., seamanship and navigation; and further, that the education in these two branches of a sailor's art ought to be carried on simultaneously by him who desires to rise to the top of his profession.

It is quite possible for a man to become a good practical seaman without any acquaintance with the art of navigation, but in that case he can only serve as a boatswain or petty officer. On the contrary, it is quite possible for a man to become even a good navigator with little knowledge of a seaman's handicraft.

Changes from Sail to Steam.—Now, in discussing this question, it must not be forgotten that the business of a sailor has been undergoing during the past forty years a singular transformation. Sixty years ago ocean steamers were non-existent. Every shipmaster was required to be both a good seaman and a good navigator. Forty years ago there were fifty foreign-going sailing ships for one steamer, now we have two steamers for every sailing ship, and, moreover, steamers almost without sails. Where this is the case seamanship is at a discount; in fact, there is no longer the necessity for what cannot be employed, viz., the handling of ships under canvas. All the other parts of seamanship remain in full vigour, but these can be acquired in a steamer quite as readily as in a sailing ship.

This state of matters is acknowledged by the Board of Trade, inasmuch as they have instituted a separate class of certificate for men brought up wholly in steamers, the examinations for which are in some respects stiffer than for the ordinary foreign-going certificates, with the one exception, that of handling a square-rigged sailing ship. The certificate conveying the right to command a sailing ship requires that knowledge and supposes the bearer to be a thorough seaman.

Qualifications of a Seaman.—To whom then may this term "*a seaman*" be applied ? and what are the necessary qualifications ? First, a seaman is one who by education and experience understands the structure of a ship, her masts, yards, sails, and rigging, and is able to perform all the handwork in connection with them, such as the sending up and down masts and yards, fitting and repairing standing and running rigging, &c.; and has a knowledge of the strength of ropes and tackles, &c., necessary for handling light or heavy weights in taking in or discharging cargo, &c.; this may be termed the trade or handicraft of a seaman, and is required of every able seaman. Secondly, how best to employ this knowledge for propelling a vessel on her voyage, or for avoiding the numberless dangers to which a ship may be exposed from wind and weather upon a voyage from one port to another—for anchoring her safely in port or getting under way—for, in fact, performing every required manœuvre. This knowledge relates to the duties of the shipmaster and his officers, and may be termed a branch of Applied Mechanics which can only be acquired by years of practice in sailing ships. The shipmaster then may be said to collate and bring into use the knowledge of the shipbuilder and the mast-maker, the rope-maker and the sail-maker, as indispensable to his training.

The Science of Navigation.—The science of Navigation, on the other hand, relates not to the ship but to her path and position on the seas. It embraces the art of pilotage, and the finding of a ship's position by the bearing of the land or its land marks, or by dead reckoning (*i.e.*, the keeping a record of the courses sailed, the distances made good, and the result calculated by the rules of Navigation); or by observation of the heavenly bodies, and thence deducing the ship's position by the rules of Nautical Astronomy.

What it Requires.—This science, with all its concomitant branches, requires, if it is to be pursued intelligently, a considerable amount of literary training and ability. As a foundation it requires a good knowledge of figures and the general principles of geometry, trigonometry, and the elements of algebra. The latter, because algebraic expressions are in such common use that it is absolutely necessary to understand the teaching of even the most elementary scientific works; and the former because they are the sciences upon which are built all the problems and formulæ of Navigation and Nautical Astronomy, and are absolutely necessary to a clear comprehension of the practical rules of the Treatises on Navigation. A knowledge of the elements of magnetism is also necessary to understand its effect upon the mariner's compass, and the manner of correcting its errors by adjustment or otherwise, so necessary in modern iron and steel ships for their safe navigation.

To the master of a steamer a knowledge of the principles of steam and the steam engine is absolutely essential, unless he is satisfied to be dependent upon the knowledge of others all his life.

How to Acquire the Necessary Knowledge—The Law Silent on this Point.—Such then being the elements of knowledge required in the shipmaster and his mates, how and where are they to be acquired? Upon this the law is silent. The one necessary condition for a foreign-going certificate is that the candidate shall have served four years at sea; of which *twelve months* must have been in a *square rigged* foreign going ship, or *eighteen months* in a *square rigged* home trade or coasting ship, within the five years previous to applying for examination; and the other three years may have been spent anywhere actually at sea. The year qualifying a second mate for a chief mate's certificate, or the year qualifying a chief mate for a master's, may be spent in any class of foreign going vessel, the only consideration being that the officer must have been in charge of a watch. This opens the door wide enough to the position of Master, which may be attained without ever serving as a Chief Mate at all, and has without doubt depreciated the Master's certificate, not only in the eyes of shipowners, but of the active members of the *personnel* themselves.

Difficulties attending Education.—This question of the education of the young sailor, with a view to subsequent command, is hedged about with difficulty. The theory evidently is, that any seaman may rise to be a master; and not only so, but the door is opened still wider, for by the regulations a carpenter, sailmaker, or cook (who at the same time works as a seaman), and can prove a good knowledge of seamanship, are admitted as candidates for examination as second mate, after six years of such service; that is to say, time so served partially in seamen's duties, counts for only "two-thirds" of that of a pure seaman. Such a theory was perhaps sufficient sixty years ago, but it was under such a theory that the whole system of education broke down and led to such a state of matters as caused legislative interference. It is such a theory which has guided all reform in connection with the mercantile marine, and paralysed any efforts in the way of education upon a sound basis. Hence no effort has been made to provide for an education suitable to the shipmaster's vocation, beyond testing such education as he may have, by his own effort, attained, and seeing whether it reaches a required standard. It is this which has led to the abandonment of all primary education in navigation, and to trust in the assistance of the "crammer" when the test is to be put into force.

Various Types of Officers.—Of course some kind of education there must be; and truly, in practice, we shall find in young sailors all shades of it, in the same way as we shall find them drawn from almost all classes in society. And so, we shall find, although abandoned in the Government scheme, various classes of ships available for absorbing the various types of sailors. The more gentlemanly type, and the better educated from the ordinary standpoint, join the more important lines of passenger and mail vessels; while the rougher type, and less educated (in the same sense) perhaps join the cargo ship and steamer. In this connection types only are dealt with and not individuals, for we may find men equally clever and well educated in either type. Nevertheless the differing types do exist.

CHAPTER V

THE PRESENT MEANS OF EDUCATION.

CONTENTS.—Education as a seaman—Training ships—Education as navigators—Where to be found—Christ's Hospital—Endowed nautical schools—Liverpool Nautical College—College of Navigation at Liverpool—School ships *Conway* and *Worcester*—Deficiency of schools in London—The Drapers' Company—Evils of the present system.

HAVING thus clearly stated the case for education, the next thing to do, is to consider the possible means there are in existence for the education of the merchant officer, and to endeavour to show how best these means can be made available.

Education as a Seaman.—It is evident that the only school for seamen is the *sailing ship*. The rudiments of a seaman's handicraft—knotting and splicing, &c.—may be taught on shore; in fact for all the higher branches—fitting and cutting rigging, &c. —the rigging loft on shore is the best place, but the seaman's knowledge of how to handle a ship, and everything belonging to her, can only be perfected by a very considerable amount of experience at sea—an experience proportioned to the intelligence and capacity of the learner.

For centuries up to 1849 every seaman served an apprenticeship, and no seaman was rated as an Able Seaman under any other condition unless on an emergency. The ablest of the apprentices rose to be mates and masters, in the ordinary course; but as there was no law on the question, inexperienced youngsters were often made mates, or even masters, by friendly owners, which gave rise to much dissatisfaction. It was one of the first causes of the Tyne seamen's petition to the House of Commons *re* loss of life at sea in 1833.

In the East India ships of the Port of London, following up the custom of the old East India Company, lads were received as midshipmen, and from the quarter deck were trained as officers. The parents of these young men paid a premium to the owners, but it was not customary to indenture them. They were thoroughly instructed both in seamanship and navigation, and after three years service were promoted to the rank of Fourth Mate and upwards as vacancies occurred; from that class sprang some of the smartest officers and masters in the Blackwall ships, and many of them passed over to the lines of mail steamers as officers after serving some time in the sailing ships.

In the year 1849, when compulsory apprenticeship was abandoned, there were enrolled 9659 apprentices, and although the number of indentures then current is not given in the returns, it must have been about 30,000. Hence it can easily be seen where our seamen came from as well as our officers. The year after the number enrolled dropped down to 5055, but that was the lowest number for the next seventeen years. The spurt in sailing shipping in 1853 to 1856 sent the number up to nearly 8000, but from that time the drop in numbers had been continuous until 1894, in which year only 1861 were enrolled, and 8455, including fishermen, were in existence. As the sailing ships disappear, which they are doing yearly, the apprentices follow, and so the school for officers diminishes. At present there seems to be no lack of young men who have passed through their four years' probation and claim a second officer's certificate, and if it could be ensured that they were all fairly educated it would leave nothing to be desired in the way of numbers.

Midshipmen, in the sense in which the term was used in the Blackwall ships, have entirely disappeared. Their place has been taken by the premium apprentices, before mentioned, whose education and treatment on board is entirely different.

There are still some owners who take apprentices on the old footing without premium; but they are few, and those lads whose parents cannot afford a premium must fight their way as boys, or ordinary seamen, until the four years' probation is past.

Although apprenticeship is no longer compulsory, the Board of Trade encourages the system by allowing the time of an apprentice to count consecutively so long as four-fifths of the time is served at sea. For all others the full time actually at sea must be made up, broken time between voyages not being allowed to count.

Lads educated in training ships* have the privilege of "half the time served on board," such ships "being allowed to count as sea service up to the limit of one year," under proper conditions as to conduct, or seamanship; but "the time so allowed is not regarded as service in a square-rigged ship." This, however, in itself, is a very considerable inducement to education in a "training ship," and should be taken advantage of where possible.

* This regulation refers only to the school ships *Worcester* and *Conway*, although it is not so expressed.

Training Ships.—Of training ships there are some dozen and a half in our ports and harbours, in addition to the "school ships for officers," the *Worcester* and *Conway*; but none available for parents who would be glad to send their sons to them for instruction on payment of moderate fees.

Five of these training ships are supported by "voluntary contribution" for destitute boys, or those whose parents are respectable but have not the means of providing for them. Several others are "Industrial Schools" for boys not absolutely criminals, but who, if not cared for, might fall into crime; and the rest are "reformatories" for young criminals. Both these latter classes are supported wholly or in part by the authorities.

None of these training ships can be esteemed as fitted for the training of young officers, although in the first of these classes a fair education is given, and to some, the elements of navigation are offered; and those boys, who are fortunate enough to be apprenticed from the ships to good owners, have a chance to succeed, by good conduct, in rising in the service. But as seminaries for seamen they serve a useful purpose, although even in that direction their efforts are limited, the average number sent to sea from them being only about 1400 per annum, of whom a goodly number go as cooks and stewards, and not as sailors.

Education as a Navigator.—It has been shown that, although the school for seamen is the ship, it is possible to teach the rudiments of a sailor's business on shore. Much more is this the case with navigation, and not only so, but it ought to begin on shore before a sea life commences.

The Navigator, as distinguished from the sailor, should have a fair literary education in early youth; he ought to be able to speak and write the English language correctly, and have a good knowledge of arithmetic in all its branches, and geography both terrestrial and physical; a fair knowledge of algebra, geometry, and trigonometry; and, if possible, a knowledge of some other European language, French or Spanish being of importance to the sailor abroad.[*]

He who attempts a sea life, in which he hopes to rise to the highest attainable position, ignorant of the sciences upon which the art of navigation is founded, sets before himself an arduous

---

[*] In a most interesting and useful lecture, on "The Study of Geography for Sailors," lately given in the rooms of the Mercantile Marine Service Association of Liverpool, Captain R. T. Miller, R.N., mentioned the great value of acquired languages; and incidentally remarked, "Spanish and French are, after our own, ... likely to be most useful to seamen, for Spanish is the official language of 962 seaports, and French that of 728 seaports, which, together with English, include most of those likely to be visited."

task in which he is more likely to fail than to succeed. It is true that no guarantee as to this kind of education is demanded by law, but for his own sake he ought to be so provided.

Why should the young sailor be permitted to start upon his career without some show of a fitting preparation? In no other profession is it the case. The lawyer, the surgeon, the engineer, and the chemist all receive a preliminary instruction in those principles of education upon which their future life is founded. Why, it may again be asked, should it not also be demanded of the sailor?

Where Education is to be Found.—Granting the necessity, where is such an education to be found? Failing any serious effort on the part of the Government to establish "Nautical Schools," such tuition must be looked for in a few municipally or privately endowed schools, or by private tuition.

Christ's Hospital.—Of the former, Christ's Hospital in London (commonly called the Blue Coat School from the old-fashioned uniform worn by the pupils) has in the past done good service. It received a special endowment from King Charles the Second for the purpose of giving "a mathematical training to a number of boys destined for the sea service," and providing an outfit for a certain number yearly. In this way hundreds of our best sailors and navigators received their training, and this to a certain extent is still kept up.

Endowed Nautical Schools.—The Trinity House school at Hull is also an old establishment which provides nautical education free for thirty sea boys. The Trinity House itself dates from the middle of the fourteenth century. This school is still doing good work.

The Mariners' School at South Shields, endowed by the late Dr. Winterbotham, the Navigation Schools of Leith and Dundee, also partially endowed, or supported by public bodies, complete the list of the endowed schools of any age.

Liverpool Nautical College.—Within the past few years the Liverpool Corporation has created and endowed a Nautical College, which is certainly the most notable public effort in aid of Nautical Training of modern times. The College was opened by Lord Brassey on December 1, 1892. "The object of the college," says the prospectus of the managers, "is not merely to supply elementary instruction in nautical science to boys who wish to follow the sea as a means of livelihood, and to give sound and efficient training to Apprentices and Officers who only wish to obtain Board of Trade certificates, ... but also to establish a Higher Grade school which shall always afford to the members of the Mercantile Marine the means of obtaining a thoroughly complete and scientific training in all the subjects embraced in a liberal technical education equally well adapted to deck officers and to marine engineers." Its success in two years is very encouraging, and it is to be hoped that many will take advantage of the "Higher Grade" school, and not rest satisfied with merely "cramming" for examinations.

College of Navigation at Liverpool.—The Mercantile Marine Service Association has also a College of Navigation in Liverpool, which is free to all its members, but open to non-members on payment of a fee. The Association also provides lectures on Shipbuilding, Stability, and Stowage of Ships, deviation of the Compass, Shipping Laws, &c., and Ambulance Classes for First Aid, &c.

School Ships "Conway" and "Worcester."—The most prominent efforts of a semi-public character are contained in the school ships *Conway*, on the Mersey, and the *Worcester*, on the Thames. These are nautical boarding-schools for the youths of the well-to-do classes who wish to follow a sea life, and whose parents are able to pay for them, much as they would do at any other public school; indeed it is clearly expressed in the *Worcester* prospectus that none but the sons of gentlemen are received, and the same may be said of the *Conway*. It is true that the ships are loaned by the Government, but to what better purpose could "obsolete war vessels" be turned? The outfit, &c., has been provided by our merchant princes, and the fees simply cover the outgoings in tuition and food. The scheme of education seems to be all that can be desired, and it is a pity that such an extension of primary education as would meet all the wants of the merchant service cannot be accomplished.

Deficiency of Navigation Schools in London.—In London all the old navigation schools are either defunct, or are converted into schools for preparation of candidates for the Board of Trade Examinations, and such a thing as a scholar attending them before going to sea, or during their four years' probation or otherwise at sea, is almost unknown. In almost all the provincial seaports there will also be found schools and teachers existing merely for the purpose of such preparation.

The Drapers' Company.—A most praiseworthy effort was made by the Worshipful Company of Drapers at the People's Palace, Mile End Road, a few years ago, to establish classes in navigation and nautical astronomy, hoping to be of use to the young sailors of the East End of London, but it fell dead from its very inception from want of a sufficient number of pupils to keep it going. As a contrast, there are hundreds of young engineers attending the mathematical and engineering classes at the People's Palace.

The London Board Schools in a few cases are prepared to teach navigation, but very few scholars apply for it; the fact being that no one now realises the necessity for any preparation for a sea life. The baneful effects of the mode in which the examinations for mercantile officers are carried out, especially the first for junior mates, has crushed all desire for preliminary teaching out of existence, except in a small minority of candidates, and all that remains is a *preliminary cram* for a few weeks, the value of which, even after passing, depends upon the scholastic grounding in mathematics which the applicant may or may not have received before going to sea—in fact, upon a mere accident.

Evils of the Present System.—Thus has the system, which was inaugurated in 1850, of examination without preliminary education, failed to bring about such an education of the mercantile marine officer as was intended and is desirable. The evils of the system, from having been raised upon a wrong foundation, are so ingrained and deep-seated, that they will only be cured by a determined effort on the part of the Marine Department of the Board of Trade to revise it thoroughly, and place it upon a true scientific basis. The most glaring evil is that careless or ignorant parents, knowing that their sons must go to school to be prepared for the examination, no longer think it necessary to have them taught the elements and principles of navigation before going to sea, and at sea such instruction is seldom given. In the case of apprentices who serve under articles of indenture, the owners to whom they are bound only contract to teach them "seamanship." Formerly, when apprentices were bound to the masters, they felt an interest in their boys, and many took a pride in their education not only as seamen but as navigators; but as the owners pocket the premiums, without which, except in rare instances, they are not taken, and as their presence on board is frequently made an excuse for a reduction in the number of A.B.'s, the masters look upon them with suspicion and sometimes with absolute dislike, showing no concern in their education. In this manner a really efficient school for officers is reduced to a vanishing point.

CHAPTER VI.

HINTS ON EDUCATION.

CONTENTS.—Elements to be acquired—The first five rules—Course recommended—To be tested by preliminary examinations—*Worcester* examinations—The nautical colleges *Conway* and *Worcester*—Little assistance given by Government, &c., to young sailors—New regulations for examinations—New element in extra-master's examination—What will be its effect?—It will be a *dilettante* exercise—The true meaning of the fifth rule of arithmetic—The two methods of education—Shipmasters' and officers' memorial for honours examination—Opinions of shipowners—Adverse to theoretical education—Officer's duty as to education—"Survival of the fittest."

FAILING any direct national aid in, or instruction as to what, the primary education of the young sailor ought to be, it will not be out of place to give some hints to parents and guardians, as well as the young sailor himself, as to the best mode of preparation for a sea life.

Elements to be Acquired.—It has already been stated that no lad should in these days go to sea, or join a ship, before he is at least fifteen years of age; the time is better employed in attaining a good scholastic training. Taking this for granted, his earlier years, up to at least that age, should be spent in acquiring a competent knowledge of the English language, so as to be able to write and speak it correctly; general history and geography, both terrestrial and physical, and, if possible, an acquaintance with the French or Spanish languages; alongside of such literary culture the theory and science of numbers, and mathematics (*i.e.*, the science of quantities) should form an important part of the sailor's education. The methods of arithmetic and algebra are comprised and illustrated in the former, and geometry and trigonometry in the latter.

The first five Rules.—As already shown, the Board of Trade examinations demand a knowledge of the "first five rules of arithmetic." But what *are they*? The term looks simple enough, but when analysed it will not be found quite so simple. To understand it, one must turn back to some of the old-fashioned treatises on arithmetic of fifty years ago, in which the methods of addition, subtraction, multiplication, and division of numbers were called the first four rules; but what the fifth rule is it would puzzle any one to tell. Such an archaic expression ought to be wiped out of the regulations. Perhaps the ancient "rule of three," is intended; that "unsatisfactory and misleading process called the 'rule of three' *which merely teaches the young student how to arrive at results without a thorough knowledge of the method by which they are attained!*"* This description might be applied without error to the present systems of nautical education and examination.

Course Recommended.—The first thing to be acquired is the abstract power of figures in all their combinations, or pure arithmetic, which carries the student through the ordinary rules relating to integral numbers, fractions, decimal fractions, and the extraction of the square and cube roots; and when these are thoroughly understood their application to the calculation of prices, quantities, &c., called commercial arithmetic, will prove easy. A knowledge of algebra, which is the science of abstract reasoning about figures by means of letters, will be of immense assistance to the student, even if carried no further than the solution of equations, and by the time it is so far conquered he will fully understand what the old rule of three means scientifically. Add to these a sufficient progress in geometry and trigonometry to enable the student to understand their application to the problems of navigation and nautical astronomy, and the primary education will be complete, fitting him to go on and study for himself the arts belonging to his profession. Such a course of education could be accomplished by any boy of fifteen of ordinary ability, and may be acquired in any good mathematical school, and under a master of any standing employed in such teaching.

The course is no more than is undergone by the pupils of the *Worcester* and the *Conway*, and many also in the few navigation schools above indicated, and no more than ought to be demanded from every young officer.

To be Tested by Preliminary Examination.—To test such an education a preliminary examination should be held by a competent professor unless proficiency is otherwise vouched for, before any examination in the problems of navigation is permitted. Such an examination is demanded in every other profession, and the education of the sailor will never be on a sound basis until it is demanded for him also. Such a course is advocated by numbers of officers in the mercantile marine, and the only difference of opinion is, as to whether such a preliminary examination should be held before, or after, the period of apprenticeship

* Hamblin Smith, Preface to "Arithmetic."

is accomplished. The writer's opinion is, that it should be held before the lad goes to sea, while the knowledge is fresh in the memory, and this would have a greater tendency to its retention. If after, it might be neglected until the time arrived for the second mate's examination, and would create the necessity, perhaps, of going to school again, and so incurring an immense loss of time in acquiring what ought to have been learnt long before, and which ought to be avoided, as any such break in a sea life is often very detrimental to after-success.

"Worcester" Examinations.—It is such an examination as the pupils on board the *Conway* and the *Worcester* pass at their final stage, as is shown by the following statistics. Out of 50 Cadets who passed out of the *Worcester* in 1895, 12 received First Class Extra certificates in general knowledge and navigation; 23 received First Class certificates, and 15 passed the ordinary standard. In seamanship, 10 passed First Class Extra; 27 First Class; and 13 Ordinary.

That the Government has admitted the value of such a preparatory course is shown by the fact, that in the case of lads so prepared on board the *Conway* and the *Worcester*, one year of the necessary four years' apprenticeship, or other sea service, required for a second mate's certificate, is remitted as being of equal value to that period of service actually at sea. It is very doubtful whether the two years on board these ships is not of more value than two years of an apprenticeship on board a modern foreign-going sailing vessel, where the apprentices are probably more occupied in scrubbing paint work, or polishing brass work, than in actual seamanship, with little or no teaching of, or exercise in, the practice of navigation.

Under existing circumstances the only thing that remains is to impress upon parents and guardians, as well as upon the young men themselves who intend to go to sea, not only the necessity for, but the exceeding value of, some such direct preparation as has been indicated; and the great desirability of their taking advantage of such means of education as may lie at their hands.

The Nautical Colleges "Conway" and "Worcester."—To those who have the means of spending, say, sixty guineas per annum for two or three years, no better means of education can be found than that provided on board the Training Colleges of H.M.S. *Conway*, on the Mersey, and H.M.S. *Worcester*, at Greenhithe on the Thames. In these colleges the pupils receive a sound English education in addition to a nautical one.

On board the *Conway* boys are admitted between the ages of 13 and 16. They must "read, write, and spell fairly, and be able to work correctly questions in the simple rules of arithmetic."

The prospectus also states that "a previous knowledge of Algebra and Euclid will be found very advantageous." The cadets are expected to remain two years, or more if necessary, but no certificate is granted under two years.

On board the *Worcester* there are two schools, an upper and a lower; to the latter pupils are admitted at from 11 to 13, and to the upper from 13 to $15\frac{1}{2}$ years of age. The preliminary education required is much the same as for the *Conway*.

In these colleges the pupils receive instruction in everything pertaining to the life of a mercantile marine officer; the discipline maintained is excellent, and every attention is paid to the pupils' well-being morally and physically. For some years a naval cadetship has been bestowed by the Admiralty upon one or two of the most deserving pupils in each ship; and several appointments to the Bengal Pilot Service are annually given by the Secretary of State for India, and to the Royal Naval Reserve as midshipmen by the Admiralty.*

To those who are not able to take advantage of such colleges, all that can be said is—seek such means as are to be found, and if no nautical school is available, try and acquire a good mathematical foundation for future work. All who are well grounded in the science of figures and geometry will find the principles thereby acquired easy of application to the practice of navigation, and a ready means of self-cultivation in the art. The examination for a second mate's certificate is of so elementary a nature that with a very little endeavour at self-training any young sailor after spending four years at sea ought to be able to pass it with little or no assistance. It only wants the desire for knowledge, but this unfortunately is not always found in the young, and those who have not a desire for study, either inbred or acquired by early training, seldom find it later in life. This is only discovered when too late; and, when a certain amount of knowledge is necessary for promotion, it is attained with much difficulty, and even then but imperfectly.

Little Assistance given by Government, &c., to Young Sailors.—The conclusion which is forced upon us is, that little assistance is given to the young sailor's education by the Government, the shipowner, or the shipmaster, and for it he must depend alone upon his own exertions. There are two methods of education for the marine officer—one, in which, without preliminary scientific education, the working rules of problems in navigation are learnt parrot-like by rote; another, an education in first principles and the scientific reasoning upon which such rules

* Many Liverpool shipowners take *Conway* boys as apprentices without premium, which is a great boon.

are based, creating an intelligent knowledge of, and reason for, their use and application, such as can alone lead to accuracy of thought and practice. It is for the young sailor himself to choose which he will follow, and upon that choice will depend much of his success in life whether as sailor or citizen. Happy will it be for him if he be well advised in time!

New Regulations for Examinations.—Before bidding adieu to the subject of education, it will perhaps be as well to say that whilst these sheets were in hand the Marine Department have issued a new set of regulations for the examination of masters and officers, which mark a very considerable advance upon those now in existence—so considerable, indeed, that they are not to come into force until the 1st of January, 1898, and thus give ample time for preparation.

For the first time the examination is to begin with a test of the writing and spelling of the candidate, by submitting him to "a quarter of an hour's dictation." This is a small step in advance, but is it enough? It is strongly maintained that it is not. What is required is to make this examination—this testing of literary knowledge—a reality, by insisting upon some proof of a knowledge of the grammar of the English language, and also of geography, unless the candidate has already passed some scholastic examination, such as that of the Junior Oxford or Cambridge, or College of Preceptors, or the highest standard in the curriculum of the Public Board, or other schools, which may be accepted as a proof of the candidate's attainments.

It is on points of general education and competent knowledge of business matters that the British sailor has shown the greatest deficiency. The Americans, in the high day of their foreign shipping trade, gave their young men whom they intended to command their merchant ships a couple of years' experience in an office before they sent them to sea. This is just the kind of education young sailors want. A gentleman who rose very quickly to a command in one of our lines of mail steamers served two years as a lad in the writer's office before going to sea, and he used to say that they were the most valuable two years of his life.

To return to the new regulations. It will be found that in each examination a large addition is made to the course now in use. A second mate will be examined in the correction of compass courses for both variation and deviation; also in finding the error of the compass by Azimuth observations. He will also be made to show that he understands how to fix the ship's position on a chart by cross-bearings, and the course to steer from one position to another on either a "true" or "magnetic" chart. He must show that he understands "the construction, use, and principle of the barometer, thermometer, and hydrometer," and also "tables of weights and measures." A chief mate, in addition to what is required in a second mate, must be able "to find the latitude and longitude" by stellar observations; know how to keep a ship's log-book, or to calculate "the internal capacity of holds and bunkers," and "a freight and its commissions."

The master, in addition to the work of a mate, must be able to calculate the latitude by the altitude of the pole-star at any time and by a meridian altitude of the moon; compute the deviation of the compass by the bearing of any object; construct a deviation curve upon a Napier diagram; answer questions as to the effect of ship's iron upon compasses; compensate the deviation by the aid of Beale's compass deviascope; counteract the effect of current upon a ship's course: and correct soundings for time and place. His knowledge of the law affecting crews and load lines; of medical treatment of scurvy; of invoices, charter parties, and bills of lading; of Lloyd's agents and their duties; the nature of bottomry, bills of exchange, surveys, averages, &c.; as also of the prevailing winds and currents of the globe, trade routes and tides, is put to the test.

A New Element in Extra Master's Examination.—So far these regulations are merely extensions of knowledge of practical rules, but when we come to the extra master's examination we find introduced as a requirement a knowledge of plane and spherical trigonometry, wherefrom he has to elucidate the scientific principles upon which the empirical rules to be found in all the ordinary treatises on navigation and nautical astronomy are constructed.

What will be its Effect?—No one will deny that this is a step in the right direction, but is it rightly timed or placed? and will it be of any practical use? Is it to be supposed that any one who has passed the three compulsory examinations without any reference to such sciences will, in middle life, set to work to acquire them simply for the sake of passing a voluntary honour examination? It is doubtful, very doubtful indeed. If an outcry has been made at the introduction of lunars into the extra examination, as being useless problems to the modern sailor, especially the steamship sailor, arising from the altered circumstances of navigation, will the outcry not be louder still when the candidates are compelled to retrace their steps and fall back upon work which should have been original in their education? And will it not have the effect of making this examination more illusory than ever and its usefulness questionable? The assertion may be confidently made that not one man in a thousand will make the attempt unless he has been fully instructed in these sciences in his youth. It must be thought of some use, or why introduce it even at the eleventh hour? The answer is left to the framers of the regulations.

It will be a Dilettante Exercise.—It may be taken for granted that no one who has not been grounded in such mathematics in youth will manage to pass this extra examination, and therefore it will remain a *dilettante exercise* for the few who have been sufficiently educated, and be useless to the service as a body; it is not, even now, required for the Royal Naval Reserve. It will certainly be a proof, if there are any to be found who will undergo and succesfully pass this examination, that some few merchant seamen are educated men; but what is required is that all shall be well educated. It is the only half-educated men who spoil any profession.

The True Meaning of the Fifth rule of Arithmetic.—Why, then, should not the Marine Department hold to the courage of its convictions, and beginning with true education at the very commencement of the sailor's career, insert a demand for such elementary scientific knowledge in the first examinations, as well as a full exposition of them in the final one? We shall then, and not till then, know what the "fifth rule" means—viz., that it is the application of the science of numbers to the solution of all questions that may meet us in nautical life, and all the functions of navigation connected therewith.

The Two Methods of Education.—We have referred to two methods of education—the one by rote, and the other by scientific training upwards from first principles. Which of these styles of education, can it be said, has been fostered by the mode of examination which has existed, with all its supposed improvements, past and present, since 1850? Surely not the latter, but the former, which neglects education till the last moment, and then permits the possibility of empirical rules being "crammed" hastily, which soon pass from the memory in which they have never been deeply embedded, leaving the mind starved and helpless, and requiring the same ground to be gone over again and again at each succeeding examination. Let us hope that, having opened out a line of education on more scientific principles in the proposed new voluntary examination for the extra master, the authorities will in time extend such principles to the compulsory examinations. The result of the new regulations will be awaited with some anxiety by all who have the future education and position of our Mercantile Marine officers at heart.

Shipmasters' and Officers' Memorial for Honours Examination.—With a view of giving an impulse to scientific education, five years ago the Shipmasters and Officers' Federation Council memorialised the Board of Trade to institute honours examinations in all the degrees from second mate upwards, which would include mathematics as a subject for examination, beginning with elementary geometry, trigonometry, &c. Before replying to the S. and O. F. Council, the Board of Trade laid the proposition before all the principal companies and firms of shipowners in the kingdom, and asked their opinion upon it. The local boards at the various ports were also asked to express an opinion. After a delay of about two years an answer was vouchsafed. Unfortunately, the replies from the shipowners, &c., were not of such a character as to afford the Board of Trade encouragement to proceed with the institution of the honours examinations, but the Board stated that " although the Department have not been able to adopt the specific suggestions of the Shipmasters and Officers' Federation, they have already decided to raise the standard of voluntary examination in compass deviation, and still have under consideration suggestions which have been made them for improving the compulsory examinations generally." This has received its fulfilment by the publication of the new regulations for examination of officers and masters. It is, however, to be regretted that the Board did not see its way to institute the honours examination for each grade, which would have easily led up to the promised examination of the master extra. It would have given the better educated a chance of proving their knowledge, and gradually have prepared the way for a more scientific training throughout, without in any way oppressing those already in the service who had not received such an early training as would fit them for such a high standard.

Opinions of Shipowners. Adverse to theoretical education.—The nature of the replies sent to the Board of Trade by shipowners is a convincing proof that the officers need not look to them for encouragement in higher education, and yet there are some who entertain a right view of the question. One of the Board's correspondents replies : " Voluntary honours examinations would attract a better class of men ; certificates from such exams. would enable them more readily to get employment in best services." Another says : " Approve generally of the proposal to institute honours exams. for all grades." Several reply, " Satisfied with present examinations ; " others say, " it would be unfair to older men ; " and several join in the opinion that " practical sailors are what owners want." These are the owners who say, " We do not want gentlemen, we want seamen to command our ships ; " and who evidently think it is impossible for a man to be a scholar and a gentlemen, and at the same time a seaman ! It is very evident our shipowners want educating as well as our seamen, and if they had been listened to there would never

o

have been any Government interference in the matter of that education.

Officers' duty as to Education.—Survival of the fittest.— Notwithstanding such ignorant and old-world ideas, it is the duty of every one who is connected with our Mercantile Marine, and has the welfare of our officers at heart, to leave no stone unturned for their improvement as scientific and practical seamen, and prove to the world that the more educated a seaman is, the better seaman he becomes. It must not be forgotten that the seamen of the present day are entrusted with the care of an instrument of commerce so complicated and of such value as was not dreamt of sixty years ago. Navigation is more complicated, more intense, than it was in the days of the sailing-ship of that period. To understand such an instrument, and to carry on such navigation, requires special ability and training, notwithstanding anything which may be said to the contrary. That there are shipowners still remaining who place no value upon such an education is manifest, but it is to be hoped they grow fewer and fewer every day. Let then our officers, encouraged by the sympathy of the better class of shipowners, look to themselves for their future success, and by constant practice, study, and daily experience, fit themselves to meet a competition which hourly grows more severe, and which can only be met by a "survival of the fittest."

PART IV.

DISCIPLINE AND DUTY IN THE BRITISH MERCANTILE MARINE.

A Paper read before Members of the Shipmasters' Society on November 22, 1894, by the Author.

CONTENTS.—Discipline and duty—Relation between the shipowner and the crew—Between the master and crew—Duties of mates, petty officers and seamen, engineers and engine-room crew—Mutual respect enjoined.

It may be remembered that in former papers on the *personnel* of our merchant fleet I have said a good deal on the personal relation to each other of the various ranks and classes usually comprising the crews of our merchant vessels, yet I by no means exhausted the subject. And as these relations have of late been widely discussed in many quarters, it seemed to me desirable that they should be placed before you in a somewhat more set and explanatory manner. So many months have passed since I undertook to do this that some of the subjects treated may appear to be matters of ancient history; still, the question is sufficiently perennial to admit of our renewed discussion of it, and at the request of your Committee I am encouraged to proceed.

I cannot but say that I approach the subject with some diffidence, feeling my inability to cope with its importance thoroughly, in either its legal or practical aspect; yet I do so with the hope that I may be able, in some measure, to throw light upon what, I fear, is in the minds of too many persons, surrounded with misapprehension, if not ignorance, from the want of giving its intent and meaning due consideration; and, with the further hope, that wherein I may fail some one with better and riper knowledge will step into the breach, and fill up my omissions, or correct me upon points wherein I may err.

Discipline and Duty.—Let us first come to a clear understanding of the terms "Discipline" and "Duty" and what they involve.

"Discipline" is defined by Webster as "Cultivation and improvement in arts, sciences, correct sentiments, morals, and manners; due subordination to authority"; then, secondarily, "Rule of government; method of regulating principles and practice; .... Subjection to laws, orders, rules, precepts, or regulations" .... and, collaterally, "Punishment intended to correct crimes or errors."

"Duty" is defined as "That which a person owes to another; that which a person is bound by any *natural* or *legal obligation*, to pay, do, or perform," and, secondarily, "Obedience, submission." Generally, then, we may say that "Duty" refers to all the acts of performance in every situation in life, and "Discipline" to the order and method in and by which such acts are regulated and carried into effect.

Now, I do not think we shall find much clearer definitions than these. They may be amplified and extended to meet varieties of situations as between man and man, but can hardly be rendered more simply. What I want you specially to observe is the dual alliance of these terms—the necessary dependence of the one upon the other. "Discipline" implies a corresponding duty, and "Duty," to be soundly performed, requires "Discipline" in all kinds of human affairs.

There is, I fear, a mistaken notion abroad that both "Discipline" and "Duty" are very one-sided affairs; that "Discipline" means the power of coercing others into doing whatever a master, employer, or any superior may please to enforce, without reference to the reasonableness, morality, or legality of the act; that "Duty" means the meek submission to such coercion, simply because it is the will of the superior. It is not so. Wherever there is, as between two parties, obligation on the one side, there is also a corresponding obligation on the other—and, before there can be any obligation at all, there must be a contract mutually entered into, or by law or custom implied. As wherever two or more work together one must be the leader, so discipline and duty necessarily imply an "instructor" and "those to be instructed"—a "governor" and the "governed." It further implies a sound moral government and a reasonable willing obedience in the governed—an experienced capability in the instructor, and a teachable attitude in the instructed—and, it goes without saying, that the better men are educated—the more civilised they are—the nearer will perfection be obtained in carrying out these principles. Having then said so much by way of definition, let us see how best they can be illustrated in their application to the service of our Mercantile Marine, and the right meaning to be attached to them in connection with life on board ship. It will be apparent that, as, of necessity, there must be differences of rank, authority, and position in the crew of a vessel, so the discussion of the terms "Discipline" and "Duty" must include a discussion of the relation of the one to the other in that crew, no matter what the department may be in which the individual work lies.

Relation between the Shipowner and the Crew.—In the first place we have the owner who employs his vessel for his own immediate profit, and for the working of the vessel he must employ a number of hands of all descriptions, with whom he contracts to pay each in his individual capacity a certain wage for the work to be performed; and he stands in the same relation to them as any other civilian who employs men at any work or trade does to his workmen. In like manner the shipmaster and the officers of all classes stand in the same relation to the owner of the ship, as do the manager and foreman of a factory to the owner of that factory. They are relatively employed and paid for conducting the necessary duties consistent with each business or trade, and possibly for the thinking out or designing much of the work to be done. The crew of a ship and the workmen in a factory are equivalent to each other, and they are employed and paid for performing the work or handicraft of the business according to each man's *training or calling*, under the foreman in each department, whose orders they contract to obey in return for their appointed wage.

From this it will be seen that the general principles which underlie the mode or method by which work is carried on in all its varied circumstances, whether on shore or afloat, are the same; and these involve a mutual obligation between the parties concerned, of which the foundation is a *contract* either written or implied.

In early days such contracts were left pretty much to the individual judgment of the parties to them, but as human nature is weak and cupidity strong, it frequently happened that the contracts came to be not only unequal, but vicious—human slavery is an instance of such inequality—and so, as nations became more civilised, the State and its Government stepped in and, to a certain extent, by just and wise laws, regulated the terms of such contracts. Of such are all laws regulating the condition of labour in factories, mines, &c., hours of work, and the like; and so, in reference to the Mercantile Marine, we find in the Merchant Shipping Acts of this country a body and system of law, by and under which the employment of all persons concerned in the navigation of our merchant vessels is to a certain extent regulated.

I have shown that employment of all kinds, whether on shore or at sea, stands upon the same moral basis; but here I must point out one very material difference between the two, which we shall have to consider. On shore, such contracts are usually for short periods of duration, frequently only from day to day, or at will on either side; so that upon any cause of disagreement the parties separate without restraint, and little harm ensues to either, for the employer can usually find another workman, and the workman another employer. Should there be any material wrong or injury sustained by either party, the civil magistrate is at hand to be appealed to and see justice done. Under such circumstances, anything like *enforced discipline* is quite unnecessary, and the question of wrong generally turns upon some idea regarding wages, the value of services, or damage incurred by the wrongful dealing of either party.

At sea a very different state of matters prevails. The seaman, like the workman, not only places his labour at the command of the employer, but he further hands himself over to the employer for a more or less extended period, under a legal contract, specifying the voyage to be undertaken, the general nature of the services to be performed, and the remuneration, &c., which is to be paid and received for such services. This restriction of the liberty of the seaman and the protracted nature of the employment makes the consideration of the discipline necessary for the due performance of duty a much more serious matter in the case of a sea voyage than in that of a workshop on shore.

This we shall find duly provided for in the Merchant Shipping Acts, which render the position of a seaman more nearly an approach to that of persons in H.M. Navy than that of the ordinary workman; but it is only a bare approach after all. The conduct of the national service is governed by statutes and articles of war, of which the operation is wholly and entirely absolute. The conduct of the merchant ship is controlled by the will and necessities of the individual owner, with very slight statutory control. The discipline may be as prudent and vigilant, the obedience may be as willingly and completely rendered, in a merchant ship, but it never can be as strictly enforced under the same penalties as in her Majesty's service. The daily life in a Queen's ship is detailed and regulated to a fault, and in a manner impossible in a merchant vessel. Of course, the more rigidly the duties are detailed, and the more vigilantly they are carried out in a merchant vessel, the nearer the approach will be; but this is possible only in the best and largest of our merchant ships, and with large crews, and staffs of officers.

Beyond the written code contained in the Merchant Shipping Acts there is an unwritten code which follows habit or custom, which may vary very much indeed, according to the kind of voyage or trade to be engaged in, or the ideas of the owner, or master, who employs, so long as the legal contract undertaken is not seriously departed from. You all know that the mode of discipline and what is required under the unwritten law or custom varies from ship to ship, or employ to employ, and the service is said to be hard or easy according to the nature of these requirements. For instance, no one would deny that life is harder on board a tramp steamer, or most of our modern sailing-ships, than that on board one of our fine mail steamers; the work being more incessant and the reliefs fewer, with a more constant strain upon the individual worker.

I now proceed to consider the facts connected with "Discipline" and "Duty" on board our merchant ships, first, as provided for by Acts of Parliament, and, secondly, as generally sanctioned by custom.

The duties of the owner I shall touch upon very slightly, as beyond the scope of this paper, and that only as far as regards his duty to his crew.

The owner may employ whom he pleases as members of his crew, with the exception of the restrictions in the Acts as to Masters, First and Second Mates, and First and Second Engineers, without regard to qualification or number. The law is very jealous of interfering with an owner in the conduct of his business, and it has only interfered on behalf of the lives and necessary comfort of those on board, or of the necessary well-being of the weaker members of the crew. To this end it has made regulations for the seaworthiness of ships, and the proper accommodation and feeding of the crew, in addition to very stringent rules as to the payment of wages, the loading of certain cargoes, &c., and subjects the owner to heavy penalties for the non-fulfilment of them.

Whatever may be the terms of contract of service between the owner, or master, of a vessel and a seaman, or apprentice, it is always an implied condition* that all reasonable means have been used to insure the seaworthiness of the ship; and this is an obligation the owner cannot contract himself out of, although he may depute its oversight to another.

Before an owner can send a ship to sea an agreement must be entered into with every member of the crew, but the onus of making the agreement is laid upon the master as the agent of the owner, who, nevertheless, is bound by its terms in regard to the

* See section 458 of 57 & 58 Vict. c. 60.

contract with the crew as to wages, food, &c.; and every such agreement must be in a form sanctioned by the Board of Trade. The master must first sign these articles himself, affixing the date. The articles must contain certain particulars, for which see section 114 of the Merchant Shipping Act, 57 & 58 Vict., 1894, but there may be added thereto any regulations as to conduct on board, and as to fines, short allowance of provisions, or as to misconduct, &c., which have been sanctioned by the Board of Trade . . . . and which the parties may agree to adopt./

Relation between the Master and the Crew.—The simple nature of the contract is that of due and proper service on the one side in return for legitimate wages, food, and accommodation on the other. The contract is required to state the capacity in which each member of the crew is to serve and the wages and food he is to receive. But here I would point to the fact that the Shipping Acts make no reference to these capacities, and look upon every person, other than a master or apprentice, simply as a seaman, and make no attempt to define each one's relative position, or the duties he has to perform. Neither is there any attempt to control the number to be carried, with one single exception, and that is as to the number of *sailors*, meaning, it is supposed, the number of A.B.s, which, under clause *b* of the 114th section of the Act, 1894, must be defined in the agreement and maintained to the end of the voyage, sickness or death alone excepted, no matter how many other persons, mates, or apprentices, for example, may be carried. Each and all form the crew, and become *responsible to the master* for the performance of their duties in the capacity for which they sign the agreement, and due obedience to his orders. Whatever questions may arise on such points, must be settled by something outside the statutes.

If we now turn to the disciplinary clauses of the principal Act, section 225, we shall find nothing to guide us as to the internal discipline or duties of the ship, but a great deal about offences against good discipline, with a statement of certain punishments to be enforced upon such offences being committed. They have a good deal to say about disobedience to *lawful command* and neglect of duty, but we are not instructed as to what a lawful command is, beyond the fact that the articles of agreement bind each member of the crew to obey the master. There is only one exception to this statement that may be urged, and that is that the mates having been, by common law or consent, considered officers of the ship, and consequently endowed with the power of command over the remaining members of the crew, a command uttered by a mate is legally a lawful command, disobedience of which is punishable under the statute. This is confirmed in clause number six of the 343rd section, where the master and mate are classed together, presumedly as alike superior to the other members of the crew, and upon whom an act of assault by any other member of the crew is accorded a set punishment; and this is the only place in the whole of the Acts where the mate is singled out from the rest of the seamen in a disciplinary point of view.

The law, then, makes the master responsible for the conduct of the ship and her crew, who, without distinction, are bound to render due obedience to his lawful commands, whether given in person or by delegation through the mates; and all beyond is left to his judgment and experience, controlled by custom. Once afloat upon the voyage, the master's government is completely autocratic, and, if true discipline is observed, should be unquestioned until again within the range of the civil authority which has the power of reviewing his acts should he have presumedly infringed the civil rights of any member of his crew.

This, I think, completes all that can be said as regards discipline or duty as provided for by Acts of Parliament, and I now proceed to see what we can discover concerning them in the light of custom, and offer a few opinions of my own upon what they ought to be, although I feel that by doing so I shall be treading upon delicate ground, which may lead to considerable difference of opinion and controversy; and I cannot but feel, after much thought and examination of the subject, that I have set myself a more difficult task than I at first anticipated.

The statute law, then, makes little distinction between the members of the crew, but when we come to state the case in the light of "custom," a great many more distinctions must be made. The merchant service now consists of two very distinct sections, viz., "sailing vessels" and "steamships." In former days, when vessels were dependent upon sail power alone, the subject would have been much more easily dealt with, but the employment of steam power has introduced elements into the composition of our crews which necessarily complicate the question.

In sailing vessels, the elements of the crew are purely nautical, master, mates, and sailors, with a few others; but in steamers we have engineers and firemen, or stokers, who form a body of men entirely alien to the calling of a sailor, but upon whom the master is now almost completely dependent for the progression of the vessel on her voyage. In a sailing-ship every operation connected with the navigation of the vessel, her sails, masts and rigging, are under the immediate control of the master and his mates; whereas, in a steamship, the control and working of the machinery necessary for the due prosecution of the voyage are in the hands of a separate body of men, whose duties are entirely distinct from those of the seamen or sailors, and are *out* of the immediate purview and control of the master, who is lacking in the necessary technical knowledge and education connected with such machinery, its general effect only being controlled by him. This, as it may have been foreseen, has sometimes led to difficulties in connection with the status and discipline of the separate bodies, of which I shall speak later on.

The connection of the owner with the general discipline of a ship may be said to end when he sends her to sea, and yet his acts may have a considerable bearing upon it afterwards. It is his duty to appoint a *competent* master in the first place, and although the law has restricted the appointment to such persons as its officers have pronounced, after due examination, to be fit for the duty, it only deals, after all, with the very fringe of the question of fitness. In former days, when seamen grew up and were educated under the eye of the owner, and were kept on year after year in his employ, his opportunities of knowing their general character and experience were seemingly greater than they are in the present day, judging from the continual changes in masters and officers which take place, except in the larger employs (such as the mail and passenger fleets of our country), in which the placing of a master in command, except after long experience as an officer, is almost unknown. The practice of dismissing officers, as well as seamen, and not unfrequently masters also, the moment a ship or steamer of the ordinary cargo type is off her voyage, has tended to destroy the continuity of knowledge and interest between them and the owner, which is greatly to be deplored; and I cannot but think that the wholesale granting of certificates, without the owner's consent or voice in the matter, by the Board of Trade, has greatly increased this practice; and since the owner can find plenty of certificated masters and officers, it has made him careless about that feeling of mutual interest which ought to reign between them.

The master having been appointed, the owner's next care is the appointment of the proper officers for navigation and engine-room service. This should be done before the lading of the ship is commenced, to enable both master and officers to make themselves thoroughly acquainted with the ship, her outfit, gear, and holds, together with all pipes and connections leading to the same. Such knowledge cannot too seriously be insisted upon, and I have been astonished at the apathy on these points displayed by some officers; but we can hardly wonder at it when we know that the appointment of officers is frequently delayed until the last moment before sailing. Such ignorance, when necessity arises, leads to difficulty and often disaster.

It is the owner's duty to see that proper accommodation is provided, and that good provisions in sufficient quantity for the voyage are supplied. Neglect of this duty has caused it to be necessary that it should be secured by governmental supervision, which has been accompanied by the usual outcry of unnecessary interference. Considerable responsibility in these matters also rests upon the master, whose clear duty it is to have due regard to the accommodation and feeding of the crew, with all that appertains to it.

Here I would enter my protest against the supply of provisions being contracted for by the master. This is the duty of the owner, and the master should be in a position to hold the scales of justice evenly between the owner and the crew, and be responsible that neither the one should suffer from extravagance nor the other from shortness of supply. If the provisioning of the crew is placed in the hands of the master there is too great temptation to unrighteous gain and consequent ill-treatment of the crew. It is no answer to this objection to say that many masters under such circumstances do their duty honourably and fairly. As a shipowner I have tried the system myself, and am satisfied that good results cannot be depended upon.

The owner having completed his duties, the vessel starts on her voyage and bids him good-bye for the time. The real work of navigation now begins, and the effect of good or bad discipline is soon felt.

The master's first duty is to muster his crew and see that all on the articles are on board. This done, before they separate and proceed to their duties, it will add materially to good discipline if the master addresses a few words to his crew, telling them what he expects from them and what he intends to do to make things pleasant for them as long as each man fairly performs his duty in his respective capacity, and especially that if any one is aggrieved or has any complaint to make, his ears will always be open to any fair and proper statement. Moreover, that it is not his habit to swear or use violent language, and that he expects both officers and men to observe the same, at all events when on duty.

I do not intend to enter into detail as to the actual work to be performed, except on points involved in the first principles of duty. The watches set and everything in due order for the voyage, the less the master interferes in the work of the ship and in giving orders to the crew (which should be done through the officers) the more likely will discipline be maintained; but his eye should be everywhere. By such a course of conduct he will the better maintain his magisterial position and make his officers respected. Above all, he should never upbraid an officer publicly. If he should find him careless, negligent, or even ignorant of what presumably he ought to know, he should take him aside and reprove him strictly and earnestly, or even instruct him, if necessary. Mere ignorance should be dealt with in a kindly spirit, but wilful negligence cannot be too severely reprimanded.

Then I say to my fellow shipmasters, do this and you may make of your officers friends and faithful fellow workers, and they will be better men at the end of the voyage than you found them at the beginning; or so incorrigible that the sooner they are sent about their business the better.

Duties of Mates.—The duty of the mates is in all things to obey the known wishes and commands of the master, and under his guidance the care of the ship and her navigation is their first concern; and here I say the "*known* wishes and commands" of the master, for if the master is not careful to communicate frequently and closely with his officers as to his ideas of duty and the manner in which he wishes it to be performed, how can they possibly *know?* There are, unfortunately, some men who think that others should know what they think and desire, without the trouble on their part of any instruction, and they become soured and ill-tempered when they fail to have their wishes carried out. To avoid such an untoward position, the master should be patient with his juniors, and carefully instruct them in those matters where they are inexperienced and in which his own riper experience qualifies him to be an instructor. Nothing but practice and experience can make a good officer. Everything must have a beginning, and if the officer evinces a desire to learn his duty, he will readily pay attention to such instruction, and he will soon be transformed from an inexperienced one into one experienced and trustworthy.

Further, the master, remembering that an officer will, or at least hopes to be, at some time in the future a master himself, not only for his own assistance, but for their instruction, should associate them with himself in the work of navigation; the charts should be open to them at all times, and he should make it their daily duty to work up all sights and reckonings for comparison with his own, and to ascertain the daily position on the chart. The more reasonable an officer's work can be made, the more interest will he feel in it, and the more likely will he be to perform his usual duties with alacrity. Good discipline requires instruction as well as command. Moreover, to what purpose is it that a junior officer is compelled to study and pass an examination in the elements of navigation and nautical astronomy if he is not afforded an opportunity when at sea of putting such studies into practice? Many a master will acknowledge the force of this, but with many more I fear it is more honoured in the breach than in the observance.

At sea, the first and principle duty of the mate is the charge of the watch, and his place is on the quarter-deck or bridge; and the safety of the ship demands that he shall be constantly there until duly relieved, notwithstanding what may be said to the contrary. Under the unwritten law which has grown up under Courts of Inquiry, the gist of which may be found in the questions propounded by the Board of Trade as the prosecuting authority, there is no doubt that an officer is required to be constantly on the watch, and nothing can relieve him of his responsibility but an express order of the master to quit his post, who then takes the responsibility on himself. It is not sufficient to say that other work of the ship of whatsoever nature demands his presence elsewhere.

Now, it is known to be a common practice for masters to expect the mates to do all kinds of work, even in the holds, during their watch on the deck in the day time, leaving only a man at the wheel on the look-out, and this without an especial order to do it, which leaves the entire responsibility on the officer, who, should a collision or any other accident occur, may lose his certificate in consequence. I have frequently inquired about this matter, and the invariable reply is, "We cannot help ourselves; if we did not do it without a direct order we should be told at the end of the voyage that our services were no longer required. We know we are running the risk, but what can we do?" The conduct of masters who expect their officers to do this is contemptible; it is not only cowardly, but criminal, and ought to be visited with the severest penalties. That such work must be performed in every ship goes without saying; and this I hold is one of the strongest arguments for the three-watch system, which would permit an officer to be employed for some hours in the daytime in superintending the work of the ship or in the holds at sea without disturbing the officer whose duty it is to be on the bridge or quarter-deck, keeping watch over the sailing of the vessel.

Duties of Petty Officers and Seamen.—I now proceed to consider the remaining members of the crew and their requisite numbers. Petty officers, such as boatswains, quarter-masters, &c., may stand aside as not necessary, although, doubtless, convenient and valuable members of a crew when carried. Able seamen must be carried, and ordinary seamen, apprentices, and boys may be carried at the option of the owner or master. Of the qualification of A.B.'s I shall not speak, as neither time nor space will permit, but shall only say that good or bad discipline is greatly dependent upon the sufficiency of the number employed; and it may be depended upon as being better where the seamen are thoroughly trained than otherwise. It is an undoubted fact, however, that the number of such men belonging to Great Britain grows less and less, and the greater number of British A.B.'s carried as such have received a very indifferent training. To what else can we attribute the large proportion of foreigners to be found in our sailing-ships especially, and also in many of our tramp steamers? On this point such returns as are rendered by the Board of Trade in their statistical reports are misleading; the correct mode would be to take the number of A.B.'s only who sign articles in British ships in any one year, distinguishing British born from foreigners, and then find the proportion. Any other method is simply throwing dust in the eyes of the public, and can never show our strength or weakness in case of a great war with other European Powers.

The question of the requisite number of sailors in ships of various classes is such a moot one at the present moment that I do not intend to discuss it here. There is, however, one point I may touch upon, as it has lately more than ever become salient; and that is the improvement in labour-saving appliances and their aid in manual labour. This has been made an excuse for reduction after reduction in the crews of our sailing-ships, until it has become almost an absurdity. Valuable in the deliberate lifting of heavy weights, anchors, topsails, &c., such mechanical aids are utterly useless in sudden squalls or changes of weather which cannot always be foreseen or prepared for, when nothing can, or will, supersede a sufficient number of hands spread over the vessel, in ensuring the necessary power to reduce sail in such emergencies. For the want of such power many a luckless ship has been swept off the face of the seas for ever.

In our steamers it would seem that if a sufficient number of deck hands to give relief in steering, look-out, sounding, and care of the lights, &c., is carried, no fault can be found. But is this always the case? I submit that this sufficiency is not attained unless there are four deck hands in each watch; that is, a distinct two hours' relief for both wheel and look-out; and, in justice to safety and the power of endurance in the men, this ought to be imperative where the voyage extends beyond forty-eight hours on a stretch.

Duties of Engineers and Engine-room Crew.—I now turn to that other portion of the crew of a steamer which her machinery necessitates, viz., the engineers and their crew of firemen and trimmers. The engineers are men who receive their early training on shore, being bred to their business in the machinery works of the country, where they are taught not only the use but the construction of the machines they are hereafter to control as sea-going engineers, and officers in command of the engine department; and their position is one of great responsibility. In the early days of steam navigation, they were men of experience in engineering shops, and were appointed upon the recommendation of the maker of the machinery, often without any experience of sea life. Ignorant of the ideas and traditions of the old-fashioned sailing master, they did not easily fall in with his ideas of discipline, cleanliness, &c., and frequently a good deal of friction was the consequence. The last forty years, however, have worked great changes. Since 1862, the engineer has been certificated, and an officer, to all intents and purposes, although nowhere distinctly so acknowledged in the statutes until the passing of this year's Act. A very few of the older uncertificated men are left, and the engineers who are now in existence are, as a rule, well-educated and able in their calling.

The discipline and duty of the engineers in their department is precisely similar to that of the ship's officers in theirs. On all points of general discipline and duty the engineers are subject to the control of the master, but for the proper working and condition of their own department—and for everything being in working order when required by the master—they are solely responsible.

The duties of the deck and engine-room crews are so distinct from each other that there should be no difficulty in the maintenance of discipline and the due performance of duty by each and all in their separate spheres. There are a few points in which the duties overlap, and which necessitate the working in accord of the separate staffs, but they are not frequent, I need not detail them, as they are well-known to you all. Where proper discipline prevails, there need be no friction, but it will, and sometimes does, occur and lead to unpleasantness. Nine times out of ten it will be found that it is not the duty, but the personal *ego* which is concerned. Some one's dignity gets hurt from trivial causes, which a moment's thought would obviate, and a fit of sulks on both sides, if not hard language, follows, and the work, as well as the discipline of the ship is disturbed. A judicious master will very soon perceive when such a screw is loose, and ought to take measures at once to set matters right by bringing the officers together, when a little quiet, kindly talk will soon obviate the difficulty. A sore which is allowed to fester is very difficult to cure.

I must now touch upon a question which has of late been much discussed, and that is the "legal status" of the engineers. A strong feeling prevails that their position as certificated officers does not receive the recognition that it ought to have, or that they deserve.

A paper was read not long ago at the Institute of Marine

Engineers by one of its members, in which, after describing the position of engineers on board merchant ships, the following may be taken as the summing up of his argument and general demand :—" The engineer's status should be *legally defined* and he should be invested with the control of the engine-room staff, *with power to enforce discipline* amongst them." . . . . " Nor should this in any way infringe upon the authority of the master, while it may go far to relieve the *strained relations* existing in very many cases between the deck and the engine-room, the result of which is the reverse of beneficial to the owner's interest." The whole paper was written from the engineer's point of view, with studied moderation, and it received a long discussion. As it acknowledges the sometimes " strained relations " to which I have referred, I may be pardoned the introduction of the subject as one which affects deck officers as well as engineers.

Generally, the question was discussed with all fairness. At the same time, a disposition was displayed on the part of some of the speakers to demand that the engineer should be *as independent of the master's control as possible*, if not altogether. In the first place it was objected that, on the articles and in the eye of the law, the engineer ranked only as a seaman, which the engineers say " detracts from their self-respect and dignity ; " but in this they differ in no respect from any other class on board our merchant ships, even deck officers.

I have shown before that the term " seaman " (for the want of a better, and for the sake of simple comprehension) is applied to all who in the agreement contract to serve the master for the specified voyage — deck officers, engineers, surgeons, pursers, stewards, &c. &c., all trades and professions alike ; it is therefore no greater hardship for the engineer than any other person. The *articles* state the capacity in which each one has to serve, and give rank and position, and it is the only means by which each seaman is distinguished from the other. Custom teaches us that the chief engineer has as full control of the working of his own department as the chief officer has of his on deck, but it is a distinctly *subsidiary department*, and has nothing to do with the direction or navigation of the vessel (beyond her locomotion at the will of the master), or any other of the multifarious duties imposed upon the master, and in which the deck officers assist him. The desire to have the " legal status " defined is simple enough in itself ; but this can hardly take place until the law takes upon itself to differentiate between all sorts and conditions of men on board ship. It leads, however, to a much broader and more serious demand, that the " engineer should be *invested with the control* of the engine-room *staff*, with *power to enforce discip-*

line." Now what is here meant by "enforcing discipline"? The chief engineer has already the power of having his orders obeyed and of seeing that every member of his staff performs his duty, and of reprimanding them if they do not, or the work of the engine-room would come to a standstill; but he has no power of administering punishment any more than the deck officer. This power the law places solely in the hand of the master, and distinct breaches of discipline must be reported to him. Anything like placing the power of personal discipline in the hands of any officer is at variance with the law, and it is this power the engineers desire to have placed in their hands without the intervention of the master. They forget, I am afraid, that it is not as the mere superior that the law places this power in the master's hands, but as the only present agent of the law when at sea, and as responsible to it for the safety of the ship and the conduct and lives of every soul on board. To invest any inferior officer with the power of punishment would create an *imperium in imperio*, which would be unendurable, and could only lead to difficulty if not disaster. The master himself has no power to inflict personal punishment or restraint unless the act of insubordination amounts to such mutinous conduct as would endanger the ship or the life of any one on board, when his power is only limited by his discretion. The only mode of punishment which can be applied to ordinary breaches of discipline, or derelictions of duty, is by fine or imprisonment, as is provided for by the statutes, and may be enforced by the civil magistrate, consular authority, or naval court, before whom the master must bring the delinquent and support the charge by due evidence of the crime. Certain fines for minor acts of insubordination may be inflicted by the master upon the discharge of his crew, with the consent of the shipping master, before whom the discharge is made. For the purpose of proper evidence of the offence, the master is obliged to enter the facts of the case in a record called the official log, which entry must be signed by the master and the mate, or any other member of the crew. This, I understand from the discussion, is regarded with dislike by the engineers as derogatory to their influence and power, and it was even proposed that the engineers should be empowered to keep an official log of their own and be able to fine their own men. The inconsistency of such a demand is remarkable, and it can only be styled as impossible, under existing circumstances.

Mr. McFarlane Gray (referring to the proposal that the Board of Trade should define the engineer's position and authority on board ship), spoke with full knowledge when he said "The Board of Trade have no authority to do anything of the sort. They

cannot interfere and tell the shipowner how he shall manage his business. The Government does not recognise anybody on board but the owner, and the captain, because he represents the owner."
. . . . "I say," he continued, "it would be contrary to the constitution of the country for the House of Commons or the Board of Trade to interfere (with any owner) and say, 'You shall give this or that authority, to certain of your foremen.'" And Mr. Gray was quite right—it would require a thorough upsetting and revision of maritime law as affecting ships and their crews to make any such definition of the engineers' status or invest them with any such power.

In connection with this question of status, there is a point which occurred to me upon first looking into the matter consequent upon the demand set forth, and that is, that in the disciplinary clause relating to assaults upon officers by other members of the crew, the engineers should be added to the masters and mates, which would clearly have the effect of ranking them as officers in the eye of the law. On perusing the new Merchant Shipping Act (57 & 58 Vict., c. 60), 1894, I find that this has been done, and I must congratulate our friends the engineers upon this recognition of their status as officers. Whether it will satisfy the ambition of the younger and more aspiring spirits amongst them, remains to be seen. Further than performing this necessary act of justice, the Board of Trade does not seem to have been able to go in answer to the demand for a definition of "legal status."

At this point I do not think it would be unseemly to speak of a yet further demand of some engineers which we shall find in the question lately propounded, viz., "Why should we not be allowed to pass and obtain certificates as masters?" Now very curiously the Board of Trade, acting within its powers, whether with more than ordinary foresight it is hard to say, laid down the rule (No. 27 in the regulations relating to the examination of masters and mates) that "Service in an engine-room will not be accepted as sea-service for a master's or a mate's certificate of competency," perceiving evidently the incongruity of the claim, inasmuch as the education and experience necessary to qualify for the one branch has no relation to that of the other, notwithstanding what may be thought to the contrary.

In many minds there is an evidently ruling desire that the engineer should supersede the sailor, for even so eminent a naval constructor as Sir Edward Reed, M.P., has almost gone the length of advocating it. Now, when our young and aspiring engineers have such an opinion placed before them by such an authority, in such an open and undisguised manner, we can hardly be surprised at the awakening of ambition. One of them gave utterance to his sentiments by advocating that "the Board of Trade should allow engineers to pass in navigation, so that they can safeguard their own interests and at the same time their owners' interests from *unscrupulous servants*" (*sic*).

One point more needs some consideration, and that is, the relative status of the mates and the engineers. In the ordinary course of duty, this can hardly give rise to any difference of opinion, for, as I have said before, their duties are so far apart that they should not in any way clash, and it is only professional jealousy on either side which can create such difficulty. Each department is under the direct control of the master, and it is only when consideration is given to what may be called the police control of the ship and the independent liberty of each section and its members, especially in foreign ports (and by foreign ports I mean any port touched at during a voyage beyond the limits of the British port of original lading and the final port of discharge within the United Kingdom), that such questions will arise.

When once the crew have signed articles and the voyage is commenced, there is no doubt that, legally, no member of the crew has a right to leave the vessel without permission of the master, or, in his absence, that of the deck officer in command. By section 223 of the Act, 1894, which is a repetition of the 246th section of the Act of 1854, any member of the crew so absenting himself without leave may be arrested by the master or any mate without warrant first obtained, which clearly establishes this position; but for the safety of the subject, the delinquent must be taken before the magistrate or consul in a foreign port if he so wishes, so that the proper facts of the case may be established. No such power is given to an engineer, but with all members of the crew he is subjected to the same discipline. This matter of leave has been a constant matter of dispute with engineers, and always will be with those engineers who arrogate for themselves "the control of the engine-room staff and power to enforce discipline."

The care of the engine-room and all its appurtenances belongs to the chief engineer. He directs how and when the engine-room crew shall be employed to fulfil his responsibilities, but the knowledge of when their services may be required rests with the master; consequently, the law gives him the sole power of saying when they may be absent from the ship, or in his absence the chief officer as his deputy. It appears to me that if true discipline is to be observed it cannot possibly be otherwise. No right-minded master would refuse such leave when the duty of the ship permitted it, and no right-minded engineer would desire that it should be otherwise. The grievance is a mere sentimental one, bred of want of self-discipline, or of self-sufficient pride. There can be only one master, and the engineer, with all the other members of the crew, contracts to, and must, be subject to his command. Any other position must necessarily "infringe upon the authority of the master," and would rather add to the existing "strained relations" for which there is no reasonable excuse, and could not possibly have a place, if all were careful to rigidly perform the duty and observe the discipline imposed upon them by their contract. In the presence of the master the mates have no disciplinary power over the engineers; but in his absence the mate becomes his legal deputy, in charge of the ship.

I think I have fairly stated the case and disposed of the demand and its feasibility, and I trust, now that the law is about to give the engineer a standing as an officer invested with authority, as well as the master and the mate, that harmony will prevail, and true discipline be accompanied by satisfactory duty. If what I have said does not meet with a cordial reception from any of my engineering friends, I can, at least, say that I am sure I shall not be accused of saying anything out of professional jealousy, but that I am only actuated by a desire to say to all alike—sailors as well as engineers—what I believe not only the law but the necessity of the case compels me to say. Until the engineer displaces the sailor altogether, the laws of our country remaining what they are, they must be content with the position accorded to them by those laws.

As to their desire to raise themselves educationally and socially, no one can accord them greater praise than I can for their endeavours, or more earnestly wish them God speed. In these qualifications as a body I hold them quite the equals of our sailors, but in so heterogeneous a company as all those composing our Mercantile Marine, there must and will be very great differences educationally and socially, whether as sailors or engineers. No one branch possesses a patent of equality in this respect, but that need not destroy the equanimity and harmony of the whole, working together for the common good, if right judgment prevails.

I should not have referred to this demand at all did I not see in it something which affects our sailor officers, and may affect them still more in the near future, unless they take heed in time.

It is a notorious fact that engineers are now appointed as superintendents of many lines of steamships in preference to sailors. Why is this? Simply because the technical knowledge possessed by engineers of the construction of modern ships and their machinery is superior, and as the superintendent's chief duty is the looking after the repair and keeping in order of the fabric of the ship, the owner places more confidence in their technical knowledge of such matters and their advice than that of our present race of shipmasters. In former days the oversight of the shipmasters was looked upon as a necessary factor in the rigging and outfit of a vessel, whereas now they are seldom consulted; and, depend upon it, unless the course of education for the sailor, and what it embraces, is seriously altered, their position will only go from bad to worse. This state of the case seriously interferes with the master's power to maintain discipline. The engineer superintendent has the ear of the owner, and he would be more than mortal if he did not favour his own cloth to the discredit of the opposing interest when differences occur. The consequence is that the sea-going engineer, confident of the support of the superintendent upon a final appeal, is apt to pay little attention to the wishes and commands of the master. It is easy to be seen how this reflects upon the discipline of the ship, and disturbs the harmony of duty. The true relation of the parties is dislocated, and although the shipmaster is master by law, with a heavy responsibility on his shoulders, he finds it difficult to maintain his authority in the face of such a state of matters.

From my point of view, nothing can mend this but a much higher technical training for those who are to command our steamers in future, to enable them to cope practically with the situation. In the early days of steam power, as applied to ships, it was deemed advantageous that an officer or master should have some knowledge of the new instrument he had to deal with, and the Board of Trade undertook to examine seamen in what is technically known as "steam." Many officers studied the question and successfully passed; but year by year the practice fell more and more into desuetude, until perhaps some half-dozen yearly take the trouble to obtain the certificate. This must always happen when examinations are voluntary. There will always be a few who will delight in attaining knowledge for its own sake; but these are always in a minority. Had such examinations been compulsory upon all steamship officers, we should not have had such complaints from the engineers that they find it difficult to get masters to understand their difficulties when they occur; nor such foolish replies as a master once made to an engineer when he informed him that he was short of *vacuum* and could not get more. "Why did you not tell me before you left——and *I would have ordered some more!*"

We may take it for granted, then, that our engineers are running our sailor officers a very hard race, and it justifies us, who ardently desire a better, fuller and more technical education for the latter, in keeping the subject alive before themselves, the Board of Trade, and the public. The want is well met in the education given on board the *Worcester*, whose highly educated and intelligent commander, Capt. Wilson-Barker, is fully alive to the wants of our sailor officers, and is doing his best in conjunction with the *Worcester* Committee to meet them. The same may be said of the *Conway*, but all that these two school-ships can do is a mere drop in the bucket to meet the clamant want.

The main factors in sound discipline are, first, KNOWLEDGE and then SELF-CONTROL. Before a man, acting in any capacity whatever, can think of or say anything about discipline in others he must have cultivated discipline and self-control in himself. How can one who gives way to fits of uncontrolled temper, or spleen, look for discipline or dutiful conduct in others? It is impossible! I would then impress upon my younger brethren especially, that to obtain good discipline it is necessary that they should acquire an intimate knowledge of their profession in all its branches—ships and their machinery, the laws of shipping and of commerce—and cultivate the art of self-control. Their lives will then be rounded by the satisfaction of performing their duties well, and of gaining the esteem of their employers and all with whom they may be brought into contact. Ignorance of one's self is the worst of ignorance. Never forget that you are always surrounded by those who see and judge your actions often more wisely than you do yourselves. Burns, the poet of Scotland, never, in all his displays of a wonderful knowledge of human nature, wrote a wiser sentence that he did when he said:

> Oh! wad some power the giftie gie us,
> *To see oursels as ithers see us,*
> It wad frae mony a blunder free us,
>   And foolish notion.

Mutual respect enjoined.—With this quotation, I commend to your thoughtful consideration and discussion my ideas on discipline and duty, and will conclude by saying that discipline and the performance of duty will always depend much more upon the mental attitude and moral character of individuals in our Mercantile Marine, whether in those who employ or command, or in those who have to obey, than upon written codes or customary formulæ. The considerate thinking man will say to himself, when differences arise, how or in what manner may I have contributed to this difference? and upon the answer will depend his capability and power of solving them, or of administering seasonable reproof when necessary. The bane of discipline is extreme selfishness.

The selfish man acts upon the principle "that he is always right and others in the wrong." Due consideration for others is one of the highest principles of true discipline, in both commander and man, and upon this depends the just appreciation and performance of duty.

Let the owner then, if he wishes the duties connected with his vessel successfully and faithfully performed, treat his master with the confidence and respect which, as his sole representative, the law as well as common-sense demands, and be careful that nothing shall be done to detract from his position and authority, either by himself or any one in his employ. He will then have the right to demand from the master in return a careful attention to his interests and regard for the safety and good management of his property.

Let the master study the interests of his owner in all things compatible with law and reason. Let him respect his officers of all classes, demanding from them a careful and diligent performance of their duties, and by his own example contribute to true discipline.

Let the officers respect the master and perform their duties with a single eye to their owner's interest and an obedient attention to the master's commands, holding their brother officers in kindly respect and esteem as fellow-workers with each other for the common good.

By such means alone can be attained that just "Discipline" and that due performance of "Duty" which ought to be the pride and the glory of every true British mariner.

POSTSCRIPT.

THE SERIOUS DECREASE IN THE NUMBER OF BRITISH SEAMEN A MATTER DEMANDING THE ATTENTION OF THE NATION.

WHILST these pages are still in the press a very serious discussion has arisen upon the gradual, but continual, falling off in the numbers of British seamen, and the consequent want of a proper reserve force for the Navy. From what has been related in the foregoing pages with regard to apprentices, there can be little doubt that this falling off began within a short period of the abandonment of compulsory apprenticeship, and has been increasing in volume, year by year, ever since. This abandonment of education for sailors has been the destruction of the British seaman. One of the many arguments used by shipowners is, that indentured apprentices are obsolete even in shore trades and professions. In this they are to some extent correct. Take for instance the engineering trade, and it will be found that indentures are now seldom entered into. Do the engineers then escape apprenticeship? By no means! Every young engineer has to serve an apprenticeship of at least four—generally five—years compulsorily. And why compulsorily? Because the Trade Union of Amalgamated Engineers is strong enough to be able to say "No man shall work alongside us as a journeyman unless he can produce his *apprentice lines!*" Many of the engineer employers would, like the shipowners, give up the employment of apprentices if they dared; but as long as the engineers are able to enforce such a regulation, the employers dare not abandon the education of engineers, or they would soon find themselves with as insufficient a supply of journeymen tradesmen as the shipowners are of seamen. Would they be able to fill up their shops with foreigners, as the shipowner does his ships? Such a thing would very soon breed a revolution in the country.

We are now beginning to grow alive to the consequences of the legislation of 1849-54, and many writers advocate a return to compulsory apprenticeship; but this apparently is impossible, as interfering with Free Trade principles; and it is very doubtful whether it would now answer the purpose, the whole system of shipowning and management having so much changed in forty years. Moreover, the British journeyman, or able, seaman, cannot exert such pressure as the engineers are able to employ in the regulation of their trade.

What then must be done? Before a reply is given, let it be settled whether the question is a national one, or not. Is an increased supply of seamen a necessity? If it should be determined that the question is not nationally important, then the shipowners may be left to deal with their business in their own way, and obtain their hands where and how they can. But if it is a national question (as some of our best naval and other authorities affirm) in which the interest of the vast body of the nation is concerned, then we must no longer look at it solely from the shipowner's point of view, but find some means of increasing our native-born marine forces, whether the shipowners like it or not. It appears that the only way in which that could be done would be to compel every British vessel to carry a crew consisting of native-born seamen to the extent of, say, four-fifths of the whole number employed, and re-enact the old law compelling British shipowners to employ none but British shipmasters. This would be no hardship on the British shipowner, as there are far more than enough qualified British masters to fill the ranks. If those foreigners who at present are employed as masters in British ships will become naturalised citizens, by all means let them remain, but only on that condition. In reply it may be said, where are we to find British seamen to fill four-fifths of our crews, seeing they are not in existence? In answer to this, it being a national question, it can only be said that the nation must find the means of creating them, and until the means can be provided, it must be a matter of compromise. It may be conceded for a short period of years that one-half of the able seamen of any ship may be foreigners; after which the proportion might be gradually reduced to one-fifth.

As it is an undoubted fact, that we have admitted foreigners for centuries to the extent of one-fourth of the crew of a British ship, but only on condition that if she had "one British seaman for every twenty tons burthen," any excess might be foreigners; and still further, that at the outbreak of every war, even that regulation had to be relaxed, when the great body of British seamen were required for and pressed into the service of the Navy, it would perhaps be unreasonable to shut out foreign seamen entirely. This very fact is, however, a strong argument in favour of our doing whatever may be possible to increase our native sea-force, seeing that the total number of able seamen

(British and foreign) now employed bears nothing like the proportion to the total number of persons employed in British vessels that it did in the first half of this century; and therefore under present circumstances to draw, say, 20,000 British seamen out of those employed would strip the Mercantile Marine of them almost completely, and leave our oversea traffic, and food supplies, entirely at the mercy of the foreigner. Can any inhabitant of these isles contemplate such a state of matters with complacency?

It would seem clear, then, that some means must be provided for the increase of our seamen, and as to the means, there are three parties to be consulted—viz., the Government, the Nation, and the Shipowners. Apparently, for over forty years neither party has done anything to assist in the education or training of the sailor, upon whom the safety of this country, according to our premiss, depends.

The Government, through its officials, has said, and still says, that it is not the province of a Government to educate the servants of the shipowner; but in such a reply the *national side* of the question is entirely ignored. The Legislature says, the shipowner requested to be relieved from the burden of the apprentice, and we thought fit, as a necessary corollary of our Free Trade policy, to relieve him, without waiting to consider what would be its effect from a national point of view.

The Shipowner says, why should we, in face of competition with the world, be compelled to educate the seaman, who may run away from us, and leave us in the lurch, after being at the expense of his education? Whilst sympathising with the shipowner on the hardship of foreign competition, we are bound in justice to ask him this question: Why should you be the only person relieved from the education of apprentices, as compared with almost every other branch of trade in the kingdom? Your refusal to educate implies that you are careless of the qualifications of your seamen, and as long as you can get your masters to recognise and sign on any sort of man as an A.B. and have no further interest in the matter, you don't intend to worry yourself about it! This indeed is not to be wondered at, considering the fact that you are able to insure yourself from loss in consequence of the *incompetence* or *mistakes* of your servants the seamen, and are, perhaps, the only employers of labour in such a happy position. In this there is no consideration for the nation or its wants. The consequence of all this is, that the nation is landed in an *impasse*—it has urgent need of more seamen, and does not know how to obtain them. Out of this dilemma, as far as the Government and the nation are concerned, there are only two courses—the Government must either train more men specially to man our ships of war, or it must do something towards the training of a greater body of seamen for general purposes, and compelling their employment in British ships.

There is another question which may be touched upon incidentally, and that is, the growing difficulty of finding employment for our increasing population, and especially of finding an outlet for numberless youths who entertain a desire for a sea life. It is not because of any diminution of that desire that so few now enter upon it, but for the want of opportunity. An opening is now only offered by shipowners to such lads as have parents who can afford to pay a premium, and who, of course, only do that in the hope that their sons will rise in the service by becoming officers on the earliest opportunity. Such lads are seldom content to serve as able seamen, when qualified, but if not immediately successful in obtaining promotion loiter about, waiting an opportunity, and, more than likely, eventually become wasters altogether.

What then is required is some means of laying hold of and educating those who show an early desire to go to sea, and it appears to the writer that the only course open is to raise up in every port in the kingdom Marine Training Schools, which should impart such an education as shall fit the pupils for a *seaman's* duty only, and not as navigators, under direct Government Supervision. This need not necessarily be carried out in Training Ships, yet the schools should be near the water, and boats be available for practice. If possible, a small brig should be provided for instruction in the use of sails, &c., but if this were found too expensive or impracticable, the very fact of teaching lads how to sail a boat would add greatly to their usefulness. Two years in such a school after a boy has passed the fifth standard in a Board School, ought to render him almost as useful as an apprentice who has served two years at sea, under ordinary conditions, and far better than nine-tenths of the ordinary seamen of the present day. Another two years as ordinary seaman or apprentice on board a sailing ship, should render him as good an Able Seaman as will be found anywhere.

In view of making such an education not only useful but necessary, the clause of the Merchant Shipping Act (57 & 58 Vict. c. 60 s. 126) must be made compulsory. There is no earthly reason why a period of service, entitling a man to be an able seaman, should not be as compulsory as a period of service for an officer, and in complying with this law the two years in a training school should be considered as quite equal to two years at sea.

Now as to the means of enabling such a scheme to be carried out, we have seen that there are objections to its being done by the Government and the Legislature, on the one hand, or by the

Shipowners on the other; each averring that it is not its, or his, especial business; but if it is a question of such national importance as very good authorities contend it is, cannot there be proposed a combined effort of all three calculated to effect the object? Cannot we avail ourselves of the common feelings of humanity to help us on the way? The sentiment of human pity for the shipwrecked mariner leads to the gathering and expenditure of large sums of money every year, for the succour of the mariner, and in prevention of loss of life by our noble Life Boat Institution and our Shipwrecked Mariners' Society, as well as Government aids for the same purpose. Would it not be quite as humane and noble a sentiment which would teach us to lay hold of the, perhaps wayward, youths of the land, and by a well-designed institution, set them on their feet, send them forward on the path of life which they have chosen, and make them useful subjects in Her Majesty's realm? There are thousands of sons of respectable parents who would willingly avail themselves of such an Institution to get to sea, but whose parents are too poor to educate them, or provide the necessary outfit, for a sea life. Under the old laws numbers of lads from the parochial schools were bound to the sea and *provided with an outfit* by the Guardians of the Poor. The law is, I believe, unrepealed, but as no Shipowner now will take such boys as apprentices, it has become virtually obsolete.

Let then the Government, the Nation and the Shipowner, join hand in hand to carry forward the good work. Let the Government insist upon British subjects in British ships—the Nation find the means to educate the youthful sailor—the Shipowner welcome him when ready, and accept him on a two years' apprenticeship—at the end of which time he will be able to stand alone. There must be "give and take" all round. It will no longer avail any one section to wrap itself up in its garment, and say "*non possumus*." The very life of the nation is at stake, and each must work for the good of all.

APPENDICES.

APPENDIX A.

A LIST OF THE SHIPS FORMING THE FLEET OF KING EDWARD THE THIRD AND THE PORTS FROM WHICH THEY WERE DRAWN.

	No. of Ships.	No. of Men.
Great Yarmouth	43	1905
London	25	662
Fowey, Cornwall	47	770
Bristol	24	608
Plymouth	26	603
Dartmouth	31	777
Sandwich	22	
Dover	21	
Winchelsea	21	
Weymouth	20	
Shoreham	26	
Southampton	21	
Newcastle	17	
Hull	16	
Lynn	19	
York	1	9
Harwich	14	
Ipswich	12	
The Mersey	1	6
Scarborough	1	19
Wrangel	1	8
Total	409	

These vessels had no cannons, as they were not heavy enough to carry them.

APPENDIX B.

DESCRIPTION OF THE SHIPMAN.

FROM CHAUCER'S PROLOGUE.

Reign of Edward the Third, Fourteenth Century.

A *Schipman* was ther wonyng* fer by west
For ought I woot,† he was of Dertemouth
He rood upon a rouncy; as he couthe
In a gown of faldyng ‡ to the Kne.
A dagger hanging on a laas § hadde he
Aboute his necke under his arm adoune
The hoote summer had made his hew all broun;
And certeinely he was a good felawe,
Ful many a draught of wyn had he ydrawe
From Burdeux ward whil that the chapman ‖ sleep,
Of nyce conscience took he no keep.
If that he faughte and had the heigher hand
By water, he sente hem hoom to every land.
But of his craft to reckne well his tides
His stremes and his dangers him besides,
His herbergh ¶ and his mone, his lodemenage**
Ther was none such from Hull to Cartage.
Hardy he was and wys to undertake
With many a tempest hadde his berd been schake.
He well knewe all the havenes, as they were
From Gootland to the Cape of Fynysterre,
And every creyke in Bretayne and in Spayne:
His barge y-cleped was the "Mandeleyne!"

* Wonyng, dwelling. † Woot, know.
‡ Faldyng, coarse serge. § Laas, belt.
‖ Chapman, merchant. ¶ Herbergh, port or anchorage.
** Lodemenage, pilotage. (Courts of Lodemenage were held at the Cinque Ports by the Wardens).

APPENDIX C.

AN ABSTRACT OF THE PASSES AND CLASSES OF MASTERS AND MATES UNDER AN ORDER IN COUNCIL, 19TH AUGUST, 1845, PRIOR TO 31ST DECEMBER, 1849.

Port.	Year.	Masters.				Mates.			
		1Ex.	1.	2.	3.	1.	2.	3.	
London	1845	—	10	2	—	—	1	—	
	1846	1	24	148	15	—	15	8	
	1847	—	20	40	2	2	9	2	
	1848	—	21	370	109	1	37	41	
	1849	—	18	274	128	1	46	38	
		1	93	834	254	4	108	89	1383
Shields (North and South) . . .	1846	—	2	30	16	—	1	—	
	1847	—	4	42	18	1	—	—	
	1848	—	1	41	18	—	—	—	
	1849	—	7	21	30	—	—	—	
		—	14	134	82	1	1	—	232
Liverpool	1846	5	—	—	—	1	—	—	
	1847	12	19	1	—	1	1	—	
	1848	1	20	5	—	2	—	—	
	1849	1	53	41	—	3	3	—	
		19	92	47	—	7	4	—	169
Plymouth	1846	—	—	3	1	—	3	3	
	1847	—	—	3	3	2	2	2	
	1848	2	6	13	4	—	3	2	
	1849	1	5	13	7	—	2	4	
		3	11	32	15	2	10	11	84
Newcastle . . , .	1846	—	—	—	1	—	1	—	
	1847	—	6	9	1	—	2	—	
	1848	—	5	15	4	1	—	—	
	1849	3	7	15	3	1	1	—	
		3	18	39	9	2	4	—	75
Forward . . .		.	.	.	.	.	.	.	1943

APPENDIX C.

Port.	Year.	Masters.				Mates.			
		1Ex.	1.	2.	3.	1.	2.	3.	
Forward		. .	. .	. .	. .	. .	. .	. .	1943
Dundee	1845	—	3	—	1	3	—	—	
	1846	—	4	3	—	2	3	1	
	1847	—	3	1	—	—	—	1	
	1848	—	2	6	1	—	2	—	
	1849	1	16	14	1	1	4	—	
		1	28	24	3	6	9	2	73
Glasgow	1846	—	1	—	—	—	—	—	
	1847	—	2	—	—	1	—	—	
	1848	1	11	3	—	2	1	—	
	1849	1	23	13	—	—	4	1	
		2	37	16	—	3	5	1	64
Portsmouth	1846	—	3	1	—	4	1	—	
	1847	1	11	9	—	—	3	—	
	1848	—	3	2	1	1	—	—	
	1849	—	3	1	—	—	2	—	
		1	20	13	1	5	6	—	46
Leith	1846	—	1	—	—	1	—	—	
	1847	4	4	—	—	2	—	—	
	1848	—	7	2	—	4	2	—	
	1849	—	14	8	—	1	4	—	
		4	26	10	—	8	6	—	54
Yarmouth	. .	—	13	10	2	1	—	2	28
Hull	. .	—	7	17	3	—	—	1	28
Milford	. .	—	—	1	—	—	1	—	2
Gloucester	. .	—	—	—	—	—	1	—	1

Total . . . 2239

APPENDIX D.

APPRENTICES IN THE MERCANTILE MARINE.

	Indentures in existence.	Indentures Enrolled.
1845	—	15,704
1850	—	5,055
1855	—	7,461
1860	—	5,616
1865	—	5,638
1870	18,303	4,241
1875	16,004	4,379
1880	14,667	3,501
1885	10,437	2,504
1890	8,650	2,167
1894	8,455	2,164

From the Board of Trade Return, June 17, 1895, "Progress of British Merchant Shipping."

(242)

APPENDIX E.

NAVIGATION CLASSES IN CONNECTION WITH SCIENCE AND ART DEPARTMENT, 1891.

Place.	School.	Teacher's Name.	Navigation	Naut. Ast.
England.				
Devonport	National School	H. C. Tarn, M.C.P.	15	—
Plymouth	Public School	C. S. Jago	3	3
South Shields	"Wellesley" Indian Training School	W. Elford	30	25
Bristol	Merchant Venturers'	P. J. J. Brooks	20	—
Portsea	Co-operative Society	W. H. T. Pain	12	—
Rochester	Mathematical School	G. Ward	10	—
Liverpool	Board School, Clint Road	W. Hewit	90	—
North Shields	Jubilee Board School	R. W. Liddell	15	—
Gorleston	Board School	R. Cook	20	—
Hull	Navigation School	Z. Scaping	95	98
Wales.				
Pencader	Grammar School	H. E. Bryant	—	6
Swansea	National Higher Grade School	W. C. Jenkins	60	—
Scotland.				
Aberdeen	Grammar School	S. Pope	20	6
Dundee	Navigation School	L. Allen	120	120
Leith	,,	J. Bolam	200	200
Row, Clyde	"Empress" Training School-ship	G. S. Deverell	40	10
Ireland.				
Rathlacken	Baugher National School	J. Munnelly	6	—
Dublin	Marine School	I. H. Colvin	25	—
Baltimore	Fishing School	C. Hounhane	30	—
,,	National School	C. Shine	25	—
Bandon	,,	F. Murphy	35	—
Colomane	Dromore ,,	J. Ryan	20	—
Drimoleague	National School	T. J. Hurley	12	—
Glandore	,,	F. McCarthy	5	—
Limerick	,,	P. O'Donovan	8	—
Macroom	,,	T. O'Brien	10	—
Queenstown	College Mission, St. Joseph	J. O'Callaghan	20	—
Skibbereen	National School	J. McCarthy	34	—
,,	Intermediate School	E. L. Hogan	20	—
,,	No. 2 National School	J. Hayes	72	—
,,	Creagh ,,	J. Hickey	12	—
,,	Killeenleagh ,,	J. McCarthy	8	—
Union Hall	Cahergal ,,	J. Collins	12	—
Waterford	Mount Zion School	Rev. J. T. Hayes	12	12
Lifford	Endowed School	F. Smith	—	12

APPENDIX F.

PASSES IN CONNECTION WITH SOUTH KENSINGTON CLASSES.

Session, 1890-91.

	Advanced Classes.				Elementary Classes.			
	1st Class.	2nd Class.	Failed.	Total.	1st Class.	2nd Class.	Failed.	Total.
Navigation	21	76	15	112	181	133	118	432
Nautical astronomy	7	17	3	27	49	38	12	99

APPENDIX G.

EDUCATIONAL STANDARD REQUIRED BY VARIOUS MARITIME POWERS FOR MASTERS AND MATES.

	France.	Holland.	Belgium.	Germany.	England.
Algebra	Yes	Yes	Yes	Yes	No
Geometry	,,	,,	,,	,,	,,
Trigonometry	,,	,,	,,	,,	,,
Mechanics	,,	No	,,	,,	,,
Physics	,,	Yes	,,	,,	,,
Steam engine	,,	,,	,,	,,	,,
Languages	,,	,,	,,	,,	,,
Winds and currents	,,	,,	,,	,,	Yes
Navigation	,,	,,	,,	,,	,,
Nautical astronomy	,,	,,	,,	,,	,,
,, survey	,,	,,	,,	,,	No
Instruments	,,	,,	,,	,,	Yes
Observations	,,	,,	,,	,,	,,

Shipping World Year-Book.

INDEX.

A

ABLE seamen, 148
Acts of 1823-4, the Reciprocity, 55
    of 1825, general revision of the marine and emigration, 55
    of 1834-5, the shipping, 57
    of 1844, the shipping, 63
Adderley's, Sir Charles, Bill, 1875, 108
Alfred the Great, 2
Aliens, reasons for employment of, 168, 169
American civil war, 1860, 99
    colonies, trade of (1731), 42
    revolt of the, 44
    competition in 1845, 73
    shipping in British ports, 99
    ships, speed of, 94
    smuggling in the West Indies, 43
    war, 1812, 52
Anne, Queen, 39
Apprentices, 57, 98, 148, 175, 197, 241
Armada, the Spanish, 26
Athelstan, King, 2

B

BALTIMORE clippers, 95
Barnes (Capt.) of the *Locksley Hall*, 113
Bell, Henry, owner of the *Comet*, 81
Blake, Admiral, 34
Board of Trade, 105, 128, 175, 185
Bounty on large ships (1694), 36
Britons', ancient, knowledge of shipbuilding, 1
Bruges: an *entrepôt* for British trade to, 1482, 23
Bubble companies, 1720, 41
Buckingham's (silk) Bill, 62
"Busses": fishing vessels, 31

C

CABOT, Sebastian, 11
Carlingford's (Lord) Bill, 1873, 105
Chamberlain's (Mr. Josh.) Bill, 1884, 120
Chancellor (Sir Richard), discovers route to Archangel, 17
Charles the Second's navigation laws, 35
Chaucer's seaman, 29, 238
Chesapeake and *Shannon*, 53
Child, Sir Joshua, 35
China trade, thrown open, 1833, 56
    English and American ships in the, 95
Cinque Ports, 2
    French rivalry with the, 5
Cod fishery, the, 16
Colony in America, the first, 34
Columbus, Christopher, 11
Comet, steam vessel, first on the Clyde, 81
Competition in shipbuilding and shipowning, effect of, 165
Cook's (James) survey of the St. Lawrence river, &c., 43
Corn Laws, repeal of the, 74
Cromwell's Act, 1657, 35
"Cunard" and "Collins'" lines of steamships, 87, 91

D

"DAPHNE," capsizing of the, 117
Denny (William), shipbuilder, 83
Discipline, true, 161
    and duty, 211
Drake, Sir Francis, 24
Drapers' Company, the, 200
Dutch trade and encroachments, 34

E

EAST India Company's fleets, 32, 37
    renewal of its charter, 1793, 47
    Company's officers, 64
    trade thrown open, 1813, 53
Education in Mercantile Marine, backward state of, 174
    (special) a necessity, 191–202
    officer's duty as to his, 210
Edward the Confessor creates the Cinque Ports, 2
Edward the First's time, trade in, 5
Edward the Third's fleet, 5, 237
Edward the Sixth and Russia, 17
Elgar (Professor) on loss of life at sea, 125
Elizabeth (Queen): her policy, &c., 21
    Spain and the Armada, 22–26
Elizabeth (Queen), Tobias' letter to, 31
Emigrants in 1817, Ill-usage of, 55
Engineers' examinations, 102
    and engine room crews, 148, 159
    advantages of the, 172
    duties of the, 222, 228
Engines, improved economy of marine, 138
England, early population of, 1
English mariners and the cod fishery, 16
    people, Froude's picture of, 13
    rovers in Queen Mary's reign, 19
Enterprise, first steam vessel to India, 84
Examinations (voluntary) of masters and officers (1845) 69–72, 239
    (compulsory) 1851, 76
    effect of lowering the standard of, 183
    new regulations for the, (1897), 206
Exports in Edward the Third's reign, great increase of, 6

F

FALMOUTH as a postal station, 87
Fishing industry, a school for sailors, 31
Flemings in London, 6
Foreign competition, principal sources of, 138
    seamen, education of, 66
Foreigners, British ships sold to, 106
Freeboard tables, 117
Free trade, 65, 93
French bounties on shipping, 100
    King's proposals for reciprocal trade (1783), 46

G

GARAY'S (Blasco) attempt at paddle-wheel propulsion of ships, 80
Gold fields of California, 94
Gray's (Mr. T.) opinion of limited liability in shipping cos., 144
Great Western, paddle steamer, 86
Great Britain, screw steamer, 89
Green (Richard) and the Americans, 93

H

HANSE Towns, the, 6, 12
Hanseatic laws, the, 3
    League, &c., 7, 17, 22
Harrison's timekeepers, 49
Hawkins, William, 16
    (John) and the slave trade, 23
Henry the Fifth's navy, 8
    Seventh's reign, state of arts and commerce in, 10
    Eighth and shipbuilding, 12
Howard, Admiral Sir Edward, 12
Hyland (Captain) on shipmasters, 58

I

INDIA, road to (fifteenth century), 8
Indian mutiny, 99
Industry, steam vessel, 82
Iron ships, &c., 84, 94

J

JAMES the First, 33
Jenkins (Professor) on loss of life at sea, 125

INDEX.

L

LARDNER (Dr.) on steam ships, 85
Legislation, hampering effect of, 51
Letters of marque, 5
Levant Company, 32
Lightning, clipper ship, 95
Limited Liability Acts, 143
Lindsay's (W. S.) opinion of British officers, 60
Liverpool, end of eighteenth century, 47
Locksley Hall case, 113
London Merchant Adventurers, 12
    Muscovite Company, 18
    passenger ships, &c., 65
"Longitude at sea," rewards offered, 48
Lord of the Isles, British clipper, 96
Lunar tables, Government grants for perfecting, 49

M

"MARCO POLO," sailing ship, 94
Marine insurance, 151
Mariners, the, 146
Martell (Mr. B.) on loss of life at sea, 116
Mary's (Queen) reign, 18
Maskelyne (Dr.), the Astronomer Royal and the Nautical Almanac, 49
Master mariner's position and duties, 152, 243
Mate's, the, position and duties, 146, 154, 169, 220, 243
Mayer's (Professor) improvements in lunar tables, 49
Mercantile Marine, *personnel* of the, 141
    as a service, 162
Monopolies, hampering effect of, 51
Montreal (port of) and grain cargoes, 116
Moorsom's new tonnage measurement, 97
Murray's (Mr.) letter to consuls, 63-75

N

NAUTICAL Almanac, (1767), 49

Nautical schools, recommendation of the Royal Commission, *re*, 175
    schools and colleges, 199, 242
Navigation, the state of, and progression, 47
    laws repealed, 21, 75
    the science of, 193
Newcomen's engine, 81
Newfoundland discovered by Cabot, 11
    Judge Prowse's history of, 30

P

PARENTS, advice to, 190
Passports to service, 187
Peninsular and Oriental Company, 87, 89
Philip of Spain and England, 25
Plimsoll (Mr.) on loss of life at sea, 104-108
Portugal friendly to England, 25, 32

R

RECIPROCITY Acts, 1824, &c., 55
Red Jacket, clipper ship, 95
Reformation, the, its effect, 16
Reform Bill and its effects, 56
Richard the First's fleet, 3
    Second's Act of Protection, 6
Right of search, 1812, 52
Rob Roy, steam vessel, 83
"Roles d'Oleron, les," 3
Royal Commissions, 59, 61, 106, 118, 121, 175
    Mail Steam Packet Co., 88
    William," steam vessel, 86
Russian Company, the, 32
    war in the Crimea, 98

S

"SAVANNAH," steam ship, 85
Screw steamers, the first, 89
Sea, lads who go to, 188
    changes in life at, 190
Seamen, education of, 66, 192
    the supply of, 42, 51, 232-236
    the past training of, and its effects on character, 60
Seymour (Sir Thomas) and his allies, 22
Shannon and *Chesapeake*, 51

INDEX.

Shipbuilding, ancient Britons' knowledge of, 1
    art school of, 31
    decline in English, 74
    fluctuations in, 131
    in 1895, 135
Shipmanagers and Limited Liability, 144
Shipmasters (British), 57, 58, 70, 113, 166, 208, 216
Shipowners (British), 61, 74, 109, 141, 151, 163, 209, 213
Shipping, state of, (1700, &c.), 41
    depression in, (1815, &c.), 54
    Acts, 1834-5, 57
    burdens on, relieved, 97
    laws consolidated, 1854, 98
    legislation, 101, 127
    property, various tenures in, 141
Ships, new tonnage laws creates improvement in, 97
    sold to foreigners, 106
    serious losses of, 115
    number of, 132
Shipwrecks, public meetings on, 58
Sir Lancelot, clipper ship, 100
Sirius, steamship, 86
Slave trade suppressed, the, 50
Sluys, battle of, 5
Smith (Francis P.), inventor of the screw propeller, 87
South Sea Company, 39
"South Kensington" schools, 177, 243

Speculation, 137
Steam propulsion, 80
    tonnage, 130
Steel Yard, the, 6
Stop-gap Act, 1875, 109
Stowage, on, 126
Suez Canal, origin of the, 102
    steam trade through, 103
Sweden's (King of) large ship, 8

T

"THERMOPYLÆ," clipper ship, 100
Thompson (Poulett), President of the Board of Trade, 64
Tobias' letter to Queen Elizabeth, 31
Tonnage in 1701, (British), 38
    in 1825   ,,   56
    laws, 96
    British, compared with foreign, 129
Trade in 1885, depression of, 121
Training ships, 197

V

VAN TROMP, Admiral, 34

W

WATT, James, 81
West of England mariners, 29
Willoughby, Sir Hugh, 17
Wreck Reports, 118

Printed by BALLANTYNE, HANSON & Co.
London and Edinburgh

A SELECTION FROM
CHARLES GRIFFIN & CO.'S PUBLICATIONS
OF
SCIENTIFIC AND TECHNICAL WORKS.

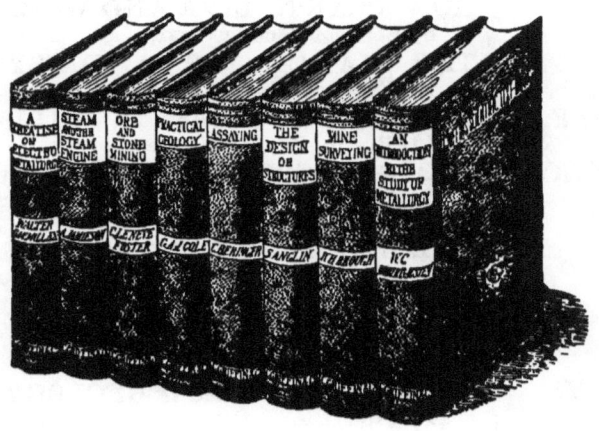

MESSRS. CHARLES GRIFFIN & COMPANY'S PUBLICATIONS may be obtained through any Bookseller in the United Kingdom, or will be sent Post-free on receipt of a remittance to cover published price. To prevent delay, Orders should be accompanied by a Cheque or Postal Order crossed "UNION OF LONDON AND SMITH'S BANK, Chancery Lane Branch."

☞ COMPLETE TECHNICAL, MEDICAL, and GENERAL CATALOGUES forwarded Post-free on Application.

LONDON:
EXETER STREET, STRAND.

GRIFFIN'S INTRODUCTORY SCIENCE SERIES.

FULLY ILLUSTRATED.

BOTANY.	OPEN-AIR STUDIES IN BOTANY. By R. LLOYD PRAEGER, B.A., M.R.I.A.,	7/6
	THE FLOWERING PLANT. By Prof. AINSWORTH DAVIS. THIRD EDITION,	3/6
	HOW PLANTS LIVE AND WORK. By ELEANOR HUGHES-GIBB,	2/6
	THE MAKING OF A DAISY. By ELEANOR HUGHES-GIBB,	2/6
BIRD-LIFE.	OPEN-AIR STUDIES IN BIRD-LIFE. By CHARLES DIXON,	7/6
CHEMISTRY.	INORGANIC CHEMISTRY. By Prof. DUPRÉ, F.R.S., and Dr. WILSON HAKE. THIRD EDITION, Re-issued,	6/ net.
	THE THRESHOLD OF SCIENCE. By DR. ALDER WRIGHT. SECOND EDITION,	6/
	CHEMICAL RECREATIONS. By J. J. GRIFFIN, F.C.S. TENTH EDITION, Complete,	12/6
	(Or in 2 parts, sold separately.)	
GEOLOGY.	OPEN-AIR STUDIES IN GEOLOGY. By Prof. G. A. J. COLE, F.G.S., M.R.I.A. SECOND EDITION,	8/6
ENGINEERING DRAWING.	I. PRACTICAL GEOMETRY, FOURTH EDITION,	4/6
	II. MACHINE DESIGN, FOURTH EDITION. By Principal S. H. WELLS, A.M.Inst.C.E.	4/6
MAGNETISM & ELECTRICITY.	By Prof. JAMIESON, late of the Glasgow and West of Scotland Technical College. SEVENTH EDITION,	3/6
MECHANICS.	By Prof. JAMIESON. SEVENTH EDITION,	3/6
THE STEAM ENGINE.	By Prof. JAMIESON. ELEVENTH EDITION,	3/6
METALLURGY.	By Prof. HUMBOLDT SEXTON, Glasgow and West of Scotland Technical College. THIRD EDITION, Revised,	6/
PHYSICS.	A TEXT-BOOK OF PHYSICS: By J. H. POYNTING, Sc.D., F.R.S., and J. J. THOMSON, M.A., F.R.S.	
	Vol. I.—PROPERTIES OF MATTER. THIRD EDITION,	10/6
	Vol. II.—SOUND. THIRD EDITION,	8/6
	Vol. III.—HEAT. SECOND EDITION,	15/
PHOTOGRAPHY.	By A. BROTHERS, F.R.A.S. SECOND EDITION,	21/

LONDON: CHARLES GRIFFIN & CO., LIMITED, EXETER STREET, STRAND.

"Boys COULD NOT HAVE A MORE ALLURING INTRODUCTION to scientific pursuits than these charming-looking volumes."—Letter to the Publishers from the Headmaster of one of our great Public Schools.

Handsome Cloth, 7s. 6d.   Gilt, for Presentation, 8s. 6d.

OPEN-AIR STUDIES IN BOTANY:

SKETCHES OF BRITISH WILD FLOWERS IN THEIR HOMES.

By R. LLOYD PRAEGER, B.A., M.R.I.A.

Illustrated by Drawings from Nature by S. Rosamond Praeger, and Photographs by R. Welch.

GENERAL CONTENTS.—A Daisy-Starred Pasture—Under the Hawthorns—By the River—Along the Shingle—A Fragrant Hedgerow—A Connemara Bog—Where the Samphire grows—A Flowery Meadow—Among the Corn (a Study in Weeds)—In the Home of the Alpines—A City Rubbish-Heap—Glossary.

"A FRESH AND STIMULATING book . . . should take a high place . . . The Illustrations are drawn with much skill."—*The Times.*
"BEAUTIFULLY ILLUSTRATED. . . . One of the MOST ACCURATE as well as INTERESTING books of the kind we have seen."—*Athenæum.*
"Redolent with the scent of woodland and meadow."—*The Standard.*

With 12 Full-Page Illustrations from Photographs.   Cloth.
Second Edition, Revised.   8s. 6d.

OPEN-AIR STUDIES IN GEOLOGY:

An Introduction to Geology Out-of-doors.

By GRENVILLE A. J. COLE, F.G.S., M.R.I.A.,

Professor of Geology in the Royal College of Science for Ireland, and Examiner in the University of London.

GENERAL CONTENTS.—The Materials of the Earth—A Mountain Hollow—Down the Valley—Along the Shore—Across the Plains—Dead Volcanoes—A Granite Highland—The Annals of the Earth—The Surrey Hills—The Folds of the Mountains.

"The FASCINATING 'OPEN-AIR STUDIES' of PROF. COLE give the subject a GLOW OF ANIMATION . . . cannot fail to arouse keen interest in geology."—*Geological Magazine.*
"A CHARMING BOOK, beautifully illustrated."—*Athenæum.*

Beautifully Illustrated.   With a Frontispiece in Colours, and Numerous Specially Drawn Plates by Charles Whymper.   7s. 6d.

OPEN-AIR STUDIES IN BIRD-LIFE:

SKETCHES OF BRITISH BIRDS IN THEIR HAUNTS.

By CHARLES DIXON.

The Spacious Air.—The Open Fields and Downs.—In the Hedgerows.—On Open Heath and Moor.—On the Mountains.—Amongst the Evergreens.—Copse and Woodland.—By Stream and Pool.—The Sandy Wastes and Mudflats.—Sea-laved Rocks.—Birds of the Cities.—INDEX.

"Enriched with excellent illustrations. A welcome addition to all libraries."—*Westminster Review.*

LONDON: CHARLES GRIFFIN & CO., LIMITED, EXETER STREET, STRAND.

THIRD EDITION, Revised and Enlarged. Large Crown 8vo, with numerous Illustrations. 3s. 6d.

THE FLOWERING PLANT,

WITH A SUPPLEMENTARY CHAPTER ON FERNS AND MOSSES,
As Illustrating the First Principles of Botany.

By J. R. AINSWORTH DAVIS, M.A., F.Z.S.,

Prof. of Biology, University College, Aberystwyth; Examiner in Zoology, University of Aberdeen.

"It would be hard to find a Text-book which would better guide the student to an accurate knowledge of modern discoveries in Botany. . . . The SCIENTIFIC ACCURACY of statement, and the concise exposition of FIRST PRINCIPLES make it valuable for educational purposes. In the chapter on the Physiology of Flowers, an *admirable résumé*, drawn from Darwin, Hermann Müller, Kerner, and Lubbock, of what is known of the Fertilization of Flowers, is given."—*Journal of Botany.*

POPULAR WORKS ON BOTANY BY MRS. HUGHES-GIBB.

With Illustrations. Crown 8vo. Cloth. 2s. 6d.

HOW PLANTS LIVE AND WORK:

A Simple Introduction to Real Life in the Plant-world, Based on Lessons originally given to Country Children.

By ELEANOR HUGHES-GIBB.

*** The attention of all interested in the Scientific Training of the Young is requested to this DELIGHTFULLY FRESH and CHARMING LITTLE BOOK. It ought to be in the hands of every Mother and Teacher throughout the land.

"The child's attention is first secured, and then, in language SIMPLE, YET SCIENTIFICALLY ACCURATE, the first lessons in plant-life are set before it."—*Natural Science.*

"In every way well calculated to make the study of Botany ATTRACTIVE to the young."—*Scotsman.*

With Illustrations. Crown 8vo. Gilt, 2s. 6d.

THE MAKING OF A DAISY;
"WHEAT OUT OF LILIES;"
And other Studies from the Plant World.

A Popular Introduction to Botany.

By ELEANOR HUGHES-GIBB,

Author of *How Plants Live and Work.*

"A BRIGHT little introduction to the study of Flowers."—*Journal of Botany.*
"The book will afford real assistance to those who can derive pleasure from the study of Nature in the open. . . . The literary style is commendable."—*Knowledge.*

LONDON: CHARLES GRIFFIN & CO., LIMITED, EXETER STREET, STRAND.

Griffin's Standard Publications

		PAGE
Applied Mechanics,	RANKINE, BROWNE, JAMIESON,	35, 46, 34
Civil Engineering,	PROF. RANKINE,	35
Design of Structures,	S. ANGLIN,	26
Bridge-Construction,	PROF. FIDLER,	26
Design of Beams,	W. H. ATHERTON,	27
Dock Engineering,	B. CUNNINGHAM,	27
Engineering Drawing,	S. H. WELLS,	27
Constructional Steelwork,	A. W. FARNSWORTH,	26
Central Electrical Stations,	C. H. WORDINGHAM,	48
Electricity Control,	L. ANDREWS,	48
,, Meters,	H. G. SOLOMON,	49
Light Railways,	W. H. COLE,	30
Sewage Disposal Works,	SANTO CRIMP,	76
Sanitary Engineering,	F. WOOD,	78
Traverse Tables,	R. L. GURDEN,	33
Locomotive Engineering,	W. F. PETTIGREW,	30
Locomotive Compounding,	J. F. GAIRNS,	30
Valves and Valve-Gearing,	CHAS. HURST,	31
Hints on Design,	CHAS. HURST,	31
Marine Engineering,	A. E. SEATON,	44
Engine-Room Practice,	J. G. LIVERSIDGE,	29
Pocket-Book,	SEATON AND ROUNTHWAITE,	44
Present Day Shipbuilding,	T. WALTON,	38
Design of Ships,	PROF. HARVARD BILES,	38
Steel Vessels,	T. WALTON,	38
Stability of Ships,	SIR E. J. REED,	38
Nautical Series,	Ed. by CAPT. BLACKMORE,	39
The Steam-Engine,	RANKINE, JAMIESON,	35, 34
Gas, Oil, and Air-Engines,	BRYAN DONKIN,	28
Boilers: Land and Marine,	T. W. TRAILL,	29
,, Steam,	R. D. MUNRO,	32
,, Kitchen,	R. D. MUNRO,	32
,, Heat Efficiency of,	BRYAN DONKIN,	28
Oil Fuel,	SIDNEY H. NORTH,	29
Machinery and Millwork,	PROF. RANKINE,	35
Pumping Machinery,	H. DAVEY,	37
Hydraulic Machinery,	PROF. ROBINSON,	37
Grinding Machinery,	R. B. HODGSON,	33
Lubrication and Lubricants,	ARCHBUTT & DEELEY,	32
Rules and Tables,	RANKINE AND JAMIESON,	36
Bonus Tables,	H. A. GOLDING,	31
Electrical Pocket-Book,	MUNRO AND JAMIESON,	48
The Calculus for Engineers,	PROF. ROBT. H. SMITH,	45
Measurement Conversions,	PROF. ROBT. H. SMITH,	45
Chemistry for Engineers,	BLOUNT & BLOXAM,	46

LONDON: CHARLES GRIFFIN & CO., LIMITED, EXETER STREET, STRAND.

FOURTH EDITION, *Revised, with Numerous Diagrams, Examples, and Tables, and a Chapter on Foundations. In Large 8vo. Cloth. 16s.*

THE DESIGN OF STRUCTURES:

A Practical Treatise on the Building of Bridges, Roofs, &c.

BY S. ANGLIN, C.E.,

Master of Engineering, Royal University of Ireland, late Whitworth Scholar, &c.

"We can unhesitatingly recommend this work not only to the Student, as the BEST TEXT-BOOK on the subject, but also to the professional engineer as an EXCEEDINGLY VALUABLE book of reference."—*Mechanical World.*

THIRD EDITION, *Thoroughly Revised. Royal 8vo. With numerous Illustrations and 13 Lithographic Plates. Handsome Cloth. Price 30s.*

A PRACTICAL TREATISE ON
BRIDGE-CONSTRUCTION:

Being a Text-Book on the Construction of Bridges in Iron and Steel.

FOR THE USE OF STUDENTS, DRAUGHTSMEN, AND ENGINEERS.

BY T. CLAXTON FIDLER, M. INST. C.E.,

Prof. of Engineering, University College, Dundee.

"The new edition of Mr. Fidler's work will again occupy the same CONSPICUOUS POSITION among professional text-books and treatises as has been accorded to its predecessors. SOUND, SIMPLE, AND FULL."—*The Engineer.*

In Medium 8vo. Handsome Cloth. Pp. i-xv + 248, with over 100 Illustrations. Price 10s. 6d. net.

CONSTRUCTIONAL STEELWORK:

Being Notes on the Practical Aspect and the Principles of Design, together with an Account of the Present Methods and Tools of Manufacture.

BY A. W. FARNSWORTH,

Associate Member of the Institute of Mechanical Engineers.

"A worthy volume, which will be found of much assistance. . . . A book of particular value."—*Practical Engineer.*

"Will be found of value to all Architects and Engineers engaged in steelwork construction."—*Building News.*

LONDON: CHARLES GRIFFIN & CO., LIMITED, EXETER STREET, STRAND.

In Large 8vo. Handsome Cloth, Gilt, Uniform with *Stability of Ships* and *Steel Ships* (p. 38). With 34 Folding Plates and 468 Illustrations in the Text. 30s. net.

The Principles and Practice of
DOCK ENGINEERING.

By BRYSSON CUNNINGHAM, B.E., Assoc.M.Inst.C.E.,
Of the Engineers' Department, Mersey Docks and Harbour Board.

GENERAL CONTENTS.

Historical and Discursive.—Dock Design.—Constructive Appliances.—Materials.—Dock and Quay Walls.—Entrance Passages and Locks.—Jetties, Wharves, and Piers.—Dock Gates and Caissons.—Transit Sheds and Warehouses.—Dock Bridges.—Graving and Repairing Docks.—Working Equipment of Docks.—INDEX.

"We have never seen a more profusely-illustrated treatise. It is a most important standard work, and should be in the hands of all dock and harbour engineers."—*Steamship.*
"Will be of the greatest service to the expert as a book of reference."—*Engineer.*

FOURTH EDITION. In Two Parts, Published Separately.

A TEXT-BOOK OF
Engineering Drawing and Design.

VOL. I.—PRACTICAL GEOMETRY, PLANE, AND SOLID. 4s. 6d.
VOL. II.—MACHINE AND ENGINE DRAWING AND DESIGN. 4s. 6d.

BY
SIDNEY H. WELLS, Wh.Sc., A.M.I.C.E., A.M.I.Mech.E.,
Principal of the Battersea Polytechnic Institute, &c.

With many Illustrations, specially prepared for the Work, and numerous Examples, for the Use of Students in Technical Schools and Colleges.

"A CAPITAL TEXT-BOOK, arranged on an EXCELLENT SYSTEM, calculated to give an intelligent grasp of the subject, and not the mere faculty of mechanical copying. . . . Mr. Wells shows how to make COMPLETE WORKING-DRAWINGS, discussing fully each step in the design."—*Electrical Review*

In Large Crown 8vo. Handsome Cloth. With 201 Illustrations. 6s. net.

AN INTRODUCTION TO
THE DESIGN OF BEAMS,
GIRDERS, AND COLUMNS
IN MACHINES AND STRUCTURES.
With Examples in Graphic Statics.

By WILLIAM H. ATHERTON, M.Sc., M.I.Mech.E.

"A very useful source of information. . . . A work which we commend very highly . . . the whole being illustrated by a large collection of very well chosen examples."—*Nature.*
"There should be a strong demand for this concise treatise."—*Page's Weekly.*

LONDON: CHARLES GRIFFIN & CO., LIMITED, EXETER STREET, STRAND.

NEARLY READY. In Handsome Cloth. With 252 Illustrations.

THE THEORY OF THE STEAM TURBINE.

A Treatise on the History, Development, and Principles of Construction of the Steam Turbine.

By ALEXANDER JUDE.

CONTENTS.—The Theory of the Steam Turbine.—Historical Notes on Turbines.—The Velocity of Steam.—Types of Steam Turbines.—Practical Turbines.—The Efficiency of Large Turbines.—The Trajectory of the Steam.—Efficiency of Turbines.—Turbine Vanes.—Disc Friction in Turbines. — Specific Heat of Superheated Steam.—Governing Steam Turbines.—Steam Consumption of Turbines.—The Whirling of Shafts.—Bibliography.—INDEX.

Works by BRYAN DONKIN, M.Inst.C.E., M.Inst.Mech.E., &c.

Now READY. FOURTH EDITION, Revised and Enlarged. With additional Illustrations. Large 8vo, Handsome Cloth. 25s. net.

A TREATISE ON
GAS, OIL, AND AIR ENGINES.

By BRYAN DONKIN, M.INST.C.E., M.INST.MECH.E.

CONTENTS.—PART I.—**Gas Engines**: General Description of Action and Parts.—Heat Cycles and Classification of Gas Engines.—History of the Gas Engine.—The Atkinson, Griffin, and Stockport Engines.—The Otto Gas Engine.—Modern British Gas Engines.—Modern French Gas Engines.—German Gas Engines.—Gas Production for Motive Power.—Utilisation of Blast-furnace and Coke-oven Gases for Power.—The Theory of the Gas Engine.—Chemical Composition of Gas in an Engine Cylinder.—Utilisation of Heat in a Gas Engine.—Explosion and Combustion in a Gas Engine.—PART II.—**Petroleum Engines**: The Discovery, Utilisation, and Properties of Oil.—Method of Treating Oil.—Carburators.—Early Oil Engines.—Practical Application of Gas and Oil Engines.—PART III.—**Air Engines.**—APPENDICES.—INDEX.

"The best book now published on Gas, Oil, and Air Engines."—*Engineer.*
"A thoroughly reliable and exhaustive treatise."—*Engineering.*

In Quarto, Handsome Cloth. With Numerous Plates. 25s.

THE HEAT EFFICIENCY OF STEAM BOILERS
(LAND, MARINE, AND LOCOMOTIVE).

With many Tests and Experiments on different Types of Boilers, as to the Heating Value of Fuels, &c., with Analyses of Gases and Amount of Evaporation, and Suggestions for the Testing of Boilers.

By BRYAN DONKIN, M.INST.C.E.

GENERAL CONTENTS.—Classification of Different Types of Boilers.—425 Experiments on English and Foreign Boilers with their Heat Efficiencies shown in Fifty Tables.—Fire Grates of Various Types.—Mechanical Stokers.—Combustion of Fuel in Boilers.—Transmission of Heat through Boiler Plates, and their Temperature.—Feed Water Heaters, Superheaters, Feed Pumps, &c.—Smoke and its Prevention.—Instruments used in Testing Boilers.—Marine and Locomotive Boilers.—Fuel Testing Stations.—Discussion of the Trials and Conclusions.—On the Choice of a Boiler, and Testing of Land, Marine, and Locomotive Boilers.—Appendices.—Bibliography.—INDEX.

With Plates illustrating Progress made during recent years, and the best Modern Practice.

"Probably the MOST EXHAUSTIVE *resumé* that has ever been collected. A PRACTICAL BOOK by a thoroughly practical man."—*Iron and Coal Trades Review.*

LONDON: CHARLES GRIFFIN & CO., LIMITED, EXETER STREET, STRAND.

FOURTH EDITION, Revised. Pocket-Size, Leather, 12s. 6d.

Boilers, Marine and Land:
THEIR CONSTRUCTION AND STRENGTH.

A HANDBOOK OF RULES, FORMULÆ, TABLES, &C., RELATIVE TO MATERIAL, SCANTLINGS, AND PRESSURES, SAFETY VALVES, SPRINGS, FITTINGS AND MOUNTINGS, &C.

FOR THE USE OF ENGINEERS, SURVEYORS, BOILER-MAKERS, AND STEAM USERS.

BY T. W. TRAILL, M. INST. C. E., F. E. R. N.,
Late Engineer Surveyor-in-Chief to the Board of Trade.

*** TO THE SECOND AND THIRD EDITIONS MANY NEW TABLES for PRESSURE, up to 200 LBS. per SQUARE INCH have been added.

THE MOST VALUABLE WORK on Boilers published in England."—*Shipping World.*

"Contains an ENORMOUS QUANTITY OF INFORMATION arrranged in a very convenient form. A MOST USEFUL VOLUME : . . . supplying information to be had nowhere else."—*The Engineer.*

FIFTH EDITION. Large Crown 8vo. With numerous Illustrations. 6s. net.

ENGINE-ROOM PRACTICE:
A Handbook for Engineers and Officers in the Royal Navy and Mercantile Marine, Including the Management of the Main and Auxiliary Engines on Board Ship.

BY JOHN G. LIVERSIDGE, A.M.I.C.E.,
Commander Engineer, Malta.

Contents.—General Description of Marine Machinery.—The Conditions of Service and Duties of Engineers of the Royal Navy.—Entry and Conditions of Service of Engineers of the Leading S.S. Companies.—Duties of a Steaming Watch on Engines and Boilers.—Shutting off Steam.—Harbour Duties and Watches.—Adjustments and Repairs of Engines.—Preservation and Repairs of "Tank" Boilers.—The Hull and its Fittings.—Cleaning and Painting Machinery.—Reciprocating Pumps, Feed Heaters, and Automatic Feed-Water Regulators. — Evaporators. — Steam Boats. — Electric Light Machinery.—Hydraulic Machinery.—Air-Compressing Pumps.—Refrigerating Machines. —Machinery of Destroyers.—The Management of Water-Tube Boilers.—Regulations for Entry of Assistant Engineers, R.N.—Questions given in Examinations for Promotion of Engineers, R.N.—Regulations respecting Board of Trade Examinations for Engineers, &c.

"The contents CANNOT FAIL TO BE APPRECIATED."—*The Steamship.*
"This VERY USEFUL BOOK. . . . ILLUSTRATIONS are of GREAT IMPORTANCE in a work of this kind, and it is satisfactory to find that SPECIAL ATTENTION has been given in this respect."—*Engineers' Gazette.*

In Large Crown 8vo, Cloth. Fully Illustrated. 5s. net.

OIL FUEL:
ITS SUPPLY, COMPOSITION, AND APPLICATION.

BY SIDNEY H. NORTH,
LATE EDITOR OF THE "PETROLEUM REVIEW."

CONTENTS.—The Sources of Supply.—Economic Aspect of Liquid Fuel.—Chemical Composition of Fuel Oils.—Conditions of Combustion in Oil Fuel Furnaces.—Early Methods and Experiments.—Modern Burners and Methods.—Oil Fuel for Marine Purposes.—For Naval Purposes.—On Locomotives.—For Metallurgical and other Purposes. —Appendices.—INDEX.

"Everyone interested in this important question will welcome Mr. North's excellent text-book."—*Nature.*

LONDON: CHARLES GRIFFIN & CO., LIMITED, EXETER STREET, STRAND.

SECOND EDITION, Revised. With numerous Plates reduced from Working Drawings and 280 Illustrations in the Text. 21s.

A MANUAL OF
LOCOMOTIVE ENGINEERING:
A Practical Text-Book for the Use of Engine Builders, Designers and Draughtsmen, Railway Engineers, and Students.

By WILLIAM FRANK PETTIGREW, M.Inst.C.E.

With a Section on American and Continental Engines.

By ALBERT F. RAVENSHEAR, B.Sc.,
Of His Majesty's Patent Office.

Contents.—Historical Introduction, 1763-1863.—Modern Locomotives: Simple.—Modern Locomotives: Compound.—Primary Consideration in Locomotive Design.—Cylinders, Steam Chests, and Stuffing Boxes.—Pistons, Piston Rods, Crossheads, and Slide Bars.—Connecting and Coupling Rods.—Wheels and Axles, Axle Boxes, Hornblocks, and Bearing Springs.—Balancing.—Valve Gear.—Slide Valves and Valve Gear Details.—Framing, Bogies and Axle Trucks, Radial Axle Boxes.—Boilers.—Smokebox, Blast Pipe, Firebox Fittings.—Boiler Mountings.—Tenders.—Railway Brakes.—Lubrication.—Consumption of Fuel, Evaporation and Engine Efficiency.—American Locomotives.—Continental Locomotives.—Repairs, Running, Inspection, and Renewals.—Three Appendices.—Index.

"The work CONTAINS ALL THAT CAN BE LEARNT from a book upon such a subject. It will at once rank as THE STANDARD WORK UPON THIS IMPORTANT SUBJECT."—*Railway Magazine.*

AT PRESS. In Large 8vo. Fully Illustrated.

LOCOMOTIVE COMPOUNDING AND SUPERHEATING.
By J. F. GAIRNS.

CONTENTS.—Introductory.—Compounding and Superheating for Locomotives.—A Classification of Compound Systems for Locomotives.—The History and Development of the Compound Locomotive.—Two-Cylinder Non-Automatic Systems.—Two-Cylinder Automatic Systems.—Other Two-Cylinder Systems.—Three-Cylinder Systems.—Four-Cylinder Tandem Systems.—Four-Cylinder Two-Crank Systems (other than Tandem).—Four-Cylinder Balanced Systems.—Four-Cylinder Divided and Balanced Systems.—Articulated Compound Engines.—Triple-Expansion Locomotives.—Compound Rack Locomotives.—Concluding Remarks Concerning Compound Locomotives.—The Use of Superheated Steam for Locomotives.—INDEX.

In Large 8vo. Handsome Cloth. With Plates and Illustrations. 16s.

LIGHT RAILWAYS
AT HOME AND ABROAD.

By WILLIAM HENRY COLE, M.Inst.C.E.,
Late Deputy-Manager, North-Western Railway, India.

Contents.—Discussion of the Term "Light Railways."—English Railways, Rates, and Farmers.—Light Railways in Belgium, France, Italy, other European Countries, America and the Colonies, India, Ireland.—Road Transport as an alternative.—The Light Railways Act, 1896.—The Question of Gauge.—Construction and Working.—Locomotives and Rolling-Stock.—Light Railways in England, Scotland, and Wales.—Appendices and Index.

"Will remain, for some time yet a STANDARD WORK in everything relating to Light Railways."—*Engineer.*

"The whole subject is EXHAUSTIVELY and PRACTICALLY considered. The work can be cordially recommended as INDISPENSABLE to those whose duty it is to become acquainted with one of the prime necessities of the immediate future."—*Railway Official Gazette.*

LONDON : CHARLES GRIFFIN & CO., LIMITED, EXETER STREET, STRAND.

FOURTH EDITION, Thoroughly Revised and Greatly Enlarged.
With Numerous Illustrations. Price 10s. 6d.

VALVES AND VALVE-GEARING:
A PRACTICAL TEXT-BOOK FOR THE USE OF ENGINEERS, DRAUGHTSMEN, AND STUDENTS.

By CHARLES HURST, Practical Draughtsman.

PART I.—Steam Engine Valves.
PART II.—Gas Engine Valves and Gears.
PART III.—Air Compressor Valves and Gearing.
PART IV.—Pump Valves.

"MR. HURST'S VALVES and VALVE-GEARING will prove a very valuable aid, and tend to the production of Engines of SCIENTIFIC DESIGN and ECONOMICAL WORKING. . . . Will be largely sought after by Students and Designers."—*Marine Engineer.*

"Almost EVERY TYPE OF VALVE and its gearing is clearly set forth, and illustrated in such a way as to be READILY UNDERSTOOD and PRACTICALLY APPLIED by either the Engineer, Draughtsman, or Student. . . . Should prove both USEFUL and VALUABLE to all Engineers seeking for RELIABLE and CLEAR information on the subject. Its moderate price brings it within the reach of all."—*Industries and Iron.*

Hints on Steam Engine Design and Construction. By CHARLES HURST, "Author of Valves and Valve Gearing." SECOND EDITION, Revised. In Paper Boards, 8vo., Cloth Back. Illustrated. Price 1s. 6d. net.

CONTENTS.—I. Steam Pipes.—II. Valves.—III. Cylinders.—IV. Air Pumps and Condensers.—V. Motion Work.—VI. Crank Shafts and Pedestals.—VII. Valve Gear.—VIII. Lubrication.—IX. Miscellaneous Details—INDEX.

"A handy volume which every practical young engineer should possess."—*The Model Engineer.*

Strongly Bound in Super Royal 8vo. Cloth Boards. 7s. 6d. net.

BONUS TABLES:
For Calculating Wages on the Bonus or Premium Systems.
For Engineering, Technical and Allied Trades.

By HENRY A. GOLDING, A.M.INST.M.E.,
Technical Assistant to Messrs. Bryan Donkin and Clench, Ltd., and Assistant Lecturer in Mechanical Engineering at the Northampton Institute, London, E.C.

"Cannot fail to prove practically serviceable to those for whom they have been designed."—*Scotsman.*

SECOND EDITION, Cloth, 8s. 6d. Leather, for the Pocket, 8s. 6d.

GRIFFIN'S ELECTRICAL PRICE-BOOK: For Electrical, Civil, Marine, and Borough Engineers, Local Authorities, Architects, Railway Contractors, &c., &c. Edited by H. J. DOWSING.

"The ELECTRICAL PRICE-BOOK REMOVES ALL MYSTERY about the cost of Electrical Power. By its aid the EXPENSE that will be entailed by utilising electricity on a large or small scale can be discovered."—*Architect.*

By WILLIAM NICHOLSON.
SMOKE ABATEMENT.
(See page 76.)

LONDON: CHARLES GRIFFIN & CO., LIMITED, EXETER STREET, STRAND.

SHORTLY. SECOND EDITION. Large 8vo, Handsome Cloth. With Illustrations, Tables, &c.

Lubrication & Lubricants:

A TREATISE ON THE

THEORY AND PRACTICE OF LUBRICATION

AND ON THE

NATURE, PROPERTIES, AND TESTING OF LUBRICANTS.

By LEONARD ARCHBUTT, F.I.C., F.C.S.,
Chemist to the Midland Railway Company,

AND

R. MOUNTFORD DEELEY, M.I.MECH.E., F.G.S.,
Chief Locomotive Superintendent, Midland Railway Company.

CONTENTS.—I. Friction of Solids.—II. Liquid Friction or Viscosity, and Plastic Friction.—III. Superficial Tension.—IV. The Theory of Lubrication.—V. Lubricants, their Sources, Preparation, and Properties.—VI. Physical Properties and Methods of Examination of Lubricants.—VII. Chemical Properties and Methods of Examination of Lubricants.—VIII. The Systematic Testing of Lubricants by Physical and Chemical Methods.—IX. The Mechanical Testing of Lubricants.—X. The Design and Lubrication of Bearings.—XI. The Lubrication of Machinery.—INDEX.

"Destined to become a CLASSIC on the subject."—*Industries and Iron.*
"Contains practically ALL THAT IS KNOWN on the subject. Deserves the careful attention of all Engineers."—*Railway Official Guide.*

FOURTH EDITION. *Very fully Illustrated.* Cloth, 4s. 6d.

STEAM - BOILERS:
THEIR DEFECTS, MANAGEMENT, AND CONSTRUCTION.

By R. D. MUNRO,
Chief Engineer of the Scottish Boiler Insurance and Engine Inspection Company.

GENERAL CONTENTS.—I. EXPLOSIONS caused (1) by Overheating of Plates—(2) By Defective and Overloaded Safety Valves—(3) By Corrosion, Internal or External—(4) By Defective Design and Construction (Unsupported Flue Tubes; Unstrengthened Manholes; Defective Staying; Strength of Rivetted Joints; Factor of Safety)—II. CONSTRUCTION OF VERTICAL BOILERS: Shells—Crown Plates and Uptake Tubes—Man-Holes, Mud-Holes, and Fire-Holes—Fireboxes—Mountings—Management—Cleaning—Table of Bursting Pressures of Steel Boilers—Table of Rivetted Joints—Specifications and Drawings of Lancashire Boiler for Working Pressures (*a*) 80 lbs.; (*b*) 200 lbs. per square inch respectively.

"A valuable companion for workmen and engineers engaged about Steam Boilers, ought to be carefully studied, and ALWAYS AT HAND."—*Coll. Guardian.*
"The book is VERY USEFUL, especially to steam users, artisans, and young Engineers."—*Engineer.*

BY THE SAME AUTHOR.

KITCHEN BOILER EXPLOSIONS: Why
they Occur, and How to Prevent their Occurrence. A Practical Handbook based on Actual Experiment. With Diagram and Coloured Plate. Price 3s.

LONDON: CHARLES GRIFFIN & CO., LIMITED, EXETER STREET, STRAND.

In Crown 8vo, Cloth. Fully Illustrated. 5s. net.

EMERY GRINDING MACHINERY.

A Text-Book of Workshop Practice in General Tool Grinding, and the Design, Construction, and Application of the Machines Employed.

By R. B. HODGSON, A.M.Inst.Mech.E.

INTRODUCTION.—Tool Grinding.—Emery Wheels.—Mounting Emery Wheels. —Emery Rings and Cylinders. — Conditions to Ensure Efficient Working.— Leading Types of Machines.—Concave and Convex Grinding.—Cup and Cone Machines. — Multiple Grinding. — "Guest" Universal and Cutter Grinding Machines. — Ward Universal Cutter Grinder. — Press. — Tool Grinding. — Lathe Centre Grinder.—Polishing.—INDEX.

"Eminently practical . . . cannot fail to attract the notice of the users of this class of machinery, and to meet with careful perusal."—*Chem. Trade Journal.*

IN THREE PARTS. Crown 8vo, Handsome Cloth. Very Fully Illustrated.

MOTOR-CAR MECHANISM AND MANAGEMENT.

By W. POYNTER ADAMS, M.Inst.E.E.

IN THREE PARTS.

Part I.—The Petrol Car. Part II.—The Electrical Car.
Part III.—The Steam Car.

PART I.—THE PETROL CAR. 5s. net.

Contents.—SECTION I.—THE MECHANISM OF THE PETROL CAR.— The Engine.—The Engine Accessories.—Electrical Ignition and Accessories. —Multiple Cylinder Engines.—The Petrol.—The Chassis and Driving Gear. —SECTION II.—THE MANAGEMENT OF THE PETROL CAR.—The Engine.— The Engine Accessories.—Electrical Ignition.—The Chassis and Driving Gear.—General Management.—GLOSSARY.—INDEX.

SIXTH EDITION. Folio, strongly half-bound, 21s.

TRAVERSE TABLES:

Computed to Four Places of Decimals for every Minute of Angle up to 100 of Distance.

For the Use of Surveyors and Engineers.

By RICHARD LLOYD GURDEN,

Authorised Surveyor for the Governments of New South Wales and Victoria.

*** *Published with the Concurrence of the Surveyors-General for New South Wales and Victoria.*

"Those who have experience in exact SURVEY-WORK will best know how to appreciate the enormous amount of labour represented by this valuable book. The computations enable the user to ascertain the sines and cosines for a distance of twelve miles to within half an inch, and this BY REFERENCE TO BUT ONE TABLE, in place of the usual Fifteen minute computations required. This alone is evidence of the assistance which the Tables ensure to every user, and as every Surveyor in active practice has felt the want of such assistance FEW KNOWING OF THEIR PUBLICATION WILL REMAIN WITHOUT THEM."
—*Engineer.*

LONDON: CHARLES GRIFFIN & CO., LIMITED, EXETER STREET, STRAND.

WORKS BY
ANDREW JAMIESON, M.Inst.C.E., M.I.E.E., F.R.S.E.,
Formerly Professor of Electrical Engineering, The Glasgow and West of Scotland Technical College.

PROFESSOR JAMIESON'S ADVANCED TEXT-BOOKS.
In Large Crown 8vo. Fully Illustrated.

STEAM AND STEAM-ENGINES, INCLUDING TURBINES
AND BOILERS. For the Use of Students preparing for Competitive Examinations. With over 800 pp., over 400 Illustrations, 11 Special Plates, and 900 Examination Questions. FIFTEENTH EDITION. Revised throughout. 10s. 6d.

"Professor Jamieson fascinates the reader by his CLEARNESS OF CONCEPTION AND SIMPLICITY OF EXPRESSION. His treatment recalls the lecturing of Faraday."—*Athenæum*.
"The BEST BOOK yet published for the use of Students."—*Engineer*.

APPLIED MECHANICS & MECHANICAL ENGINEERING.
Vol. I.—Comprising Part I., with 568 pages, 300 Illustrations, and 540 Examination Questions: The Principle of Work and its applications; Part II.: Friction; Gearing, &c. FIFTH EDITION. 8s. 6d.

"FULLY MAINTAINS the reputation of the Author."—*Pract. Engineer*.

Vol. II.—Comprising Parts III. to VI., with 782 pages, 371 Illustrations, and copious Examination Questions: Motion and Energy; Graphic Statics; Strength of Materials; Hydraulics and Hydraulic Machinery. FOURTH EDITION. 12s. 6d.

"WELL AND LUCIDLY WRITTEN."—*The Engineer*.

*** *Each of the above volumes is complete in itself, and sold separately.*

PROFESSOR JAMIESON'S INTRODUCTORY MANUALS
Crown 8vo. With Illustrations and Examination Papers.

STEAM AND THE STEAM-ENGINE (Elementary
Manual of). For First-Year Students. ELEVENTH EDITION, Revised. 3/6.

"Should be in the hands of EVERY engineering apprentice."—*Practical Engineer*.

MAGNETISM AND ELECTRICITY (Elementary Manual
of). For First-Year Students. SEVENTH EDITION. 3/6.

"A CAPITAL TEXT-BOOK . . . The diagrams are an important feature."—*Schoolmaster*.
"A THOROUGHLY TRUSTWORTHY Text-book. PRACTICAL and clear."—*Nature*.

APPLIED MECHANICS (Elementary Manual of).
Specially arranged for First-Year Students. SEVENTH EDITION, Revised and Greatly Enlarged. 3/6.

"The work has VERY HIGH QUALITIES, which may be condensed into the one word 'CLEAR.'"—*Science and Art*.

A POCKET-BOOK of ELECTRICAL RULES and TABLES.
For the Use of Electricians and Engineers. By JOHN MUNRO, C.E., and Prof. JAMIESON. Pocket Size. Leather, 8s. 6d. SEVENTEENTH EDITION. [See p. 48.

LONDON: CHARLES GRIFFIN & CO., LIMITED, EXETER STREET, STRAND.

WORKS BY
W. J. MACQUORN RANKINE, LL.D., F.R.S.,
Late Regius Professor of Civil Engineering in the University of Glasgow.

THOROUGHLY REVISED BY
W. J. MILLAR, C.E.,
Late Secretary to the Institute of Engineers and Shipbuilders in Scotland.

A MANUAL OF APPLIED MECHANICS:

Comprising the Principles of Statics and Cinematics, and Theory of Structures, Mechanism, and Machines. With Numerous Diagrams. Crown 8vo, cloth. SEVENTEENTH EDITION. 12s. 6d.

A MANUAL OF CIVIL ENGINEERING:

Comprising Engineering Surveys, Earthwork, Foundations, Masonry, Carpentry, Metal Work, Roads, Railways, Canals, Rivers, Waterworks, Harbours, &c. With Numerous Tables and Illustrations. Crown 8vo. cloth. TWENTY-SECOND EDITION. 16s.

A MANUAL OF MACHINERY AND MILLWORK:

Comprising the Geometry, Motions, Work, Strength, Construction, and Objects of Machines, &c. Illustrated with nearly 300 Woodcuts, Crown 8vo, cloth. SEVENTH EDITION. 12s. 6d.

A MANUAL OF THE STEAM-ENGINE AND OTHER PRIME MOVERS:

With a Section on GAS, OIL, and AIR ENGINES, by BRYAN DONKIN, M.Inst.C.E. With Folding Plates and Numerous Illustrations. Crown 8vo, cloth. SIXTEENTH EDITION. 12s. 6d.

LONDON: CHARLES GRIFFIN & CO., LIMITED, EXETER STREET, STRAND.

PROF. RANKINE'S WORKS—*(Continued)*.

USEFUL RULES AND TABLES:

For Architects, Builders, Engineers, Founders, Mechanics, Shipbuilders, Surveyors, &c. With APPENDIX for the use of ELECTRICAL ENGINEERS. By Professor JAMIESON, F.R.S.E. SEVENTH EDITION. 10s. 6d.

A MECHANICAL TEXT-BOOK:

A Practical and Simple Introduction to the Study of Mechanics. By Professor RANKINE and E. F. BAMBER, C.E. With Numerous Illustrations. Crown 8vo, cloth. FIFTH EDITION. 9s.

⁎ *The* "MECHANICAL TEXT-BOOK" *was designed by* Professor RANKINE *as an* INTRODUCTION *to the above Series of Manuals*.

MISCELLANEOUS SCIENTIFIC PAPERS.

Royal 8vo. Cloth, 31s. 6d.

Part I. Papers relating to Temperature, Elasticity, and Expansion of Vapours, Liquids, and Solids. Part II. Papers on Energy and its Transformations. Part III. Papers on Wave-Forms, Propulsion of Vessels, &c.

With Memoir by Professor TAIT, M.A. Edited by W. J. MILLAR, C.E. With fine Portrait on Steel, Plates, and Diagrams.

"No more enduring Memorial of Professor Rankine could be devised than the publication of these papers in an accessible form. . . . The Collection is most valuable on account of the nature of his discoveries, and the beauty and completeness of his analysis. . . . The Volume exceeds in importance any work in the same department published in our time."—*Architect*.

BY W. VINCENT SHELTON (Foreman to the Imperial Ottoman Gun Factories, Constantinople):

THE MECHANIC'S GUIDE: A Hand-Book for Engineers and Artizans. With Copious Tables and Valuable Recipes for Practical Use. Illustrated. *Second Edition*. Crown 8vo. Cloth, 7/6.

LONDON: CHARLES GRIFFIN & CO., LIMITED, EXETER STREET, STRAND.

THIRD EDITION, *Thoroughly Revised and Enlarged. With 60 Plates and Numerous Illustrations. Handsome Cloth. 34s.*

HYDRAULIC POWER

AND

HYDRAULIC MACHINERY.

BY

HENRY ROBINSON, M. INST. C.E., F.G.S.,

FELLOW OF KING'S COLLEGE, LONDON; PROF. EMERITUS OF CIVIL ENGINEERING, KING'S COLLEGE, ETC., ETC.

CONTENTS —Discharge through Orifices.—Flow of Water through Pipes.—Accumulators. —Presses and Lifts.—Hoists.—Rams.—Hydraulic Engines.—Pumping Engines.—Capstans. —Traversers. — Jacks. — Weighing Machines. — Riveters and Shop Tools. — Punching, Shearing, and Flanging Machines.—Cranes.—Coal Discharging Machines.—Drills and Cutters.—Pile Drivers, Excavators, &c.—Hydraulic Machinery applied to Bridges, Dock Gates, Wheels and Turbines.—Shields. — Various Systems and Power Installations.— Meters, &c.—INDEX.

"The standard work on the application of water power."—*Cassier's Magazine.*

Second Edition, Greatly Enlarged. With Frontispiece, several Plates, and over 250 Illustrations. 21s. net.

THE PRINCIPLES AND CONSTRUCTION OF

PUMPING MACHINERY

(STEAM AND WATER PRESSURE).

With Practical Illustrations of ENGINES and PUMPS applied to MINING, TOWN WATER SUPPLY, DRAINAGE of Lands, &c., also Economy and Efficiency Trials of Pumping Machinery.

BY HENRY DAVEY,

Member of the Institution of Civil Engineers, Member of the Institution of Mechanical Engineers, F.G.S., &c.

CONTENTS —Early History of Pumping Engines—Steam Pumping Engines— Pumps and Pump Valves—General Principles of Non-Rotative Pumping Engines—The Cornish Engine, Simple and Compound—Types of Mining Engines—Pit Work—Shaft Sinking—Hydraulic Transmission of Power in Mines—Electric Transmission of Power—Valve Gears of Pumping Engines — Water Pressure Pumping Engines — Water Works Engines — Pumping Engine Economy and Trials of Pumping Machinery—Centrifugal and other Low-Lift Pumps—Hydraulic Rams, Pumping Mains, &c.—INDEX.

"By the 'one English Engineer who probably knows more about Pumping Machinery than ANY OTHER.' . . . A VOLUME RECORDING THE RESULTS OF LONG EXPERIENCE AND STUDY."—*The Engineer.*

"Undoubtedly THE BEST AND MOST PRACTICAL TREATISE on Pumping Machinery THAT HAS YET BEEN PUBLISHED."—*Mining Journal.*

LONDON: CHARLES GRIFFIN & CO., LIMITED, EXETER STREET, STRAND

Royal 8vo, Handsome Cloth. With numerous Illustrations and Tables. 25s.

THE STABILITY OF SHIPS.

BY

SIR EDWARD J. REED, K.C.B., F.R.S., M.P.,

KNIGHT OF THE IMPERIAL ORDERS OF ST. STANILAUS OF RUSSIA; FRANCIS JOSEPH OF AUSTRIA; MEDJIDIE OF TURKEY; AND RISING SUN OF JAPAN; VICE-PRESIDENT OF THE INSTITUTION OF NAVAL ARCHITECTS.

"Sir EDWARD REED's 'STABILITY OF SHIPS' is INVALUABLE. The NAVAL ARCHITECT will find brought together and ready to his hand, a mass of information which he would otherwise have to seek in an almost endless variety of publications, and some of which he would possibly not be able to obtain at all elsewhere."—*Steamship.*

THE DESIGN AND CONSTRUCTION OF SHIPS. By JOHN HARVARD BILES, M.INST.N.A., Professor of Naval Architecture in the University of Glasgow. [*In Preparation.*

THIRD EDITION. Illustrated with Plates, Numerous Diagrams, and Figures in the Text. 18s. net.

STEEL SHIPS:
THEIR CONSTRUCTION AND MAINTENANCE.

A Manual for Shipbuilders, Ship Superintendents, Students, and Marine Engineers.

By THOMAS WALTON, NAVAL ARCHITECT,
AUTHOR OF "KNOW YOUR OWN SHIP."

CONTENTS.—I. Manufacture of Cast Iron, Wrought Iron, and Steel.—Composition of Iron and Steel, Quality, Strength, Tests, &c. II. Classification of Steel Ships. III. Considerations in making choice of Type of Vessel.—Framing of Ships. IV. Strains experienced by Ships.—Methods of Computing and Comparing Strengths of Ships. V. Construction of Ships.—Alternative Modes of Construction.—Types of Vessels.—Turret, Self Trimming, and Trunk Steamers, &c.—Rivets and Rivetting, Workmanship. VI. Pumping Arrangements. VII. Maintenance.—Prevention of Deterioration in the Hulls of Ships.—Cement, Paint, &c.—INDEX.

"So thorough and well written is every chapter in the book that it is difficult to select any of them as being worthy of exceptional praise. Altogether, the work is excellent, and will prove of great value to those for whom it is intended."—*The Engineer.*

AT PRESS. In Handsome Cloth. Very fully Illustrated.

PRESENT-DAY SHIPBUILDING.

For Shipyard Students, Ships' Officers, and Engineers.

By THOS. WALTON,
Author of "Know Your Own Ship."

GENERAL CONTENTS.—Classification.—Materials used in Shipbuilding.—Alternative Modes of Construction.—Details of Construction.—Framing, Plating, Rivetting, Stem Frames, Twin-Screw Arrangements, Water Ballast Arrangements, Loading and Discharging Gear, &c.—Types of Vessels, including Atlantic Liners, Cargo Steamers, Oil carrying Steamers, Turret and other Self Trimming Steamers, &c.—INDEX.

LONDON: CHARLES GRIFFIN & CO., LIMITED, EXETER STREET, STRAND.

GRIFFIN'S NAUTICAL SERIES.
Edited by EDW. BLACKMORE,
Master Mariner, First Class Trinity House Certificate, Assoc. Inst. N.A.;
AND WRITTEN, MAINLY, by SAILORS for SAILORS.

"THIS ADMIRABLE SERIES."—*Fairplay.*   "A VERY USEFUL SERIES."—*Nature.*
"EVERY SHIP should have the WHOLE SERIES as a REFERENCE LIBRARY. HANDSOMELY BOUND, CLEARLY PRINTED and ILLUSTRATED."—*Liverpool Journ. of Commerce.*

The British Mercantile Marine: An Historical Sketch of its Rise and Development. By the EDITOR, CAPT. BLACKMORE. 3s. 6d.
"Captain Blackmore's SPLENDID BOOK . . . contains paragraphs on every point of interest to the Merchant Marine. The 243 pages of this book are THE MOST VALUABLE to the sea captain that have EVER been COMPILED."—*Merchant Service Review.*

Elementary Seamanship. By D. WILSON-BARKER, Master Mariner, F.R.S.E., F.R.G.S. With numerous Plates, two in Colours, and Frontispiece. FOURTH EDITION, Thoroughly Revised. With additional Illustrations. 6s.
"This ADMIRABLE MANUAL, by CAPT. WILSON BARKER, of the 'Worcester,' seems to us PERFECTLY DESIGNED."—*Athenæum.*

Know Your Own Ship: A Simple Explanation of the Stability, Construction, Tonnage, and Freeboard of Ships. By THOS. WALTON, Naval Architect. With numerous Illustrations and additional Chapters on Buoyancy, Trim, and Calculations. NINTH EDITION. 7s. 6d.
"MR. WALTON'S book will be found VERY USEFUL."—*The Engineer.*

Navigation: Theoretical and Practical. By D. WILSON-BARKER and WILLIAM ALLINGHAM. SECOND EDITION, Revised. 3s. 6d.
"PRECISELY the kind of work required for the New Certificates of competency. Candidates will find it INVALUABLE."—*Dundee Advertiser.*

Marine Meteorology: For Officers of the Merchant Navy. By WILLIAM ALLINGHAM, First Class Honours, Navigation, Science and Art Department. With Illustrations, Maps, and Diagrams, and *facsimile* reproduction of log page. 7s. 6d.
"Quite the BEST PUBLICATION on this subject."—*Shipping Gazette.*

Latitude and Longitude: How to find them. By W. J. MILLAR, C.E. SECOND EDITION, Revised. 2s.
"Cannot but prove an acquisition to those studying Navigation."—*Marine Engineer.*

Practical Mechanics: Applied to the requirements of the Sailor. By THOS. MACKENZIE, Master Mariner, F.R.A.S. SECOND EDITION, Revised. 3s. 6d.
"WELL WORTH the money . . . EXCEEDINGLY HELPFUL."—*Shipping World.*

Trigonometry: For the Young Sailor, &c. By RICH. C. BUCK, of the Thames Nautical Training College, H.M.S. "Worcester." THIRD EDITION, Revised. Price 3s. 6d.
"This EMINENTLY PRACTICAL and reliable volume."—*Schoolmaster.*

Practical Algebra. By RICH. C. BUCK. Companion Volume to the above, for Sailors and others. SECOND EDITION, Revised. Price 3s. 6d.
"It is JUST THE BOOK for the young sailor mindful of progress."—*Nautical Magazine.*

The Legal Duties of Shipmasters. By BENEDICT WM. GINSBURG, M.A., LL.D., of the Inner Temple and Northern Circuit: Barrister-at-Law. SECOND EDITION, Thoroughly Revised and Enlarged. Price 4s. 6d.
"INVALUABLE to masters. . . . We can fully recommend it."—*Shipping Gazette.*

A Medical and Surgical Help for Shipmasters. Including First Aid at Sea. By WM. JOHNSON SMITH, F.R.C.S., Principal Medical Officer, Seamen's Hospital, Greenwich. THIRD EDITION, Thoroughly Revised. 6s.
"SOUND, JUDICIOUS, REALLY HELPFUL."—*The Lancet.*

LONDON: CHARLES GRIFFIN & CO., LIMITED, EXETER STREET, STRAND.

GRIFFIN'S NAUTICAL SERIES.

Introductory Volume. Price 3s. 6d.

THE
British Mercantile Marine.

By EDWARD BLACKMORE,

MASTER MARINER; ASSOCIATE OF THE INSTITUTION OF NAVAL ARCHITECTS;
MEMBER OF THE INSTITUTION OF ENGINEERS AND SHIPBUILDERS
IN SCOTLAND; EDITOR OF GRIFFIN'S "NAUTICAL SERIES."

GENERAL CONTENTS.—HISTORICAL: From Early Times to 1486—Progress under Henry VIII.—To Death of Mary—During Elizabeth's Reign—Up to the Reign of William III.—The 18th and 19th Centuries—Institution of Examinations — Rise and Progress of Steam Propulsion — Development of Free Trade—Shipping Legislation, 1862 to 1875—"Locksley Hall" Case—Shipmasters' Societies—Loading of Ships—Shipping Legislation, 1884 to 1894—Statistics of Shipping. THE PERSONNEL: Shipowners—Officers—Mariners—Duties and Present Position. EDUCATION: A Seaman's Education: what it should be—Present Means of Education—Hints. DISCIPLINE AND DUTY—Postscript—The Serious Decrease in the Number of British Seamen, a Matter demanding the Attention of the Nation.

"INTERESTING and INSTRUCTIVE . . . may be read WITH PROFIT and ENJOYMENT."—*Glasgow Herald.*

"EVERY BRANCH of the subject is dealt with in a way which shows that the writer 'knows the ropes' familiarly."—*Scotsman.*

"This ADMIRABLE book . . . TEEMS with useful information—Should be in the hands of every Sailor."—*Western Morning News.*

FOURTH EDITION, *Thoroughly Revised. With Additional Illustrations. Price 6s.*

A MANUAL OF
ELEMENTARY SEAMANSHIP.

BY
D. WILSON-BARKER, MASTER MARINER; F.R.S.E., F.R.G.S., &c., &c.
YOUNGER BROTHER OF THE TRINITY HOUSE.

With Frontispiece, Numerous Plates (Two in Colours), and Illustrations in the Text.

GENERAL CONTENTS.—The Building of a Ship; Parts of Hull, Masts, &c.—Ropes, Knots, Splicing, &c. — Gear, Lead and Log, &c. — Rigging, Anchors — Sailmaking — The Sails, &c. — Handling of Boats under Sail — Signals and Signalling—Rule of the Road—Keeping and Relieving Watch—Points of Etiquette—Glossary of Sea Terms and Phrases—Index.

*** The volume contains the NEW RULES OF THE ROAD.

"This ADMIRABLE MANUAL, by CAPT. WILSON-BARKER of the 'Worcester,' seems to us PERFECTLY DESIGNED, and holds its place excellently in 'GRIFFIN'S NAUTICAL SERIES.' . . . Although intended for those who are to become Officers of the Merchant Navy, it will be found useful by ALL YACHTSMEN."—*Athenæum.*

*** For complete List of GRIFFIN'S NAUTICAL SERIES, see p. 39.

LONDON: CHARLES GRIFFIN & CO., LIMITED, EXETER STREET, STRAND.

GRIFFIN'S NAUTICAL SERIES.

SECOND EDITION, *Revised and Illustrated.* Price 3s. 6d.

NAVIGATION:
PRACTICAL AND THEORETICAL.

BY DAVID WILSON-BARKER, R.N.R., F.R.S.E., &c., &c.,

AND

WILLIAM ALLINGHAM,
FIRST-CLASS HONOURS, NAVIGATION, SCIENCE AND ART DEPARTMENT.

With Numerous Illustrations and Examination Questions.

GENERAL CONTENTS.—Definitions—Latitude and Longitude—Instruments of Navigation—Correction of Courses—Plane Sailing—Traverse Sailing—Day's Work—Parallel Sailing—Middle Latitude Sailing—Mercator's Chart—Mercator Sailing—Current Sailing—Position by Bearings—Great Circle Sailing—The Tides—Questions—Appendix: Compass Error—Numerous Useful Hints, &c.—Index.

"PRECISELY the kind of work required for the New Certificates of competency in grades from Second Mate to extra Master.... Candidates will find it INVALUABLE."—*Dundee Advertiser.*

"A CAPITAL LITTLE BOOK ... specially adapted to the New Examinations. The Authors are CAPT. WILSON-BARKER (Captain-Superintendent of the Nautical College, H.M.S. 'Worcester,' who has had great experience in the highest problems of Navigation), and MR. ALLINGHAM, a well-known writer on the Science of Navigation and Nautical Astronomy."—*Shipping World.*

Handsome Cloth, Fully Illustrated. Price 7s. 6d.

MARINE METEOROLOGY,
FOR OFFICERS OF THE MERCHANT NAVY.

BY WILLIAM ALLINGHAM,
Joint Author of "Navigation, Theoretical and Practical."

With numerous Plates, Maps, Diagrams, and Illustrations, and a facsimile Reproduction of a Page from an actual Meteorological Log-Book.

SUMMARY OF CONTENTS.

INTRODUCTORY.—Instruments Used at Sea for Meteorological Purposes.—Meteorological Log-Books.—Atmospheric Pressure.—Air Temperatures.—Sea Temperatures.—Winds.—Wind Force Scales.—History of the Law of Storms.—Hurricanes, Seasons, and Storm Tracks.—Solution of the Cyclone Problem.—Ocean Currents.—Icebergs.—Synchronous Charts.—Dew, Mists, Fogs, and Haze.—Clouds.—Rain, Snow, and Hail.—Mirage, Rainbows, Coronas, Halos, and Meteors.—Lightning, Corposants, and Auroras.—QUESTIONS.—APPENDIX.—INDEX.

"Quite the BEST publication, AND certainly the MOST INTERESTING, on this subject ever presented to Nautical men."—*Shipping Gazette.*

*** For Complete List of GRIFFIN'S NAUTICAL SERIES, see p. 39.

LONDON: CHARLES GRIFFIN & CO., LIMITED, EXETER STREET, STRAND.

GRIFFIN'S NAUTICAL SERIES.

SECOND EDITION, REVISED. With Numerous Illustrations. Price 3s. 6d.

Practical Mechanics:
Applied to the Requirements of the Sailor.
By THOS. MACKENZIE,
Master Mariner, F.R.A.S.

GENERAL CONTENTS.—Resolution and Composition of Forces—Work done by Machines and Living Agents—The Mechanical Powers: The Lever; Derricks as Bent Levers—The Wheel and Axle: Windlass; Ship's Capstan; Crab Winch—Tackles: the "Old Man"—The Inclined Plane; the Screw—The Centre of Gravity of a Ship and Cargo—Relative Strength of Rope: Steel Wire, Manilla, Hemp, Coir—Derricks and Shears—Calculation of the Cross-breaking Strain of Fir Spar—Centre of Effort of Sails—Hydrostatics: the Diving-bell; Stability of Floating Bodies; the Ship's Pump, &c.

"THIS EXCELLENT BOOK . . . contains a LARGE AMOUNT of information."—*Nature.*

"WELL WORTH the money . . . will be found EXCEEDINGLY HELPFUL."—*Shipping World.*

"NO SHIPS' OFFICERS' BOOKCASE will henceforth be complete without CAPTAIN MACKENZIE'S 'PRACTICAL MECHANICS.' Notwithstanding my many years' experience at sea, it has told me *how much more there is to acquire.*"—(Letter to the Publishers from a Master Mariner).

"I must express my thanks to you for the labour and care you have taken in 'PRACTICAL MECHANICS.' . . . IT IS A LIFE'S EXPERIENCE. . . What an amount we frequently see wasted by rigging purchases without reason and accidents to spars, &c., &c.! 'PRACTICAL MECHANICS' WOULD SAVE ALL THIS."—(Letter to the Author from another Master Mariner).

WORKS BY RICHARD C. BUCK,
of the Thames Nautical Training College, H.M.S. 'Worcester.'

A Manual of Trigonometry:
With Diagrams, Examples, and Exercises. Price 3s. 6d.
THIRD EDITION, Revised and Corrected.

*** Mr. Buck's Text-Book has been SPECIALLY PREPARED with a view to the New Examinations of the Board of Trade, in which Trigonometry is an obligatory subject.

"This EMINENTLY PRACTICAL and RELIABLE VOLUME."—*Schoolmaster.*

A Manual of Algebra.
Designed to meet the Requirements of Sailors and others.
SECOND EDITION, Revised. Price 3s. 6d.

*** These elementary works on ALGEBRA and TRIGONOMETRY are written specially for those who will have little opportunity of consulting a Teacher. They are books for "SELF-HELP." All but the simplest explanations have, therefore, been avoided, and ANSWERS to the Exercises are given. Any person may readily, by careful study, become master of their contents, and thus lay the foundation for a further mathematical course, if desired. It is hoped that to the younger Officers of our Mercantile Marine they will be found decidedly serviceable. The Examples and Exercises are taken from the Examination Papers set for the Cadets of the "Worcester."

"Clearly arranged, and well got up. . . A first-rate Elementary Algebra.—*Nautical Magazine.*

*** For complete List of GRIFFIN'S NAUTICAL SERIES, see p. 39.

LONDON: CHARLES GRIFFIN & CO., LIMITED, EXETER STREET, STRAND.

GRIFFIN'S NAUTICAL SERIES.

SECOND EDITION, Thoroughly Revised and Extended. In Crown 8vo.
Handsome Cloth. Price 4s. 6d.

THE LEGAL DUTIES OF SHIPMASTERS.

BY

BENEDICT WM. GINSBURG, M.A., LL.D. (CANTAB.),
Of the Inner Temple and Northern Circuit; Barrister-at-Law.

General Contents.—The Qualification for the Position of Shipmaster—The Contract with the Shipowner—The Master's Duty in respect of the Crew: Engagement; Apprentices; Discipline; Provisions, Accommodation, and Medical Comforts; Payment of Wages and Discharge—The Master's Duty in respect of the Passengers—The Master's Financial Responsibilities—The Master's Duty in respect of the Cargo—The Master's Duty in Case of Casualty—The Master's Duty to certain Public Authorities—The Master's Duty in relation to Pilots, Signals, Flags, and Light Dues—The Master's Duty upon Arrival at the Port of Discharge—Appendices relative to certain Legal Matters: Board of Trade Certificates, Dietary Scales, Stowage of Grain Cargoes, Load Line Regulations, Life-saving Appliances, Carriage of Cattle at Sea, &c., &c.—Copious Index.

"No intelligent Master should fail to add this to his list of necessary books. A few lines of it may SAVE A LAWYER'S FEE, BESIDES ENDLESS WORRY."—*Liverpool Journal of Commerce.*
"SENSIBLE, plainly written, in CLEAR and NON-TECHNICAL LANGUAGE, and will be found of MUCH SERVICE by the Shipmaster."—*British Trade Review.*

SECOND EDITION, Revised. With Diagrams. Price 2s.

Latitude and Longitude:
How to Find them.
BY W. J. MILLAR, C.E.,
Late Secretary to the Inst. of Engineers and Shipbuilders in Scotland.

"CONCISELY and CLEARLY WRITTEN . . . cannot but prove an acquisition to those studying Navigation."—*Marine Engineer.*
"Young Seamen will find it HANDY and USEFUL, SIMPLE and CLEAR."—*The Engineer.*

FIRST AID AT SEA.

THIRD EDITION, Revised. With Coloured Plates and Numerous Illustrations, and comprising the latest Regulations Respecting the Carriage of Medical Stores on Board Ship. Price 6s.

A MEDICAL AND SURGICAL HELP
FOR SHIPMASTERS AND OFFICERS
IN THE MERCHANT NAVY.

BY WM. JOHNSON SMITH, F.R.C.S.,
Principal Medical Officer, Seamen's Hospital, Greenwich.

*** The attention of all interested in our Merchant Navy is requested to this exceedingly useful and valuable work. It is needless to say that it is the outcome of many year PRACTICAL EXPERIENCE amongst Seamen.
"SOUND, JUDICIOUS, REALLY HELPFUL."—*The Lancet.*

*** For Complete List of GRIFFIN'S NAUTICAL SERIES, see p. 39.

LONDON: CHARLES GRIFFIN & CO., LIMITED, EXETER STREET, STRAND.

GRIFFIN'S NAUTICAL SERIES.

NINTH EDITION. Revised, with Chapters on Trim, Buoyancy, and Calculations. Numerous Illustrations. Handsome Cloth, Crown 8vo. Price 7s. 6d.

KNOW YOUR OWN SHIP.

By THOMAS WALTON, NAVAL ARCHITECT.

Specially arranged to suit the requirements of Ships' Officers, Shipowners, Superintendents, Draughtsmen, Engineers, and Others,

This work explains, in a simple manner, such important subjects as:—Displacement.—Deadweight.—Tonnage.—Freeboard.—Moments.—Buoyancy.—Strain.—Structure.—Stability.—Rolling.—Ballasting.—Loading.—Shifting Cargoes.—Admission of Water.—Sail Area.—&c.

"The little book will be found EXCEEDINGLY HANDY by most officers and officials connected with shipping. . . . Mr. Walton's work will obtain LASTING SUCCESS, because of its unique fitness for those for whom it has been written."—*Shipping World.*

BY THE SAME AUTHOR.

Steel Ships: Their Construction and Maintenance.
(See page 38.)

FIFTEENTH EDITION, Thoroughly Revised, Greatly Enlarged, and Reset Throughout. Large 8vo, Cloth. pp. i-xxiv+708. With 280 Illustrations, reduced from Working Drawings, and 8 Plates. 21s. net.

A MANUAL OF
MARINE ENGINEERING:
COMPRISING THE DESIGNING, CONSTRUCTION, AND WORKING OF MARINE MACHINERY.

By A. E. SEATON, M.I.C.E., M.I.Mech.E., M.I.N.A.

GENERAL CONTENTS.—PART I.—Principles of Marine Propulsion. PART II.—Principles of Steam Engineering. PART III.—Details of Marine Engines: Design and Calculations for Cylinders, Pistons, Valves, Expansion Valves, &c. PART IV.—Propellers. PART V.—Boilers. PART VI.—Miscellaneous.

"The Student, Draughtsman, and Engineer will find this work the MOST VALUABLE HANDBOOK of Reference on the Marine Engine now in existence."—*Marine Engineer.*

EIGHTH EDITION, Thoroughly Revised. Pocket-Size, Leather. 8s. 6d.

A POCKET-BOOK OF
MARINE ENGINEERING RULES AND TABLES,
FOR THE USE OF
Marine Engineers, Naval Architects, Designers, Draughtsmen, Superintendents and Others.

By A. E. SEATON, M.I.C.E., M.I.Mech.E., M.I.N.A.,
AND
H. M. ROUNTHWAITE, M.I.Mech.E., M.I.N.A.

"ADMIRABLY FULFILS its purpose."—*Marine Engineer.*

LONDON: CHARLES GRIFFIN & CO., LIMITED, EXETER STREET, STRAND.

WORKS BY PROF. ROBERT H. SMITH, Assoc.M.I.C.E.,
M.I.M.E., M.I.El.E., M.I.Min.E., Whit. Sch., M.Ord.Meiji.

THE CALCULUS FOR ENGINEERS AND PHYSICISTS,
Applied to Technical Problems.
WITH EXTENSIVE
CLASSIFIED REFERENCE LIST OF INTEGRALS.
By PROF. ROBERT H. SMITH.
ASSISTED BY
R. F. MUIRHEAD, M.A., B.Sc.,
Formerly Clark Fellow of Glasgow University, and Lecturer on Mathematics at Mason College.

In Crown 8vo, extra, with Diagrams and Folding-Plate. **8s. 6d.**

"PROF. R. H. SMITH's book will be serviceable in rendering a hard road AS EASY AS PRACTICABLE for the non-mathematical Student and Engineer."—*Athenæum.*

"Interesting diagrams, with practical illustrations of actual occurrence, are to be found here in abundance. THE VERY COMPLETE CLASSIFIED REFERENCE TABLE will prove very useful in saving the time of those who want an integral in a hurry."—*The Engineer.*

MEASUREMENT CONVERSIONS
(English and French):
28 GRAPHIC TABLES OR DIAGRAMS.

Showing at a glance the MUTUAL CONVERSION of MEASUREMENTS in DIFFERENT UNITS

Of Lengths, Areas, Volumes, Weights, Stresses, Densities, Quantities of Work, Horse Powers, Temperatures, &c.

For the use of Engineers, Surveyors, Architects, and Contractors.

In 4to, Boards. **7s. 6d.**

** Prof. SMITH's CONVERSION-TABLES form the most unique and comprehensive collection ever placed before the profession. By their use much time and labour will be saved, and the chances of error in calculation diminished. It is believed that henceforth no Engineer's Office will be considered complete without them.

Pocket Size, Leather Limp, with Gilt Edges and Rounded Corners, printed on Special Thin Paper, with Illustrations, pp. i-xii + 834. Price 18s. net.

(THE NEW "NYSTROM")
THE MECHANICAL ENGINEER'S REFERENCE BOOK
A Handbook of Tables, Formulæ and Methods for Engineers, Students and Draughtsmen.

By HENRY HARRISON SUPLEE, B.Sc., M.E.

"We feel sure it will be of great service to mechanical engineers."—*Engineering.*

LONDON: CHARLES GRIFFIN & CO., LIMITED, EXETER STREET, STRAND.

SECOND EDITION. In Large 8vo. Handsome Cloth. 16s.
CHEMISTRY FOR ENGINEERS.
BY
BERTRAM BLOUNT, AND **A. G. BLOXAM,**
F.I.C., F.C.S., A.I.C.E. F.I.C., F.C.S.

GENERAL CONTENTS.—Introduction—Chemistry of the Chief Materials of Construction—Sources of Energy—Chemistry of Steam-raising—Chemistry of Lubrication and Lubricants—Metallurgical Processes used in the Winning and Manufacture of Metals.

"The authors have SUCCEEDED beyond all expectation, and have produced a work which should give FRESH POWER to the Engineer and Manufacturer."—*The Times.*

For Companion Volume by the same Authors, see "CHEMISTRY FOR MANUFACTURERS," p. 71 *General Catalogue.*

In Handsome Cloth. With about 50 Illustrations. 3s. 6d. net.
THE ELEMENTS OF CHEMICAL ENGINEERING.
BY J. GROSSMANN, M.A., PH.D., F.I.C.,
Chemical Engineer and Consulting Chemist.
WITH A PREFACE BY
SIR WILLIAM RAMSAY, K.C.B., F.R.S.

CONTENTS.—The Beaker and its Technical Equivalents.—Distilling Flasks, Liebig's Condensers.—Fractionating Tubes and their Technical Equivalents.—The Air-Bath and its Technical Equivalents.—The Blowpipe and Crucible and their Technical Equivalents.—The Steam Boiler and other Sources of Power.—General Remarks on the Application of Heat in Chemical Engineering.—The Funnel and its Technical Equivalents.—The Mortar and its Technical Equivalents.—Measuring Instruments and their Technical Equivalents.—Materials Used in Chemical Engineering and their Mode of Application.—Technical Research and the Designing of Plant.—Conclusion.—Chemicals and Materials.—INDEX.

WORKS BY WALTER R. BROWNE, M.A., M.INST.C.E.

THE STUDENT'S MECHANICS:
An Introduction to the Study of Force and Motion.
With Diagrams. Crown 8vo. Cloth, 4s. 6d.

"Clear in style and practical in method, 'THE STUDENT'S MECHANICS' is cordially to be recommended from all points of view."—*Athenæum.*

FOUNDATIONS OF MECHANICS.
Papers reprinted from the *Engineer.* In Crown 8vo, 1s.

Demy 8vo, with Numerous Illustrations, 9s.
FUEL AND WATER:
A Manual for Users of Steam and Water.
BY PROF. FRANZ SCHWACKHÖFER OF VIENNA, AND
WALTER R. BROWNE, M.A., C.E.

GENERAL CONTENTS.—Heat and Combustion—Fuel, Varieties of—Firing Arrangements: Furnace, Flues, Chimney—The Boiler, Choice of—Varieties—Feed-water Heaters—Steam Pipes—Water: Composition, Purification—Prevention of Scale, &c., &c.

"The Section on Heat is one of the best and most lucid ever written."—*Engineer.*

SECOND EDITION, REVISED AND ENLARGED.
With Tables, Illustrations in the Text, and 37 Lithographic Plates. Medium 8vo. Handsome Cloth. 30s.

SEWAGE DISPOSAL WORKS:
A Guide to the Construction of Works for the Prevention of the Pollution by Sewage of Rivers and Estuaries.

By W. SANTO CRIMP, M.Inst.C.E., F.G.S.,
Late Assistant-Engineer, London County Council.

"Probably the MOST COMPLETE AND BEST TREATISE on the subject which has appeared in our language."—*Edinburgh Medical Journal.*

Beautifully Illustrated, with Numerous Plates, Diagrams, and Figures in the Text. 21s. net.

TRADES' WASTE:
ITS TREATMENT AND UTILISATION.
A Handbook for Borough Engineers, Surveyors, Architects, and Analysts.

By W. NAYLOR, F.C.S., A.M.Inst.C.E.,
Chief Inspector of Rivers, Ribble Joint Committee.

CONTENTS.—I. Introduction.—II. Chemical Engineering.—III.—Wool De-greasing and Grease Recovery.—IV. Textile Industries; Calico Bleaching and Dyeing.—V. Dyeing and Calico-Printing.—VI. Tanning and Fellmongery.—VII. Brewery and Distillery Waste.—VIII. Paper Mill Refuse.—IX. General Trades' Waste.—INDEX.

"There is probably no person in England to-day better fitted to deal rationally with such a subject."—*British Sanitarian.*

In Handsome Cloth. With 59 Illustrations. 6s. net.

SMOKE ABATEMENT.
A Manual for the Use of Manufacturers, Inspectors, Medical Officers of Health, Engineers, and Others.

By WILLIAM NICHOLSON,
Chie Smoke Inspector to the Sheffield Corporation.

CONTENTS.— Introduction. — General Legislation against the Smoke Nuisance. — Local Legislation.—Foreign Laws.—Smoke Abatement.—Smoke from Boilers, Furnaces, and Kilns. — Private Dwelling-House Smoke. — Chimneys and their Construction. — Smoke Preventers and Fuel Savers. — Waste Gases from Metallurgical Furnaces. — Summary and Conclusions.—INDEX.

"We welcome such an adequate statement on an important subject."—*British Medical Journal.*

SECOND EDITION. In Medium 8vo. Thoroughly Revised and Re-Written. 15s. net.

CALCAREOUS CEMENTS:
THEIR NATURE, PREPARATION, AND USES.
With some Remarks upon Cement Testing.

By GILBERT R. REDGRAVE, Assoc. Inst. C.E.,
Assistant Secretary for Technology, Board of Education, South Kensington,
AND CHARLES SPACKMAN, F.C.S.

"We can thoroughly recommend it as a first-class investment."—*Practical Engineer.*

LONDON: CHARLES GRIFFIN & CO., LIMITED, EXETER STREET, STRAND.

ELECTRICAL ENGINEERING.

SECOND EDITION, *Revised. In Large 8vo. Handsome Cloth. Profusely Illustrated with Plates, Diagrams, and Figures.* 24s. net.

CENTRAL ELECTRICAL STATIONS:
Their Design, Organisation, and Management.
By CHAS. H. WORDINGHAM, A.K.C., M.INST.C.E., M.INST.MECH.E.,
Late Memb. of Council Inst. E. E., and Electrical Engineer to the City of Manchester;
Electrical Engineer-in-Chief to the Admiralty.

ABRIDGED CONTENTS.

Introductory.—Central Station Work as a Profession.—As an Investment.—The Establishment of a Central Station.—Systems of Supply.—Site.—Architecture.—Plant.—Boilers—Systems of Draught and Waste Heat Economy.—Coal Handling, Weighing, and Storing.—The Transmission of Steam.—Generators.—Condensing Appliances.—Switching Gear, Instruments, and Connections.—Distributing Mains.—Insulation, Resistance, and Cost.—Distributing Networks.—Service Mains and Feeders.—Testing Mains.—Meters and Appliances.—Standardising and Testing Laboratory.—Secondary Batteries.—Street Lighting.—Cost.—General Organisation.—Mains Department.—Installation Department.—Standardising Department.—Drawing Office.—Clerical Department.—The Consumer.—Routine and Main Laying.—INDEX.

"One of the MOST VALUABLE CONTRIBUTIONS to Central Station literature we have had for some time."—*Electricity.*

In Large 8vo. Handsome Cloth. Profusely Illustrated. 12s. 6d. net.

ELECTRICITY CONTROL.
A Treatise on Electric Switchgear and Systems of Electric Transmission.

By LEONARD ANDREWS,
Associate Member of the Institution of Civil Engineers, Member of the Institution of Electrical Engineers, &c

General Principles of Switchgear Design.—Constructional Details.—Circuit Breakers or Arc Interrupting Devices.—Automatically Operated Circuit-Breakers.—Alternating Reverse Current Devices.—Arrangement of 'Bus Bars, and Apparatus for Parallel Running.—General Arrangement of Controlling Apparatus for High Tension Systems.—General Arrangement of Controlling Apparatus for Low Tension Systems.—Examples of Complete Installations.—Long Distance Transmission Schemes.

"Not often does the specialist have presented to him so satisfactory a book as this.... We recommend it without hesitation to Central Station Engineers, and, in fact, to anyone interested in the subject."—*Power.*

SEVENTEENTH EDITION, Thoroughly Revised and Enlarged. 8s. 6d.

A POCKET-BOOK
OF
ELECTRICAL RULES & TABLES
FOR THE USE OF ELECTRICIANS AND ENGINEERS.
By JOHN MUNRO, C.E., & PROF. JAMIESON, M.INST.C.E., F.R.S.E.
With Numerous Diagrams. Pocket Size. Leather, 8s. 6d.

GENERAL CONTENTS.

Units of Measurement.—Measures.—Testing.—Conductors.—Dielectrics.—Submarine Cables.—Telegraphy.—Electro-Chemistry.—Electro-Metallurgy.—Batteries.—Dynamos and Motors.—Transformers.—Electric Lighting.—Miscellaneous.—Logarithms.—Appendices.

"WONDERFULLY PERFECT.... Worthy of the highest commendation we can give it."—*Electrician.*

"The STERLING VALUE of Messrs. MUNRO and JAMIESON'S POCKET-BOOK."—*Electrical Review.*

LONDON: CHARLES GRIFFIN & CO., LIMITED, EXETER STREET, STRAND.

ELECTRICAL ENGINEERING.

JUST OUT. In Large 8vo. Profusely Illustrated. 8s. 6d. net.

WIRELESS TELEGRAPHY.
BY GUSTAVE EICHHORN, PH.D.

CONTENTS.—Oscillations.—Closed Oscillation Systems.—Open Oscillation Systems.—Coupled Systems.—The Coupling Compensating the Aerial Wire.—The Receiver.—Comparative Measurement in the Sender.—Theoretical Results and Calculations in respect of Sender and Receiver.—Closely-Coupled Sender and Receiver.—Loose-Coupled Sender and Receiver.—Principal Formulæ.—The Ondameter.—Working a Wireless Telegraph Station.—Modern Apparatus and Methods of Working.—Conclusion.—Bibliography.—INDEX.

JUST OUT. Large 8vo, Handsome Cloth, with 334 Pages and 307 Illustrations. 16s. net.

ELECTRICITY METERS.
BY HENRY G. SOLOMON, A.M.Inst.E.E.

CONTENTS.— Introductory. — General Principles of Continuous-Current Meters.—Continuous-Current Quantity Meters.—Continuous-Energy Motor Meters.—Different Types.—Special Purposes, *i.e.*, Battery Meters, Switchboard Meters, Tramcar Meters.—General Principles of Single- and Polyphase Induction Meters.—Single-phase Induction Meters.—Polyphase Meters.—Tariff Systems.—Prepayment Meters.—Tariff and Hour Meters.—Some Mechanical Features in Meter Design.—Testing Meters.—INDEX.

"An earnest and successful attempt to deal comprehensively with modern methods of measuring current or power in electrical installations."—*Engineering.*

"Trustworthy information. . . . We can confidently recommend the book to every electrical engineer."—*Electricity.*

ELECTRIC SMELTING AND REFINING.
BY DR. W. BORCHERS AND W. G. McMILLAN.
SECOND EDITION, Revised and Enlarged. 21s. net.

ELECTRO-METALLURGY, A Treatise on.
BY WALTER G. McMILLAN, F.I.C., F.C.S.
SECOND EDITION, Revised and in Part Re-Written. 10s. 6d.

ELECTRICAL PRACTICE IN COLLIERIES.
BY D. BURNS, M.E., M.INST.M.E.
(See page 58 General Catalogue.)

GRIFFIN'S ELECTRICAL PRICE-BOOK.
EDITED BY H. J. DOWSING.
(See page 31.)

LONDON: CHARLES GRIFFIN & CO., LIMITED, EXETER STREET, STRAND.

THIRD EDITION, Revised, Enlarged, and Re-issued.   Price 6s. net.

A SHORT MANUAL OF
INORGANIC CHEMISTRY.

BY

A. DUPRÉ, Ph.D., F.R.S.,

AND

WILSON HAKE, Ph.D., F.I.C., F.C.S.,
Of the Westminster Hospital Medical School.

"A well-written, clear and accurate Elementary Manual of Inorganic Chemistry. . . . We agree heartily with the system adopted by Drs. Dupré and Hake. WILL MAKE EXPERIMENTAL WORK TREBLY INTERESTING BECAUSE INTELLIGIBLE."—*Saturday Review.*

"There is no question that, given the PERFECT GROUNDING of the Student in his Science, the remainder comes afterwards to him in a manner much more simple and easily acquired. The work IS AN EXAMPLE OF THE ADVANTAGES OF THE SYSTEMATIC TREATMENT of a Science over the fragmentary style so generally followed. BY A LONG WAY THE BEST of the small Manuals for Students."—*Analyst.*

LABORATORY HANDBOOKS BY A. HUMBOLDT SEXTON,
Professor of Metallurgy in the Glasgow and West of Scotland Technical College.

OUTLINES OF QUANTITATIVE ANALYSIS.
FOR THE USE OF STUDENTS.

With Illustrations.   FOURTH EDITION.   Crown 8vo, Cloth, 3s.

"A COMPACT LABORATORY GUIDE for beginners was wanted, and the want has been WELL SUPPLIED. . . . A good and useful book."—*Lancet.*

OUTLINES OF QUALITATIVE ANALYSIS.
FOR THE USE OF STUDENTS.

With Illustrations.   FOURTH EDITION, Revised.   Crown 8vo, Cloth, 3s. 6d.

"The work of a thoroughly practical chemist."—*British Medical Journal.*
"Compiled with great care, and will supply a want."—*Journal of Education.*

ELEMENTARY METALLURGY:
Including the Author's Practical Laboratory Course.   With many Illustrations.   [See p. 66 *General Catalogue.*

THIRD EDITION, Revised.   Crown 8vo.   Cloth, 6s.

"Just the kind of work for students commencing the study of metallurgy."—*Practical Engineer.*

LONDON: CHARLES GRIFFIN & CO., LIMITED, EXETER STREET, STRAND.

Griffin's Chemical and Technological Publications.

		PAGE
Inorganic Chemistry,	Profs. Dupré and Hake,	50
Quantitative Analysis,	Prof. Humboldt Sexton,	50
Qualitative ,,	,, ,,	50
Chemistry for Engineers,	Blount and Bloxam,	46
,, ,, Manufacturers,	,, ,,	71
Foods and Poisons,	A. Wynter Blyth,	72
Tables for Chemists,	Prof. Castell-Evans,	79
Dairy Chemistry,	H. D. Richmond,	73
Dairy Analysis,	,,	73
Milk,	E. F. Willoughby,	73
Flesh Foods,	C. A. Mitchell,	74
Practical Sanitation,	Dr. G. Reid,	78
Sanitary Engineering,	F. Wood,	78
Technical Mycology,	Lafar and Salter,	74
Ferments,	C. Oppenheimer,	75
Toxines and Anti-Toxines,	,, ,,	74
Brewing,	Dr. W. J. Sykes,	75
Bacteriology of Brewing,	W. A. Riley,	75
Sewage Disposal,	Santo Crimp,	47
Trades' Waste,	W. Naylor,	47
Smoke Abatement,	Wm. Nicholson,	47
Paper Technology,	R. W. Sindall,	81
Cements,	G. R. Redgrave,	47
Water Supply,	R. E. Middleton,	77
Road Making,	Thos. Aitken,	79
Gas Manufacture,	W. Atkinson Butterfield,	77
Acetylene,	Leeds and Butterfield,	77
Fire Risks,	Dr. Schwartz,	77
Petroleum,	Sir Boverton Redwood,	61
——(Handbook),	Thomson and Redwood,	61
Ink Manufacture,	Mitchell and Hepworth,	81
Glue, Gelatine, &c.,	Thos. Lambert,	81
Oils, Soaps, Candles,	Wright & Mitchell,	71
Lubrication & Lubricants,	Archbutt and Deeley,	32
India Rubber,	Dr. Carl O. Weber,	81
Painters' Colours, Oils, &c.,	G. H. Hurst,	80
Painters' Laboratory Guide,	,,	80
Painting and Decorating,	W. J. Pearce,	80
Dyeing,	Knecht and Rawson,	82
Dictionary of Dyes,	Rawson and Gardner,	82
The Synthetic Dyestuffs,	Cain and Thorpe,	82
Spinning,	H. R. Carter,	83
Textile Printing,	Seymour Rothwell,	83
Textile Fibres of Commerce,	W. I. Hannan,	83
Dyeing and Cleaning,	G. H. Hurst,	84
Bleaching, Calico-Printing,	Geo. Duerr,	84

LONDON : CHARLES GRIFFIN & CO., LIMITED, EXETER STREET, STRAND.

Griffin's Geological, Prospecting, Mining, and Metallurgical Publications.

		PAGE
Geology, Stratigraphical,	R. ETHERIDGE, F.R.S.,	52
" Physical,	PROF. H. G. SEELEY,	52
" Practical Aids,	PROF. GRENVILLE COLE,	53
" Open Air Studies,	" "	19
Mining Geology,	JAMES PARK, F.G.S.,	55
Prospecting for Minerals,	S. HERBERT COX, A.R.S.M.,	55
Food Supply,	ROBT. BRUCE,	54
New Lands,	H. R. MILL, D.Sc., F.R.S.E.,	54
Ore and Stone Mining,	SIR C. LE NEVE FOSTER,	56
Elements of Mining,	" "	56
Coal Mining,	H. W. HUGHES, F.G.S.,	56
Practical Coal Mining,	G. L. KERR, M.Inst.M.E.,	58
Elementary "	" "	58
Electrical Coal Mining,	D. BURNS,	58
Mine-Surveying,	BENNETT H. BROUGH, A.R.S.M.,	57
Mine Air, Investigation of,	FOSTER AND HALDANE,	57
Mining Law,	C. J. ALFORD,	57
Blasting and Explosives,	O. GUTTMANN, A.M.I.C.E.,	58
Testing Explosives,	BICHEL AND LARSEN,	58
Mine Accounts,	PROF. J. G. LAWN,	57
Mining Engineers' Pkt.-Bk.,	E. R. FIELD, M.Inst.M.M.,	57
Petroleum,	SIR BOVERTON REDWOOD,	61
A Handbook on Petroleum,	THOMSON AND REDWOOD,	61
Oil Fuel,	SIDNEY H. NORTH,	29
Metallurgical Analysis,	MACLEOD AND WALKER,	60
Microscopic Analysis,	F. OSMOND & J. E. STEAD, F.R.S.,	60
Metallurgy (General),	PHILLIPS AND BAUERMAN,	60
" (Elementary),	PROF. HUMBOLDT SEXTON,	66
Getting Gold,	J. C. F. JOHNSON, F.G.S.,	59
Gold Seeking in South Africa,	THEO KASSNER,	59
Cyanide Process,	JAMES PARK, F.G.S.,	59
Cyaniding,	JULIAN AND SMART,	59
Electric Smelting,	BORCHERS AND M^cMILLAN,	67
Electro-Metallurgy,	W. G. M^cMILLAN, F.I.C.,	67
Assaying,	J. J. & C. BERINGER,	66
Metallurgical Analysis,	J. J. MORGAN, F.C.S.,	66
Metallurgy (Introduction to),	SIR W. ROBERTS-AUSTEN, K.C.B.,	63
Gold, Metallurgy of,	DR. KIRKE ROSE, A.R.S.M.,	63
Lead and Silver, "	H. F. COLLINS, A.R.S.M.,	64
Iron, Metallurgy of,	THOS. TURNER, A.R.S.M.,	65
Steel, "	F. W. HARBORD,	65
Iron-Founding,	PROF. TURNER,	68
Precious Stones,	DR. MAX BAUER,	68

LONDON: CHARLES GRIFFIN & CO., LIMITED, EXETER STREET, STRAND.

www.ingramcontent.com/pod-product-compliance
Lightning Source LLC
Chambersburg PA
CBHW032047230426
43672CB00009B/1506